SERVANT TO
THE SERVANTS

SERVANT TO THE SERVANTS

Roy C. Wilhelm, Hand of the Cause of God

By
Joel Nizin, Kathryn Jewett Hogenson, and Gary L. Hogenson

BAHÁ'Í
PUBLISHING

EVANSTON, ILLINOIS

Bahá'í Publishing
1233 Central St., Evanston, IL 60201
Copyright © 2023 by the National Spiritual Assembly of the Bahá'ís of
the United States
All rights reserved. Published 2023
Printed in the United States of America ∞
26   25   24   23   1   2   3   4

Library of Congress Cataloging-in-Publication Data

Names: Nizin, Joel, author. | Hogenson, Kathryn Jewett, author. |
    Hogenson, Gary L., author.
Title: Servant to the servants : Roy C. Wilhelm, hand of the cause of God /
    by Joel Nizin, Kathryn Jewett Hogenson, and Gary L. Hogenson.
Description: Wilmette, IL : Bahá'í Publishing, 2023. | Includes
    bibliographical references and index.
Identifiers: LCCN 2023002270 | ISBN 9781618512260 (paperback) |
    ISBN 9781618512277 (epub)
Subjects: LCSH: Wilhelm, Roy. | Bahais—United States—Biography. |
    Hands of the Cause of God—United States—Biography.
Classification: LCC BP395.W55 N59 2023 | DDC 297.9/3092 [B]—
    dc23/eng/20230206
LC record available at https://lccn.loc.gov/2023002270

Cover design by Carlos Esparza
Book design by Patrick Falso

To my favorite and only wife Vickie René,
my dearest daughters Zia Tahirih and Anisa Jamal,
and my parents, Florence and Harry Nizin,
who are together forever in the Abhá Kingdom.

CONTENTS

PUBLISHER'S NOTE

This book contains provisional English translations of letters of 'Abdu'l-Bahá. These letters, which were addressed to and sent to their respective recipients, should not be regarded as authorized translations of authenticated documents but are included for their historical value. Many of the photos in the book come from the US Bahá'í National Archives, which has been abbreviated as "USBNA" in the photos' citations.

ACKNOWLEDGMENTS

In 1980, for the first time, my wife and I attended the Annual Souvenir Picnic of 'Abdu'l-Bahá in Teaneck, New Jersey. As new nearby residents of the area, this event and the Wilhelm property where it was held immediately captured our hearts and imaginations. I wanted to know more, much more, and was fortunate that Ben Kaufman, Iris Tarafdar, Don Kinney, and other longtime Bahá'ís informally shared their memories with me about the early history of the Faith in New Jersey. This beginning led me to investigate further the story of that unique Bahá'í property with its log cabin and antique car, the Annual Picnic, and Roy Wilhelm—who started it all. It was soon apparent to me that there was a dearth of printed material, so I set a personal goal to document the history of that special property and event. Of course, Roy Wilhelm himself soon became the focus of my search.

For the last three decades I have spent many odd moments in dusty Bahá'í archives. These included those of Baltimore, Chicago, Philadelphia, and Washington, DC. Close to home, I searched the archives of the Bahá'í communities of New York City, and the following communities in New Jersey: Englewood, Teaneck, North Hudson, Ridgewood, and Jersey City. Other archival and government records I explored included North Lovell Historic Society, Maine Historical Society, Bergen County Office of Deeds and Records, and the Division of Old Records at the New York City Department of Records & Municipal Archives, among others. The Maine General Hospital, Lewiston, now called Central Maine Medical Center, allowed limited

1

access to medical records. I wish to express my gratitude to everyone who assisted me with accessing materials at those archives.

I wish to express special thanks to the National Spiritual Assembly of the Bahá'ís of the United States for granting me access to its institutional records. The United States Bahá'í National Archives was a treasure trove of information, so I wish to thank its archivist Roger Dahl and his assistant Lewis Walker, who were invaluable help. Later, Edward Sevcik assisted in his role as the new archivist.

The International Bahá'í Archives at the Bahá'í World Center kindly shared correspondence and archival photographs.

Over time, I had the opportunity to have a number of informal conversations with those who knew Roy Wilhelm or information about him. These included the following people who have now departed for the next world: Mildred Mottahedeh; 'Alí Nakhjavání; Loretta Voltz; and especially Betty D'Arujo, who told me stories of her father, Carl Scheffler. Face-to-face and phone interviews with other individuals helped fill in several gaps. For those both named and unnamed, I am truly thankful.

Many friends guided my prolonged efforts and read nascent portions of this manuscript. Diane Iverson and James Mangan contributed additional information including several recorded interviews. Angelina Allen shared her research on John Bosch. Carol Rutstein made available documents from her father Curtis Kelsey. Graham Hassall's interview of Dudley Blakely was particularly helpful. Keith Korbut shared his keen interest in the REO touring automobile. Jay Levin's research contributed additional history for the town of Teaneck. Fran Pollitt offered insights on the Speckled Mountain, Maine period of Roy's life. The president of Kohler industries shared data on the power plants that were used to light the shrines in Haifa. Everett C. Golden III, President and COO of Otis McAllister, Inc., explained the 1962 demise of the R. C. Wilhelm corporation after its merger in 1957. Rodrigo Tomás helped with the investigation of Roy's time spent in Costa Rica and his son, Rodrigo Tomás Jr., provided the photograph of the coffee cupping process. Marybeth

Vargha assisted with producing the map of the Wilhelm New Jersey property.

Even though the Covid-19 pandemic, which played havoc with many people's lives, made possible the many hours necessary to transform years of research into prose, my attempts to create an actual manuscript were not successful. Fortunately, Nat Yogachandra of the United States Bahá'í Publishing Trust offered the brilliant suggestion to collaborate with Kathryn Jewett Hogenson and Gary Hogenson as coauthors. That successful joint venture has resulted in this work. Weekly video conferencing sessions over many months and a delightful weekend together cemented our friendship.

A substantial component of this collaboration was the addition of several experienced authors and editors, including Dr. Michael Penn, Angelina Allen, Mary K. Makoski, and Jean Gould. Their assistance, editorial guidance, and meticulous checking of footnotes and grammar resulted in major revisions of the text over numerous iterations.

The staff of the Bahá'í Publishing Trust—including Nat Yogachandra, general manager; Bahhaj Taherzadeh, senior editor; and Christopher Martin, associate editor—were superb in their continual guidance, encouragement, and insights. I am also grateful to Martha Schweitz, Director of the Office of Review, for her helpful comments.

None of this would have been possible without the loving assistance, encouragement, and understanding of my wife, Vickie René Nizin, and daughters Zia Tahirih Rayner and Anisa Jamal Alabastro.

Joel Nizin

Ridgewood, New Jersey

January 20, 2023

PROLOGUE

Who was Roy Cochran Wilhelm? No doubt many of the readers of this book were first attracted to it not by his name, but by Roy's title *Hand of the Cause of God*. Bahá'ís want to know more about the individual lives of this unique, select band of fifty souls* who, for a short time, beginning during the Faith's Heroic age and continuing into the Formative age, served in exemplary ways as learned teachers and protectors of the Cause. Thus, for most Bahá'ís, the title *Hand of the Cause* brings to mind images of earlier believers who seem, with hindsight, to have been saints who accomplished tasks far beyond the capacity of others. Yet each one of them was quite mortal and certainly flawed; nonetheless, they rose above those very human traits to achieve great service, often by walking undaunted through the fires of tests. Each and every one of them is worthy of a closer look because they provide timeless inspiration and models for the generality of believers now and in the future. Anyone studying these extraordinary lives should ask: What can be learned from these stellar individuals?

---

* Bahá'u'lláh appointed four Hands of the Cause, all of whom were living at the time. 'Abdu'l-Bahá appointed four Hands posthumously; however, there are hints that 'Abdu'l-Bahá made other posthumous appointments for which the documentation is missing at present. Shoghi Effendi appointed ten Hands posthumously and thirty-two who were living at the time of appointment. Roy was the last Hand appointed posthumously. (Please see "Hands of the Cause of God" at http://bahai-encyclpedia-project.org).

How can lessons from those exemplary lives be applied to present challenges and goals?

Roy Wilhelm—a quiet, gentle though iron-willed soul with a strong sense of humor—is generally not as well-known as many of the other Hands. His relative obscurity leads naturally to the question: What were those elements of his life that led Shoghi Effendi, upon learning of Roy's passing, to cable the Bahá'í world that he was "qualified to join the ranks of the Hands of the Cause of God?" The Guardian's message lauded his exemplary devotion, saintliness, indomitable faith, and his outstanding services to the administrative institutions of the Faith, whether local, national, or international. In the same message, Shoghi Effendi referred to Roy as "an immovable pillar," and assured him of an everlasting reward in the Abhá Kingdom. He also bestowed upon Roy the honorific *Herald of the Covenant.*[1]

Roy's distinguished career as a servant to 'Abdu'l-Bahá and Shoghi Effendi can be likened to the span of an arch, where the carefully chiseled and shaped stones of teaching, obedience, generosity, devotion, and service were held together by the keystone of his resolute faith. Many of his services were carried out behind the scenes, confidentially and without fanfare, but that did not make them any less important to the progress of the Cause.

One only needs to examine the life of Roy Wilhelm to find an example of excellence in every variety of Bahá'í service: spreading the Faith far and wide, administering the organization of its affairs at both the national and local level, and protecting it from those who attempted to create disunity or attack it. He was also instrumental in the development of the material assets of the Faith, not only in North America but also in other parts of the world, especially at the Center of the Faith in the Holy Land. He possessed a sterling character and was selfless, loyal, unfailingly kind, generous, trustworthy, and obedient to the guidance of the Faith. Besides those virtues, Roy was a practical man who always put the needs of the Cause ahead of his personal and material interests. He applied his knowledge acquired as a successful businessman—such as paying attention to his clients, acting in a timely manner, and never forgetting details—to his service to the Cause.

Years working as a salesman and serving customers enhanced his capacity to introduce the Faith to those who had never encountered it before, to accompany new believers, and to support the teaching work of other Bahá'ís. His expertise in organizing and running his own company, preparing budgets, and managing and scrutinizing financial statements fortified his administrative work on Local and National Assemblies, particularly when serving as an officer. Because his administrative service coincided with the period when those world-shaking institutions were in their infancy, he played a significant role in establishing policies and procedures that are still used by Bahá'í institutions around the globe. He strove tirelessly for more than four decades to ensure the erection of the House of Worship in North America—the Mother Temple of the West. He also did everything in his power to assist 'Abdu'l-Bahá and Shoghi Effendi during the critical phases of development of the World Center. Furthermore, one of Roy's most valuable qualities was his innate ability to get along with anyone from any walk of life while at the same time exercising sound judgment. Little wonder then, whenever mischief or disunity threatened the Faith, he was often called upon to protect the Cause by privately counseling those who had strayed from the straight path. He unfailingly arose without hesitation whenever he was asked to take on delicate, difficult assignments.

Roy's life also exemplifies that of a Chief Steward—another title given to the Hands—without ever knowing that he would be included amongst that most venerated group. From the time when Roy first awakened to the verities and beauty of Bahá'u'lláh's message during the early years of the twentieth century, he never deviated from his distinctive life of humble service to the Cause. The bright light of such service, however, is not a flash of lightning, but rises slowly above the horizon like the morning sun, for his qualities as a Hand of the Cause of God emerged over a lifetime filled not only with service, but also effort focused upon spiritual growth, dedication, study, patience, weathering tests one after the other, and instant obedience. This work seeks to portray, however inadequately, Roy's mystical and hard-won transformation from a prosperous American businessman into a spiritual titan. When he reached the end of his life, he had become the much-loved immovable pillar of the Cause of God whom generations long into the future will admire and extol.

1 / A FRAGRANT BEAN

Bursts of sunlight broke through the black clouds, and as quickly as the tropical downpour arrived, it disappeared. The aging cargo ship, having completed a pitching and rolling journey across the Gulf of Mexico, at last bumped up against the creaking pilings at the port, and its engine fell silent. When his ship arrived at Puerto Limón—a small, isolated port on the Caribbean Coast of Costa Rica—Roy, probably for the first time, heard shouts in Spanish and Creole-English rather than American English coming from the sweat-drenched workers scrambling to make fast and unload the ship. Up on the slippery deck, the young man from the Midwest made his way to the rail in search of the gangway. With a look of confident optimism mixed with a touch of apprehension, he turned back and waved farewell to the handful of passengers and crew before making his way carefully down the gangplank that led from the ship to the pier. With his heavy baggage tugging at his arms, Roy gasped for breath in the steamy air as he took his first steps into an exotic world—the antithesis of his Ohio roots.

Once on firmer ground, Roy was directed to a small shack with a sign in Spanish that read *Aduana*—which means *customs house* in English. Inside, he was told to place his belongings on a table, where an agent pawed through them. Next, his bags were weighed, and Roy then paid the required duty on his few possessions. As he waited for the customs agent to complete his tasks, a quick survey of the unfamiliar surroundings may have brought on brief pangs of regret that he had left the comforts of his homeland. But ahead lay what he anticipated to be an adventure. His arrival in Limón at this Central

American tropical port was one stop on Roy's lifelong journey to experience the wider world.[1]

In the closing years of the nineteenth century, Limón was a fever-infested, backwater settlement with fewer than three thousand inhabitants. But change was underway in the little country of Costa Rica, and the town was on the cusp of becoming a city. In 1890, the narrow-gauge railroad connecting that port with the country's principal cities to the west had been completed. At last, previously inaccessible regions were now open to commerce. This most basic of railway lines snaked through lowland swamps and soaring mountain passes. The raging rivers, steep granite mountains, soggy wetlands, and impassable roads had long served as natural barriers to developing commerce between Costa Rica and other countries. After years of financial insolvency, engineering nightmares, and thousands of worker deaths from accidents, yellow fever, malaria and other diseases, the railroad had at last opened for business to passengers and cargo.[2]

Leaving behind the noxious smells of tar and the harbor's sloshing black water, Roy walked from the custom house along narrow congested streets, where he had to sidestep muddy rain-filled holes as he sought lodging. After a night's sleep in a typical, spartan, roach-and-flea-infested establishment, his primary goal the next morning was to find the train station. Shopkeepers, roadside vendors, and their customers would no doubt have noticed the lanky American as he passed, while Roy's sensitive nose would have been assaulted by the unusual mix of pungent smells from discarded vegetables mingled with the sweet fragrance of fruits and flowers. The primary street cleaners were flocks of protected and valued turkey vultures that diligently went about their unending work of consuming all malodorous fruits, vegetables, and food items tossed out of the windows and doors of shops and houses. Peering into the unlit stores, Roy might have noticed sparsely stocked shelves—a subtle reminder of the challenges of living in such a remote outpost. If he had stopped to make a purchase or had asked for directions, Roy would have been able to figure out the local Caribbean-accented English, for most of the residents he encountered were descended from previously enslaved Africans who had been transported to Limón from Jamaica and other English-speaking Caribbean locations to work on banana plantations and the railway construction.

As soon as he arrived at the station, Roy purchased a ticket to his next stop: San José, the country's capital city. When the train departed for the cooler altitude of the central valley, clouds of steam, followed by smoke and soot from the puffing engine, no doubt drifted past Roy's window and settled on his shoulders and pant legs as he tried to get comfortable on the hard wooden seat. Any clammy breeze blowing through open windows would have offered paltry relief from the humid coastal heat. Roy, a fastidious dresser, was not wearing clothes for the tropics, a problem he could remedy in San José. Although the train trip was less than a hundred miles, the slow journey consumed most of the day and afforded Roy the opportunity to get a good look at his new home.

At first, the train rumbled across the swampy lowlands, past wobbly shacks on stilts, each nestled among a handful of cacao trees or small groves of broad-leafed banana trees. Every few miles, the train slowed or stopped to pick up or drop off passengers and freight in isolated towns with names such as *Moín* and *Siquirres*. In many places, only a small platform stood beside the tracks.

Most likely, the tropical landscape unfolding before him was different from what Roy expected. Guide and history books about Central America usually only highlighted the populated, economic, and political centers of a country, so anything he may have read prior to leaving the United States was probably focused mainly on San José and the surrounding cities in the higher elevations of the central valley. If he had stood on the platform at the rear of the train, Roy would have surveyed the panorama of sugar cane and long waving grasses punctuated by palm trees. Occasionally, other varieties of tall trees adorned with orange, yellow, or red blossoms would have presented a vibrant, multicolored vista unlike anything Roy had ever seen other than perhaps in picture books.

The Limón, Costa Rica Train Station in the 1920s, some years after Roy was there. (Public stock images, James Dearden Holmes photographer)

The train slowed almost to a crawl once it left the coastal plain and began its steep ascent toward the capital. As it made its way through tunnels of lush vegetation that brushed the sides of the cars, the passengers could feel the engine labor as it climbed the rolling foothills. Perhaps for the first time, Roy would have noticed that the comfort of hearing Creole-English, as he had in Limón, had been replaced with unfamiliar Spanish. By the time the train arrived in the cooler, busy agricultural outpost of Turrialba, it had climbed to an elevation of over two thousand feet since leaving the coast. During this brief stop, vendors rushed from window to window, scurried through the cars, and offered the riders drinks, bananas, tortillas, cheese, and hard-boiled eggs—welcome fare for hungry travelers. Over the next forty miles, the train ascended another three thousand feet to reach Cartago. After a brief stop in that quaint colonial capital, with its one-story white stucco buildings with red tile roofs, they were once again on their way.

On both sides of the track, leaping and chattering white-faced monkeys entertained the passengers, while a chorus of songs and squawks rang out from the menagerie of forest birds. This, along with the breaking rapids of the Reventazón River below and streams cascading from soaring cliffs above would have created an exciting landscape for the young traveler. Over the next twenty miles, the train descended from its mountain zenith toward the vast central plateau and the town of San José. The volcano Irazú came into view, providing Roy with his first look at rows of emerald-green coffee bushes carpeting the rolling foothills. These shade-loving shrubs were his reason for coming to Costa Rica. The volcano, thankfully quiet at that moment, provided the rich earth that made the country's coffee exceptionally tasty. At last, the train lurched to a stop, and Roy stepped out onto the platform into the center of the world that would be his new home—a place with a different language and an unfamiliar culture.

Anecdotal references and recollections by friends unravel threads of Roy's journey to and life in Costa Rica. However, the details of how he traveled there, and of the nearly two years he owned his coffee farm, remain a mystery. What inspired this young man from the Great Lakes basin to leave the known for the unknown? Was he traveling alone, or with a friend or family member? Was there someone waiting for him when he arrived? How did he become interested in growing, importing, and selling coffee and ultimately making it his life's singular business interest and livelihood? The answers to these questions may never be known.

San José, with an abundance of urban businesses, was the political, economic, social, and cultural center of Costa Rica. The tropical

Belle Époque city was swiftly modernizing following the installation of residential and commercial electric lights, telegraph lines and the recently added luxury of private telephones. Though oxcarts still clattered through its streets carrying cargoes of vegetables, bricks, and coffee, electric trolleys had replaced many of the earlier horse-drawn ones used for transporting people.

When Roy left the train station in the northeast corner of San José, he encountered streets, businesses, and homes unlike any he had experienced during his travels in the United States. On his way to the center of town along the magnificent tree-lined Avenida de las Damas—then a Parisian-inspired boulevard—he would have passed by older buildings—remnants of the time San José had been a Spanish colonial crossroads, but was then in the process of becoming a great European-style city.[3] Turning onto a side street, he would have carefully made his way down narrow sidewalks bounded largely by crumbling one-story adobe structures, which were then being replaced by more substantial multistory neoclassical buildings fashioned from brick and marble. Surrounded by parks and plazas, a new national theater (Teatro Nacional), reminiscent of the grandeur of the Palais Garnier opera house in Paris, was under construction, paid for by taxes on the owners of the numerous coffee farms, or *fincas*.

As impressive as San José was, Roy was not seeking a city in which to live. The verdant green of nearby suburbs and the surrounding countryside—the coffee farms—had drawn him to this lush spot in Central America. An exploding demand for coffee had sped up Costa Rica's race to join the modern world. Notwithstanding the wealth and power of the small number of coffee barons and their plantations, many of the farms in Costa Rica had fewer than a dozen hectares under cultivation where rich volcanic soil, the perfect amount of seasonal rainfall, and shaded mountain slopes at three- to five-thousand feet elevations produced high-value Arabica beans. Even today, the fertile highlands surrounding Costa Rica's central valley continues to be reputed as the best area for growing coffee in that country.

Sufficient evidence exists to conclude that at some time between 1896 and 1901, Roy owned a coffee farm in the environs of San José, but its exact location and size are unknown. Typically, the center of most farms in Central America was a two-room adobe house topped with red terracotta barrel roof tiles clinging to the side of a small hill. It would be decades before electricity and indoor plumbing would extend beyond city centers, so Roy most likely heated water and cooked food on a cast iron, wood-burning stove. The morning work on a farm started early, and bedtime arrived early as well, although inside most modest farmhouses, kerosene lanterns were lit for a short period after sunset in order to finish up the last of the daily chores or to read a few lines from a favorite book. Stands of banana trees provided shade for chickens that were pecking at the ground in search for insects next to the farm's garden patch.

Roy would have needed someone to carry out the numerous chores of running his small farm and to watch over his property. When it was time to harvest his coffee, he would have also had to hire pickers when the coffee cherries turned from green to red. Often, entire families—father, mother, grandparents, and children—would scramble from bush to bush, meticulously plucking the red cherries, and carefully leaving the green ones for a later round of harvesting. A large woven basket, *la cajuela,* would be tied around each picker's waist leaving both hands free to work the coffee bushes. Once the baskets were filled, the cherries would be dumped into a colorfully decorated oxcart for transport down the mountain to a cooperative processing plant, the *beneficio.* There the coffee cherries would be washed, the pulp would be removed, and the remaining beans would be left to ferment. Finally, the beans would be scrubbed and laid out on a large concrete patio to dry in the sun. The clean, dry, green coffee beans, ready for export, would then be loaded into burlap bags.

Roy's coffee growing endeavor in the highlands of Costa Rica, coupled with his earlier experience mastering the art of selling unroasted coffee beans to retailers, restaurants, and hotels through-

Roy inspects coffee trees, about 1896 (US Bahá'í National Archives)

out New England, laid the foundation on which Roy would build his fortune.

Roy's own background and point of view reflected that of the majority White citizenry of the United Stated during his upbringing. As an adult, he was both knowledgeable and proud of his family's history, which could be traced back to the earliest days of the European colonization of North America. His ancestors—including the famous Captain Myles Standish, head of the militia for the Pilgrims at Plymouth Colony in Massachusetts—were among some of the first English settlers to make their home in New England. His German forefathers from the Wilhelm side of the family helped settle the wilds of Pennsylvania. He was well aware that he came from tough, courageous people. As a child, he had listened to stories told by his elderly relatives, who still remembered accounts of those pathfinders. Long before his own birth in 1875, Roy's family settled in the west of the

Appalachian Mountains due to events that occurred eight decades earlier. In the years following the American Revolution, a treaty ending wars against the Native peoples of the Ohio Valley made it possible for White settlers to move westward across the mountains towards the Great Plains.* Roy's forbearers arrived with the earliest European immigrants to settle among the western foothills in the rolling fertile land through which the Muskingum River flowed to join the Ohio River. Roy's ancestors helped cut timber used for road construction, built ferries to cross rivers in eastern Ohio, and cleared woodlands for farms. They were blacksmiths, tanners, millers, farmers, and lawyers; in fact, several of them earned their livelihoods through multiple trades. As pillars of their communities, Roy's ancestors left their marks on many local institutions, including churches and local governments.[4]

Roy's hometown, Zanesville, Ohio, was established in 1794 at the point where the Licking River met the Muskingum River. Initially settled as a small trading post along a trail blazed earlier by Native peoples, Zanesville began to resemble a town when its streets were laid out five years later.[5] Its unusual Y-shaped bridge, crossing both streams, became its best-known landmark. As the two rivers flowed through the town, they were just deep enough to handle flat-bottomed steamboats that transported passengers and goods throughout the region. Dams were constructed across both rivers, and water was channeled to turn the wheels of mills along their banks, and, eventually, to generate electricity for the town's growing number of small factories. Taking advantage of that well-situated location, Zanesville developed a diverse economy. Craftsmen and entrepreneurs made everything from furniture to coffins, saddles and harnesses to

---

* In 1795, the US government signed a treaty with the Western Confederacy that ended the Northwest Indian War. The Nations included in the Confederacy were the Iroquois Confederacy, Seven Nations of Canada, Shawnee, Lenape, Kickapoo, Chickamauga Cherokee, and others. In exchange for land in what is now Ohio, Michigan, and Illinois, the Native peoples were promised funds, goods, and the assurance of yearly payments.

mattresses, beer and baked goods to doors and window blinds. For a short time, it became a textile center.

View of Zanesville, Ohio, about 1900 showing the confluence of the Licking and Muskingum Rivers and the famous Y-Bridge (Courtesy of the Ohio History Connection)

In 1890, when Roy was a teenager, Zanesville's first major pottery factory was opened to take advantage of the rich clay deposits found in the area. Pottery would become the primary product for which the city was known. By that time, Zanesville was already an industrial hub for the region with a thriving central commercial area and burgeoning residential neighborhoods. Frame two-story houses with front porches lined the unpaved streets in neat rows. All-in-all, Zanesville was a good place to live for a middle-class family like the Wilhelms.

During Roy's childhood, the city's population more than doubled, from 10,011 in 1870 to 21,009 according to an 1880 census.[6] While growing up, he would have encountered people from a variety of backgrounds, especially immigrants from Germany and Ireland. Moreover, he would have also come into contact with numerous Black citizens, since during the years prior to the Civil War, Zanesville had been an important stop on the "Underground Railroad," the clandestine system set up to help enslaved people from the Southern States flee to regions where slavery was no longer legal. Though many escaped enslaved people only passed through the city, a significant number remained to fully become part of its growing community as free men and women.

At the time Roy was born on September 17, 1875—a mere ten years after the end of the Civil War—having a college education was rare; his father, John Otis Wilhelm, was one of the privileged exceptions to this rule. The son of a farmer, he first studied at Denison University, then completed his studies at Ohio Wesleyan University. Otis established a business as a wholesale merchant specializing in clothing and hats for women. The vagaries of selling for a living meant that it took years of hard work before Otis prospered. The family lived in a boarding house close to the Muskingum River[7] when Roy was young, but twenty years later, the Wilhelms owned a spacious clapboard home at 38 Thurman Street and could afford the services of a live-in housekeeper.[8]

Anna Laura Cochran Wilhelm, Roy's mother, who was usually called Laurie,[9] was born and raised in the small Ohio town of McConnelsville, downstream on the Muskingum River from Zanesville. Laurie's father, John Lowry Cochran, owned a tobacco factory that produced cigars. He died only two months before she was born, so she was raised by her widowed mother, Elvina Williams Waterman Wilson, who remarried at least once. Laurie had older siblings, half-siblings, stepsiblings, and young cousins within the large households in which she grew up. For a time, her family lived on a farm with her stepfather. Later the family moved back into McConnelsville where they lived with an uncle, and her older brothers found work in

Otis and Laurie Wilhelm in front of Zanesville home, 1896 (USBNA)

the family cigar business. On New Year's Eve, 1874, Laurie married Roy's father and moved with him to Zanesville.[10]

Even though Roy was educated in local public schools, his proficiency with language bespoke a more cultivated background, most likely because of his father's educational achievements. It seems, nevertheless, that Roy did not like school. When he was a teenager, fed up with the demands of his teachers, he slipped away from Zanesville to find his own way in life. His family searched for him, found him, and brought him home. But his restlessness and dissatisfaction with his circumstances continued. He ran away again, but this time he was careful to leave no clues that would make it possible to track him. Searching for a means to support himself, he found a job selling pottery. It would be the first of many jobs he would take on as a traveling salesman, or "drummer."[11]

The itinerate life suited young Roy despite his parents' anguish over never being certain of his whereabouts. He did not complete high school, which was not uncommon in the late nineteenth century. Frequently, many students in their mid-teens left school to find work because their families needed their labor or the income contributed from their job. During this period in the United States, anyone with intelligence, audacity, and a willingness to work diligently could still get along in life without educational credentials. Roy possessed these traits which, when mixed with his pleasing personality and folksy sense of humor, made him an asset to any employer. He quickly learned to manage his earnings and accumulate savings, and he learned a valuable lesson about trust and assessing a man's character when he once was swindled out of his savings.[12]

During his early career as a salesman, he sold a variety of products until he found one that struck his fancy. Coffee would take him from the highways of America to the mountains of Central America and finally to the center of commerce in New York City.[13] Most likely this lifetime interest began when he became a salesman—a job that also brought out the theatrical side of his personality—for the Victor Coffee Company. An 1898 newspaper article* reported how he put on a sales show worthy of a small circus:

> The Shapleigh Coffee Company of Boston is advertising its "victor" coffee in this city in a way which attracts much attention. The outfit came in a handsomely equipped car made specially for the purpose and which now stands on a sidetrack in the Fitchburg (railroad) yard. The company is represented by Roy C. Wilhelm, who has with him two men and five beautiful grey horses. Mr. Wilhelm uses a horse and a buggy to drive

---

* The words used in the story reflect the language of the time in which it was written.

about the city and calls upon the merchants, while four of the horses are driven abreast by Mr. Brown, a stalwart African, who plays the cornet. The establishment is very showy and gives the small boys an idea that a circus has "struck" the city. The horses and whole outfit are carried in the (rail) car from place to place and the men, excepting Mr. Wilhelm, live in the car, which is supplied with many conveniences. The party will be in this city for two or three days.[14]

Victor Coffee label with its chariot logo

It is easy to imagine men, women and children lining the streets to witness this five-horse parade: a man dressed in an exotic costume standing in a chariot and four spirited gray horses straining at the reins, followed by a young man in a horse and buggy going from shop to shop with his coffee bags. The sales show not only gave Roy plenty of experience standing before crowds of people but also gave him the opportunity to work closely with his Black colleague, who drove the chariot and tended the horses. How long Roy participated in this tiny coffee circus is unknown, but it must have afforded him moments of fun.

By the time Roy returned to the United States after his sojourn in Costa Rica, he was still only in his mid-twenties. Nevertheless, he had already learned most aspects of the coffee business from the tree to the table. He had the beginnings of what he would need to make the fragrant bean his life's work.

1896 portrait of Roy Wilhelm (USBNA)

The Coffee Exchange and, consequently, the American coffee trade was concentrated around a few blocks of lower Manhattan in New York City, close to the waterfront, where Atlantic steamers docked, and Wall Street crossed Front Street. There, rows of coal yards and stables stood next to storehouses overflowing with the commodities and trade goods of the nation. Burly longshoremen wheeled bags of green coffee down gangplanks of ships arriving from Brazil and Central America, then the bags were piled high in Front Street warehouses.[15] Naturally, this was exactly the neighborhood in which to set up business as a coffee broker. New gold letters, spread across the second-floor window at number 104 at the foot of Wall Street, read: "R. C. Wilhelm & Co."[16] Thus, Roy began his career as a green coffee importer in the heart of the financial and wholesale mercantile district. What a fortuitous time to be an entrepreneur in that greatest of American ports!

View of New York City from the water in 1902 (New York City Archives, public stock images)

Roy settled into this unique city, perhaps the most cosmopolitan and modern city in the world at the time. Its residents were no longer the descendants of Dutch and English colonists but had become a diverse mixture of humanity. A flood of immigrants from the economically depressed regions of Europe had inundated the United States throughout the almost fifty years after the American Civil War.[17] For many of these hopeful newcomers, their first home after they stepped onto the soil of the New World was the lower eastern section of that port city, not far from the docks and commercial hub of Wall Street. When Roy established his office near that area, the lower east side was still an exotic, world-in-miniature filled with overcrowded, vermin-infested, disease-ridden tenements. Wave after wave of the poor and ambitious replaced earlier immigrants who were beginning to prosper economically and to finally be able to escape that section of Manhattan. Slowly, Russian, Irish, Italian, and eastern European families spread across the city and began to change, more and more, the culture of New York.

Besides having a diverse population, New York had other unique features. For example, it was the first city to install electric lines and power plants, so by 1900, it had conquered darkness in many of its neighborhoods. Electric trolleys and automobiles had begun to replace the thousands of horses that clopped through its cobbled streets every day. This exchange in modes of transport gradually eliminated the stench from the tons of horse manure that had befouled the city air for centuries.[18] Manhattan's towering skyline was visible proof that Elisha Otis's invention of the safety elevator a few decades earlier had made it practical to construct buildings taller than five stories. Advancements in construction practices, low-cost and abundant steel, as well as the development of the steel girder also made possible the growing number of "skyscrapers."[19]

104 Wall Street, where Roy Wilhelm's Office was located on the corner of the second floor. (Photograph from the 1940s Tax Photo Collection, Works Progress Administration, and New York City Tax department)

In 1903, Roy's embryonic coffee brokerage received both a market and capital boost when he partnered with Robert Vickery, a Boston-based green coffee importer with a long history in the trade in New York and New England.[20] Together they expanded their company until Vickery's retirement in 1917. Roy then dissolved that enterprise and opened a new company under the rubric of Roy C. Wilhelm & Co., Inc. at the same 104 Wall Street address. A new partner, Alfred H. Hart, joined Roy and his father, Otis, to reconstitute its board of directors. On the eve of the Great Depression in 1929, Hart passed away, and Roy became the sole owner and director of the company.[21]

The business of coffee is multifaceted, and Roy became an expert in every aspect of it. The process began with a grower on a plantation or tiny farm in a country somewhere between the latitudinal bands circling the globe where the finicky coffee tree grew well. As a broker, Roy had to know as much as possible about the origin and quality of the 69-kilogram (152 pounds) bags of green coffee beans he bought and sold, including the elevation, climate, and soil conditions of each farm, as well as each year's rainfall.[22] His brief experience as a coffee grower in Costa Rica gave him a different perspective from most of the other New York brokers. To further ensure the quality of his wares, he vigilantly tracked the harvesting, processing, storage, and shipping movements of each lot he bought. His clients were roasters, packers, and wholesalers, who sold to retailers, who then sold to restaurants and other consumers. Traditionally, coffee was first roasted in iron pans—whether in a coffeehouse, home, or over a soldier's campfire—then ground before it could be brewed. Coffee became a more convenient beverage when large rotary roasters came into use and roasted beans were ground, packed, and sold by neighborhood stores.

By the time Roy set up his business, larger companies—such as his primary clients, Maxwell House and Beech-Nut—began supplying roasted coffee in bags and one-pound tin cans. In 1901, a further innovation improved selling coffee to the consumer when Hills Brothers Company became the first company to package their coffee in vacuum-packed tins, which retained the freshness of the grounds.

This innovation signaled the final demise of the tiny roasting shops and coffee mills scattered throughout the country.[23]

Roy's key employee during these early years was Margaret Raymond, a graduate of Gloversville Business School (NY) in bookkeeping and stenography.[24] She managed his correspondence, checked shipping reports and warehouse receipts, and followed up with customers and suppliers. Of course, she quickly became accustomed to her boss's well-known sense of humor. Noting his humorous alter-ego signature, *A. Fragrant Bean,* which Roy sometimes scribbled on the bottom of letters to friends, must have brought a smile to her face.

The reputations of many brokers in the coffee trade were often darker than the brew itself, as the industry was rife with reports of deceit and misbranding. Brokers lied about the origin, classification, and quality of their beans. Worse yet, unscrupulous sellers would sometimes put stones and other heavy objects in bags of green coffee to increase their weight. One notorious incident that circulated among the traders on the street was the discovery that an iron stove had been concealed in a bag of coffee from Jamacia. Cutting corners and other forms of dishonesty, though tolerated conduct for many in the trade, were regarded as deplorable and disgraceful under the banner of R. C. Wilhelm & Co. Even though Roy was in a freewheeling competitive business and had to work hard to set himself apart from others in the trade while still turning a profit, over time, his resolute honesty resulted in his firm gaining a reputation for its integrity.

In order to raise the standards and practices of the coffee trade, Roy became a founding member of the Green Coffee Association of New York City, a standards board for writing coffee contracts, setting steamship and rail freight rates, settling disputes, and formulating rules of arbitration. Because of his upstanding character, his refined palate, his fair and honest dealings with suppliers and clients, and his expertise, he was often called upon to arbitrate quality or origin dispute cases. He also compiled a Green Coffee Shrinkage table used by buyers and sellers to facilitate weight loss calculations.[25]

Roy became a regular contributor to "coffee culture" awareness by giving lectures and writing articles for the industry's foremost publication, the *Tea & Coffee Trade Journal*, on topics such as detecting the essences of coffee, or judging its flavor by the roasting process, or the best techniques for making an excellent cup of coffee.[26] But he also had an exceptional nose to detect coffee's subtle aromatic characteristics and a sense of taste capable of detecting acidity, astringency, and thinness and thickness in the cup of coffee. The art of "cupping" coffee to test for aroma, flavor, and body came into practice about the time he began his career in the business. Clarence Bickford, of C.E. Bickford and Co., an early pioneer in developing standards and a market for high-quality coffee from Central America, is attributed with having introduced the cupping procedure in the marketplace.[27] Importers such as Roy no longer had to judge beans by appearance, color, size, imperfections, or qualities such as broken, unripe, or undeveloped. As a cupper, with his sensitive and experienced nose and palate, combined with roasting and then brewing a weighted amount of the selected beans, he and other cuppers would loudly slurp small amounts of coffee from a large spoon to aerate the sample as a way to detect the elusive components and volatile essence in the cup.

One commentator, mentioning trends in the coffee industry, not only discussed these developments but also cited Roy's company by name as an example of a business with honest, transparent practices:

> Having discovered the cup merit of high grown Pacific Slope Central American coffees, Bickford set about reinventing the coffee trade to suit his vision of it. He created the blind cup test to prove the merit of the Centrals against those beans which hitherto had brought premiums in the market. And he made it stick. Once roasters began to examine offerings for their cupping merit, values were revolutionized. Blending, for the first time, was put on a taste basis. Within a dozen years, importers and brokers throughout the land were advertising as did R.C. Wilhelm & Co. of New York in a 1905 edition of The Spice Mill "Cup Selections-Only."[28]

Rodrigo Tomás of Costa Rica demonstrates cupping coffee to determine its quality and origin

The New York Coffee Exchange was the clearing house for trades, but importers such as Roy built the warehouses, controlled the trade, and set prices. During his decades in the business, Roy was often selling in a market with little price elasticity when consumption was sometimes in decline. Wars, economic depressions, frosts, and rainfall each contributed to the supply and demand volatility of the coffee market. His intricate knowledge of not only coffee but also finances, shipping, international trade, and other business matters was crucial to his success as he navigated the ups and downs of the times and the markets.

During Roy's lifetime, coffee became America's most popular beverage. By 1940, the country imported seventy percent of the world's coffee crop. Within a few decades after his passing in 1951, coffee had, after water and tea, become the world's favorite beverage.[29] Roy played an important role in the development of the industry, especially in setting standards, and in the process, the coffee industry made him wealthy. However, his integrity and the knowledge he had gained about the complex fruit of the *coffea arabica* bush were not the only attributes that set him apart from his colleagues in the industry. He was also distinguished by how he used the material and business resources he had acquired through his business. His prosperity not only gave him the funds he could use to better the world, but his ownership of the company also meant he could freely structure his time and serve the Bahá'í Faith whenever he was needed. Without those little fragrant beans, Roy would have trodden a much rockier path of service in his striving to bring the healing message of the Bahá'í Faith to mankind.

2 / TURNING POINT

When Roy's beloved mother wrote to inform her only child that she had accepted a new religion, he immediately became concerned. He knew well that his mother was a restless, lifelong seeker of spiritual truth, a church hopper, and a voracious reader of religious tracts. Consequently, when she gave her heart to a strange sounding new faith from Persia, he was hardly surprised that she had committed to one that appeared to offer a less conventional road to salvation. But he also feared she may have taken a wrong turn, perhaps leading her down a dangerous pathway. The new religion wasn't even Christian.[1]

The women in Roy's family had been religious seekers for at least three generations beginning with his maternal great-grandmother, Sarah Thomson Williams, who Roy met only once when he was about age ten. She was remembered for being an active member of the Methodist Episcopal Church, a Protestant denomination, spawned in England as an offshoot of the Anglican Church during a period of religious fervor in the years leading up to the American Revolution. With Bibles in their saddlebags, the denomination's itinerant American preachers rode on horseback across the vast countryside of the English colonies where they converted thousands of the far-flung frontier settlers through their down-to-earth approach to Christianity. Methodism emphasized the love of God for man and the idea that He could be worshipped under any circumstances: in the field, in the factory, in the shop, or at the entrance to a coal mine. As one of the most rapidly growing churches in the region along the eastern seaboard, Methodism also advocated rigorous moral standards and required its followers to eschew alcoholic beverages and card playing—both of which were very much a part of American daily life during the formative years of the new Republic. In his youth, when he was a paid singer in a Methodist church's choir, Roy became immersed in the teachings of his great-grandmother's religion every Sunday morning.[2]

Another spiritual seeker among his ancestors was Roy's maternal grandmother, Elvina* Williams Cochran Wilson, who tragically lost her husband to cholera two months before she gave birth to Roy's mother. As a result, Roy's grandmother was left to raise a number of children by herself.[3] Perhaps this great loss, at such a pivotal moment in her life, may have led Roy's grandmother to search for a more mystical approach to spiritual truth than even that of her own Methodist mother.

Though Roy always considered his maternal grandmother to be highly intelligent and religious by nature, he could not recall her ever attending a church. She did not believe in paying clergy to promote the word of God. Her understanding was that Jesus of Nazareth had preached God's Message for humanity freely throughout His ministry and that He had instructed His disciples to do the same. For Elvina, this was the only proper approach to spreading God's Word. Instead of spending time sitting in a church pew, she studied the Bible intensely and became convinced from her extensive knowledge of that Holy Book that the time for the fulfillment of prophecies was near. She spoke to her grandson about her conclusions and admonished him to be vigilantly watchful for the Promised One—the return of the Messiah—who would usher in the Kingdom of God on earth.[4]

Roy's parents took him to a local Presbyterian church to provide him with a basic education in Christianity. One fruit of his Sunday

---

* Roy's maternal grandmother was married at least three times. Her first name is given in records as *Elvina, Melvina,* and *Alvina,* and Roy's handwritten notes indicate that he was uncertain about her first name. (USBNA, Roy C. Wilhelm papers, M-46, Box 3).

school instruction was his lifelong familiarity with the Bible and his ability to quote scripture. Despite the Wilhelm family's participation in that Protestant congregation, his mother's spiritual thirst was never quenched. Like her mother and grandmother before her, Laurie began her own search, which came to include exploring religious teachings such as Christian Science and various other new American religious movements, many of which drifted further and further afield from those of conventional Protestant Christianity. Her search took her even onto the paths of religions apart from Christianity. Her son observed his mother's quest from the sidelines, asking himself, "What next?" The one conviction—which her own mother had firmly planted within her—that propelled her forward was the belief that the Great Day of God was near and that it would, perhaps, come during her own lifetime. She was determined not to miss the Promised One when He made His appearance.[5]

Portrait of the Wilhelm Family from 1902. Left to right: Otis, Laurie, Roy. (USBNA)

While Roy, far away from his parents, was focused on himself and making his way in the world, his mother found among her Zanesville neighbors a kindred spirit, Laura Jones. Laurie and Laura shared the same ardent desire to find the promised Spirit of Truth if He was on earth. The two often discussed and pondered how they might go about discovering Him. Sadly, Laurie lost her spiritual ally when her friend moved to Chicago; however, what may have at first seemed to be a loss would prove to be the greatest blessing of her life, for it was there that her former neighbor and fellow seeker first encountered the Bahá'í Faith.[6]

The Bahá'í Faith in the West began quietly in the parlor of a Chicago businessman in the early summer of 1894.[7] The four inquirers after truth present that historic June evening had come hoping to obtain spiritual instruction from a Lebanese immigrant. Ibrahim Kheiralla was the only Bahá'í in the Americas at the time, albeit a less than satisfactory spokesperson of the Faith for many reasons, including character faults which would be his undoing a few years later. He himself was a new believer with only a cursory knowledge of the Faith's teachings and history, and much of what he had learned from his Bahá'í teachers in Egypt was either incorrect or incomplete. To make matters worse, what he did not know about the Faith, he made up. However, having been educated in Protestant schools, he was familiar with Biblical prophecy and applied it to teaching the Faith, thereby enthralling his eager listeners. Only after weeks of lessons would he finally reveal the identity of God's latest Messenger, Bahá'u'lláh, Who had recently passed away in the Holy Land in 1892.[8] Despite Kheiralla's shortcomings, the spirit of divine truth flowing through that impure channel was strong enough to capture a growing number of hearts, one of which belonged to Roy's mother's friend and former neighbor, Laura Jones.

Laurie's inner joy can only be imagined when she opened a fat envelope from her friend in Chicago and read its contents about the Bahá'í Faith. Fortunately, by late 1898 or early 1899 when she would have received the letter, Americans had already begun to visit Bahá'u'lláh's Son, 'Abdu'l-Bahá, in the Holy Land and were sending back reports of the true teachings of the Bahá'í Faith. Within the few brief years that had passed since those first introductory lessons in a Chicago home, hundreds had embraced Kheiralla's version of the Faith and carried it across the country, from New York City to Oakland, California. Laura had also tucked a small pamphlet about the Faith into the envelope along with an early English translation of The Hidden Words of Bahá'u'lláh—concise words of spiritual wisdom similar to the Book of Proverbs in the Bible. As soon as Laurie read this sacred Bahá'í scripture, she immediately knew her quest was at an end. She had indeed found the Promised One for Whom she and her mother had searched through many decades.

When Roy's mother, her heart full to bursting with the good news, wrote to him about the new religion, he may have been preparing to leave the United States or was perhaps already living in Costa Rica. A newspaper clipping about 'Abdu'l-Bahá that also included a picture of Him was enclosed in her letter. The photograph had been taken decades before when He was younger, so with His dark, long hair and beard, He looked every bit like the image many Americans held in their minds of Jesus. Roy understood from that brief account that many regarded 'Abdu'l-Bahá as a return of the Spirit of God. He was, however, unimpressed, and scribbled on the margins of the article, "Strange if true," and returned it to his mother.[9]

A short time after Roy left Costa Rica and settled in New York City, his parents came to visit. His mother was the sole Bahá'í in central Ohio and, of course, was eager to meet other Bahá'ís, so Roy obliged her by accompanying her to Bahá'í gatherings around the city. He was not yet genuinely interested in pursuing the Faith for himself but instead hoped that, by learning more about it, he could show her that it was "a fad born of the anti-Christ."[10]

The New York Bahá'í community was established when the polymath Arthur Pillsbury Dodge moved there in late 1897 from Chicago, where he learned about the Faith by attending Kheiralla's classes.[11] He lost no time in introducing his newfound religion to those around him. Among his friends was Howard MacNutt, another businessman and an internationally known cricket player, who quickly embraced the Cause. Dodge felt unqualified to give more than a superficial summary of the Faith, for he had been instructed by his teacher to share its teachings cautiously and secretly, just as it was being propagated in Kheiralla's Ottoman Empire homeland, where its followers were persecuted. Dodge, therefore, invited Kheiralla to come to New York for an extended visit to conduct Bahá'í classes. Besides MacNutt and his wife, other members of that first Manhattan class included James and Isabella Brittingham, a couple from New Jersey who had heard about the Faith through James' sister. The Brittinghams and Howard MacNutt became important to the early development of the Faith in the United States and would become Roy's friends.

In the winter of 1898–1899, Kheiralla traveled with a group of Americans to the Holy Land where, for the first time, they all met the head of the Faith, 'Abdu'l-Bahá. Kheiralla was given a welcome worthy of a hero who had achieved a glorious victory. He alone could be credited with introducing and spreading the Bahá'í Faith in North America—a signal achievement. But accolades were insufficient for him. Kheiralla wanted to be formally placed in charge of the American Bahá'í community with a commensurate salary. When these rewards for his efforts were not forthcoming, he rebelled against 'Abdu'l-Bahá, unveiling his true character in the process.[12] When Kheiralla's attempt to wrest control of the American Bahá'í community erupted in 1899, the New York Bahá'í community became embroiled in this unfortunate affair. Most of its believers stood steadfastly allegiant to 'Abdu'l-Bahá, due in part to His sending knowledgeable Persian Bahá'ís to fortify the nascent community. One of these was the renowned scholar Mírzá Abu'l-Faḍl, who not only tutored the Americans in the authentic teachings of the Faith but wrote an introductory text for them, which was translated into English and published.[13] The New York Bahá'ís were still recovering from this traumatic period of disunity when the Wilhelms began to attend meetings in 1902.[14] Despite having lost the teacher who first introduced them to the Faith, the community gained something much better—frequent direct communications with 'Abdu'l-Bahá Himself. The spirit of the community was rising and had become anchored upon a surer foundation.

Those who established the Faith in New York were stalwart believers, at least four of whom would be named Disciples of 'Abdu'l-Bahá after their passing. These included one of the first believers to accept the Faith in Chicago—William Hoar, a Canadian businessman who had relocated to New York where he and his family became vital members of the community. The Hoars and Dodges had made a pilgrimage to the Holy Land together in 1900, where their steadfastness had been strengthened by offering prayers at the tomb of Bahá'u'lláh and by spending many hours with 'Abdu'l-Bahá. These families: the Dodges, MacNutts, Hoars and Brittinghams—spiritual giants all— were the primary leaders of the New York area Bahá'í community in 1902. Howard MacNutt, in particular, was a gifted speaker and often the one who conducted introductory classes. These sessions focused upon the basic truth that God had sent a new Messenger into the world, Bahá'u'lláh, and that His Son, 'Abdu'l-Bahá, was the one to Whom all should turn as their guide after Bahá'u'lláh's passing in 1892.

The first Bahá'í gathering the Wilhelms attended was held at the Dodge home. There Roy met the Hoars and two members of the first group of Westerners to visit 'Abdu'l-Bahá: Dr. Edward Getsinger, a homoeopathic physician from Michigan who had taken up residence in the New York area; and May Maxwell, who would become a treasured, lifelong friend. Though born in New York and raised across the Hudson River in New Jersey, May had already become the spiritual mother of the Paris Bahá'í community and, at the time she first met Roy, was newly married to a Canadian architect and living

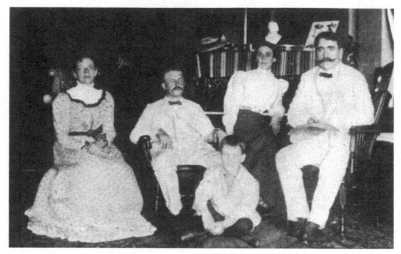

1898, the Dodge and Hoar families. Left to right: Elizabeth Ann Dodge,
Arthur Pilsbury Dodge, Ann Mason Hoar, William Hoar, child on floor
is unidentified (USBNA)

in Montreal.[15] Remembering his first encounter with the Bahá'í community, Roy would say later that he became "conscious of a strong heart attraction before much understanding came."[16]

In His Writings to the Western Bahá'ís, 'Abdu'l-Bahá repeatedly emphasized the importance of unity and that the believers should love one another—a goal not always easy to achieve as forceful personalities emerged and clashes between members began to erupt within this small but growing group. The initial gatherings of believers in the United States relied heavily on references to the Bible, especially prophecies fulfilled by the coming of Bahá'u'lláh. Many of the people investigating the Faith were also interested in the subject of metaphysics and previously had been involved in other unconventional religious movements, such as New Thought and Theosophy. These seekers often diverted group discussions toward the pondering of dreams and miracles, and although his mother found these topics fascinating, they did not interest Roy.[17] The few authentic Bahá'í scriptures available in English at the time (usually ineptly translated) were coveted and memorized. Any time a new letter or Tablet arrived from 'Abdu'l-Bahá, it was read aloud at the next gathering then copied and circulated among the friends.

Over the first five years of the twentieth century, several dozen Americans made the journey to 'Akká in Ottoman-held Palestine and returned to the United States with glowing faces reflecting the transformation within their hearts. These pilgrims traveling to and from the Holy Land generally passed through New York, affording the friends living in that port city the privilege of hearing their accounts firsthand. They all understood the significance of their time in the Holy Land, and several of them wrote about their experiences and circulated printed versions of their notes.

After his mother returned to Zanesville, Roy continued to be drawn to Bahá'í gatherings. Some were held in rented rooms at Carnegie Hall, and others were held at the Manhattan homes of the Dodge and MacNutt families. Through his continued study of the Faith, Roy was never able to prove that it was fraudulent, a fad, or a passing fancy of his mother's; instead, over time, he was surprised to find himself increasingly attracted to it, and after a year of attending meetings, he finally accepted that it was indeed from God.[18] His heart had been moved and awakened.[19] But his commitment was far from solid despite his growing involvement in the Bahá'í community. He began to include visits to Bahá'ís during his business travels around the country, and he often offered his services as a speaker. Within two or three years, he identified himself as a Bahá'í and was listed on the membership rolls that existed at the time.

During those early years of the Faith in North America, there was no formal method of enrollment. Lists of names were kept for administrative purposes, especially in the New York and Chicago areas, but the primary method by which someone entered the Faith was to write to 'Abdu'l-Bahá. Even after doing so, there was no requirement that the new Bahá'í relinquish membership in another religion. Apparently, after Roy decided he was indeed a Bahá'í, he did not write to 'Abdu'l-Bahá; so, in 1904, 'Abdu'l-Bahá, wrote to him first:

Roy Wilhelm in 1902 (USBNA)

He is God!

O thou attracted to the Beauty of the Glorious One!

No letter has ever been received from you; but I am always trusting in the Bounty of God that He may reveal to thee the mysteries of the Perfect Wisdom, so that thou mayest comprehend the occult [sic] of the Universal Reality and that the Light of Guidance may shine as the ray of the Morn of Truth!

Upon thee be greeting and praise

Signed Abdul Beha Abbas[20]

This Tablet was followed on October 18, 1904, by a second letter from 'Abdu'l-Bahá to Roy, in response to an (apparently mistaken) report from Mírzá Abul-Faḍl stating that Roy wished to fully defray the costs of sending a Bahá'í teacher from New York to India:

May the Glory of El Abha be upon him!

O thou attracted to the Lights of the Sun of Truth!

His honor, Abel Fezail, [sic] gave me the news that thou desirest to diffuse the Fragrances of the Divine Rose Garden! This intention is very splendid and this purpose is a Divine Inspiration!

Happy! Happy! That thy design is (to assist) that the Manifest Light may shine upon the Universe and the Cloud of Mercy may shower upon the mortals!

If thou send Mr. Harris to India, that he may guide the heedless ones, it is very pleasing and advisable and great results are hoped for.

I beg of God, that thou mayest by confirmed in the service of the Kingdom and become the appearance of Divine Blessing in the contingent world!

(Signed) Abdul Beha Abbas[21]

Although Roy sent a letter responding to 'Abdu'l-Bahá, its contents are unavailable at this time. He along with a few others did, however, provide some of the necessary funds for the young New York lawyer, Hooper Harris, along with a traveling companion, to journey to India to spread the Faith. This was the first time Roy helped to deputize another believer's travels to teach the Cause and would not be the last. By December 1904 'Abdu'l-Bahá had composed the following response to Roy, suggesting that He knew He was writing to a sincere seeker of truth who was not yet a confirmed believer.

O servant of God!

The contents of thy letter was replete with Spiritual feelings, and was a source of pleasure and of joy.

Of my freedom thou hast expressed great joy. I am free, although I should remain in prison. All the fortresses and castles shall not confine me, and the dungeon cannot bring me under the narrow bondage of the world.

The Spirit is ever soaring even if the body be in the depths. What can these ignorant creatures do? They might imprison the body, but the Spirit they cannot: the Spirit will ever soar in the atmosphere of Eternal bliss and glory.

Therefore, neither the prison is a cause of sorrow nor freedom from it a source of joy.

When thou findeth the way to the Kingdom, the earthly world shall be of no account, and when thou art illumined, the darkness will not affect thee—nay, rather the four corners of the earth will then be radiant and every thorn will become a rose and a rose garden.

Upon thee be greeting and praise

(Signed) Abdul Baha Abbas.[22]

Even though 'Abdu'l-Bahá Himself seemed to be reaching out to Roy to strengthen his beliefs, Roy's connection to the Bahá'í Faith was growing but still tenuous, and he had other things on his mind besides the newfound Faith. For instance, he was building his business, and the demands of day-to-day life in Manhattan undoubtedly consumed him. Because he had a unique talent for sales, the ability to manage money, and had acquired expertise in his trade, by 1907, he was well on the way to achieving success as a coffee broker. Indeed, he had become prosperous enough to reside in a modest apartment located within the newly developed West Side neighborhood of Morningside Heights.[23] It was close to the campus of Columbia University, which was surrounded by many multistory residential buildings that were under construction, as well as new office buildings to house various medical and religious institutions.[24]

Throughout his life, Roy organized his day according to his own strict rituals. He was known to prefer an unwavering distinctive style of business attire: polished leather shoes, a dark wool suit in winter and a tan khaki one in summer, and a crisp white shirt always embellished with a bow tie—his signature wardrobe detail. He left home at the same time each morning and returned in the evening according to a fixed schedule.[25] He ran his office with efficiency, for that was, to his mind, only good business practice. On rare occasions, however, his well-ordered world was jolted by something unexpected that required him to forsake his usual practices, leaving him a bit flummoxed, especially when the unexpected became the unexplainable.

Perhaps the most noteworthy of such incidents occurred one day while he was sitting on his bed changing his shoes—something he routinely did with little thought. On that occasion, most likely in 1905 or 1906, his room suddenly underwent a magical transformation! He found himself no longer in his New York bedroom, but in an unfamiliar room in another part of the world. Gazing around, he found that the walls had become whitewashed plaster, and instead of his furniture, a divan stood against a wall. Stranger still, he was no longer alone. Standing near him was a Man with a majestic bearing and an unusually long, luxurious, black beard who was dressed in an oriental-style gown. The Man came to him, then removed a ring from His finger and placed it on Roy's. He next removed a ring from Roy's hand and placed it on His own. Then, as quickly as the vision began, the scene disappeared, and Roy found himself back in his bedroom. He was wide awake.[26]

At the time, Roy thought to himself that such an odd experience should never be mentioned aloud, lest his sanity be questioned. Unlike many of his mother's acquaintances and his Bahá'í friends, the metaphysical realm continued to hold little attraction for him. No, he had been successful in building his business because he was a practical man of action with scant interest in the tales of dreamers. Having never sought out the mystical, he could not begin to guess the identity of the Man in his vision or figure out why there was an exchange of rings. His vision was a bizarre mystery he was determined to keep to himself as a closely guarded secret.[27]

A number of Bahá'ís from the United States, especially from New York and Chicago, traveled to the Holy Land between 1900 and 1905.[28] No doubt the Wilhelms heard many stories recounted by these pilgrims, especially following the visits of the Dodge, Hoar, and MacNutt families. In 1905, Roy's father, who was still residing in Zanesville, wrote to 'Abdu'l-Bahá and asked for permission to visit the Holy Land as a pilgrim. The response Otis received probably surprised all three Wilhelms. 'Abdu'l-Bahá began by summoning Otis to faith by telling him, "It is time for thee to free thyself from every thought and to be busy with the thoughts of God, to be of service to Him, and to free thyself of all else save Him." He went on to say that, for unstated reasons, Otis's request to come to the Holy Land as a pilgrim was denied and explained that "on account of the hindrances which are unlimited, you must wait until [a] suitable time." Yet, Otis's "revered son is privileged to come here. . ."[29]

Otis would later have the opportunity to meet 'Abdu'l-Bahá when He visited the United States, but he never traveled to the Holy Land as a pilgrim. Perhaps this response to Roy's father can best be understood from comments 'Abdu'l-Bahá made to Roy's friend, Corinne True, while she was a pilgrim, to the effect that there is a certain time for each believer when they should make their pilgrimage.[30] He explained to her that if a pilgrim comes who is not thirsting for the gifts of the spirit, what he receives during his visit will taste bitter, and it would have been better had he not come. But if the believer is truly longing for spiritual enlightenment, what he imbibes during his time in the Holy Land will taste sweet.[31]

Roy's business continued to grow and prosper, so in 1907, when his mother requested and received permission from 'Abdu'l-Bahá to visit 'Akká, he was not only able and willing to help make the journey possible for her, but also to serve as her travel companion.

At age thirty-one, Roy was already an experienced traveler, but most likely his fifty-six-year-old mother had never left the United States until the day in early March when they sailed from New York to the United Kingdom. They first spent time in London, the perfect place for Americans to adjust to a different culture because they at least spoke the language.[32] From England, they crossed the Channel to Europe and continued their journey overland to a Mediterranean seaport, where they boarded another ship to Port Said, Egypt.[33] When they disembarked, they were met by Bahá'ís living in Egypt who lovingly assisted them with preparations for the last leg of their journey to the Holy Land. During that brief stopover lasting several days, the Wilhelms had a serendipitous reunion with Thornton Chase, the first American Bahá'í, as well as with three other Bahá'ís from Chicago who were returning from their pilgrimage.[34] Roy and his mother must have listened attentively to their friends' reports of their experiences in 'Akká. After several days of loving companionship with both the Egyptian and American Bahá'ís, the Wilhelms embarked once again, this time on a Russian steamer sailing north along the eastern coastline of the Mediterranean.[35]

Roy and his mother's departure from Egypt was delayed by several days because of one of the severe dust storms that were common at that time of year. High winds, carrying fine particles of sand the color of burnt umber, blew in from the deserts of Africa and Asia, filling the air with a dusty haze that made it difficult to breathe and impossible to see beyond the end of a city block. When their voyage north was at last underway, the persistent desert winds continued to whip up the waves and made the next leg of their journey uncomfortable as the ship pitched and rolled through the turbulent sea.

The next morning, after an undoubtedly stressful night, Roy and his mother obtained their first hazy glimpse of the Holy Land—the land of the Bible they had heard about all their lives. At midday, the ship anchored in the choppy waters at the ancient port of Jaffa, the seaport that for thousands of years had served pilgrims on their way to the holy city of Jerusalem. Then, departing on the last leg of its journey, the ship steamed northward, hugging the coast as it made its way toward the port of Haifa, where at last Roy and his mother would disembark.[36]

What an exciting moment it must have been when, after many weeks of travel, Roy and his mother finally caught their first sight of Haifa tumbling down the lower slopes of Mount Carmel to the edge of the Mediterranean Sea. The rapidly growing city was developing new neighborhoods, which spread out far beyond the original three walls that had enclosed it for the last two hundred fifty years.

As it sailed into the port, the ship passed the neat red-tiled-roof buildings of the German Templar Colony. The Wilhelms could see that the streets of the colony were laid out in a neat grid pattern, with its principal avenue stretching to the beach, where the Germans had built their own wharf. The colony, founded by a German religious sect anticipating the return of Christ, had brought modern and organized systems of agriculture, construction, and industry with them when they settled in Haifa in the middle of the nineteenth century. The colony's European look made it stand out among the jumble of surrounding buildings. Roy would come to know that colony well in the years ahead.

It was almost sunset when the ship dropped anchor about a mile from the beach at the back of the bay. The town's modest commercial wharf could only accommodate the smallest of vessels; therefore, rowboats from different touring companies, each hoping for paying customers they could ferry to shore, raced to the ship. Roy helped his mother to the precarious spot at the edge of the ship's deck, where they were instructed to climb, one at a time, down the rope ladder into one of the rocking, waiting boats. The small launches bobbed up and down in the heavy surf, which made clambering aboard the rowboats from the large seagoing steamer both difficult and dangerous. When they were finally on dry land, the Wilhelms at once proceeded to the nearby customs house, where their entry into the Ottoman Empire was quickly processed. A carriage was found to take them to the Hotel Carmel, which was the city's newest hotel and catered to Westerners. It was located at the bottom of the German Templar Colony's main street.[37] Cook's Travel Agency, which most likely arranged the Wilhelm's travel, had set up its office adjacent to the hotel.

That evening, Roy and his mother sent messages to the addresses of two Bahá'ís living in Haifa, but they were informed that both had traveled to the other side of the bay, to the city of 'Akká. They then recalled the name of another Bahá'í who they knew lived in Haifa. He was the father of a Persian Bahá'í they had met in the United States. After they sent him a message, this believer arrived at their hotel early the next morning to greet them and to invite them to his home. After a delightful meal with his family, their host offered to take the Wilhelms to the unusual stone structure located halfway up the side of Mount Carmel, which 'Abdu'l-Bahá had built to serve as the burial place of the Báb.[38] During the last year of His life, Bahá'u'lláh had pointed to a spot on the mountain and directed 'Abdu'l-Bahá to erect a worthy mausoleum for the Prophet-Herald there. Carrying out this command was one of 'Abdu'l-Bahá's greatest accomplishments. Unbeknownst to the believers residing in the Holy Land, the sacred remains of the Báb were already concealed in the Haifa Bay vicinity, but it was not yet safe for them to be laid to rest in the waiting shrine. Nonetheless, the building was already venerated by the Bahá'ís.

Roy asked his host if he could be excused so that he could go to the future Tomb of the Báb ahead of the others to take photographs. The one-story structure was laid out in six rooms. Only one door was open when Roy circled the building. Through the doorway he glimpsed a group of men seated and visiting with one another. Peering inside, Roy pointed to his camera as a gesture to gain permission to use it, and they nodded their assent. He then noticed an elderly man wearing a ring, the kind he had seen before on the hands of Persian believers, with a Bahá'í symbol engraved on it. He approached the wearer and whispered in his ear the universal Bahá'í greeting in Arabic, "Alláh-u-Abhá." The startled fellow immediately cried out and embraced the American, kissing him on both cheeks. Tears welled up in the old man's eyes at the joy of meeting a believer from the West—a miracle to those who had endured persecution for the Faith in the Muslim world. The others, eager to welcome Roy themselves, crowded around him. Just as when he first encountered the Bahá'ís in Egypt, Roy found to his delight that the Faith dissolved all barriers between East and West. United in the Faith of Bahá'u'lláh, they were all brothers.[39]

The next morning, the message Roy and his mother had been awaiting reached them—they were asked to proceed to the home of 'Abdu'l-Bahá without delay. It was Tuesday, April 23. Roy lost no time obtaining the services of a high-bodied carriage to take them

The Shrine of the Báb in 1909 (USBNA)

to 'Akká on the other side of the bay.[40] The journey out of Haifa was unforgettable for the Wilhelms, their heads full of happy high expectations reinforced by the beauty of the surrounding mountains, plains, and sea. Springtime in the Holy Land is glorious as months of rain bring forth a profusion of wildflowers. During late April, the region is at the apex of loveliness before the coming dry season turns the landscape to brown and gold. That day, the rocky hillsides were verdant with all shades of green. Patches of scarlet poppies and mounds of yellow mustard flowers blended with vibrant golden crown daises, accented by dozens of other varieties of blossoms of every hue that created swathes of color in the open spaces at the city's edge. The Wilhelms' hearts must have danced like the vivid petals of the windflowers—anemones—that fluttered in the breeze as their carriage made its way through the town and onto the road towards 'Akká.[41]

Poorly maintained roads made the beach circling the half-moon bay the fastest and easiest route between Haifa and 'Akká. The carriage sped along the firm sand at the water's edge, occasionally running through the surf where waves lapped at the bottoms of their seats. Twice, the carriage forged shallow rivers where they emptied into the Mediterranean.

Roy studied the travelers who passed them along the way. Some with rifles slung over their shoulders were on horseback, but many more, their long tunics flapping in the wind, were on foot. As the carriage approached the northern portion of the crescent beach, the four-thousand-year-old white city of 'Akká—visited by Saint Paul and Marco Polo, and whose impregnable stone walls had withstood Napoleon's lengthy 1799 siege—rose from the sand and sea. Offshore, near its sea gate, a few boats tugged their anchor lines in the breaking swells.

The nine-mile journey from Haifa along the sand had taken over an hour, and at last they left the beach for firmer ground. After a short drive down the tree-lined road paralleling the beach, they arrived at the only land gate into the prison city. It was about two o'clock in the afternoon. The gate's towering wooden doors and internal ninety-degree turn made it an easily defended passageway. Proceeding cautiously, the carriage threaded its way through the maze of the crowded Crusader city along narrow, untended streets, where the Americans were bathed in a sea of vile odors. When they turned from one lane into another, the driver cracked his whip to warn oncoming traffic, for the rumbling carriage left little room for others to pass. At last, they reached the northwest corner of the town and arrived at a large gate framed by a high wall with a house built over its top. Passing through the gate, they entered a sizeable open area in which stood an old building, known as the House of 'Abdu'lláh-Páshá, that originally had been constructed to serve as a palace. The carriage creaked to a stop beneath the archway of the entrance, where several men were expecting their arrival. The men greeted them with shouts of "Welcome, welcome!"

Stepping down from the carriage, their hearts pounding, the two Americans were directed through a small wooden gate, sheathed in metal, that opened into the building. Once inside, they observed that the rectangular building, which contained many apartments, enclosed a central square inner courtyard. Turning to the left, they were led past an ornamental garden to a long, steep stairway covered with flowering vines. Carefully climbing to the top of the worn, uneven stone steps, they reached their journey's end.[42]

The House of 'Abdu'lláh-Páshá about 1907, showing steps
leading from inner courtyard to entrance of the apartments
of 'Abdu'l-Bahá (USBNA)

The young man serving as their escort led them through a modest dining room and into a corner room where, from one side, they could see over the city's crumbling walls to the Mediterranean. Another window looked out onto a garden at one end of the open area through which their carriage had just passed. Below their window, a tent had been pitched near a small fountain. They were pleased to learn that they were to be the guests of 'Abdu'l-Bahá and that this was to be their room. The chamber, though spacious, was plain and economically furnished, with iron beds laid out with immaculately clean white cotton linens, a simple washstand, and woven straw matting for rugs. After inquiring if they had everything they needed, their escort then advised them to rest.[43] But how was it possible to rest when they were so excited, when they were anticipating meeting at last the Person they had traveled half a world to see?

They did not have to wait long before 'Abdu'l-Bahá appeared at their door. He approached them with outstretched arms and greeted them with a hearty "Welcome! Welcome!"[44] He hugged Roy so tightly that Roy thought his ribs had been cracked.[45] It was the first time Roy had ever been hugged by another man, and it happened so quickly that he did not have time to offer instead the customary American handshake.

'Abdu'l-Bahá directed them to a divan along one wall of the room where He sat with one of them on each side. Taking Laurie's hand in His, He put His other arm around Roy. With the aid of an interpreter, He began to speak to them in Persian. First, He wanted them to know that He had been awaiting their arrival and that they had reached 'Akká through the assistance of God. Next, 'Abdu'l-Bahá inquired about the believers in the United States. Roy and his mother informed Him that the believers were well and becoming more unified. This news made their Host very happy. He commented that the more the Bahá'í friends became united, the more they would receive divine confirmations. It was important that the followers of Bahá'u'lláh love each other to the point that they would be willing to sacrifice themselves for their fellow believers. He then made a statement that must have surprised the Wilhelms. He told them that they represented all the American believers, and that He could see them all within Roy's and Laurie's faces, for they were shining. He reiterated that He had been waiting a long time for them to come to the Holy Land and was grateful to God for their arrival. The Wilhelms responded by saying that they also thanked God for that bounty and hoped to be worthy of the privilege of pilgrimage. 'Abdu'l-Bahá assured them that they would become more worthy.[46]

Thus began six days in the prison-house, their paradise.

Alas, 'Abdu'l-Bahá was very busy with His many responsibilities and unable to spend every minute with His pilgrim guests. They often had to content themselves with only visiting with Him at meal-times and an occasional hour or so when He was able to get away.[47] Everyone, from the highest official to the lowliest peasant, came to Him for advice and assistance, for He was renowned throughout the region for His wisdom, knowledge, justice, and compassion. He settled disputes, answered theological questions from other Faiths, gave advice to local officials, and provided practical assistance to many in need. On the ground floor below the family's living quarters was a room set aside to meet with the many people who wished to speak with Him.

Roy found the daily parade of visitors to that room to be remarkable, not only because of how much 'Abdu'l-Bahá gave of Himself but also because He did so without regard to the status or background of the person. Old rivalries and hatreds between religions and ethnicities were anathema to Him. The Jew, the Muslim, the Druze, the Turk, the Christian, the European, and the Bedouin—anyone and everyone—was warmly welcomed to His reception room and mingled there in peace with others, even their enemies. What made this even more notable was that 'Abdu'l-Bahá continued to be a prisoner under house arrest by direct order of the Sultan.[48] Soldiers, stationed about the compound, watched every move 'Abdu'l-Bahá and His guests made. The governor himself resided in the house perched above the gate to 'Abdu'lláh-Páshá. The walls had ears. However, despite His lack of wealth and temporal power, 'Abdu'l-Bahá was nonetheless the most influential person in that region of Palestine.

One sight that deeply touched Roy occurred on their third day in 'Akká. Friday was the Sabbath, a day of rest for Muslims and the day on which 'Abdu'l-Bahá paid homage to the Islamic roots of the

Faith by attending the noon services of a mosque. However, this act of respect was not the most noteworthy part of His routine, for every Friday morning around seven o'clock He devoted time to the poor, the lame, the blind, and the infirm, who flooded the front area of the property just below the Wilhelms' window. Roy watched from above as His Host moved from person to person and slipped coins, often the only means of sustenance for these guests, into the hands of most of them. He radiated love and compassion as He whispered words of encouragement, sympathy, or advice to those whom the rest of the world had forgotten or had chosen to ignore. This weekly routine was not His only time with the poor, the sick, and the downtrodden, for the Americans also observed that He would slip away before daybreak to minister to them in their homes.[49]

The Wilhelms were not the sole Bahá'í pilgrims present at that time in the Holy Land. Others that had also traveled from the West included three single women: Edith Sanderson, a wealthy Bahá'í from California living in Paris; Wellesca "Aseyeh" Allen (later Dyar) from Washington, DC; and Ruby Jean "Hebe" Moore (later Struven), a sister of Roy's friend, Lua Moore Getsinger, from New York State. Hebe would also become a lifelong friend and later played a significant role in assisting Roy during the last years of his life.[50] During the evenings, the Western pilgrims were joined by Eastern pilgrims, most of whom had traveled to the Holy Land by foot from Persia, the Cradle of the Faith. These Eastern pilgrims made an indelible impression on Roy as he listened to their stories of enduring intolerable persecution in the path of God.[51]

Throughout the six days, Roy must have heard many things from the lips of 'Abdu'l-Bahá, but he did not include most of them in his published account of his pilgrimage. Two minor matters were discussed with his Host; one was important to Western believers and the other regarded one of his own problems. First, Roy asked 'Abdu'l-Bahá about the proper spelling of the name *Bahá'u'lláh* in English, because Westerners spelled it phonetically several different ways.[52] The personal issue dealt with Roy's health, which was not good. In fact, he was up late many nights because he did not feel well, and he usually found that 'Abdu'l-Bahá was also awake and busy work-ing.[53] Roy's Host demonstrated how to prepare a type of porridge with goat's milk, from a specific variety of grain, which would aid in improving his health. Ever after, Roy would follow 'Abdu'l-Bahá's directions almost fanatically and eat it daily.[54]

Although most Western pilgrims took copious notes during their time with 'Abdu'l-Bahá, Roy apparently wrote little if anything about private conversations he had with his Host. However, Roy did describe one talk, which particularly stirred him, that 'Abdu'l-Bahá gave during a meal. The talk was an example of how well 'Abdu'l-Bahá understood the Christian backgrounds of the American believers and how He used Christ as an example to explain concepts to them.

'Abdu'l-Bahá began by speaking of God's Messengers; that is, His Manifestations such as Abraham, Moses, Jesus, Muhammed, the Báb, and Bahá'u'lláh. Whenever any of these Messengers appeared, They were always opposed and rejected by the very people They were sent to raise up. Their followers were likewise persecuted. The accusation laid against these Holy Ones was that They were corrupting society's laws and destroying the predominant religion of Their times. Jesus was accused of being a liar; consequently, many people oppressed Him. Yet, in the end, Christ was victorious, and much of the world fell under His influence and sway. Ultimately, those who denied Him and tried to undermine His message were thwarted.

'Abdu'l-Bahá continued by focusing on what the handful of Jesus' followers had accomplished. Despite their small numbers, the spiritual power they exercised through Christ overcame all obstacles and illuminated the world. This portion of the talk must have been a balm to the hearts of His listeners because the number of Bahá'ís, especially in the West, was miniscule.

'Abdu'l-Bahá then remarked that only eleven disciples remained faithful at the time of Christ's martyrdom; and He added that of these, Simon Peter, the greatest disciple, denied his connection to Jesus three times out of fear.[55] On the other hand, when Bahá'u'lláh passed away, He left behind many thousands of believers willing to give their lives for His Faith. The enemies of the Faith killed thousands of these Bahá'ís in gruesome ways, yet these martyrs faced their ends with such bravery that rather than cry out or complain of torture, they died while invoking the name of God. 'Abdu'l-Bahá then commented that this comparison is an indication of the future greatness of the Bahá'í Cause.[56]

Roy later wrote about his overall sense of 'Abdu'l-Bahá's household during these magical six days:

> That which most impresses the pilgrim to the "Most Great Prison" at 'Akká, is the spirit of sacrifice. Nowhere have I witnessed such love, such perfect harmony. The desire of those in that prison was to serve one another.
>
> In our Western liberty it is difficult to realize the bitter antagonism and hatred which exists in the East between the followers of the several great religious systems. For example, a Jew and a Muhammadan would refuse to sit at meat together: a Hindu to draw water from the well of either. Yet, in the house of 'Abdu'l-Bahá we found Christians, Jews, Muhammadans, Zoroastrians, Hindus, blending as children of the one God, living in perfect love and harmony.[57]

The last meal the Wilhelms shared with 'Abdu'l-Bahá must have evoked thoughts of Christ's last supper with His disciples when Jesus broke and shared His bread with them.[58] 'Abdu'l-Bahá performed the same act. He "broke a quantity of bread into His bowl; then asking for the plates of the pilgrims, He gave to each of us a portion." When the meal was finished, He said, "I have given you to eat from My bowl—now distribute My Bread among the people."[59]

The Wilhelms' time with 'Abdu'l-Bahá had come to an end, but their pilgrimage had not. The Wilhelms had two more places to visit before leaving the 'Akká area, one of which was the singularly most important element of their pilgrimage—praying and paying homage at the Shrine of Bahá'u'lláh. They were driven to the estate at Bahjí, about two miles outside of the city walls, where Bahá'u'lláh spent His final years before passing away in 1892. Much of the property was under the control of the descendants of Bahá'u'lláh who opposed 'Abdu'l-Bahá's position as Head of the Faith, so the mansion at Bahjí was not available to visit.

Mansion of Bahjí in 1900 (USBNA)

The earthly remains of Bahá'u'lláh had been laid to rest in the former residence of Bahá'u'lláh's son-in-law, beneath the floor of the simple, unadorned, one-story building across from the western side of the mansion. 'Abdu'l-Bahá had beautified that holy shrine with gardens on two sides. The roof over the center of the building had been raised to accommodate high glass transom windows on all four sides, and a garden had been planted in the central hall adjoining the room that held the Tomb of Bahá'u'lláh. The Wilhelms removed their shoes outside of the entrance and, with great reverence, were ushered into the Bahá'í Qiblih,* the most sacred spot on earth. When Roy and his mother finally left the shrine, a gardener who was waiting outside for them filled their arms with roses and carnations.[60]

Leaving Bahjí to return to Haifa, the Wilhelms made a stop at the Garden of Riḍván, a green oasis in the arid landscape where Bahá'u'lláh had often rested beneath the shade of its mulberry trees.

---

* The Qiblih is the geographic point to which the faithful should turn in prayer. For Christians and Jews, the Qiblih is Jerusalem; for Muslims, it is Mecca.

Shrine of Bahá'u'lláh and surroundings, 1919 (Bahá'í Media Bank)

The garden was situated on a manmade island formed by a small river that had been diverted to create a millpond. The centerpiece of the bucolic place was a tiered fountain whose splashing waters provided soothing relief from even the hottest of late summer days. The old blue and white bench suspended above the stream, where Bahá'u'lláh had loved to sit, was still there and His favorite spot marked off with potted plants.

This lovely garden was a perfect capstone to the Wilhelms' time in 'Akká, but it would be more than a pleasant interlude for Roy. It also would be a life-changing turning point. Roy and his mother were guided to a little white building at one end of the garden and shown the room where Bahá'u'lláh would stay, sometimes overnight.

When he stepped into the simply furnished room with white-washed, plaster walls, Roy was stunned. It was the very room he had seen in his vision that day while changing his shoes in New York! Not having been previously subjected to visions or other strange experiences, Roy had never spoken to anyone about this unusual occurrence. When he entered that room at the end of the garden, any doubts he still entertained about the truth of the Faith vanished. From that moment, he was indeed a steadfast believer. 'Abdu'l-Bahá would later explain to Roy that the vision meant that Bahá'u'lláh had wedded him to His Faith by exchanging rings with him.[61]

Building at the Riḍván Garden where Bahá'u'lláh would stay (Bahá'í Media Bank)

The Wilhelms returned to Haifa that evening and left three days later. They sailed down the coast as far as Jaffa and from there took the narrow-gauge railway up into the central hills of Judaea to Jerusalem. While in the ancient holy city of the Prophets, the Wilhelms visited the birthplace of Jesus in nearby Bethlehem, as well as the Mount of Olives.

'Abdu'l-Bahá had spoken to the Wilhelms about their journey home and had asked them to visit with Bahá'ís in Cairo, Paris, and London. Roy and his mother, of course, complied by altering their plans to add stops at all these cities. Finally, on June 27, 1907, after over four months of travel, the Wilhelms reached New York after

Interior of the Room of Bahá'u'lláh at the Riḍván Garden, which Roy saw
in a vision (Bahá'í Media Bank)

having embarked from Southampton, England, on June 22 on the
S.S. New York.[62]

Roy summarized his pilgrimage by saying that "the true Journey
and the real Meeting is of the spirit, for only that 'cup' which one
carries there is filled."[63]

More than a year after his pilgrimage, in a letter to a friend, Roy
expressed his belief in the Bahá'í Faith, for he had attained not simply
faith, but certitude based upon reason. The concept that all religions
come from God made sense to him. He also acknowledged that
becoming a Bahá'í had made him a better person. He explained to
one friend that

> . . . I accept it because it works. It accomplishes what all of
> the systems have been theorizing about, and again, its broad

principles of recognizing the truth in all systems are so much more Christ-like than the <u>practice</u> of our systems, each of which attempts to unify the world through the destruction of all the other systems and the consuming of their flowers into their own. Another reason is that I find it is helping my individual self to undergo a refining process which, although my progress seems very slow and laborious, has yet taught me a certain something I never knew before.[64]

Roy looked back on his life as a Christian, during which he thought that service to his church and Faith meant giving ten percent of his income to charity—tithing—and that it was not only sufficient, but "doing a great deal."[65] After he became a Bahá'í, his understanding changed, and he realized that that was far from enough, and that he must exert a much greater effort to serve God.[66]

In 1909, 'Abdu'l-Bahá Himself stated that Roy had become truly a firm and steadfast believer. In response to a letter from Roy, He said that the contents of his letter "were faith and assurance and illumined by the manifest Light, and its significance was firmness and stead-fastness in the Most Great Testament."[67] This was not all, however. 'Abdu'l-Bahá went beyond praising Roy's services to the Faith and his present state of belief; in addition, He assured him that "ere long thou shalt increase thy capacity and ability and wilt be assisted in performing universal service in the Cause."[68]

3 / FLOWERING IN NEW JERSEY

Roy and Laurie had much to think about following their pilgrimage, especially once they returned home and were reunited with Otis. Transformed after basking in the light emanating from the Holy Places and presence of 'Abdu'l-Bahá, they each had a richer understanding of the Faith and renewed hope for better things to come. In June 1907, shortly after returning to New York, Roy wrote a letter to one of the believers in the Holy Land who then passed it on to 'Abdu'l-Bahá.[1] He received a treasured reply from 'Abdu'l-Bahá Himself in which He twice addressed Roy as one who was firm in the Covenant and then reminded him of his time as a pilgrim in the Holy Land. 'Abdu'l-Bahá wrote, "Although the length of your stay in this Most Great Prison was very short, yet I hope that it may become like unto the oil, which no sooner comes into touch with the fire, then it becomes ignited. Therefore, God willing, important outcomes will be the outcome of this visit."[2] 'Abdu'l-Bahá stressed to Roy that such a privilege should lead to action, saying, "Be thou firm in the Cause and be engaged in service. Awaken the souls and make mindful the (heedless) minds. The Spiritual outpourings will become uninterrupted and the meetings of heart-to-heart constant. Rest thou assured upon the Favor and Bounty of the Beauty of Abha."[3]

This guidance must have generated questions in Roy's mind along with a stronger desire to serve the Faith. What did it mean to be firm in the Covenant? He loved 'Abdu'l-Bahá and was willing to follow His guidance. Was that what it meant? Furthermore, he was already engaged in serving the Faith, so what more should he do? The Bahá'í

Writings repeatedly remind the reader that the most praiseworthy way to serve God is to spread His divine teachings. As a man gifted in the art of sales, Roy was already telling others about the Faith long before he himself became confirmed in his own beliefs during his time in the Holy Land. Buoyed by his pilgrimage, he redoubled his efforts and seized any opportunity to share the message of the coming of Bahá'u'lláh with those who crossed his path. When traveling for his business, he constantly met new people with whom he could share the good news that God had not left mankind alone in darkness, but had sent a new Messenger, as promised in the Bible. Just as with selling any product, he knew he had to bring up the Faith multiple times with many people before he found one soul who would listen with genuine interest and not simply out of politeness. On occasion, he encountered an individual eager to know more.

In early March 1908, less than a year after his return from the Holy Land, while on a business trip to Pittsburgh, Roy found an individual who would not only listen but would also become an outstanding Bahá'í teacher. Arriving at his hotel late in the evening, Roy was informed that the hotel's kitchen was closed for the night, but that he could find a meal at Child's, a nearby restaurant. When he walked into that establishment, he was surprised to see that, despite the lateness of the hour, the restaurant was filled to capacity. He learned that most of the customers had come to Pittsburgh to attend an interdenominational religious convention in support of the Christian foreign mission movement. There was hardly any table space left, so the head waitress made room for him at the back of the restaurant close to a table full of women.[4]

Roy was not one to eavesdrop; however, he could not help but overhear the impassioned conversation of the women dining beside him. They were engrossed in a dispute centered on ideas about how to spread the message of Jesus Christ to those whom one of the diners called "the heathen," referring to those who still lived in the pre-industrial world and had not yet heard of Christianity. That woman emphatically stated her conviction that those unfortunate souls would not go to heaven because they were not Christian, and what a pity that was indeed! This sentiment upset the woman next to her who countered with her own firm belief that there was only one Creator who loved all His creation, so she was certain that those who had never encountered Jesus must not really be lost. This challenge was met with coolness, with each woman holding silently to her own opinions. Roy held his tongue, resisting his impulse to explain the Bahá'í teaching that all the revealed religions of the world came from the same source, the One True God. But just as he resolved not to say anything, the women all rose to leave. Given the cramped seating, he had to get up from his chair to allow the women, with their flowing skirts and brimmed hats, room to pass. This brief gesture presented Roy the salesman with an irresistible opportunity to speak up.[5]

He began by saying that he could not help but overhear their conversation and asked their permission to make a few comments. He then gave his best two-minute summary of the Bahá'í Faith. He also told of his recent visit with his mother to the Holy Land where he had observed that people born into other religious systems said prayers and lived righteous lives much like Christians. It was clear to him that the non-Christians he encountered also sought to create true brotherhood. One woman who had remained silent throughout the spirited dinner conversation seemed interested in what he said and slipped him her business card as she passed by. Printed on the card was the name "Martha Root," and it indicated that she was the Society and Religion editor for the *Pittsburgh Post* newspaper.[6] In that instant, the beginning of what would become an historic relationship between two spiritual titans began.

Roy's new inquirer after truth was a plain woman, who made up for her austere appearance with a towering intellect and the ability to make her way in the male-dominated world of journalism. Like Roy, Martha, three years his senior, was also born in Ohio; however, she was raised in a small town nestled in the Alleghany mountains of the northwestern corner of Pennsylvania near Lake Erie, where her father owned a variety of prosperous businesses. Her family were high-minded, churchgoing, solid middle-class citizens. She counted among her distant relations the renowned internationalist, winner of the Nobel Peace Prize, Secretary of State and diplomat Elihu Root—a connection that would prove invaluable when Martha served the Bahá'í Faith internationally.[7] Martha was well educated at a time when few women were afforded this advantage, studying first at Oberlin College and then earning a degree from the prestigious University of Chicago.[8] Like her dinner companions, she was attending—most likely as a journalist—the first international convention of the Young People's Missionary Movement of the United States and Canada.

After Roy returned home, he sent Martha a Bahá'í book, along with a note, in the hope that he could further her interest in the Faith. Martha—who will forever be widely extolled as one of the foremost Bahá'ís produced by the West—chose not to read it and gave the book to a person she knew had unconventional religious interests. She did, however, send Roy a polite acknowledgement, which seemed to indicate that the door to future conversations remained open, if only a crack. Being the persistent salesman that he was, Roy did not drop his prospect, even after learning the fate of the book. Some months later, he was again passing through Pittsburgh on business and offered to meet Martha, and she agreed. This time, on January 23, 1909, they enjoyed a meal together at a different restaurant, the Farmer's Restaurant. For almost two hours, the journalist listened attentively and asked intelligent questions about Roy's religion. Upon returning to New York, he sent another book, and this time she read it.[9]

Martha's conversations with Roy marked the beginning of her spiritual transformation and of a deep, abiding friendship with Roy and his parents. Though Roy started Martha on a path of investigation that would lead to her complete commitment to the new Faith, he was not the only Bahá'í who would influence her along her spiritual journey. Almost a year would elapse after that lunch with Roy in Pittsburgh before her heart was totally won over to the Cause of Bahá'u'lláh.[10]

Martha Root (USBNA)

Having been advised by 'Abdu'l-Bahá to serve the Cause and to teach it to others, Roy began to write to Him on a regular basis after his 1907 pilgrimage so that he could report his activities. He was especially diligent in telling Him about those he was instructing in the Faith, such as Martha. These letters delighted 'Abdu'l-Bahá, Who responded by reiterating the importance of Roy's teaching work:

> . . . Thank thou God thou wert assisted in teaching the maid-servant of God, Mrs. . . ., and supplicate Him that thou

mayest be confirmed in the guidance of innumerable souls. The confirmation of the Kingdom is with thee. Rest thou assured. Loosen thy tongue with the utmost fluency and eloquence and summon the souls to the Kingdom, explain the proofs and give forth the arguments, and instruct the people in the exhortations and advices of God.[11]

A few years later 'Abdu'l-Bahá again expressed the pleasure Roy's reports gave Him, especially his travel to spread the Cause, and He promised Roy greater things to come as a result of his efforts, saying: "Thou hast written that during these days thou hast travelled to different parts, have seen different assemblies in every city, which are beautifully organized, and are engaged in the service of the Kingdom. Ere long thou shalt behold greater things than these."[12]

Roy and his mother were always willing to assist those new to the Faith to become more fully part of the Bahá'í community. Roy hosted gatherings for inquirers in his New York City apartment and did what he could to ensure that those coming into the Faith had access to information and Bahá'í fellowship. Among these new believers were a French-Canadian architect, Louis Jean-Baptiste Bourgeois, and his wife Alice. For several months starting in 1904, the Bourgeois had been tutored in the teachings of Bahá'u'lláh and the Bahá'í Faith in the Boston parlor of Mary Hanford Ford, a renaissance woman with far-reaching interests in topics such as spirits, art, literature, religion, mysticism, numerology, and the women's suffrage movement.[13] In addition to Mary Ford, the Bourgeois also received further instruction about the Faith and 'Abdu'l-Bahá from teachers such as Marie Watson and Eaton Moses, as well as Roy. After Louis and Alice moved to New York City during the winter of 1906–1907, they enrolled in the Faith. This turned out to be fortuitous for both Roy and Louis. Not only did the two become friends, but Roy also needed the services of an architect, so it followed that he would hire his new friend, Bourgeois.

The allure of country living had never left Roy, even though his upper westside home in Morningside Heights made his commute to and from his lower Manhattan Wall Street office manageable. In 1908 he was searching for another place to live and found the backwoods tranquility of rural Bergen County, across the Hudson River, more to his taste than his urban home. Most of New Jersey had remained farmland despite its proximity to New York City, but this situation too was changing. Suburbs sprang up as forests were cleared and houses were built on what had been farmers' fields. The Wilhelms were drawn to the West Englewood area, where lots were being laid out on the former estate of William Walter Phelps. These lots provided city dwellers an attractive alternative to the congested metropolitan life on the other side of the river.

Phelps, like Roy forty years later, had desired to flee the dirt and noise of the city, eventually purchasing over twenty-five hundred acres in an orchard-filled farming community overflowing each spring with a vast array of cherry, peach, apple, and pear blossoms. Initially, Phelps was only looking for a rural summer residence for his family, but their Dutch colonial house was soon enlarged to become a sprawling, 350-foot-long mansion. The son of railroad baron and financier, he inherited his father's considerable fortune and soon moved permanently to Teaneck, where he spent the rest of his life. And Phelps loved trees. He planted approximately six hundred thousand of them, including over seventy thousand Norway Spruces, some of which would later be used by Roy to construct a log cabin. Phelp's legacy was evident in the wooded lots the Wilhelms purchased, especially the majestic trees Phelps planted to line miles of winding carriage trails.[14]

About a decade before Roy and his father purchased their first lots, the township of Teaneck was incorporated and began to take on the attributes of a distinct community. The name *Teaneck* was a relic of the Dutch colonization of the area, for "Tea" or "Tee" is Dutch for *bordering on a stream*, and *neck* indicates a curved section of land.[15] After the British took control of the area away from the Dutch, they kept the name but over time changed its spelling from *Teeneck* to *Teaneck*. The original Dutch name well described the area because it was well-watered, and its rolling terrain bordered wetlands that spilled into rivers.

When Roy and his father purchased lots at the top of a hill in West Englewood*—then an unincorporated village within Teaneck Township—it was still a forested, undeveloped area but on its way to becoming a select residential community.[16] The 1900 census records show the entire population of Teaneck as only 768. A decade later, the population of the little village had almost tripled to over two thousand residents. This growth resulted from Phelps extending his Northern Railway line, making the town a convenient train ride away to the center of Manhattan. For Roy, Teaneck appeared to be an ideal location—close enough to commute to his office yet far enough away from the city center to be surrounded by nature. There, he could build a suitable home where he and his parents would be comfortable, on a corner lot situated in the peaceful suburban woodland. Best of all, the Bourgeois Family had also purchased a lot close to Roy's and were constructing their own home there.

Louis Bourgeois had an unusual background, which may in part explain why his wandering spirit was attracted to a new religion. He

---

* Eventually a total of fifteen contiguous lots would be purchased, which Roy ultimately donated to the National Spiritual Assembly of the United States. These included the ones that were the site of the 1912 Souvenir Picnic where 'Abdu'l-Bahá was present (Bergen County, New Jersey, Clerk's Office, Land Records).

had inherited his mother's far-reaching curiosity and her love for art. His creativity and talent with a pencil naturally led to his passion for drawing, especially architectural drawing. From a young age, he was not only artistic but fascinated by the complexity of mechanics and building structures. While still a youth, he found work as a clerk with a company in Québec that built churches, and this job satisfied many of these facets of his personality.[17]

During his early adulthood, an unexpected tragedy redirected Louis' life and was perhaps the pivotal event sparking his spiritual quest: his young wife died shortly after the birth of their third child, leaving him to raise their three young children by himself. As if that loss by itself was not sufficient to turn his world upside down, the debts from his late wife's medical expenses forced him to look for a more lucrative position, so he took a job as an apprentice to a sculptor. This forced career change turned out to be a blessing because his new employer discovered that he clearly possessed a talent for working with marble and granite. To help him hone that skill, Louis was given a scholarship to study sculpture at the famed *École des Beaux-Arts* in Paris.[18]

What he studied or how long he remained at the school remains uncertain, but within a few years Louis was wandering around Europe, absorbed in the close study of the classical architecture of Rome and ancient Greece. During his travels, he also developed an interest in learning about religions other than Christianity. His journey through Turkey, Egypt, and Persia exposed him to the world of Islam, a faith rarely encountered in North America.[19] For the first time in his life, he was immersed in the rich architectural styles, religious traditions, and poetry of the Middle East. The intricate designs with their complex tracery, curves, filigree, and elaborate ornamentation as used in Islamic structures would have been especially captivating to him because of his sensibilities as an artist and as an engineer.

After returning to North America, Louis continued his spiritual search while working with architectural firms around the United States. He went from Chicago to Omaha, to San Francisco, and finally to Los Angeles, where he met the woman who would become his second wife, Alice de Longpré.[20] Alice's father was the French artist Paul de Longpré, whose paintings of flowers were very popular. He commissioned Louis to design a house, as well as most of its ornamentation, for his three-acre estate in the newly established community of Hollywood. Louis was also hired to tutor de Longpré's three daughters in French. Years later, Louis married de Longpré's middle daughter, Alice.

Louis and Alice Bourgeois (USBNA)

As Louis' architectural skills grew and his professional reputation rose, he never stopped searching for a faith to which he could give his heart. He moved east to Boston where, for the first time, he encountered Bahá'ís. The Bourgeois family then moved to New York, where they met the Wilhelms at Bahá'í gatherings and became confirmed believers. Later, talking about his spiritual quest for a religion he could embrace, Louis explained that "I had a strong psychic feeling that the Christ spirit was astir in the world and that I should design the temple for this spirit."[21]

In 1908, Roy and his parents commissioned Louis to design their home—a more mundane, more earthly assignment than a "temple for this spirit." Two years earlier, Louis and Alice had completed their own family home on Alicia Street in Teaneck, a short walk from Roy's property. After accepting the Wilhelms' project, Louis sat down at his desk and started drawing up the plans for the modest, two-story, stucco-finished house—his first design for a Bahá'í. As Roy's parents had already sold their Zanesville home, the Bourgeois family opened their home to them to provide a temporary place for the Wilhelms to stay while their house was under construction. As fellow believers who were living together for months, the two families drew even closer together.

Louis' design for the Wilhelm homestead was both charming and practical. Situated at the top of a steep hill, the spacious though modest house was adorned simply and economically with smooth rocks

The Teaneck home of the Bourgeois family, which was visited by
'Abdu'l-Bahá in 1912. It was designed by Louis Bourgeois,
who is seated in a rocking chair.

collected from the river at the bottom of the hill. The rocks, arranged in columns running the full height of the house, gave the stucco residence the rustic look Roy favored. Its wide front porch, which opened onto the terrace that ran along the front of the house, provided ample seating when the weather was fine. The main front room, which

Front and rear views of the Wilhelm home in Teaneck as it appeared in 2022. 'Abdu'l-Bahá stayed in the front bedroom on the left. (Bryan Weber, photographer)

opened into the dining area, could be used as a parlor, which made it perfect for gatherings. Exposed wooden millwork added to the warm ambience, and the plentiful number of large windows made the home bright and cheerful. Few houses had been built around it by 1908, so for many years, the home appeared to be situated in a forest.

The Wilhelms did not wait long to landscape the area closest to the house, and within a few years, they added other beautiful features, such as a wisteria-covered pergola. Later, on the top of the hill near the road, they built a tennis court, perhaps because Otis loved to play that game. Then, along the back of the property, Roy built a smaller frame building with a garage to not only house Roy's vehicles but also to serve as a residence for those he employed to take care of the property.

The Wilhelm tennis court with the rear of the home in the background. Today, the location of the court is a parking lot. (USBNA)

Almost as soon as the Wilhelms moved into their new home, they opened it to Bahá'ís and to those interested in the Faith. Roy and his parents became well acquainted with their neighbors and actively took part in the general life of the West Englewood community. Even before they occupied the house, the Wilhelms invited all the Bahá'ís from the New York area to a picnic at their property. Roy's home became another tool he used to serve and teach the Faith. Happily settled in New Jersey, the three Wilhelms became a team devoted to Bahá'í service.

Within a year of Roy's move to Teaneck, Louis' and Roy's service to the Cause would connect in ways other than merely supporting each other's Bahá'í gatherings. Over time, both men would become intimately involved in raising up a Bahá'í Temple in North America. To understand how their two paths merged, it is important to explore the history of this project that would have major implications for both friends.

It all began when, in 1903, the American believers learned that Bahá'ís in Turkmenistan, just across the border from Iran, were building a House of Worship—a "Dawning Place of the Praise of God" (called in Persian, *Mashriqu'l-Adhkár*), a type of building ordained by Bahá'u'lláh.[22] Houses of Worship were not meant to be meeting halls, but rather grand nine-sided edifices dedicated to quiet prayer—majestic, inviting, and beautiful. The building under construction would serve as the spiritual heart of the community of 'Ishqábád (modern day Ashgabat) as a place where people of all faiths could come to pray and meditate. Surrounding it, institutions such as schools, medical clinics, lodgings for travelers, and drug dispensaries would arise to serve the community. As the Faith grew and expanded, every city and town would eventually come to revolve around a House of Worship and its subsidiary institutions. One individual was providing most of the funds for the construction work in 'Ishqábád, though believers from many other countries were contributing as well.

This first ever House of Worship inspired the American Bahá'ís. If their fellow believers could erect such a Temple in a remote place without the material resources available in the United States, couldn't they do the same? Thus, the believers in North America began to discuss the possibility of erecting such a building. 'Abdu'l-Bahá encouraged them to follow the example of their co-believers in the Orient, but vocal skeptics, surveying the community's resources, warned that such an undertaking was beyond the capacity of the infant North American community. The reality was that the small local communities struggled to collect funds simply to rent halls for meetings and to publish Bahá'í literature, and so they could not be expected to construct and maintain a building akin to a grand cathedral.

'Abdu'l-Bahá Himself settled the matter in 1907 with His unequivocal instructions to one American believer. The month or so before the Wilhelms reached 'Akká, a well-to-do matron from Chicago—Corinne Knight True, with her young daughter, Arna—were in the Holy Land as pilgrims. Corinne True was one of the strongest proponents for an American House of Worship and had already taken steps to promote it. She had brought with her to Haifa a petition with over eight hundred signatures from people around the country willing to support a House of Worship raised up in the Chicago area, the focal point of America's heartland.

This petition, which she worked diligently to compile, brought great joy to the heart of 'Abdu'l-Bahá. He carefully instructed her as to what needed to be done and charged her with making the House of Worship her life's work—and she did. Shortly after her visit, three men who served on the Bahá'í governing council for Chicago, the House of Spirituality (as it was then called), arrived at the home of 'Abdu'l-Bahá as pilgrims. Arthur Agnew, accompanied by Thornton Chase and Carl Scheffler, had been asked by the House of Spirituality to put forth questions to 'Abdu'l-Bahá about the prospect of a Temple. 'Abdu'l-Bahá politely but firmly informed the three men that He had already given His instructions to Mrs. True, and that they would need to obtain the answers to their questions from her. This response had the effect of indirectly highlighting the importance of women serving in leadership positions in the Faith. He emphasized that the raising up of a House of Worship was of the utmost importance and that building it was not a mere suggestion, but necessary.

Over the next year, Bahá'í communities, especially those in Chicago, New York, and Washington, DC, sent letters back and forth to one another about what steps needed to be taken to construct a House of Worship. Mrs. True wrote to 'Abdu'l-Bahá proposing that a conference be held to discuss how to bring the Temple into existence. She also suggested inviting each Bahá'í community to send a representative to the conference. Finally, after much wrangling, a date was set for the period of the Bahá'í New Year in March, 1909. Over seventy communities with three or more believers were asked to send representatives, and thirty-six did so. The delegates would participate in Chicago's Bahá'í New Year celebration, after which they would tour two lots, which had already been purchased as a potential site, located north of the city and close to Lake Michigan. Then on Monday, March 22, they would· get down to the real business at hand—creating a national organization essential to making the Temple a reality.

Before the delegates convened in Chicago, a number of prominent Bahá'ís from large communities envisioned that the Chicago House of Spirituality would oversee the project, with a committee representing the country-at-large assisting that board. But this arrangement was not what the majority of delegates desired. Instead, the delegates adopted the vision that the Temple would belong to all North Americans, not simply the Chicagoans. It would serve as a continental symbol, a visible ideal, even for those who would never be privileged to worship within it. In any case, there was already a growing recognition that the Faith, with communities spread from coast to coast, needed a national organization, if for no other reason than to coordinate the production of Bahá'í literature. Therefore, the House of Worship was not to be a meeting place solely for the Bahá'í community within whose environs it was located. Rather, the Temple would be used by everyone, and it would be a tangible means of uniting the people of North America.

In the third-floor billiard room of the True Family's house, a constitution was drafted, and the newly born national body was given a most awkward name: Bahá'í Temple Unity. The members of the organization decided to hold conventions annually and to elect an executive board that would carry out the directives of the annual Convention in the intervening months. The members realized that the new entity had to be established on a sound legal basis in order for the organization to own property, enter into contracts, and manage bank accounts. Fortunately, among the delegates were several lawyers, notably Albert Hall of Minnesota, as well as a professional architect, Charles Mason Remey of Washington, DC who were able to assist the consultation with practical advice.

When it came time to consider the membership of the Executive Board, the delegates decided to appoint a committee from among themselves to nominate a slate of candidates to ensure that all the large communities were represented.

If the delegates could have looked far into the future, they would have discovered to their amazement that they were planting the tiny seed that, in the fullness of time, would sprout and grow into the first institutions of the Bahá'í Administrative Order—a new pattern for ordering the affairs of humanity based upon the principles set forth by Bahá'u'lláh. In hindsight, the role of the organization was not simply to raise up a building. Rather, it was about learning to work together and to make decisions through the divinely ordained process of consultation. The work before them was permeated with challenges and obstacles. They had resolved to build, with scant resources, a magnificent House of Worship to the Glory of God. The fruit of their labors would be more stunningly wonderful than they could imagine at that moment when they assembled on Corrine True's front porch for a photograph to memorialize the historic gathering.[23]

To underline the significance of the 1909 Chicago convention, by a "strange coincidence," it was held on the same day as another monumental event.[24] At the time the delegates were meeting, 'Abdu'l-Bahá was placing the sacred remains of the Báb in their final resting place on Mount Carmel—one of many remarkable connections between the Shrine of the Báb and the Mother Temple of the West.

Roy was not a delegate and therefore did not attend the Chicago convention in 1909. Nonetheless, he became the center of a minor

Some of the participants in the 1909 National Convention, which established the Bahá'í Temple Unity and elected its Executive Board. The group posed on the front porch of the True home in Chicago. (USBNA)

disagreement during its proceedings. The delegates decided that New York needed two representatives, not one. The New York community was contacted while the sessions were underway, and the response from that community was that it had chosen Roy as its second delegate. This created confusion in Chicago because he was not present. After further discussion, the delegates determined that the New York lawyer, Mountfort Mills, who was present and who would later work closely with Roy on Bahá'í affairs, should serve as his proxy.[25]

When the results of the election of the Executive Board were announced at that first Temple Unity Convention, Roy was not among those named; however, by the time the next Convention was held the following year, he was already serving on it. Perhaps he had been appointed to fill a vacancy, though the surviving records are unclear. By late summer of 1909, Roy was receiving messages from 'Abdu'l-Bahá about his services on that Board as well as the

New York Board of Council, which was the governing body for the Bahá'ís living in New York. 'Abdu'l-Bahá wrote that "Thy membership in the Spiritual Assembly of New York is very acceptable and seasonable: also thy chairmanship of the Executive Board for the services of the Mashrek-el-Azkar. I ask the Lord of Hosts for victory in thy behalf and that thou mayest be surrounded by His Bounties."[26]

Over the course of the next few years, the Executive Board seldom met. Most of its work was focused on raising the funds necessary to complete the purchase of the building site in the suburbs of Chicago. However, Roy did begin to regularly attend the annual Conventions from 1910 forward and usually attended the Executive Board meetings.

Though Roy missed the historic first meeting of Bahá'í Temple Unity, he visited Chicago sixty days after the meeting concluded when several of the delegates were still there. He reported that he was very affected by their reports of that gathering:

> I reached Chicago some sixty days after the Convention last year, but several members were still in the city, and do you know it seemed to me that the spirit was still very strong there. I am not of the emotional kind, rather too matter-of-fact, I guess, but at that Sunday meeting several of the visitors spoke, and to my astonishment I was so overcome that my feelings nearly swamped me—an entirely new experience for me.[27]

Clearly, Roy took to heart 'Abdu'l-Bahá's guidance after his 1907 pilgrimage to be actively involved in service. Not only was he engaged in the national work of raising up a House of Worship, but he also became fully committed to the administration of the Faith for the New York metropolitan area following his 1909 election to its Board of Council, which began to call itself, prematurely, the New York Spiritual Assembly. Spiritual Assemblies were ordained by Bahá'u'lláh, but the time for their election had not yet arrived. (Furthermore, "Assembly" was the term used in Western Bahá'í communities until the mid-1920s to refer to the entire membership of a locality, not its governing council.)

The history of the Board of Council for New York went back to 1900 when it was first elected, predating by a couple of years the Wilhelms' first introduction to that community. During its first years, the Council did the best it could to organize its work, even though it lacked any authoritative guidance about how to administer a Bahá'í community. Regrettably, several of the Persian believers sent to North America to instruct the friends in the verities of the Faith were themselves confused about many points of Bahá'í administration. One important misstatement they conveyed to their eager students was that, even though women had the right to vote in elections, only men could serve on Bahá'í administrative bodies. Given that the United States did not fully grant suffrage to its female citizens until 1920 with the passage of the 19th Amendment to the Constitution, this restriction was accepted by many believers without question, even though women constituted the majority of active members of the community. 'Abdu'l-Bahá would clarify that they had been misinformed regarding women's service on administrative bodies of the Faith, and as a result of His guidance, women began to be elected. Furthermore, the governing committees in major cities such as New York and Chicago had little authority beyond managing funds, taking care of major administrative duties such as renting spaces for gatherings, and ensuring that the Faith was publicized and its literature produced. They could not make determinations regarding whether or not a point of view was true to the Bahá'í teachings, nor could they decide issues of membership status.[28] They did, however, provide valuable experience in administration that would make the later transition to Local Spiritual Assemblies easier.[29]

As it happened, Roy was elected to the New York governing council in 1909 as part of a concerted effort to unseat other members, because two factions had developed within the community. His election at that time was ironic because Roy was usually a peacemaker,

The original New York City Board of Council elected in 1900. Seated second from the left is Howard MacNutt, standing on his left is William Hoar, and seated to Hoar's right is Arthur Dodge. (USBNA)

even though he had keen insight into the machinations of the believers who created difficulties. No evidence exists that he was part of either faction. This disunity created by dominant personalities would continue for some time and become one of the challenges of serving on the New York Board of Council. However, this experience provided Roy with the opportunity to learn about another important area of service: protecting the Faith. He became a voice of reason and a quiet counselor who could often find a point of unity when problems arose that created ill-feelings between believers. His presence would help that community heal its rifts over the years ahead.[30]

Roy never ceased teaching the Faith as he traveled the country for his company. Many of Wilhelm & Co.'s important clients were the big coffee roasters headquartered in major cities of the Northeast, but others were scattered across the country, from its heartland to the Pacific shore. His company's goal was to have only one client in each major market. Reaching distant customers in Chicago, Los Angeles, San Francisco, and the Northwest cities in Oregon and Washington required long journeys by train, so Roy's business travels allowed him to connect with and assist Bahá'ís all over the country. In whichever city he stopped, he would urge local Bahá'ís to arrange a venue where he could speak about God's latest revelation. Whether he was meeting only one or two souls in a parlor or many listeners in an overflowing hotel banquet hall, Roy would always show up wearing a suit and his signature bowtie to lovingly speak about the great new day brought by Bahá'u'lláh.

On one such occasion, during a business trip to Tacoma, Washington, in 1909, Roy was invited by Valeria Kelsey to give a talk in her home "on the Bahá'í Movement." This new Bahá'í was also anxious for him to meet with her sixteen-year-old son, Curtis, who of all her children seemed to have a spiritual sensitivity. As a teenager, however, Curtis did not share his mother's enthusiasm for her new-found religion, or for any religion for that matter. He had explored a few conventional religions at his mother's insistence and had even branched out to fringe faiths and the occult before rejecting them all.

The day Roy came to his home, Curtis preferred to hide out in the basement with his woodworking tools until his mother's New York visitor was gone. Valeria, however, thought that if Roy talked to her son, he might listen. Overhearing their conspiracy at the top of the stairs, Curtis knew he was trapped and braced for a long, boring sermon. But Roy, perhaps because of his own youthful rebellions, well understood the young man's reticence to listen to a stranger talk about religion. So, instead of speaking about the Bahá'í Faith, Roy instead focused solely on what Curtis was doing in the basement. He asked about woodworking and watched Curtis demonstrate how to turn a length of wood on a lathe. Impressed with the young man's skills, he invited Curtis to help him set up a woodshop at his Teaneck home. Although happy that the coffee merchant from the East didn't engage him in "religious talk," Curtis was not keen to abandon his bucolic life in the Pacific Northwest for the city, so he declined the invitation. Roy's cryptic response—"Well, you never know about these things; strange things happen"—must have baffled the youth. But God had other plans for Curtis.[31]

Through Curtis, Roy would cultivate his ability to nurture new believers and mentor a promising young man. A lifelong close relationship began that day in the basement that would be further cemented in the Holy Land.

4 / JOYOUS DAYS:
'ABDU'L-BAHÁ IN AMERICA

". . . hearts will be bound together, spirits blended and a new foundation for unity established. All the friends will come. They will be my guests. They will be as the parts and members of one body. The spirit of life manifest in that body will be one spirit. The foundation of that temple of unity will be one foundation. Each will be a stone in that foundation, solid and interdependent. Each will be as a leaf, blossom or fruit upon one tree. For the sake of fellowship and unity I desire this feast and spiritual gathering."[1] 'Abdu'l-Bahá

In the early autumn of 1910, momentous news reached the Bahá'ís in America: as a result of the Young Turks Revolution, 'Abdu'l-Bahá had been released from a lifetime of imprisonment,[2] and He was no longer in Palestine. Free at last to leave the Levant, He sailed from the Holy Land to Egypt, escaping the clutches of those who wished Him harm and would try to prevent His departure, including members of His own family.[3] Naturally, the first thought of His American flock when they heard that good news was that He should come to the United States, so they immediately sent appeals imploring Him to visit. His consistent response was that He would be drawn to their shores only by their unity, and not before that condition was met.[4]

Roy was a member of the Executive Board of Bahá'í Temple Unity when it sent a letter to the believers across North America describing in detail what was needed if they wanted 'Abdu'l-Bahá to come to them, emphasizing how they could outwardly manifest unity by supporting the drive to collect funds to build the Temple. The American Bahá'ís already understood the importance of erecting the House of Worship, for it was the one tangible goal given to them by 'Abdu'l-Bahá Himself, yet the total sum needed to begin the project had not been contributed. The Board reminded the friends of the significance of the Temple by calling their attention to 'Abdu'l-Bahá's admonition to several pilgrims from Chicago that it would be "the *cause* of the confirmation of the believers. It has a great effect because it is the beginning of the foundation . . . This *building* will be the *cause* of *Unity* and *prosperity* of the Cause."[5]

The letter went on to recount what 'Abdu'l-Bahá had told an unnamed pilgrim the previous year when asked if He would come to America. He responded that He would if the House of Worship was built. When the pilgrim had an opportunity to speak to 'Abdu'l-Bahá in private, he asked the question again. His countenance changed, and He became very serious as "a great majesty" came over Him. He replied, "If the ground in America is well prepared so that much work can be done for the Cause." He concluded by saying that building the House of Worship would prepare that ground.[6] The Board therefore appealed to the believers to work and pray in unity until the Temple was built, and it warned that, given 'Abdu'l-Bahá's sudden departure from the Holy Land, the friends should make more efforts for the Temple "lest 'Abdu'l-Bahá come upon us suddenly and 'find us sleeping.'"[7]

When 'Abdu'l-Bahá arrived in France in the late summer of 1911, the Americans became even more hopeful that He would soon cross the Atlantic Ocean. Instead, He returned to Egypt in November, after informing the Americans that He hoped to come to the New World the following spring.[8] This was the joyful news that the friends throughout North America had longed to receive.

For years, the Bahá'ís in North America had become intensely interested in providing practical assistance to their fellow believers in Persia,* the Cradle of the Faith, by sending funds, teachers, nurses, and a doctor to establish schools and medical clinics there. Most of those who went to Iran were women who focused primarily on improving the well-being of women and girls. North American Bahá'ís were asked to sponsor individual students at the Bahá'í schools. Roy was apparently assisting with this effort and wrote to 'Abdu'l-Bahá that he wished to travel to Iran. 'Abdu'l-Bahá first replied enthusiastically that Roy should go,[9] but in a second letter sent months later from Egypt, it was clear that the situation had changed. The new guidance Roy received dissuaded him from making that trip because 'Abdu'l-Bahá would be coming to visit him instead. 'Abdu'l-Bahá wrote:

> A cable was sent to you in answer to your cable communication to the effect that you may remain in America. The aim is this: as in these days great revolution and internal disorder exists in Persia, therefore travelling in that country is very difficult. You stay in America till I come so that we may meet each other. It is my hope that it may become better than the Persian trip and that we may associate with each other with the utmost joy and fragrance and communicate with each other through the Breaths of the Holy Spirit.[10]

In response to this happy news of a probable visit, Roy sent $1,000** to 'Abdu'l-Bahá to assist with His upcoming travels to America. The money was gratefully accepted and then returned to Roy with a request that it be used in pursuit of humanitarian goals.

---

* Iran.

** The sum of $1,000 dollars would be equivalent to more than $28,000 in 2022 US dollars. This amount was probably enough to pay for all of 'Abdu'l-Bahá's personal expenses while in North America, though it would not have covered the expenses of His entourage.

The privilege of financially supporting 'Abdu'l-Bahá's Western journey would be given solely to the Bahá'ís in the East. The letter read:

> With regard to the sum of $1,000 which you sent, I was made very happy with your endeavors, and I will never forget this kindness of yours. I ask for you the Divine Blessings and I have accepted this sum. But, as there is no ceremony between us, and as the expenses of my journey have been prepared, furthermore, as to accumulate is the manner of worldly people, not permissible to 'Abdu'l-Bahá—for the Christ has said "O God! Give us our daily bread"—therefore I am returned these $1,000 so that you may spend it yourself, in my name, in good works for humanity . . .[11]

The Executive Board of the Bahá'í Temple Unity, as the only national Bahá'í committee then in existence in North America, lost no time in preparing for the hoped-for visit of 'Abdu'l-Bahá. It called upon the communities across the United States and Canada to consider the importance of the upcoming national Convention in April 1912, and asked them to make early preparations to select delegates.[12] This was followed shortly thereafter by details for the next Convention, which the Board hoped that 'Abdu'l-Bahá would attend. It also expected that He would consecrate the site for the future House of Worship during the Convention period. The Board was certain that many of the friends, in addition to the delegates, would be present at the special Convention, so it asked local communities to send in advance an estimate of the number of those planning to attend in order for adequate preparations to be made.[13] Roy's head must have been spinning as he and his colleagues contemplated the preparations needed to organize such an historic gathering in Chicago, not to mention Roy's other responsibilities as a member of the New York Board of Council, which was also planning for 'Abdu'l-Bahá's visit to its community.

In the early morning hours of April 11, 1912, the steamship *Cedric* completed her voyage across the Atlantic, passing the Statue of Liberty as she churned her way through the harbor to finally settle into her berth alongside a New York pier. From the upper deck, 'Abdu'l-Bahá watched as the ship passed the immense statue symbolizing the ideals upon which the United States was established as a country. He remarked at that moment, "There is the new world's symbol of liberty and freedom. After being forty years a prisoner I can tell you that freedom is not a matter of place. It is a condition. Unless one accept dire vicissitudes he will not attain. When one is released from the prison of self, that is indeed a release."[14]

While tugboats were still guiding the ship toward her berth, most of the members of the New York Bahá'í community stood on the pier eagerly awaiting His arrival. Newspaper reporters had already been ferried out to the *Cedric* to begin interviewing the religious leader from the East. Finally, around noon, the ship's passengers began to disembark, but 'Abdu'l-Bahá was not among those coming down the gangplank. He sent word to the believers anxious for even a brief glimpse of Him that they should leave, and He would meet with them later that day at the home of the Kinney family. There is no record of Roy waiting at the pier, but most likely he was there, especially considering pier 18 was only about three miles from his office.

Thus 'Abdu'l-Bahá's travels across the United States began—a spiritual journey that would forever transform not only countless hearts but the nature of the American Bahá'í community. Roy, often working behind the scenes to make practical arrangements for 'Abdu'l-Bahá, would play a prominent role throughout this great and sacred adventure.

Over the course of the next two weeks, Roy and his parents had many opportunities to meet with 'Abdu'l-Bahá at both the homes of believers in Manhattan and at the venues of His public speaking engagements. It seems likely that Roy, and probably his parents, attended 'Abdu'l-Bahá's first public address at the Church of the Ascension on April 14, three days after His arrival. His talk was the main sermon delivered at the customary Sunday morning worship service. The large, affluent Episcopal Church was so crowded that some members of the congregation and many visitors were seated on chairs placed in the aisles.

When it was His time to speak, 'Abdu'l-Bahá did not begin from behind the pulpit, but instead, with His long robes flowing, He paced back and forth across the chancel steps in front of the altar. He began His impromptu remarks by referring to Saint Paul's letter to the Corinthians in the New Testament, which a clergyman had just read aloud to the congregation. He then turned to His theme—the oneness of mankind, the overarching message of most of His talks in North America. He also emphasized the importance of the spiritual development of not only individuals but civilization, a bold point to make in the heart of the one city that best exemplified all facets of materialism. By the time the service concluded with 'Abdu'l-Bahá's chant of a prayer in Persian, the hearts of His listeners were overflowing.[15]

On April 20, 'Abdu'l-Bahá boarded a train in New York to travel to Washington, DC, where an excited Bahá'í community was waiting for Him on the platform. For the next eight days, He met with many prominent people in the nation's capital, as well as those who stood on the lower rungs of Capitol Hill society. He made a point of visiting poorer neighborhoods as well as giving special attention to Black believers and their friends who endured deep-seated rejection due to racial prejudice within the greater community. Overall, His visit to Washington was a triumph and set the Americans more firmly on the road of advocating racial unity. Then, early on the evening of April 28, He was once again on a train, this time headed toward Chicago, where He would arrive the following day. This is where Roy, a delegate to the national Convention, which had already convened, would next catch up with Him.

'Abdu'l-Bahá had numerous reasons to visit Chicago. It was where Americans first encountered and became committed to the Faith. These new believers spread out from that city in the heartland of the continent, establishing within a decade fledgling communities from the Atlantic to the Pacific.[16] One of the city's suburbs, the Village of Wilmette, had been chosen as the site for the future House of Worship, and the greater metropolitan Chicago area had become the hub of the work of Bahá'í Temple Unity. Most important of all, the fifth National Convention would be underway during 'Abdu'l-Bahá's time there.

Even though the National Convention was two days into its work when He arrived, alternative engagements had already been arranged for 'Abdu'l-Bahá by the time He stepped down from the train the night of April 29. One of the most important commitments on 'Abdu'l-Bahá's schedule was addressing the national convention of the National Association for the Advancement of Colored* People (NAACP), the foremost organization working for the rights of the oppressed Black segment of the population. He was keenly interested in the work being done by this and other progressive organizations in the city, such as Jane Addams' innovative Hull House, that were striving to improve the plight of those who were oppressed or poor, for He wished to encourage and strengthen their efforts.

Having convened on the 27th, the Bahá'í National Convention had already completed most of its agenda before 'Abdu'l-Bahá arrived in Chicago. The organizers had anticipated that He would attend it from beginning to end; however, 'Abdu'l-Bahá apparently did not wish to participate in the Convention deliberations, and He instead

---

* In 1912, the word "colored" was the preferred word for Black citizens in the United States. Over time, other words have been used to designate that segment of the population. This work has chosen to use the current preference, "Black."

'Abdu'l-Bahá addressing those who came for the dedication of the Temple
property as part of the 1912 National Convention. (USBNA)

gave the delegates the freedom to carry out the business before them
without the distraction of His presence. On the evening of the 30th,
after all business sessions were concluded, 'Abdu'l-Bahá entered the
spacious Drill Hall of the Masonic Temple, which was filled to overflowing with more than a thousand Bahá'ís representing the widespread communities of Canada and the United States. Many of the
pillars of the Bahá'í Faith in North America, including Roy, were
present.

With every eye fixed upon Him, 'Abdu'l-Bahá walked majestically
up the aisle to the podium. He began his remarks by discussing the
spiritual importance of the House of Worship, which would be "con-
ducive to unity and fellowship . . ." He said, however, that "The real
temple is the very Word of God; for to it all humanity must turn,
and it is the center of unity for all mankind. . . ."[17] After discussing
the Bahá'í message of the oneness of mankind and world peace, He
concluded His remarks with a prayer for America.[18]

An event took place the next day that those who were privileged to be present, such as Roy, would always remember: the laying of the cornerstone of the House of Worship by 'Abdu'l-Bahá. The crowd of more than three hundred Bahá'ís, and others interested in the event, came by automobile and taxi to the open field that the Bahá'í Temple Unity planned to purchase. The site was full of tall grass, shrubs, and the occasional tree. Nearby were modest buildings which, once acquired, would be torn down as the Temple rose. Across the street, waves washed against the shore of Lake Michigan. On the other side of the large meadow, an iron bridge spanned a canal. The center of the property had been cleared for the event, and a large, white canvas tent had been erected there to shelter the guests from the capricious northern Illinois spring weather. Inside, three hundred chairs had been arranged in concentric circles, divided by nine aisles, and standing room was available inside the perimeter of the tent.

'Abdu'l-Bahá overseeing the laying of the cornerstone of the Temple
(USBNA)

The dedication of the Temple land was set for 11:00 o'clock in the morning. The crowd, using the opportunity to visit with their fellow believers from across the country, waited anxiously for the arrival of 'Abdu'l-Bahá. An hour passed, yet there was no sign of Him or His entourage. The members of the increasingly restless crowd, alternately sitting for a while and then standing, wandered in and out of the tent. The Bahá'ís started to wonder aloud what might have happened to 'Abdu'l-Bahá, though those who had been traveling with Him the previous weeks had already learned that He was not governed by clocks, for, to Him, there were matters more important than keeping to a schedule.

Finally, two hours after the appointed time, 'Abdu'l-Bahá arrived in a taxi. Excitement pulsed through the crowd as many rushed to where the vehicle had stopped. They were puzzled and disappointed when the door opened, Corinne True got in, and the taxi drove off. What many of them may not have yet known was that her young son had died the night before, so 'Abdu'l-Bahá wanted to comfort her and called to her from the taxi. Several blocks away, the taxi stopped in a public park, and 'Abdu'l-Bahá and Corinne got out and walked together.

At last, 'Abdu'l-Bahá returned to the Temple site and walked into the center of the tent. After His brief remarks, He left the tent, with everyone following closely behind Him, and went to the site of the groundbreaking ceremony. The organizers of the event had assumed He would bring a cornerstone with Him, but He had not done so. Indeed, because a design for the building had yet to be chosen, it was premature to lay a cornerstone for any reason other than as a ceremonial memento of the dedication. Moreover, most of the ground the crowd was trampling upon had not yet been purchased.[19]

The lack of a proper cornerstone was not a problem because for years, the believers had said prayers around a stone already on the site. Several years before the morning's groundbreaking ceremony, Nettie Tobin, a widow and seamstress from Chicago, had, with much difficulty, dragged, pushed, and shoved a misshapen hunk of discarded construction stone to the site. Over time, this stone had become a

Corinne True, whose son died the night prior to the Temple land
dedication. Like Roy, she would be named a Hand of the Cause of God.
(USBNA)

focal point around which local believers stood and said prayers.
'Abdu'l-Bahá called for it to be brought to Him. Then, assisted by
a few others, and using first a special decorative golden trowel and
then a sturdier shovel and pickaxe, He ceremoniously created a hole
within which to place the stone. This was spiritually significant to the
believers from Christian backgrounds because it seemed to fulfill the
biblical prophecy that the stone which the builders rejected became
the cornerstone of the Temple.[20] (That stone, now a historic relic,
is displayed in the lower level of the House of Worship in approxi-

mately the spot where ʻAbdu'l-Bahá placed it that first day of May in 1912.[21])

In early 1912, before ʻAbdu'l-Bahá sailed from Egypt for New York, Roy sent Him a photograph of the new Wilhelm residence in Teaneck, no doubt with an invitation to stay there while He was in America. In reply, ʻAbdu'l-Bahá wrote that "Your portrait and the photograph of our house have both reached me . . . The sight of your portrait brought joy to my heart, because it is luminous and celestial; and looking at the photograph of your house, I saw the charm of the spot and the beauty of the environment, and the perfection of its buildings . . ."[22] He continued, "Your house is my house: there is no difference whatsoever between yours and mine . . ." However, Roy's offer of hospitality was left an open question because, "as far as where I am to stay is concerned, I must do what wisdom commands."[23]

Over the course of the first three months of His travels in North America, ʻAbdu'l-Bahá's arduous journey had been from one metropolitan center to the next. His days were fully scheduled. Except for a brief Hudson Valley respite in the green hills surrounding Lake Mohonk, He had been immersed in the urban congestion and gray concrete canyons of Boston, Chicago, Washington DC, Cleveland, and New York City. His travels, drawing press attention and listeners by the thousands from every segment of the population, became a paean to diversity.[24] His audiences ranged from foreign diplomats to the homeless in New York's infamous Bowery neighborhood. Whether speaking before an audience of affluent church members, delivering a lecture to university students, or meeting with a group of disadvantaged children, His overarching message was the same—the oneness of mankind.[25]

When considering the various titles of 'Abdu'l-Bahá—*the Servant of Bahá, the Master, the Perfect Exemplar, the Mystery of God*—it becomes easy to overlook His human side. The friends witnessed His radiant, majestic presence and heard His reassuring yet commanding voice and forgot the toll a lifetime of physical deprivation had taken on His body. Having suffered decades of meager access to nourishment or medical care, He was racked by the aches and pains of rheumatism caused by sleeping in cold damp places as a prisoner, as well as by other chronic ailments. Whether in the Holy Land or during His travels, 'Abdu'l-Bahá would have to seek opportunities to restore His health and spirit. As summer arrived in Manhattan, so did heatwave upon heatwave, which wore Him down when He was already exhausted because of his relentless schedule of travel and meetings. Consequently, the invitation from the friends in Montclair, New Jersey, to visit their town arrived at an ideal moment. Nestled at the foot of the Blue Hills of the Watchung Mountain range, Montclair, though only twelve miles outside of New York City, was pleasant and green—just the sort of place where 'Abdu'l-Bahá could escape Manhattan's oppressive summer heat for a few days and recuperate from the ardors of his travel and the many burdens He constantly bore.[26] This respite brought Him closer to Roy's home.

One way in which Roy was able to assist 'Abdu'l-Bahá during His stay in Montclair was to make available to Him the use of Roy's large automobile. Like many people of his generation, Roy was fascinated by the rapidly developing new mode of transportation—automobiles—and he owned several during a time when they were not yet widely owned by average Americans. While many of his peers were driven by chauffeurs during those early days of the still-unreliable horseless carriage, Roy preferred to drive himself. In 1911, he bought a four-door REO Touring Car that could easily carry four passengers, in addition to the driver. By definition, a touring car did not have a fixed roof, only a folding canvas top to provide a measure of protection from sun, rain, and dust. Built in Lansing, Michigan by the company founded by Ransom E. Olds (REO) of the Oldsmobile nameplate, Roy's automobile had a formidable 30-horsepower, four-cylinder engine. With its shining kerosene taillight warning off other drivers, it was rugged enough to climb the steep hills of the back roads of the New Jersey countryside, yet elegant enough to drive up Broadway Avenue in New York City. Advertisements for the car listed it for $1,350, including a top and windshield, making it almost twice as expensive as a similarly equipped though less robust but more popular Model T touring car, which sold for $780, from Henry Ford's company. The following incident involving the REO most likely took place while 'Abdu'l-Bahá rested in Montclair.

One day 'Abdu'l-Bahá asked Roy to drive Him to Newark, New Jersey, in order to visit a man. Delighted to be of service, Roy agreed without hesitation, and picked up 'Abdu'l-Bahá (and most likely, sev-

REO automobile used by Roy to take 'Abdu'l-Bahá from place to place within the New York metropolitan area in 1912

eral members of His entourage) in the REO. Naturally, Roy asked for
the name and address of the man in Newark, but either 'Abdu'l-Bahá
did not know or did not care to say; He was, nonetheless, anxious to
depart. Puzzled, Roy drove off toward Newark. When they arrived
at that city, Roy, uncertain where he was supposed to take 'Abdu'l-
Bahá, began driving up one street and down another. A short time
later, as Roy recalled, "a man came running out of his house yelling
at the top of his lungs, 'Abdu'l-Bahá, 'Abdu'l-Bahá!'"²⁷ Roy stopped
the car, and everyone went to the stranger's home, where the mystery
man and 'Abdu'l-Bahá entered into a long discussion. This was but
one example of 'Abdu'l-Bahá's supernatural knowledge, for He knew
that the fellow, unknown to the Bahá'í community, was searching
for Him that day. 'Abdu'l-Bahá did not need to know his name or
address, because He was guided by divine inspiration. Roy subsequently learned that this unidentified man later became an ardent
follower of Bahá'u'lláh.²⁸

Even before 'Abdu'l-Bahá went to Montclair, memories of wonderful picnics in the Holy Land must have come into His mind. His
family had often escaped the heat and congestion of bleak 'Akká—a
densely populated, walled city lacking any vegetation—by holding
picnics beneath the towering pines adjoining the open fields outside
the city's walls. There, their faces would be cooled by the refreshing
breezes blowing across the land from the Mediterranean Sea. After
months of exhausting travel, a gathering of His American friends
in the dappled shade of a garden where they could enjoy a simple
repast together would provide a different and welcome dimension
to His visit to North America. In such a setting, there would be no
rigid protocols such as those required in hotel banquet rooms, lecture
halls, or church sanctuaries. His guests at a picnic would be able to
relax, perhaps with a little less starch in a loosened collar or a bonnet

pushed back off the forehead. Unity would be enhanced by bringing the friends together for a day of fellowship and harmony in a pastoral spot. Where could 'Abdu'l-Bahá find such a garden to host the picnic He desired? He stated exactly what He wanted, saying:

> I am about to leave the city for a few days rest at Montclair. When I return, it is my wish to give a large feast of unity. A place for it has not yet been found. It must be outdoors under the trees, in some location away from city noise—like a Persian garden. The food will be Persian food.[29] When the place is arranged, all will be informed, and we will have a general meeting in which hearts will be bound together, spirits blended and a new foundation for unity established. All the friends will come. They will be my guests. They will be as the parts and members of one body. The spirit of life manifest in that body will be one spirit. The foundation of that temple of unity will be one foundation. Each will be a stone in that foundation, solid and interdependent. Each will be as a leaf, blossom or fruit upon one tree. For the sake of fellowship and unity I desire this feast and spiritual gathering.[30]

Those responsible for arranging 'Abdu'l-Bahá's picnic did not have to consider many options because they already knew where to turn to find a perfect site. The loving hospitality and courtesy shown by the Wilhelm family to all who came to their Bergen County home had attracted seekers to the Cause ever since the Wilhelms had taken up residence there. Many seekers had attended the household's regular Bahá'í gatherings and had become members of the Faith through Roy's and his parents' efforts. Roy had already hosted large gatherings on the lawn of his West Englewood home, so having another large event on his family's expansive property was perhaps less daunting for the Wilhelms than for others in the community, especially if they could be assisted by the Bourgeois family living close by.

Roy had begun hosting picnics in 1908, when over one hundred Bahá'í friends from New York and the surrounding area had held a picnic in the open fields and woods next to their home, even though it was still under construction. Roy had even arranged for hay wagons to pick up sixty or seventy of the friends from the Hudson River ferry landing to bring them up to their property for the day.[31] Consequently, Roy was not surprised when, in April 1912, the organizing committee approached him about using his property for 'Abdu'l-Bahá's Unity Feast. Roy replied that he and his family were willing to help.[32] A short time later, Howard MacNutt confirmed that West Englewood had been selected and that, with a meager budget of $100 set by 'Abdu'l-Bahá, the arrangements should proceed.[33]

Although the Wilhems knew there would be plenty of room for the hundreds of anticipated guests in the woods, gardens, and lawns surrounding their home, nonetheless, they must have been both euphoric and anxious about holding such an important event.[34] How many guests could be realistically expected? Would they have enough food? What would their neighbors think? Would they be able to make 'Abdu'l-Bahá comfortable? What should they do if it rained?

Roy, along with Howard MacNutt and the Kinneys in New York, began planning immediately for the gathering. People throughout the New York City area received a printed invitation to join 'Abdu'l-Bahá on Sunday, June 29 1912, for an afternoon picnic in suburban New Jersey. Dishes, cutlery, and cups were acquired. New galvanized ash cans were used for cooking the large quantities of fried chicken, as well as Persian rice dotted with pieces of lamb and vegetables. These dishes were all prepared at the Kinney's large Manhattan kitchen on the morning of the picnic. The food was then transported across the Hudson River to the Wilhelm home by three taxis in the same large ash cans.[35] Roy recruited a neighbor to help him clear out the underbrush and most of the poison ivy in the grove below the house. To exemplify the picnic's worldwide unifying message, Herman Pauley provided various national flags to decorate the event, which were arranged across the arc of the grove's circle. Every element of the occasion was planned carefully and well executed.

The day of the highly anticipated picnic arrived. Since early morning, excited guests had been wandering through the trees and up and

ABDUL BAHA

INVITES YOU TO BE PRESENT AT A UNITY FEAST
WHICH WILL BE CELEBRATED

SATURDAY, JUNE 29TH, 1912

AT

WEST ENGLEWOOD, N. J.

(NEAR THE HOME OF R. C. WILHELM)

TAKE 1.15 P. M. TRAIN AT WEST 42D STREET FERRY—
WEST SHORE RAILROAD—TO WEST ENGLEWOOD
STATION.

THIS INVITATION IS EXTENDED TO BAHAIS ONLY.
IT IS CONSIDERED ADVISABLE THAT NO CHILDREN
SHOULD BE PRESENT.

PLEASE REPLY IMMEDIATELY IF YOU WISH TO ATTEND.

MRS. E. B. KINNEY
780 WEST END AVENUE
NEW YORK CITY

Invitation to 'Abdu'l-Bahá's picnic at the Wilhelm home in
1912. (Courtesy of Joel Nizin)

down the hilly Wilhelm lawn anxiously looking forward to 'Abdu'l-Bahá's appearance. Meanwhile, at the rented house in Montclair, 'Abdu'l-Bahá began His day by greeting a stream of children who came to visit Him. Only a couple of members from His retinue remained with Him as the rest had been dispatched early that morning to the Kinney's home in Manhattan to help with cooking the Persian dishes for the picnic.[36] Although He was located less than twenty miles away, 'Abdu'l-Bahá's journey by tram required that He change trams four times, going into and back out of New York City to reach Teaneck. 'Abdu'l-Bahá, the Mystery of God, walked with His thoughts always on the world of the spirit, even as he paid attention to the day-to-day world of being. Unsurprisingly, then, He focused on those children who had arrived before dawn to see Him rather than preparing to leave for the picnic. That He had a particular train to catch did not matter. He arrived at the station just as the tram was starting down the rails, but seemingly miraculously, He was still able to get on board.[37]

Eager to escort 'Abdu'l-Bahá on the steep trek up to the Wilhelms' home, a group waited impatiently at the West Englewood train station that sultry morning. When He arrived at last, they enveloped Him as He stepped from the train. Though 'Abdu'l-Bahá, was much older than most of those accompanying Him on His way to the picnic, the group had to scramble to keep up with Him. The house, gardens and lawns at the Wilhelm property were already a beehive buzzing with activity, as family and visitors rushed to make everything ready for 'Abdu'l-Bahá, the Host of the gathering. Everyone wanted the special occasion to be perfect. At the sight of His white turban, the cacophony of chattering voices echoing through the surrounding woodland faded to silence. For a moment, only the hum and chirp of summer insects could be heard. He broke the silence by cheerfully calling out greetings to His guests as He continued trekking up the steep dirt road and onto the Wilhelms' property. An excited murmur from the hundreds assembled rose up, flooding the woods with waves of audible joy because He was now among them.

Exhausted from His morning exertions and the heat, 'Abdu'l-Bahá hastened to the refuge of the Wilhelm home, taking a few precious minutes to rest. Soon, however, He emerged from the house and strolled across the green, flower-lined lawn, perfuming the gardens with the fragrances of His beaming presence. The gentle breeze that accompanied Him stirred the hearts of the jubilant friends as He joined the crowd.[38] A covey of Bahá'ís encircled Him as He began walking down the hill to the grove. Along the way, He would sometimes pause and sit on the ground, with His back leaning against the rough bark of a pine tree. At other times, He would beckon a few of the friends standing close to Him to join Him for an intimate moment of communion.

The hill below the house created a natural amphitheater. 'Abdu'l-Bahá continued to walk to the bottom of the slope to a point where the woods created an evergreen backdrop. From there, He briefly paused before turning to look back up the hillside, to survey the crowd that had followed Him. He begin to address the assembled multitude above Him. Just as with His other talks in North America, the central theme of 'Abdu'l-Bahá's talks that day—He would give several—was the oneness of mankind. The event itself was labeled the "Feast of Unity."[39] Pacing back and forth in the shade of the tall pine trees, He exhorted the friends to ". . . have neither will nor desire of your own but seek everything for the beloved of God and live together in complete love and fellowship."[40]

Taking breaks from addressing the crowd, 'Abdu'l-Bahá retreated from time to time to the shade found in a corner of the Wilhelms' front porch, where He engaged in animated conversations whenever approached by one of the friends. Whether with Black or White, affluent or poor, Christian, Muslim, Jew, or Bahá'í, His countenance projected the spirit of welcome and goodwill toward all of God's people.

Group photograph of many of those who attended the 1912 picnic. 'Abdu'l-Bahá is on the left with members of His entourage behind Him. (USBNA)

Roy noted that the beginning of the day, "was excessively hot. One of the hottest muggiest* days that I remember in our long residence in West Englewood."[41] The hours passed, but the stifling heat never abated. Peering up through the trees, a few clouds could be seen dot-

---

* *Muggy* is an American word for hot, humid weather.

ting an otherwise bright blue sky, not that unusual for a New Jersey summer afternoon. Just before the meal was ready to be served the weather changed.[42] Suddenly a gust of wind swept over the grounds, the bushes began to rustle, and the trees started to sway. Then, to the surprise and dismay of the crowd, threatening black clouds appeared in the south, followed by other gusts of wind and the crash of thunder. The first splatter of giant rain drops hitting the tables sent many people scrambling back up the hill to the Wilhelm house for cover.

Unruffled, 'Abdu'l-Bahá rose and, with His entourage following a few paces behind, calmly walked toward the road at the top of the hill beyond the Wilhelm property. He continued walking until He reached a lone chair that had been left by the roadside. There, beneath a sky thick with dark roiling clouds, flashing lightning and booming thunder, He sat perfectly still for a few moments. He then held out His hands to detect any sprinkling of rain, but there was none. Roy and his parents watched with concern, for their special Guest was now exposed to lightning. As quickly as the storm had arrived, it dissipated. The blazing sun reemerged from between the scattering clouds, and an azure canopy once again enveloped the festive Teaneck gathering.[43] 'Abdu'l-Bahá got up from the chair and walked back to the Wilhelms' pine grove where the friends were anxiously waiting for Him to return.[44]

From Juliet Thompson's poetic description of the storm, the incident has seemed to have attained a mystical quality as it entered oral Bahá'í lore, for many who heard about it said that somehow the Holy Man from the East had performed a miracle willing away the clouds with His heavenly gaze. One could easily interpret the sudden change in weather as a miracle, for one of 'Abdu'l-Bahá's titles was the *Mystery of God*. Were there not other examples of miraculous or unexpected moments during His visit to America?[45] Roy, however, did not believe the storm's passing was anything more than a typical New Jersey summer weather pattern.[46] In any event, 'Abdu'l-Bahá did perform one genuine miracle that day—unifying diverse people who would normally refrain from socializing with each other; for the occasion was held during the period when people generally only socialized with those who were like themselves. In 1912, in the United States, class, religious, cultural, and racial divisions were pronounced such that each group functioned within its own constrained world, with restrictions often enforced by law.. The picnic demonstrated that the Cause of God could overcome all manmade barriers that separated people.

'Abdu'l-Bahá with the crowd at the West Englewood picnic.
(USBNA)

The group photographs and movie taken that day vividly illustrate the power of 'Abdu'l-Bahá to bring diverse people together. In one photograph, Black and White children are gathered happily together around their Host—a sight almost never seen in the United States where racial prejudice ran deep and was the most critical problem facing American society. During the picnic itself, wealthy believers mingled with housekeepers and factory workers. Protestants enjoyed their lunch alongside Catholics. Persians, Germans, Irish, English, new immigrants, and those with deep roots in America ate together; all felt welcome, all felt loved, and all felt accepted.

Tables decorated with pale yellow paper tablecloths and orna-
mented with jonquils and bowls of fruit[47] were arranged in a large circle on the lawn, where guests listened, spellbound, to 'Abdu'l-Bahá's
words. While the friends enjoyed their exotic Persian fare, 'Abdu'l-
Bahá walked among them whispering blessings, and annointing them
with attar of rose. The vial of the sweet-scented oil seemed too small
to hold sufficient perfume to anoint such a crowd, so one woman,
fearing He would be embarassed if it ran out, followed Him with a
bottle of water so He could continue to anoint the friends once the
attar of rose ran out. But the little bottle was never empty. When He
had finished placing the fragrant oil on every forehead, He turned to
the woman and gave her the bottle which, to her surprise, still had
perfume left inside.[48] For those gathered beneath the trees, the scent
of rose would linger not only for this day but also for the rest of their
lives. Whenever they encountered the fragrance of roses in the future,
it would trigger a flood of memories of that glorious day and the
wonderful picnic with 'Abdu'l-Bahá.

'Abdu'l-Bahá's remarks to the friends were often lighthearted, yet
sprinkled throughout them were serious admonitions. Throughout
the day, He reminded the friends of their greater spiritual task—to
look beyond their material interests toward attaining the virtues of
God. He called upon them to understand that they were the ones
charged "to uplift the cause of unity among the nations of the
earth."[49] He wanted His listeners to understand the importance of
their spiritual nature. Embedded in His comments was the theme
that, foremost in this "New Day" and "New Hour,"[50] was the attainment of unity:

Such gatherings as this have no equal or likeness in the world of
mankind, where people are drawn together by physical motives
or in furtherance of material interests, for this meeting is a pro-
totype of that inner and complete spiritual association in the
eternal world of being.

True Bahá'í meetings are the mirrors of the Kingdom
wherein images of the Supreme Concourse are reflected. In them

the lights of the most great guidance are visible. They voice the summons of the heavenly Kingdom and echo the call of the angelic host to every listening ear. The efficacy of such meetings as these is permanent throughout the ages.[51]

Over the course of the day, 'Abdu'l-Bahá gave what were later characterized as four separate addresses. He also engaged in numerous conversations with individuals and smaller groups.[52] From dawn to dusk on that hot June day, a wave of over three hundred guests* ebbed and flowed through the Wilhelms' lovely grounds. Friends, seekers, and the curious came from nearby and from as far away as California, Maine, and everywhere in between. Few gathered there that day could have fully understood His cryptic words and what they would mean to future generations of Bahá'ís. He not only inspired His listeners, but helped them see the spiritual and historical significance of that glorious picnic amid the pines:

> This assembly has a name and significance which will last forever. Hundreds of thousands of meetings shall be held to commemorate this occasion, and the very words I speak to you today shall be repeated in them for ages to come. Therefore, be ye rejoiced, for ye are sheltered beneath the providence of God. Be happy and joyous because the bestowals of God are intended for you and the life of the Holy Spirit is breathing upon you.
>
> Rejoice because the breaths of the Holy Spirit are directed to you!
> Rejoice, for the heavenly table is prepared for you.
> Rejoice, for the angels of heaven are your assistants and helpers.
> Rejoice, for the glance of the Blessed Beauty, Bahá'u'lláh, is directed to you.

---

* The estimates of the crowd range from 200 to 350. Based on the group photographs, three hundred seems a reasonable assumption. It was a fluid crowd, with people coming and going for hours.

Rejoice, for Bahá'u'lláh is your Protector.
Rejoice, for the everlasting glory is destined for you.
Rejoice, for the eternal life is awaiting you.[53]

'Abdu'l-Bahá'í seated on the front porch of the Wilhelm home.
Left to right standing: Edward "Saffa" Kinney, Lua Getsinger, Otis
Wilhelm. Seated: Mírzá 'Ali-Akbar Nakhjavání, Dr. Ameen Fareed,
unknown, unknown, 'Abdu'l-Bahá, unknown, woman on right is
Carrie "Vaffa" Kinney, in front of her is Roy Wilhelm, and man in
front on right is unknown. (USBNA)

As the historic day drew to a close, the rising moon flickered through
the branches high above the shrinking crowd still lingering at the
Wilhelms' property. After such a sweltering day, the setting sun
brought little relief from the afternoon's hot sticky weather, and provided only a steamy, insect-filled twilight. Those reluctant to leave,
perhaps a hundred or more, plus a few of the Wilhelm's neighbors,
waited for 'Abdu'l-Bahá's last words, unwilling to miss anything He
said.[54] While the friends took their seats in a big semicircle on the
lawn surrounding the front verandah, 'Abdu'l-Bahá approached, sat

down beside them, and answered their many questions. At one point, waving His arms and kicking up dust, He paced along the dirt road in front of the house while He gave a spirited response to a question asked by one of the guests.[55] As darkness fell, at His request, the haunting melody of a prayer chanted in Persian filled the still evening air.[56] Juliet Thompson captured His eloquent final words encouraging them to "vivify the world"[57] in the poetic prose of her diary entry:

> To me the most beautiful scene of all came later, when the Master returned to us after dark. About fifty or sixty people had lingered, unable to tear themselves from Him. The Master sat in a chair on the top step of the porch, some of us surrounding Him . . . Below us, all over the lawn, on each side of the path, sat the others, the light summer skirts of the women spread out on the grass, tapers in their hands to keep off mosquitoes. In the dark, in their filmy dresses, they looked like great moths and the burning tips of the tapers they waved like fireflies darting about. Then the Master spoke again to us saying His talk "was a resounding Call to us to arise from the tomb of self in this Day of the Great Resurrection and unite around Him to vivify the world." Before He had finished He rose from His chair and started down the path still talking, passing between the dim figures on the grass with their lighted tapers, talking till He reached the road, where He turned and we could no longer see Him. Even then His words floated back to us—the liquid Persian, Ali-Kuli Khan's beautiful, quivering translation, like the sound of a violin string. "Peace be with you," this was the last we heard, "I will pray for you."[58]

The picnic was over, the crowd was gone, and the daily routines of life would begin to return to West Englewood, but the memory of that historic gathering would endure not only in the hearts and minds of all who were present that day, but down through the ages.

Exhausted but glowing with inner happiness, the Wilhelms walked up the lane for a late-night dinner of the leftover Persian rice which was being served at the Bourgeois home.[59] Sleeping in Roy's own spacious room on the first floor, 'Abdu'l-Bahá spent the night with the Wilhelms, while the rest of His entourage, except for the individual who took care of His personal needs, stayed at other Bahá'í homes in the neighborhood.

Roy observed that 'Abdu'l-Bahá carried no baggage, not even personal effects in His pockets, so he became concerned about His comfort after such a long, hot, humid day. He learned that 'Abdu'l-Bahá's devoted attendant, Mírzá Assadu'lláh, ensured that His clothes were cleaned each night and ready for Him the following morning.[60] Despite generous offers, Mírzá Assadu'lláh[61] could not be convinced to accept the comfort of a bed or couch that night, saying he preferred to sleep in a space on the floor next to 'Abdu'l-Bahá's room. Later that evening, Roy checked with his neighbors to ensure the other Persian visitors were comfortably settled for the night. Finding everyone to be satisfactorily situated, he returned home late. Because he was familiar with the layout of his house, he did not turn on the lights but rather felt his way in the dark. All of a sudden, he tripped over Mírzá Assadu'lláh sleeping on the floor, which caused Roy to stumble and hurtle into the dining room table.[62]

Arising at 6:00 o'clock the following morning, 'Abdu'l-Bahá immediately began His day no matter whether others were awake at that hour or not. While 'Abdu'l-Bahá strolled in the empty, peaceful gardens, Roy—ready to drive Him to the places He wished to visit— brought the REO around to the front of the house. The following is Roy's wonderful recounting of that morning, and it is a second episode of searching for an individual through the assistance of the Holy Spirit rather than earthly directions:

One of the Persians, a delightful young man in the entourage (Varqá) said that 'Abdu'l-Bahá met a minister here yesterday and He promised to call on him. "He is ready to go now." "Who is this minister," I asked. "I don't know" was the reply. "Where does he live?" "I am sorry but I don't know—but 'Abdu'l-Bahá wants to go and call on this minister." "Besides

113

its pretty early, isn't it?" "No, 'Abdu'l-Bahá is ready to go now." Someone who happened to be there, one of the believers said that I think I know that minister, I heard Him talking to him yesterday and he is a friend of our neighbors on ??? Street. "It is pretty early, I don't suppose they will be up yet." "But He said He is ready to go." I went across Bogert Street to the back door of a neighbor and rapped on the door and in a minute rapped a little louder on the door and finally a head came out of the window above me—"What do you want?" "This is Mr. Wilhelm and I am sorry to disturb you but I would like to know the name of that minister that was here yesterday because 'Abdu'l-Bahá would like to call upon him." "That was Reverend Gulick and he liked 'Abdu'l-Bahá very much and 'Abdu'l-Bahá said he was going to call upon him." "Where does he live?" "He lives up in Dumont." "Where in Dumont?" "We don't know" "Thank you very much, we will try and find out." So we got into the little car and started up the road and 'Abdu'l-Bahá was quite puzzled that the stores were not open and most of the people weren't up. How was I going to find this revered gentleman in Dumont?

I asked when I got to the edge of town, one or two passerby's, [sic] but they didn't know. I was still going along on the main street and suddenly behind us we heard somebody shouting and running slowly and I looked and here came Reverend Gulick in his shirtsleeves. He was just getting dressed and had heard the car pass and saw 'Abdu'l-Bahá. He ran down the stairs and out into the street and shouted to him "'Abdu'l-Bahá! 'Abdu'l-Bahá." We went and parked in his house and he took us upstairs and we had a very nice little visit. I remember 'Abdu'l-Bahá said I promised you that I would come to your home and now I am here. He seemed extremely happy to see 'Abdu'l-Bahá and after that 'Abdu'l-Bahá said now we will return home.[63]

Once the visit with Reverend Gulick was over, Roy resumed their drive through the rural New Jersey countryside toward Morris Plains and the residence of the Persian Consul-General, Mr. Haigazoun

Topakyan, for a second visit with that diplomat. What a privilege for Roy to personally drive 'Abdu'l-Bahá on that beautiful sunny day! They would have been enchanted driving over the verdant rolling landscape where occasional streams and dense thickets enhanced the view along the dusty road.[64]

Waiting expectantly, the Consul-General, his staff, and several distinguished guests greeted 'Abdu'l-Bahá and ushered Him inside the Persian court, ". . . a building in the garden built after the old style of Persian architecture," for a barbecue lunch.[65] The diplomatic implications of the visit were important enough for the luncheon to be reported in the *New York Herald* and *New York Sun*.[66] Consul-General Topakyan was the representative of the government of 'Abdu'l-Bahá's homeland—that same government which first imprisoned and exiled Bahá'u'lláh and His family. Topakyan himself was a declared enemy of the Faith and continued to persecute its followers. Although he talked about the need for peace in the world and about the pervasive injustice in his country, his motivation for inviting the spiritual and administrative head of the Bahá'í Faith to his official residence remained uncertain. That 'Abdu'l-Bahá accepted the invitation demonstrated His forgiveness and willingness to treat an enemy as a friend.

'Abdu'l-Bahá gave permission to the celebrated photographer, Gertrude Käsebier, to take photos of Him and the other guests at the table. After lunch and a stroll through the gardens, 'Abdu'l-Bahá sat and answered questions while the reporters took down His words for their newspapers. He spoke of His impressions of New York and its greatness as well as the burden that excessive materialism brought to society. Accustomed to the niceties and protocols required of a diplomatic host, Topakyan "was most courteous and humble in 'Abdu'l-Bahá's presence, to such an extent that he refused to sit without permission."[67] That afternoon, with the sun below the western horizon, the Consul-General escorted 'Abdu'l-Bahá to a waiting car, and together they drove to his nearby residence. There, 'Abdu'l-Bahá was able to rest, have a light refreshment, and sit on the lawn while Persian music playing on a phonograph filled the night air.[68] At the end of the visit, Roy drove 'Abdu'l-Bahá back into New York City. His rest in the New Jersey countryside had come to an end.

'Abdu'l-Bahá at Morristown, New Jersey, as a guest of the Persian Consul who, despite being an enemy of the Faith, treated his guest as a friend that day. Roy accompanied 'Abdu'l-Bahá during that visit, then drove Him back to New York. (USBNA)

Two weeks after the visit to the Consul-General, the summer weather continued to be unbearable. On July 14th, 'Abdu'l-Bahá addressed the congregation of the All Souls Unitarian Church in New York, speaking again about the oneness of the world of humanity, the equality of men and women, and principles of divine religion.[69] That evening, Roy drove his REO into Manhattan to retrieve 'Abdu'l-Bahá and drive Him to His next engagement. This service provided Roy with a double bounty, for he would also take 'Abdu'l-Bahá to spend the night once again at the Wilhelm family's West Englewood house. 'Abdu'l-Bahá must have been delighted to leave the city and drive into the cooler, arboreal landscape for a quiet evening in Roy's comfortable home, especially because the unrelenting heat had taken a toll on His health. Moreover, the picnic two weeks earlier had aroused interest among friends and neighbors of the Teaneck Bahá'ís, so that afternoon He shared the Bahá'í teachings with a small group of inquirers at the Wilhelm house. Darkness fell, and the cicadas began their noisy serenade while the small party walked up the street to the home of Louis and Alice Bourgeois. After an evening of gracious hospitality and a delicious meal, they listened to 'Abdu'l-Bahá's remarks before strolling back to the Wilhelm home for the night.[70]

The next morning, Roy drove 'Abdu'l-Bahá back to Manhattan. On the way to the hotel, 'Abdu'l-Bahá said He wanted to make an important stop. One of Roy's friends and a dedicated believer was Charlotte Segler, a twenty-nine-year-old bookkeeper. She lived with her invalid mother, Bertha Segler, an elderly native of Germany who had worked as a seamstress* after being widowed when her daughter was less than two years old.[71] Charlotte was very excited by 'Abdu'l-Bahá's presence in New York City and had taken every opportunity to hear Him speak, including attending the picnic at Teaneck. A few days after His arrival in New York, Charlotte, hoping to catch a glimpse of Him, stood and waited in the company of two other believers on the sidewalk outside the Riverside Drive apartment where He was staying. They were rewarded for their efforts when they spotted Him sitting by a window. They then got up the courage to wave to Him, and He waved back. Curious, 'Abdu'l-Bahá then sent Lua Getsinger to find out who they were. Another time, Charlotte was delighted to unexpectedly encounter 'Abdu'l-Baha on her way to work one morning. He was standing at the corner of Broadway and 79th Street with one of His interpreters. They exchanged cheery greetings and a "thrilling handshake!" On one occasion, Roy charged Charlotte with delivering a package of letters to 'Abdu'l-Bahá, a small service which delighted her. Charlotte recounted what must have

---

* This information about the Seglers is derived from census documents available on http://ancestry.com.

been the general sentiment among the New York believers during the times 'Abdu'l-Bahá was in their midst saying that "It was really a marvelous experience in those days to be able to meet our Adored One in the streets of busy New York! The believers lived in an atmosphere of radiant happiness."[72]

For Charlotte, there had been one highlight of the West Englewood picnic, which would remain among her cherished memories. As that wonderful day turned to night and most of the friends returned to their homes, Charlotte could not help but linger. Wandering the area, she chanced upon 'Abdu'l-Bahá walking all alone in the moonlight in the Bourgeois' garden. Summoning her courage, she took advantage of this unexpected encounter to ask Him to visit her mother. He replied in English, "I come."[73] On July 11, a messenger from 'Abdu'l-Bahá's entourage informed the Seglers that they should come to Him instead early the following Sunday morning. The excited family began to prepare for the treasured visit. But those plans suddenly changed. After 10:00 in the evening on July 13th, the doorbell rang while Charlotte was taking a bath. She first thought that, at that hour, someone must have pressed the button by mistake, so she ignored it. When it rang again, she hurriedly got out of the tub and slipped on her bathrobe. Waiting at her door was Grace Ober, who was assisting 'Abdu'l-Bahá as a housekeeper, with a message from Him, telling her that He would come to visit them at their home. When 'Abdu'l-Bahá learned that Charlotte's mother had difficulty walking, He said that it would not be just for her to make the effort to come to Him.[74]

On July 15th Charlotte returned home from work during her lunch break to find her mother waiting for her by their door in a state of excitement. She greeted her daughter by saying, "guess what!" Roy had brought 'Abdu'l-Bahá to see her that morning. They had climbed three flights of stairs to get to the humble apartment. 'Abdu'l-Bahá showered Bertha with loving kindness and inquired about the accident that had fractured her hip. He assured her that she would be well again. Charlotte said that she would "never forget my darling mother's radiant joy and excitement over the marvelous visit!" Bertha told her that 'Abdu'l-Bahá had such a majestic walk that "she could not resist telling Him that the feeling which came over her when she saw Him was that He was the Christ."[75] After that visit, 'Abdu'l-Bahá asked after her mother every time He saw Charlotte and paid her mother one last visit shortly before He departed from the United States.[76]

'Abdu'l-Bahá's second visit to the Wilhelm home would be His last. Ahead lay months of travel that would eventually take Him west to San Francisco, Oakland, and Los Angeles. However, before His journey west, Roy had the good fortune to be present during His stop at Green Acre, a retreat center in Maine near Portsmouth, New Hampshire.

Green Acre was not then a Bahá'í-owned facility. It had been established by Sarah Farmer, a farsighted woman who was keenly interested in the life of the spirit as well as in social causes. She, with the help of others, especially Phoebe Hearst, a wealthy California widow, purchased a four-story inn that overlooked the Piscataqua River, not far from where it emptied into the Atlantic Ocean. The area's rolling lawns and fresh air made it an ideal spot for Bostonians and New Yorkers seeking to escape from the daily drudgery of those large cities. While reveling in its pastoral surroundings, Green Acre visitors could gain enlightenment and intellectual stimulation from renowned speakers.

In 1901, Farmer made a visit to the Holy Land, during which she discovered the Bahá'í Faith. Her open heart accepted it almost immediately. From that point on, the programs at Green Acre began to include Bahá'í speakers and topics, though many of the earlier programs continued as before. Phoebe Hearst, the primary benefactress of Green Acre, having learned of and accepted the Faith through other channels, wholeheartedly approved of the facility's use for Bahá'í gatherings.[77]

'Abdu'l-Bahá at Green Acre with members of His entourage. The Inn is in the background. (USBNA)

After a restful several weeks in cooler Dublin, New Hampshire, 'Abdu'l-Bahá journeyed to Green Acre, where hundreds of Bahá'ís and others joyfully awaited His arrival. They not only lined the long dirt drive leading to the inn to greet Him, but they also had worked together to place hundreds of colorful paper Japanese lanterns along the drive to make it as festive as possible.

Roy was there. Years later, one of Roy's friends recounted one story he heard from Roy about 'Abdu'l-Bahá's visit to Green Acre. Early one evening, a special dinner had been prepared for 'Abdu'l-Bahá and the hundreds of people who had flocked to Green Acre to be with Him. Everything was ready in the dining room of the inn, yet 'Abdu'l-Bahá continued to remain outside on the broad porch that surrounded three sides of the building. He was absorbed in surveying the dirt road leading to the inn. After some time watching the road, a solitary man appeared. He made his way up the rutted track and finally stepped onto the porch. The exhausted fellow was ragged, dirty and unkempt. 'Abdu'l-Bahá directed several men, including Roy, to furnish the new arrival with spare articles of their own clothing. Roy and the others immediately complied. The unexpected guest was sent to wash, shave, and put on the borrowed clothes while everyone's dinner continued to get cold.[78]

At last, Fred Mortensen, who had traveled all the way from Minnesota to see 'Abdu'l-Bahá, emerged, clean and presentable. Only then was 'Abdu'l-Bahá ready to eat. The story of Fred Mortensen became legendary. He had spent time in prison and learned about the Faith from his lawyer, Albert Hall, who served with Roy on the Temple Unity Executive Board. Mortensen had no money for a train ticket, yet he was so determined to meet 'Abdu'l-Bahá that he stowed away on top of and underneath rail cars to make the lengthy journey to Maine. It was not only dangerous, but an illegal way to travel.

'Abdu'l-Bahá knew how Mortensen got there, and, after gentle prodding, Mortensen confessed to Him that he had indeed traveled just as 'Abdu'l-Bahá suspected. What Mortensen found at Green Acre was not judgment but love, not only from 'Abdu'l-Bahá but also from the other believers who interacted with him, including Roy, who would make use of Mortensen's audacity and courage a few years later to serve as the courier of funds needed by 'Abdu'l-Bahá during wartime. Fred and his family became active Bahá'ís and ardent servants of the Cause in the years following his unorthodox travel by rail.[79]

'Abdu'l-Bahá did not return to New York for months. After leaving Green Acre, He made one or two other stops in New England before heading West, including a brief visit to Montreal, Canada. By September, He had reached California where most of His time was spent in the San Francisco Bay area. While traversing the Western states by train, He learned of the untimely passing of Thornton Chase, who had crossed paths with the Wilhelms on their way to Haifa in 1907. Thornton was especially significant because he had been designated the first American believer. Because of Thornton's passing, 'Abdu'l-Bahá unexpectedly added a brief visit to Los Angeles and its environs to His California itinerary—where His westward journey ended. There, He made a pilgrimage to Thornton's grave site, located in a cemetery in Inglewood, a suburb of Los Angeles.

Finally, the time had come for 'Abdu'l-Bahá to bring to a close His visit to North America. There, along the shores of the Pacific Ocean, He turned His face back toward the East and began the long journey home.[80] He recrossed the United States, arriving for the last time in New York on November 11.

Roy had longed to accompany 'Abdu'l-Bahá on the western leg of His journey across America and Canada, but 'Abdu'l-Bahá did not wish for him to do so. Instead, He gently told Roy that he had spent enough time away from his business and must turn his attention to it again.

O thou my dear son!

Your letter was received. As it has been for sometime that thou wert away from the center of commerce, I desired that thou mayest reach there as soon as possible, therefore I did not ask you to come. Nevertheless thou art always with me. The memory of your face never escapes my thought. I hope from the Favors of the Blessed Perfection that day by day thou mayest become more illumined and more spiritual.[81]

Knowing that 'Abdu'l-Bahá's departure from the United States was imminent, the New York Board of Council arranged for a large banquet in His honor at the Great Northern Hotel on November 23. No doubt, Roy was involved in that event as a member of the Board. Hundreds of Bahá'ís attended. During that memorable evening, 'Abdu'l-Bahá went from table to table anointing each attendee with attar of roses as He had at the picnic.[82]

The day finally came that the believers in the United States had long dreaded, the one when 'Abdu'l-Bahá would take His leave of them.

The final banquet to honor 'Abdu'l-Bahá while in North America, held at the Great Northern Hotel by the New York Bahá'í community a few days before His departure from New York for England. (USBNA)

The previous night, a farewell gathering was held for the New York believers at the Kinneys' spacious home, which seemed fitting since His first meeting with the friends in America also took place there. Just as with 'Abdu'l-Bahá's arrival more than ten months earlier, no evidence exists that Roy was among those at the pier on December 5 to see 'Abdu'l-Bahá off as He sailed for England. Whether he was there in person or not, unquestionably his heart was present.

5 / TWIN DUTIES

Roy C. Wilhelm will be forever remembered as one of the select group of fifty believers designated Hands of the Cause of God. During his lifetime, the meaning of that title was neither fully appreciated nor well understood. Four Hands of the Cause had been named by Bahá'u'lláh, but because they resided in Iran, Roy and most Western believers had few, if any, opportunities to interact with them, and Westerners were largely unaware of the services they rendered in the East. During the 1950s, after Roy's passing, the station and role of Hands of the Cause would be defined more fully. These trustworthy, capable lieutenants would be charged with two primary fields of action: namely, the propagation and protection of the Faith.[1] Over the decade following 'Abdu'l-Bahá's visit to the United States, Roy would be repeatedly called upon to carry out both of those critical roles. Yet, while doing so, he was unaware that his responsibilities and actions were of those of a Hand of the Cause. Early on, 'Abdu'l-Bahá recognized that Roy had within him sterling qualities that were yet to be cultivated and while in the United States, He took steps to both temper and enhance Roy's character. 'Abdu'l-Bahá also tutored this steadfast American businessman with guidance he would need to serve Him over the course of many years as one of His most trusted lieutenants within the fledgling community in North America.

Many years after 'Abdu'l-Bahá's 1912 visit, Roy told a friend about an incident that illustrates how 'Abdu'l-Bahá strove to improve Roy's character. The incident was also indicative of 'Abdu'l-Bahá's confidence in Roy's ability to accept correction. One day while

'Abdu'l-Bahá was in New York City, He summoned Roy to meet Him at 2:00 o'clock that afternoon. Roy canceled his other plans and arrived at 'Abdu'l-Bahá's residence before the appointed hour. He was directed to a sitting area and asked to wait. The time passed, yet 'Abdu'l-Bahá did not come out to meet him. Roy continued waiting, checking his watch, anxiously fidgeting, and pacing the floor. One hour became two, then the clock chimed four o'clock. During what seemed an interminable delay, Roy was certain that his pacing back and forth had worn the carpet thin. At last, 'Abdu'l-Bahá appeared. The entire purpose of the meeting had been to teach Roy patience, a lesson driven home by 'Abdu'l-Bahá in comments He made to Roy that afternoon.[2]*

On another occasion, while walking alone with 'Abdu'l-Bahá and his interpreter, Dr. Zia Baghdadi, in a Chicago park, 'Abdu'l-Bahá gave Roy a warning. With gravity in His voice, 'Abdu'l-Bahá spoke to Roy about people using their association with the Faith to solicit money from individual believers. Roy took this admonition to heart, and, from that time forward, advised others that any claims of financial distress should only be directed to the institutions of the Faith, rather than to an individual of means. Many of the friends knew that Roy had money, and occasionally someone would approach him for financial help. He had to learn to balance listening to his head while still listening to his heart.[3]

Periodically, Roy's lessons arrived in the form of a letter. Shortly before 'Abdu'l-Bahá came to the United States, He wrote to Roy, candidly setting forth proof of the perfidy of the first Bahá'í teacher in America, Ibrahim Kheiralla, who had been expelled from the Faith as a Covenant-breaker—that is, one who strove to usurp or undermine the authority of the legitimate head of the Faith. Though Roy had not been one of Kheiralla's students and most likely never met him,

---

* Blakely recounted the gist of the conversation between 'Abdu'l-Bahá and Roy but did not record the specifics of what was said.

126

some of his Bahá'í friends had first been introduced to the Faith by Kheiralla, and their former teacher, along with his dwindling group of followers, continued to exercise a little influence within the Bahá'í community. 'Abdu'l-Bahá warned Roy about Kheiralla, lest more problems arose.[4]

Similarly, in 1913, setting forth confidential details, 'Abdu'l-Bahá wrote to Roy about the lack of sincerity of a well-known American believer.[5] In the Tablet, 'Abdu'l-Bahá emphasized His own patience in working with that individual, as well as His unwillingness to listen to gossip about him. As Roy read through the account, he would have noted the various and numerous ways in which 'Abdu'l-Bahá showered love upon the wayward Bahá'í in order to keep him from continuing down a crooked path. 'Abdu'l-Bahá had even given that person choice assignments and had provided the funds for him to carry them out. Finally, however, 'Abdu'l-Baha was left with little choice but to intervene in a more direct and forceful manner because, despite His efforts, the man had continued down the road of treachery. Even then, however, 'Abdu'l-Bahá said nothing about this man's disloyalty to the generality of the friends, and He continued to demonstrate His love for him. 'Abdu'l-Bahá's example was a tutorial in how to appropriately manage—and love—someone who was creating problems within the community. Roy would repeatedly draw upon this valuable lesson in the years ahead, especially because 'Abdu'l-Bahá's loving method had the desired effect. Roy would be able to witness firsthand that the individual did reform, and became a truly trustworthy believer.[6]

A few years after Roy received guidance from 'Abdu'l-Bahá about managing difficult believers, he was faced with an incident where he had to put this and other Bahá'í principles into practice. While attending a Bahá'í gathering, he was confronted by an aggressive community member who disagreed with him about a point of Bahá'í policy. With other people looking on, that person sternly lectured Roy, stating unequivocally why she believed his understanding of those principles was wrong. Relating the incident later, Roy reported that throughout the harangue, "I made no reply. It is sometimes better to listen to unreason in silence."[7] He was relieved that, at the time, only Bahá'ís were present to witness the embarrassing scene created by his attacker. Once Roy and his critic were no longer with the group, but alone together, the attack resumed. He wrote about the unfortunate encounter to his friend, Agnes Parsons, who knew about the incident, saying that "I had a quite lively twenty minute session."[8] He told Agnes how he sparred with the one who so adamantly disagreed with him:

> Certain points I tried to <u>drive</u> home . . . and it was a drive, though I don't know whether they penetrated. When "force" and "fight fight fight" is openly advocated in a Bahai meeting as the one way that good can overcome evil, we might just as well save our steam. Abdul Baha said . . . 'Verily we will administer unto them (the enemies of the Cause) & quaff from the cup of non-resistance.'"[9]

Correspondence Roy received from 'Abdu'l-Bahá was particularly insistent about adherence to one directive: requiring authenticated credentials from anyone arriving from Persia or Palestine claiming to be Bahá'í. On December 30, 1912, 'Abdu'l-Bahá cabled Roy from London:

RECEIVE NO PERSIAN EVEN MY FAMILY WITHOUT AUTHOGRAPHIC PERMISSION COMMUNICATE ALL FRIENDS.[10]

After conveying this message to the editor of the national Bahá'í newsletter, misgivings about publishing such a seemingly direct statement began to fester in Roy's mind because the text of the cable would be seen in print by a wide cross-section of people. He confessed to the editor that "I usually rush ahead at express speed and do my sane thinking afterwood [sic]." He had concluded that there were undoubtedly innocent, soft-hearted readers of the publication who would be disturbed by the cable and not understand the reason for the directive, so he suggested ways it could be stated in a less blunt manner. In obedience to 'Abdu'l-Bahá, Roy had, however, already notified all the leading U.S. and Canadian communities of the directive.[11]

A few months later, in another strongly-worded Tablet, written in 'Abdu'l-Bahá's own handwriting, Roy was once again cautioned to refrain from associating with anyone coming from the Middle East without proper authorization from 'Abdu'l-Bahá Himself. It appeared there was a conspiracy among a group of Middle Eastern enemies of the Faith to go to the West and claim to be Bahá'ís with the intention of disrupting and harming the American Bahá'í community. 'Abdu'l-Bahá's translator, Ahmad Sohrab, sensing that this was an unusually important letter, wrote to Roy restating the contents of 'Abdu'l-Bahá's letter so the Americans would not fail to recognize its significance.[12] Roy was tasked with ensuring these instructions were disseminated to all North American believers. At least once after Roy received these general warnings, 'Abdu'l-Bahá wrote to him about specific individuals traveling to the United States.[13] On other occasions, He wrote to Roy about trustworthy believers coming from Iran and not only affirmed that they were coming to America with His blessing but also asked Roy to assist them.[14]

One of the best barometers of 'Abdu'l-Bahá's trust in Roy was His use of Roy's Manhattan office as His primary North American post office. Roy and his staff became the communication center responsible for receiving cables and letters from 'Abdu'l-Bahá and then forwarding them throughout the United States and Canada to their intended recipients. Sometimes this service presented a challenge. For example, if a cable or letter did not state the recipient's name, Roy had to either use his own knowledge to determine its destination or send an inquiry back to 'Abdu'l-Bahá asking for further clarification. Americans also entrusted Roy with dispatching their messages to the Holy Land. Much of what passed through his hands was confidential; it was therefore vital for him to ensure that his staff could be trusted as well.

With all that Roy did to serve 'Abdu'l-Bahá, he must have been humbled by the encouragement and praise 'Abdu'l-Bahá lavished upon him in letter after letter. The following expression of gratitude for all the behind-the-scenes tasks the coffee broker carried out during the 1912 visit was but one example:

> During the days of my sojourn in America the services that thou didst render shall never be forgotten. They are always remembered. Thank thou God that thou has been confirmed in the services of the Cause of God, faithfulness in the Kingdom of Abha and steadfastness in the Testament and the Covenant. This Bestowal is a splendor from the Lights of the Kingdom of Abha and this assistance is from the Breaths of the Holy-Spirit. It causes the ascension of the spirit of man to the world of God and it will bestow illumination upon the pure in heart.[15]

'Abdu'l-Bahá's reference to the Testament and the Covenant may have raised questions in Roy's mind, but within less than a decade he would more fully comprehend the meaning of those words.

In August 1913, 'Abdu'l-Bahá wrote a particularly noteworthy letter to Roy that was printed in the September issue of *Star of the West*. It further expounded upon the importance of firmness and steadfastness in Bahá'u'lláh's Covenant:

> The Confirmation of the Kingdom of Abha shall descend uninterruptedly upon those souls who are firm in the Covenant. Thou hast well observed that every firm one is assisted and aided and every violator is degraded, humiliated and lost. It is very astonishing that people are not admonished. . . This Covenant is the Covenant of His Holiness Baha-o-llah. Now its importance is not known befittingly; but in the future it shall attain to such a degree of importance that if a King violates to the extent of one atom he shall be cut off immediately.[16]

Less than a year later, in April 1914, 'Abdu'l-Bahá wrote another highly significant letter to the believers in the United States, and He again sent it through Roy. It addressed a source of confusion among the believers that was generating disunity: lack of understanding of

'Abdu'l-Bahá's station. To a significant number of Western believers, the One they had come to know and love during His journey throughout Europe and North America seemed to be the embodiment of the spirit of Christ—perhaps His long awaited Second Coming. It was difficult for many Bahá'ís from Christian backgrounds to conceptualize how He, with all His perfections, was only a humble servant in relationship to His Father, Bahá'u'lláh, the Manifestation of God for this day. The lengthy epistle explained the stations of the Báb and Bahá'u'lláh as well as His own station. Summarizing His theme, 'Abdu'l-Bahá stated unequivocally that "The Blessed Perfection is Unique and Peerless. He is Single in His Identity and is sanctified and holy above any qualifications. I am beneath His Shade and the Servant at His Threshold."[17]*

In the summer of 1914 during the early days of World War I, 'Abdu'l-Bahá made plain His charge to Roy that he had a role to play in defending the Faith, and He enjoined the one He often addressed as His son[18] to "be a vigilant guard for the impregnable fort of the Cause of God and protect it against the intrusion of the ignorant."[19] 'Abdu'l-Bahá went on to spell this out at length:

> (Judas) Eschariot** [sic] must not be forgotten; the Divine sheep must be constantly guarded against devouring wolves; the light of the Cause of God must be protected from contrary winds by means of a chimney; the oppressed fowls must be

---

* In 2021, the Universal House of Justice published an authorized, improved translation of the Tablet. The quoted section in its new version reads: "My purpose is to show that the Blessed Beauty hath neither peer nor likeness. He is unique in His essence, and holy and sanctified in His attributes. I am under His shadow and the servant of His Threshold." *Light to the World*, #46, par. 7.

** Judas Iscariot was the disciple of Jesus who betrayed Him, leading to Jesus' arrest and crucifixion. Feeling great remorse for what he set in motion, Judas committed suicide. See the Gospel of Matthew 27: 1–5.

shielded against the birds of prey; blooming roses should be saved from the outstretched hands of injustice and the lambs of God must be fortified against the fierce of ravenous animals.

Were it not for the protecting power of the Covenant to guard the impregnable fort of the Cause of God, there would arise, among the Bahais, in one day, a thousand different sects as was the case in former ages. But in this Blessed Dispensation, for the sake of the permanency of the Cause of God and the avoidance of dissension amongst the people of God, the Blessed Beauty (may my soul be a sacrifice unto Him) has through the Supreme Pen written the Covenant and the Testament; He appointed a Center, the Exponent of the Book and the annuller of disputes. Whatever is written or said by him is conformable to the truth and under the protection of the Blessed Beauty he is infallible. The express purpose of this last Will and Testament is to set aside disputes from the world.[20]

Over the years, Roy must have thought back to that particular letter when, as a member of Spiritual Assemblies, he had to confront several perilous episodes of violation of the Covenant or other disunifying mischief. Indeed, within a few months after receipt of that letter, Roy was asked to meet with someone whom 'Abdu'l-Bahá had declared a Covenant-breaker.[21] 'Abdu'l-Bahá approved of how Roy handled the assignment and reminded him of the importance of normally avoiding such people. He instructed Roy that "When He (Bahá'u'lláh) says, associate with all religions with joy and fragrance, by this is meant the human kind [sic] and not the wicked."[22]

Roy had come to appreciate that an essential element of protecting the Faith was living up to its principles and that only by living a Bahá'í life would others be attracted to the Cause. During the 1916 annual convention, he emphasized this insight when addressing his fellow believers by talking about one of his conversations with 'Abdu'l-Bahá in New York. 'Abdu'l-Bahá said that if the Bahá'ís in that city had lived up to just one of the principles of the Faith from the time when the Faith was first established there (less than fifteen years earlier), and if they had actively delivered the message of the Cause of God, it would have had such an effect that by the time of His visit, half of the population of New York would have already become Bahá'í. This astonishing comment got Roy thinking. He told his listeners that "I sharpened my pencil and figured out that if I had done my part 7183 would have caught the Bahai spirit."[23]

Despite his work to protect the Faith, Roy never dwelt upon the challenges confronting the Bahá'ís; his main interest was always spreading the good news that God had sent humanity a new Messenger Who would alleviate the world's suffering. Roy was by nature an optimistic person who wished to see as many people as possible drawn to Bahá'u'lláh and His teachings. From the time he first began attending Bahá'í meetings, Roy was concerned about the lack of quality Bahá'í literature in English, especially inexpensive pamphlets and small tracts that could be handed to inquirers. After all, how could the Faith be spread widely when it did not have introductory literature to freely give away? How could both those exploring the Faith and new believers increase their understanding of the Cause without access to its Sacred Writings? Because he thought like a salesman and was a man of action, Roy was determined to do what he could to rectify this deficiency. First, he enthusiastically served on various national committees responsible for the review and publication of literature.[24] But assisting others to publish Bahá'í works was not enough; he went through the Holy Writings that had already been translated and created two compilations of quotations he felt were suitable for the general public. He formatted the selections into two pamphlets, with the tiniest one only two inches square and the other slightly larger. Roy christened his creations "Big Ben" and "Little Ben" after the famous clock tower and its smaller replica that had impressed him during his 1907 visit to London.[25]

When Roy first introduced and sold his "Bens" at the 1917 National Convention, the booklets, with their signature blue covers, were an instant success, selling out the first printing of fifteen thousand copies at that gathering.[26] Clearly, there was a tremendous need for such literature. Or, as Roy put it: "Well, it seems that the little-blue-booklet-for-inquirers started a veritable snowball rolling—an avalanche of orders swamped me."[27] Soon, sixty-five thousand copies of a revised second edition were printed.[28] Over the decades, these small compilations were translated into multiple languages, often at the urging of his friend, Martha Root, who usually traveled the globe with at least one of her trunks stuffed full of them. Roy even offered a suggestion as to how to use his Bens:

> I keep a dozen or two of these booklets upon my dresser at home and each morning before I start out I load myself with a couple of each: during the day's round one can usually find some opportunity to speak an "earnest word," and these provide ammunition both large and small according to the size and fierceness of the game.[29]

> If each Bahai in America could daily [give?] the story to one soul, it would bring the Melody to a hundred thousand ears in a single moon.[30]

Roy sent a few Bens to 'Abdu'l-Bahá, Who responded that they were "exceedingly praiseworthy" and asked him to send hundreds more to the Holy Land.[31] Later, 'Abdu'l-Bahá cautioned him not to place the booklets in public places because "their dignity and worth will thereby decrease."[32] This was a lesson about how to treat the sacred word with reverence, because these were not tracts, but rather compilations of Sacred Writings. Roy's production of the booklets evoked more praise from 'Abdu'l-Bahá, Who said that "His Holiness Bahá'u'lláh is well pleased with you, and I am also satisfied and content."[33]

The teaching booklets produced by Roy Wilhelm, known as the "Bens," came in two sizes (Joel Nizin photographer)

By the 1930s, when Shoghi Effendi, employing his masterful command of English, authoritatively translated a number of volumes of the Holy Writings, Roy's Bens became outdated because they relied on earlier, less accurate renderings. Other Bahá'ís also began to produce alternative introductory literature as Bahá'í publishing expanded and became more sophisticated. Nonetheless, the Bens will long be remembered as a significant milestone along the path of spreading the Faith to the far corners of the earth. Over the years, hundreds of thousands of Bens were distributed across the globe.

Roy's close work with a printer to produce his Bens gave him an education in the realities of publishing. He learned about the finer points of the preparation and costs of producing and distributing printed materials and applied this invaluable knowledge when serving on publication committees and assisting with other Bahá'í printing projects. Always factoring in practical considerations and how to keep costs as low as possible, Roy knew how to get a job done the right way. His booklets were popular because they were inexpensive, dignified, and easy to fit inside a pocket.

Roy also took an active role in carrying out another area of Bahá'í publishing—that of distributing periodicals. In 1910, when two

Chicago believers, Gertrude Buikema and Albert Windust, created a national newsletter—first called *Bahá'í News*—it became so successful that within a few years it was circulating outside of the United States in a handful of other countries. 'Abdu'l-Bahá suggested a new name for the newsletter, *Star of the West*.[34] Roy helped to offset a major portion of the newsletter's expenses by paying the rent on office space for the Chicago-based journal.[35] Years later, he served on its governing board.

Roy's work on publications is another example of his diligence in protecting the interests of the Faith. He had taken opportunities to speak with 'Abdu'l-Bahá about producing introductory Bahá'í literature in 1912 and had been instructed that, under the circumstances at that time, it would be wise to print only as much literature as there was interest in it, for Bahá'í literature should not be haphazardly scattered far and wide.[36] Roy also came to appreciate the importance of ensuring that Bahá'í scripture be published reverently and with clear authentication. This realization led him to ask 'Abdu'l-Bahá additional questions, and he rigorously conveyed the answers he received from the Holy Land to those working on Bahá'í publications to ensure the guidance was carried out. In that vein, he wrote the following to a staff member of the *Star of the West*:

> If the Tablets we circulate do not contain the name of the translator and the date, to whom they were sent, etc., or from what books they were taken, it will lay us wide open to abuses on the part of the nakazeen [Covenant-breakers] later. Also Abdul-Baha has directed that we call him by no other name, and such titles as "His Holiness", etc. are prohibited. He said to me when he was in New York that the pronouns "he", "his" etc., when applied to Baha'o'llah and the Bab should be capitalized ("the purpose being to attract the attention of the people"), but he said that when they were used in connection with Abdul Baha's name, they are not to be capitalized.[37] I do not want to appear overfussy, good brother, but I know there is a wisdom in strict obedience in these matters, and so I feel that great

caution should be used before Tablets or extracts are generally circulated.[38]

Even though World War I made correspondence between the United States and the Holy Land intermittent and unreliable, a letter from 'Abdu'l-Bahá got through to Roy. It provided detailed instructions about Bahá'í publications, and it specified that certain works could continue to be printed and circulated, but directed that all others would have to first be reviewed, either by a committee of the Temple Unity Executive Board or, after the hostilities ceased, in the Holy Land. This principle of review of Bahá'í publications was new and not especially appealing to American Bahá'ís, who were long accustomed to writing whatever they wished about the Faith.

The problem was that even though the letter appeared to be authentic, it did not bear 'Abdu'l-Bahá's signature, and the lack of a signature provided the excuse for those who did not want a national review committee to put the letter aside. Roy, simply the messenger, was innocently caught in the middle. In a letter received after the War, 'Abdu'l-Bahá affirmed the contents of the letter Roy had received, again stating that all publications had to be reviewed at the national level (rather than locally) in order to ensure that the Faith was represented with accuracy, with dignity, and with consideration to the timeliness of the published material.[39]

Summer arrived in New Jersey. Six months had passed since 'Abdu'l-Bahá had sailed from New York for Europe, and it had been almost a year since the Unity Picnic was held in Teaneck. With the one-year anniversary coming up, Roy and his parents decided to organize another picnic. No gathering at the Wilhelm property would ever be as special as the one graced with the presence of 'Abdu'l-Bahá, but perhaps this picnic could help reinforce His lesson that day about the importance of spiritual fellowship, love, and unity among diverse people. Friends from throughout the greater New York area again made the journey to the sylvan property on Sunday, June 29, 1913, bringing with them picnic hampers full of good things to eat. With a soft breeze from the north and moderate temperatures and humidity, the weather was more pleasant than the sultry temperatures the crowd had endured the previous year.[40] There beneath the shade of the towering pines, the friends basked in the memory of that wonderful occasion. The words spoken by 'Abdu'l-Bahá as He had paced the Wilhelms' lawn were read aloud to the 1913 picnickers and again filled their hearts—a reminder of the importance of unity, of the coming together of all people, and of the elimination of prejudices. Unity could never be achieved without effort, and the good feelings from the year before needed to be constantly renewed.

Roy wrote to 'Abdu'l-Bahá to report the picnic and received an unexpected reply. 'Abdu'l-Bahá wished the picnic to be held annually as a souvenir of His visit to North America, saying, "That annual, memorial meeting will be the souvenir of Abdul Baha, especially when it is passed with infinite delight and gladness."[41] This guidance became a charge that Roy would faithfully carry out—to hold an annual "Souvenir Picnic" at his West Englewood property. The word *souvenir*—referring to a tangible reminder of a visit to a place—must have resonated with Americans at a time when they were traveling more and often returned home with a tangible memento of their experience in hand. Despite an occasional interruption, 'Abdu'l-Bahá's directive would continue to be fulfilled perpetually under the supervision of Bahá'í institutions, regardless of war, pandemics, inclement weather, economic crisis, and the like. The picnic not only reminds each new generation of 'Abdu'l-Bahá's historic 1912 visit but of the need to continue the work of breaking down all barriers between people.

Participants at the 1926 Souvenir Picnic (USBNA)

One of those most deeply touched by the 1912 picnic at the Wilhelms' home was the family's friend, Martha Root, and she wanted to express that inspiration through action.[42] Since that first encounter with Roy in the Pittsburgh restaurant, she had become a devoted, knowledgeable believer as well as a close friend to all three Wilhelms. Opportunities to spend time with 'Abdu'l-Bahá, such as at the Unity Picnic, stoked the fire within her to share the message of the new day with as many people as possible. She was already an experienced international traveler, having toured Europe with her family as a youth, and, years later, covering a sporting event in Ireland as a reporter. This taste of the world beyond the borders of North America created within Martha an insatiable longing to spread the Faith by traveling not only across the country (like Roy), but around the globe. After consulting Charles Mason Remey, who had considerable experience living and traveling abroad, she devised a proposal that she wanted to present to 'Abdu'l-Bahá for His blessing. Her plan was to ask her employer, a Pittsburgh newspaper, to continue to pay her salary as well as cover her expenses in exchange for articles she would write about her travels.

Roy introduced her proposal to 'Abdu'l-Bahá when he met with Him in New York on November 12. 'Abdu'l-Bahá responded that Martha had underestimated not only the expenses involved, but also the hardship of the journey she proposed, especially the difficulties of traveling within Persia. He asked that she remain in Pittsburgh for the time being. However, He did not close the door on the idea and stated at the end of His discussion with Roy that, "If any paper will ensure her salary and expenses fully, she may go."[43]

'Abdu'l-Bahá's response to Martha's proposal was not what she had hoped for. Her spiritual brother tried to help her view it as being for the best and wrote:

> I don't believe this will be as much of a disappointment to you as it was a year ago. I think too, Martha, it is a mistake to strain too hard to <u>create</u> <u>conditions</u>. I believe in trying to be in shape to grasp opportunities <u>when</u> they come and then to lay low for the arrival of the when, and I doubt if your whenly [sic]* for this big jaunt has yet arrived, though I some how feel in my bloomin' bones that it <u>will</u> <u>come</u>.[44]

Though Martha was not destined to travel to Europe, the Holy Land, and Persia as soon as she wished, she did get to explore and have fun with the Wilhelms that summer of 1913 by joining them on a monthlong vacation excursion around the Northeast by automobile. Only a few weeks after the second annual Souvenir Picnic, they began their drive from suburban New Jersey to enjoy the natural beauty of the New England countryside.

Even though Roy's parents did not exhibit a strong desire to see the world through travel, their son did. In his youth, Roy had been an archetype of America on the move, exemplifying the energy created by waves of people in motion as they traveled from place to place, often in search of greener pastures.

---

* Roy enjoyed making up words if doing so added humor.

Roy's own history—running away from home when he was a teenager, venturing far from Ohio to explore other regions of the country as a salesman, disappearing for two years in the highlands of Central America as a young adult, and traveling to the Holy Land as a pilgrim—was full of signs that he was not only curious about the wider world, but anxious to experience it firsthand. Until the start of the twentieth century, most travel was usually undertaken for business, for visiting relations, or for migration. Leisure travel in 1913 continued to be primarily the purview of the well-to-do. However, as travel by train became safer, more comfortable, and more affordable, railway companies began to promote recreational travel by building resort hotels and spas at desirable vacation sites. Nevertheless, for the average American, travel only stopped being a luxury when more reliable and less expensive automobiles began to rumble along the rutted dirt byways crisscrossing the American landscape. In a few short years, especially following the introduction of the everyman's Model-T Ford automobile in 1908, an era of "purposeless wandering" began.

Because of their mutual devotion to the Faith and interest in the wider world, Roy and Martha Root were kindred spirits. She had become an honorary Wilhelm family member, calling Laurie and Otis her second parents. By this time, the family was well settled in their West Englewood home, and Roy's coffee brokerage was expanding, so a deluxe vacation trip—dining out and staying in hotels—could easily fit within their budget. But the Wilhelms cared nothing for fancy resorts. Their holiday was going to be a camping trip—no soft hotel beds, no hot baths or meals served on delicate china plates—for they were going to revel instead in the beauty of nature, in the great outdoors. The past year, which had included 'Abdu'l-Bahá's visit, had been strenuous, filled with busy schedules, and marked by the family members' scurrying from event to event. Now, they all longed for a bit of relaxation and recuperation.

Preparation started weeks before, when Roy began converting his 1911 REO touring car, now named *The Lady*, into the equivalent of a modern-day camper. They could not rely on easily locating stores where they could purchase more than basic food items and fuel, so much of what they needed was strapped, screwed, or hung somewhere on the car. The back of the vehicle became a mobile chuck wagon,* complete with a self-contained stove to cook meals. Awnings and a large umbrella for shade or to keep out the rain could be deployed at a moment's notice. Uncertain of where the next place to buy gasoline or to have the car repaired might appear, they carried extra gasoline, oil, auto parts, and grease. Weatherproof bags containing a tent, rope, blankets, ample bedding, food, and cooking utensils were fastened to the running boards next to tent poles. Dozens of other smaller items were tucked under seats and stuffed in corners until every nook and cranny of the car was filled, leaving just enough space for the "four gypsies,"** as they dubbed themselves. And they were off on a great adventure!

The REO fully outfitted for the 1913 tour of New England. Roy Wilhelm is standing next to the automobile, which is parked at the Wilhelm home. (USBNA)

---

* Cowboys in the Western United States would take a "chuck wagon" on cattle drives to serve as a mobile kitchen.

** The word *gypsy,* meaning a nomadic or free-spirited person, has also been used with a capital "G" as a name for the Roma people. In the twenty-first century, the appellation *Gypsy,* when applied to the Roma, is considered a racial slur. The Wilhelms and Martha Root used the term in the more general sense of happy wanderers.

Over the next four weeks—Roy, the chief engineer; Otis, in charge of the commissary; Laurie, the poet-cook; and Martha, the navigator, affectionately referred to as "Peelot"—explored over thirteen hundred breathtaking, bumpy miles of rural New England. They bounced over rough roads in Connecticut, slept in a farmer's field in Vermont, and ate beneath the shade of elm trees in Massachusetts. Occasionally they received invitations to dine with friends or strangers in their homes or allowed themselves a night in the comfort of an inn. Mostly they were on their own, bathing one day in a cold New Hampshire lake and then, in the evening, swatting mosquitos while setting up the tent in the fading twilight. Except when sitting by themselves in the quiet of the night beneath a canopy of stars, privacy was rare. For a month, the four were bound together within the confines of the REO, camping, enjoying nature, making new friends, sometimes singing, other times laughing and talking, all the while further cementing their bonds of personal affection. Surviving a trip together with family or friends without generating lasting friction is an achievement, but when there is real unity, an *esprit de corps* is built, and deeper understanding and love for each other becomes evident.

No doubt, with four avid teachers of the Faith on board the REO, there must have been many times when they took advantage of an encounter to introduce someone to Bahá'u'lláh. For Martha, this rugged experience would serve as the bootcamp she needed to prepare for a future of service to the Faith—a service often fraught with material hardships and dangerous travel to remote corners of the earth where she would carry Bahá'u'lláh's message. So too, after getting to know Martha much better, Roy learned to anticipate her—how she thought, what she needed, and how she went about life. This deeper understanding of his Bahá'í sister enabled him to know when and how to throw her a lifeline when she needed one.

When they returned to New Jersey, Roy and Martha together penned a long article about the trip, which was published in the January 10, 1914, edition of *Collier's Weekly.** It even included some of

---

* See Appendix B for the full Collier's article.

The Wilhelms and Martha Root with the REO during their 1913 New England tour (Roy, who is not in the photograph, probably took it.) (USBNA)

their photographs. After the magazine article about the trip appeared, Roy bragged in his playful folksy style in a letter to his friend, Ella Cooper,* that the payment they received for the article nearly paid for the expenses of the trip, adding that roughing it was a "Nice way to gypsy** if one is fond of wood smoke, Khaki suits, spiders,

---

* Ella Goodall Cooper was among the first group of Western believers to visit 'Abdu'l-Bahá during the winter of 1898–1899. The daughter of a wealthy shipping company owner and wife of a renowned cardiologist, Ella was one of the most important leaders of the Faith on the West Coast. She and her mother, Helen Goodall, at their Oakland, California home, became the center of most of the activity in that region. Ella would serve with Roy on the Executive Board, the National Spiritual Assembly, and on various committees. They were kindred spirits, playfully addressing each other as BroRoy and SisElla.

** Please refer to footnote 2 on page 142. The word *gypsy* as used by Roy in the letter was meant to denote merry wandering and was not a reference to the Roma people. Because of its offensive connotations, the word *gypsy* is no longer widely used. (For a history of its usage in the United States, see the Merriam-Webster Dictionary.)

daddy-longlegs, bacon and eggs, spud-de-pommes in ashes and such-like [sic]."[45]

In that same letter to Ella, Roy diverged from his lighthearted account of the trip to discuss what had been bothering him in the months after that relaxing summer vacation. Working daily in the heart of New York's financial district, Roy felt that the happy spirit generated by the excursion had dissipated as he kept abreast of the news about the deteriorating situation in Europe. After his humorous comments, he turned more inward and serious, confessing to another of his Bahá'í sisters that he had a strong sense that the world was not right—a feeling so strong that he was reluctant to make long-term plans:

> I don't know just what's biting me, but even in business affairs I don't like to make a contract for even 90 days ahead. I think very many of us feel that there is some change taking place, or going to, but we don't know just what. Maybe it's like white mice when they're given a taste of the X-ray. But whatever it is to be, or whatever the result, I feel that its all a part of our education. Even the broiling of a lobster helps 'im manifest in a higher form of life, I suppose! But I don't have that feeling of depression about it any more. We must be stand-patters.[46]

When 'Abdu'l-Bahá toured North America and Europe, He warned of an impending global disaster—a war—multiple times. He clearly foresaw that the nations of Europe were careening toward a deep precipice and never shied away from saying so.[47] In the summer of 1914, 'Abdu'l-Bahá's uncanny ability to read the times and so foretell the future proved to be correct. In late June, what first seemed to be a minor incident—the assassination of the heir to the Austro-Hungarian throne by a small group of rebels in a remote region of that vast empire—rapidly exploded into a full-blown war which, in quick succession, drew in most of the great powers of Europe by early August. Even though the United States, under the leadership of President Woodrow Wilson, stayed aloof from this Old

World conflict, the country could not help but be affected by it. As a nation whose majority of citizens were immigrants from Europe or their descendants, it was hard for the average American to refrain from taking sides. While many of the elite sided with the United Kingdom, France, and Russia against Germany, Austria, and the Ottoman Empire, many others were adamant that the United States should remain neutral.[48]

Weeks before the spark ignited Europe, 'Abdu'l-Bahá wrote to Roy and assigned him to the post at which He wished him to remain for the time being—Roy's Wall Street office in lower Manhattan. Roy had written to Him about his frequent journeys across the country, which were increasingly motivated by his desire to spread and assist the Faith and less by his business. He wanted to continue his travels for the Faith with 'Abdu'l-Bahá's blessings. 'Abdu'l-Bahá acknowledged his praiseworthy efforts and said that Roy did not have "any personal aim" such as touring, "nay rather thy ultimate hope is to render service unto the Divine Kingdom."[49] His trips for both the Faith and his company pleased 'Abdu'l-Bahá immensely, but for now, Roy was to stay at home and concentrate on his business affairs. Like most letters addressed to him during this period, it begins by praising Roy for his steadfastness, saying that "like unto a solid mountain thou are unshakable in the Straight Path and save service in the Kingdom of God thou has no other hope and aim."[50] Then came the new guidance:

Now thou art again intending to make another extensive journey. If during this trip, thy absence from New York will not affect the normal state of thy trade, then it is very acceptable: but if on the other hand the long time consumed in the voyage will react upon thy commerce and at present it is in a condition of prosperity, and growth, then select someone else to make this journey in thy place. However such an one must be a firm soul and eloquent. Then after finding such a person, send him traveling around instead of yourself.[51]

Over the next few years, Roy faithfully carried out this injunction, not only by remaining at his office where he continued to serve as the Bahá'í community postman, but also by assisting others to travel to spread the faith. Martha, for example, would circle the planet four times with him ever at the ready as her safety net and cheerleader.

Roy knew that 'Abdu'l-Bahá's continued insistence that he take care not to neglect his business affairs in order to serve the Faith did not arise from a desire for Roy to contribute more money to the Cause. The embodiment of generosity, Roy was always willing to share his growing material wealth. This kind of generosity was not, however, what 'Abdu'l-Bahá wanted. He only wanted Roy's heart and had written a letter to this effect to Roy only a few months earlier:

> Concerning the fund: all that you and the steadfast believers of God have belongs to me. Whenever anything is needed I will unquestionably refer the matter to you. But at present it is not needed at all. I do not ask the friends to give up their money; but I ask the giving up of the heart and the soul—thus may they sacrifice their lives in the Path of God. This is the real contribution, otherwise it has no importance whatsoever.[52]

By the autumn of 1914, the flames of war were consuming more and more of Europe, beginning with the atrocities and devastation committed in little Belgium as German boots marched across it on their way to invade France. The conflagration then spread to the east toward the Holy Land, where the Ottoman Empire had entered the war on the side of Germany.

Back in Roy's world, Martha was, despite the expanding conflict, eager to begin traveling outside the United States to bring the Bahá'í Faith to places around the world where it was not yet known. Only someone as persistent and focused as Martha would consider a journey traversing Europe at such a time. Yet she was determined to go and, in addition, to reach the Holy Land as part of her itinerary. She did not even wait for good weather when booking passage to cross the Atlantic but sailed from New York in cold, stormy January 1915. Roy must have had his misgivings and fears, but if Martha was set on going—for she was as immovable in her resolve as he was—he would make good use of the opportunity by using her as a courier to deliver the princely sum of $2,000 in gold to 'Abdu'l-Bahá, Who needed it because of the war. She safely reached British-held Egypt, but after weeks of trying, she never obtained the necessary permission to enter Ottoman Palestine. However, she was able to find a trustworthy means of transferring the gold from Egypt to 'Abdu'l-Bahá. With this feat accomplished, though disappointed that she was not allowed to deliver Roy's gold to 'Abdu'l-Bahá herself, she departed for India, away from the main theaters of the war.[53]

Martha Root (left), Harry Randall (right), and Agnes Alexander (back far right) on the porch of the inn at Green Acre, 1918 (USBNA)

Unrestricted German submarine warfare against military as well as neutral civilian vessels prevented Martha from returning home across the Atlantic Ocean, so she continued her journey by heading east which gave her the opportunity to visit Bahá'ís in Burma, Japan, and Hawaii before arriving back in the United States through the port of

San Francisco.[54] Though Roy was eager to see Martha and to hear in detail about every aspect of her journey, her account would have to be conveyed to him by letter for the time being, as she had to return to Pittsburgh and then to her hometown, where her aging parents required her attention.[55] She was already a Bahá'í heroine, an inspiration to many, but her story was only beginning.

6 / MOVING FORWARD

In the summer of 1916, five Bahá'ís, each living in a different area of the United States or Canada, opened their mailboxes and, to their surprise, found a postcard from Haifa. Set forth in tiny writing were Tablets from 'Abdu'l-Bahá addressed to the region where each of the five lived. These signal Tablets were written on postcards to increase the odds they would make it unimpeded through the censored wartime mails. Using an atlas, 'Abdu'l-Bahá had adopted the publication's arrangement of the American states into four geographic regions. He then addressed a Tablet to each region, with a fifth addressed to the entire country of Canada.[1] These five messages were the first installment of a collection of Tablets—now known as the Tablets of the Divine Plan—written during the war years. The Tablet addressed to the northeastern states was sent to a New Yorker and fellow member of that city's Board of Council, Hooper Harris, rather than to Roy. Each Tablet included instructions and a prayer for teaching the Faith in the named region.[2] After their receipt, committees for each sector were appointed, and the focus of the North Americans expanded from raising money for the Temple to raising up souls.[3] Both were daunting tasks.

'Abdu'l-Bahá's visit had been the catalyst for significantly raising the level of contributions needed to complete the purchase of the Temple land. In the early twentieth century, that alone was a herculean achievement for a community which at that time was predominantly composed of women, most of whom were of modest means. 'Abdu'l-Bahá instructed the Executive Board to refrain from starting construction on the House of Worship until enough funds had been collected to avoid the need for a bank loan. However, without an architectural design, the Temple remained a hazy dream, and donations were slow in coming. The Executive Board was still the only nationwide, elected institution, so naturally it assumed responsibility for other matters, such as carrying out the mandates laid out in the five regional Tablets, publishing books and newsletters, and organizing annual Conventions.[4]

While the Great War raged with increasing intensity across the oceans, Roy found ample ways to stay occupied on the less turbulent shores of America, far from the conflict. He continued to serve intermittently on the Executive Board of the Temple Unity. When not a member of that Board, he was still often asked to attend its meetings as a designated consultant. Roy was not only involved with pressing national issues, but also continued to serve as a member of the New York Board of Council, which oversaw the largest Bahá'í community in North America. One of its major tasks was hosting most of the national Conventions at Manhattan hotels.

Roy and his parents, especially his mother, continued to provide hospitality at their West Englewood home for those wishing to learn more about the Faith. Their home also became a place for the local Bahá'ís to hold meetings, and after the war, 'Abdu'l-Bahá would comment favorably, saying, "Praise be to God thy home is the place wherein I have been and at present in that garden and that house spiritual gatherings are held and seeking souls attain unto guidance."[5] As the number of new believers in the Teaneck area grew through their efforts, Roy's thoughts turned to the needs of the Bahá'ís in the New Jersey suburbs, many of whom made the lengthy trek into Manhattan to attend Bahá'í events. Was it time to have a larger meeting space closer to home? This thought also appealed to Roy's desire to create something new. He hit upon the unusual idea of building a log cabin.

What he did not anticipate when he decided to construct one was the future significance of his project. The cabin would become one of the most iconic Bahá'í buildings in North America.

The tradition of log homes came to the New World with the immigrants from places with an abundance of trees, especially the Scandinavian region of northern Europe. The first settlers from Europe found the eastern seaboard of North America covered by a vast forest stretching from the ocean to the western edge of the Appalachian Mountains. Before planting crops and erecting buildings, trees had to be cleared. The plentiful wood naturally became the primary building material. To create a building entirely of logs did not require expensive, hand-forged nails or a saw; only an axe and adze combined with muscle power were needed. A man alone or with the help of a family member or friend could quickly cut, notch, and square enough logs to construct an adequate, warm, and secure shelter in just a few days. Once a roof was added, clay or wattle was pounded into the seams between the logs to keep out wintry drafts. Against one wall, field stones were usually piled high to build a hearth and chimney for cooking, warmth, and light. The loft over the rafters provided storage and a warm place to sleep during winter.

By the twentieth century, the log cabin had become a romantic part of American lore.[6] They continued to be built, but primarily as rustic retreats in which to escape the modern life and return to a simpler one. No longer the shelter of the impoverished, log cabins became instead durable vacation hideaways—lakeside cottages or mountainside retreats—for the urban affluent to escape the city's summer heat and bad air.

Roy began to build his cabin at what would have seemed to most of his contemporaries to be an inopportune time. By 1917, the world—as everyone had known it before the war began—had been turned upside down. The newspapers Roy read reported new atrocities every day as senseless slaughter in the muddy trenches of France horrified humanity, Russia descended into civil war, and the Pacific seas echoed with the boom of naval cannons. After the United States entered the conflict, all building materials were diverted to the war effort. It was within this turbulent milieu that Roy, always comfortable with modern technological advances while still savoring aspects of a simpler life, started his new construction project.

The north side of Evergreen Cabin in 1923 (USBNA)

What possessed this man, with an up-to-date office in New York, to build a log cabin a few yards behind his modern house? He most likely wanted to craft something out of wood with his hands. When he started the odd project, neighbors must have already been curious about the fastidious man in a bowtie with his constant flow of unorthodox, exotic visitors. They hardly raised an eyebrow when he built his modern tennis court—an unmistakable sign of affluence—but why had he started raising goats in a neighborhood that was becoming a residential suburb as new construction replaced the forest? And then there was the Japanese Torii* at the edge of his property. The towering gate built of two log pillars with two log crossbeams must have been just one more peculiarity to baffle his neighbors. (Often

---

* Torii gates are found in Japanese Shinto Shrines. They symbolize the entry into the sacred space of the shrine from the profane outside world.

Evergreen Cabin interior in 1920 during construction (USBNA)

traveling to the West Coast, Roy had become familiar with Japanese symbols, and certainly Martha Root and Ella Goodall stoked his interest in the Japanese people.) To those paying attention to this suburban bachelor, Roy was a quirky mix of rustic and sophisticated urban businessman.

Roy's thriving business consumed most of his week, but, beginning with the first warm weather of 1917, he devoted each Wednesday and Saturday to felling and hauling trees from the woods surrounding his home. For Roy, this activity was an enjoyable way to relax. Certainly, the cabin would be a place for him to unwind and enjoy recreational activities, but he never lost sight of his greater goal of providing a space where people who were uncomfortable going to a private home would be willing to attend Bahá'í gatherings in a neutral, informal setting.[7] Over the next nine years, beginning with the purchase of additional lots,[8] his Evergreen Cabin took shape in the shadow of

A view of the torii taken at the 1946 Souvenir Picnic (USBNA)

the main house. He started the project with only his father's help, and together, they shoved, pushed, lifted, and wrestled the three-hundred-pound logs into place.

Roy's friendship with Curtis Kelsey had continued and strengthened since that day the two met in the Kelsey basement. The Kelseys had moved to the New York area, and, as Roy requested at that first encounter years before, Curtis assisted Roy with creating a woodworking shop in his Teaneck basement. As one who loved working with his hands, Curtis gladly joined the Wilhelms in building Evergreen Cabin when it was time to clear the ground and pour the concrete foundation. The three men worked without formal architectural plans, laying out a 13 x 25-foot,* two-story log cabin with a large verandah. Timbers, culled from the many dying Norway Spruces planted on the property four decades earlier by Walter Phelps, were augmented by white cedar logs imported from Canada. Curtis, in his early twenties, missed his Pacific Northwest home with its basement

* Approximately four by eight meters.

156

woodworking shop, so the opportunity to cut trees, shape logs, and saw planks was a perfect weekend antidote to his job at his father's company in New York City. The three had just started the building, however, when Curtis received his military draft notice. Before long, Roy's junior assistant was on his way to Europe as an infantryman.[9]

When Curtis returned home after the end of World War I, wood chips flew faster as work on the cabin resumed—that is, until the day Curtis met Roy for lunch at a restaurant in lower Manhattan.

In early 1919, correspondence once again began to flow from 'Abdu'l-Bahá to the world outside of Palestine with renewed intensity. After not having received personal correspondence from 'Abdu'l-Bahá over the past two and a half years, Roy was elated to finally get another letter from Haifa. 'Abdu'l-Bahá began by assuring him that He was in good health, saying, "we have passed these years of war in joy and gladness," and, "praise be to God, the darkness of oppression has passed away and the light of justice has dawned and a just government [Great Britain] has been ministering to this land."[10] Regarding correspondence with the Holy Land, Roy was informed that "the hinderances and obstacles have been eliminated," so the way was clear for direct communication.[11] In another letter written a few weeks later to Martha Root, 'Abdu'l-Bahá praised Roy, telling her, "His honor, Mr. Roy Wilhelm is in reality a true servant. He has no thought save service to the Kingdom of Abha and is therein engaged day and night."[12]

Almost as soon as it was possible to travel from the Holy Land when the hostilities ceased, 'Abdu'l-Bahá's secretary and English translator, Ahmad Sohrab, persuaded 'Abdu'l-Bahá to allow him to return to the United States. The embodiment of worldly ambition, Sohrab was sent to America in 1901 when he was a teenager to serve the Bahá'í scholar, Mírzá 'Abu'l-Fadl, on behalf of 'Abdu'l-Bahá. He had been instructed to return to Egypt with 'Abu'l-Fadl, but ignoring

'Abdu'l-Bahá's clear directive, he never left the country until ordered to accompany 'Abdu'l-Bahá back to Haifa in 1912.[13] Throughout the war, Sohrab was fixated on returning to the West, even writing to Bahá'ís in the United States asking them to finance his return. While he longed to be back in America, he wrote detailed daily accounts of 'Abdu'l-Bahá's activities and sayings, often sending them to the *Star of the West* for publication. He endured the hardships of the war at 'Abdu'l-Bahá's side, making him not only a source of invaluable information, but also a hero. When he arrived in New York, he was feted as one.[14]

The most important items Sohrab included in his luggage were several metal cylinders containing carefully rolled parchments. These precious scrolls were the remaining Tablets of the Divine Plan. Rendered in beautiful calligraphy, they constituted the blueprint for the spiritual conquest of the planet and would later be designated as one of the three charters of the Faith.* They would serve forever as the underpinning of all efforts to systematically spread the Cause to every nook and cranny of the world. As soon as Sohrab arrived in New York in early 1919 and delivered the remaining sacred Tablets, the Executive Board knew that the Tablets had to be promulgated in a special way.[15]

With the return of peace and the resumption of unrestricted travel, the North American Bahá'ís were looking forward to the 1919 National Convention, and the planners anticipated a larger than usual attendance when it convened in April at the prestigious McAlpin Hotel in New York City. The Convention would celebrate 'Abdu'l-Bahá's liberation after four years of constant danger. Moreover, there was hope that the Convention would restore unity by healing a traumatic rift that had torn apart segments of the American

---

* Shoghi Effendi designated the Will and Testament of 'Abdu'l-Bahá, the Tablets of the Divine Plan, and the Tablet of Carmel as the three charters. The first document outlines the administrative order, the second sets forth the worldwide teaching plan, and the third underlies the establishment of the World Center on Mount Carmel.

Bahá'í community. The controversy, ignited by a small breakaway group in Chicago called "The Reading Room," would likely have been avoided or quickly resolved if it had been possible to obtain direction from the Holy Land.[16] Now that guidance was flowing from the source of spiritual illumination in a growing torrent, tempers had cooled, and most believers were willing to forgive and move on from the past. Moreover, with the remaining Tablets safely delivered, the special ceremony arranged for dramatically unveiling the parchments promised to make the gathering not only joyful and memorable, but historic. As a featured speaker, Sohrab, enthusiastically related story after story from the Holy Land, enthralling the Bahá'ís gathered from across the continent. The Convention was a total success and was undoubtedly the happiest since 'Abdu'l-Bahá had attended in person in 1912.[17] Roy attended the Convention, and, most likely, so did one or both of his parents. It marked the turning of a corner for the North American Bahá'í community, for they had not only been charged to construct the Temple but had also been given the primary responsibility for taking the Message of Bahá'u'lláh to myriad places around the globe, many of which they had never even heard of before.

The remainder of the Tablets, which were received after the War, listed countries, territories, and islands throughout the world that needed to be opened to the Faith. Where to begin? The challenge of carrying out these directives seemed beyond the capacity of the North Americans with their limited resources, yet everyone left the Convention determined to conquer the planet for Bahá'u'lláh. They knew they could rely upon divine assistance. Some began to consider moving or traveling to faraway lands.

Martha Root was in the vanguard of those anxious to meet the challenge of the Tablets of the Divine Plan. Having already received 'Abdu'l-Bahá's blessing, she had laid out her next journey even before the second batch of Tablets were disseminated. The formal unveiling was just her starting gun before she sprinted off to other shores, this time headed south. She was among the first from America to begin what became a systematic process of carrying the Faith to the places named in the Tablets—a heroic, sacrificial endeavor that was finally

Women and girls who unveiled the Tablets of the Divine Plan at the 1919
National Convention in New York City (USBNA)

concluded in 1990 when the last places named in the Tablets were
finally opened to the Faith.[18] Less than two months after the convention, and after attending the 1919 annual picnic at Roy's home,
Martha sailed from New York for a five-month journey throughout
much of South America, her trunks stuffed with a large supply of
Roy's teaching pamphlets, the Bens.[19]

Meanwhile in North America, after the entire collection of Tablets was formally introduced, the Executive Committee decided to
appoint a nineteen-member committee, including Roy, to devise a
plan to carry out the directives set forth in the Tablets. The following
year, Roy was reappointed to that committee of nineteen, but there
is no indication that it ever accomplished anything noteworthy other
than producing a newsletter, perhaps because its membership was
scattered across the continent, making it impossible to meet.[20]

Another significant issue had also been languishing during the war,
awaiting further guidance from 'Abdu'l-Bahá—namely, the selection
of a design for the House of Worship. In 1909, one of the first acts of

the newly created Executive Board was to publicly invite architects to submit designs. Seventeen Bahá'ís and other architects did so within the deadline. Roy's neighbor, Louis Bourgeois, sent a hastily made drawing that was not well developed, but it was a start.

When no decision was forthcoming, the architects continued to refine their designs. Charles Mason Remey, who also served intermittently on the Executive Board, began circulating designs in a variety of architectural styles, hoping to win the honor of designing what all Bahá'ís believed would become a world-famous edifice. William Sutherland Maxwell, a Bahá'í who had been Remey's friend at Ecole des Beaux Artes, where both of them had been students of architecture, also continued to work on his own Temple design.[21] As a prominent Canadian architect, Maxwell had already designed churches and government buildings. (And Maxwell's wife, May, had been present at Roy's first Bahá'í gathering, becoming one of his good friends.)

From the beginning of their friendship, Roy encouraged Louis to submit a design for the Temple. To give 'Abdu'l-Bahá an idea of the experienced architect's capabilities, when the Wilhelms went on pilgrimage in 1907, they carried with them Louis' drawings for The Hague's majestic, eight-sided Peace Palace, which he had designed jointly with another architect.[22] 'Abdu'l-Bahá dismissed the drawings after a brief glance with the sole comment, "The Bahá'í Temple will have nine sides." When this remark was reported to Louis, he was disappointed, but he learned the lesson of adhering closely to 'Abdu'l-Bahá's directives, for He was only willing to consider designs for the Bahá'í Temple, not concepts for comparable buildings.[23]

In the first letter Roy received from Him after the war, 'Abdu'l-Bahá asked to be remembered to Louis, recalling the July evening He visited the Bourgeois home for dinner, which He said was "a night that we passed in joy and fragrance."[24] 'Abdu'l-Bahá then requested that Roy forward his neighbor's current design of the House of Worship to the Holy Land because He was anxious for construction to begin.[25] After 'Abdu'l-Bahá studied Louis' design, He wrote to Roy that Louis "has indeed striven hard" and that "Blessedness awaiteth him and a goodly home."[26]

Plaster model of Bourgeois design for the Bahá'í House of Worship,
which is today displayed in the lower level of that building (USBNA)

In 1920, 'Abdu'l-Bahá directed that the delegates to the next
National Convention should choose the design for the Mother Temple of the West. Though a number of architects were vying for the
commission, the three designs that dominated the competition had
been submitted by the three Bahá'í architects: Charles Mason Remey,
William Sutherland Maxwell, and Louis Bourgeois. Roy was the first
person to address that joyous gathering in New York, delighting
the audience with his humor and reminding them that the house of
'Abdu'l-Bahá is "the home of laughter and exultation."[27]

Then the contest for the prize of the Temple commission began.
After a full day of presentations about the advantages and disadvan-
tages of the three foremost designs, most delegates found themselves
drawn to Louis's submission. Going to great trouble and sacrificial
expense, Louis had commissioned a large plaster model of his design,
which was on display at the convention. It had been exhibited the
previous June at the Souvenir Picnic and at other locations. Bour-

geois' nine-sided, ornate dome seemed to have mystical, dreamlike qualities inherent in its ethereal, unique beauty. Many who viewed his model were convinced that Louis' account of being divinely inspired was true.[28] It was the overwhelming favorite at the Convention and received the most votes. Now Roy, as a member of the Executive Board, would have to work with his neighbor to bring Louis's vision into reality. The choice of the Bourgeois design also meant that the Wilhelms would lose their dear neighbors to the little town of Wilmette, Illinois, where Louis and Alice would take up residence near the Temple land so that Louis could complete the plans for the building's details while overseeing the construction.

Roy's coffee business continued to grow, making him moderately affluent. The end of the Great War sent coffee prices skyward, "the highest it has been in nearly quarter century," Roy reported, "and still climbing."[29] 'Abdu'l-Bahá had assured Roy that He would pray for him to be prosperous.[30] To assist him in his expanding business, Roy hired a local believer, Nellie Hope Lloyd,* who had shown great capacity when working with Roy to organize New York Bahá'í events, especially during 'Abdu'l-Bahá's visit to the city. He relied upon her to assist with the Bahá'í communications still passing through his office. But that was not the only way his office served the Cause. His reputation within the business community gave Roy important connections in the finance world, and he took advantage of this to introduce prominent people to the Faith. For example, one time,

---

* Though very few details of her life are known, Nellie Hope Lloyd, born in 1876, was close in age to Roy, and she never married. Other than in wartime, married women were not usually hired prior to the 1960s, unless they were beyond childrearing years. They also usually had to have their husband's permission to accept employment. Nellie, born in New York City, was the daughter of Irish immigrants. (Records from http://Ancestry.com)

Roy hosted a luncheon in honor of J. W. Robertson Scott, author of bestselling books on English and Japanese economics. Other guests that day included George E. Roberts, the former head of the U.S. Mint and author of a major economic bulletin, as well as Roy's Bahá'í friends, international lawyer Mountfort Mills, and Harry Randall, the owner of a successful Boston shipping company. He was already in the process of introducing the Faith to Roberts and Scott.[31]

When Roy first established his coffee brokerage, it may have been true that his business practices were not yet up to Bahá'í standards. Once, 'Abdu'l-Bahá, demonstrating His knowledge of English, used a common American idiom when He told Roy that He wanted him to be a "straight shooter." Roy, who always strove to be obedient to 'Abdu'l-Bahá, took this advice literally. He purchased two pistols, set up targets in his backyard, and practiced shooting. Of course, the sound of gunshots concerned his neighbors. Finally, his friend Curtis Kelsey gently suggested that perhaps 'Abdu'l-Bahá did not mean for him to become a marksman, but to be more direct and honest in his business practices. Roy realized that his friend's interpretation of "straight shooter" was the correct one and apparently made adjustments in how he conducted his business affairs.[32]

Roy's professional reputation for excellence and overall business integrity and knowledge proved especially useful as the actual construction of the House of Worship got underway. At one point, the Executive Board asked him for advice when a supplier wanted to charge more for building materials than what some of the other Bahá'ís thought was fair. He responded that he was opposed to the Faith taking legal action against the contractor, stating that he "would go any reasonable length, yes, even stand some abuse, rather than enter litigation."[33]

'Abdu'l-Bahá not only showered Roy with praise in every letter but also once acknowledged how much trouble He gave him, saying, "Although I trouble you very much, yet I supplicate God's assistance and favor (for you), because the troubles you are taking are for the sake of God. Surely great rewards will follow one after the other."[34]

By the end of World War I, the bright twinkle of lights made major cities in America and Europe seem almost like nighttime fairylands, thanks to widespread use of Thomas Edison's electric generators and lightbulbs. Beginning in New Jersey, large power plants had also been constructed and wires strung along tall poles lined street after street in Manhattan. Gone was the flickering, yellow glow from oil lamps and candles or the white light and hiss of gas lamps. The marvel of the electric light was still only to be found within large cities in both the United States and Europe. Small towns and villages, which could not afford to install power plants, would have to wait to be brought into the electric age over the next two decades. Electricity to light a farmhouse and barn would only arrive in the neglected corners of the United States during the Great Depression of the 1930s after the initiation of the New Deal's Rural Electrification Act.[35] In the meantime, ambitious and creative businesses set to work to develop innovative technologies to fill dark voids in the areas not yet served by electric power plants. Companies such as Delco in Ohio and Kohler in Wisconsin designed and built compact, self-contained electric generators capable of charging a bank of storage batteries. Once they owned a generator, a farmer and his family could, for the first time, enjoy a few hours of quiet illumination after sunset to milk the last cow, to darn a sock, or to read a passage from the family Bible before going to bed.

Roy was deeply affected by 'Abdu'l-Bahá's recounting of the Báb's imprisonment in the oppressive, lightless fortress of Máh-Kú, and how that illustrious Manifestation of God was deprived of even a single lighted candle during His years of incarceration. Hearing this account from 'Abdu'l-Bahá sparked a desire within Roy to illuminate the Báb's holy resting place with the light of a thousand candles by employing an electric generator, for the city of Haifa still lacked municipal electricity. In 1919, he wrote to 'Abdu'l-Bahá and offered to purchase a generator and ship it to Haifa.[36] This offer was generous because the plants were expensive, each costing two thousand dollars, and the total expense rose even higher by the time the expenditures for installation and shipping were added. Roy must have been elated when 'Abdu'l-Bahá accepted his gift, but also surprised, perhaps even stunned, when the response came back with a request not for one generator, but for three.[37] This was beyond Roy's budget, but obediently, without hesitation, he ordered three diesel Kohler generators, which he judged to be the best available. Although Roy's coffee business was doing well, he would need the equivalent of more than $100,000* to cover all costs, and a short-term loan would be necessary. 'Abdu'l-Bahá followed up the request by saying, "As to the electric light (plant), thou wilt, surely, do thy best."[38] As a testament to Roy's character, no words of this financing reached the ears of those in the Holy Land. 'Abdu'l-Bahá, also asked Roy to send a suitably skilled electrician to oversee the installation of the electrical system for illuminating the Shrine of the Báb because no one in Haifa knew how to install the equipment and lights.[39] Roy knew just the person to send.

Roy and Curtis had just finished eating lunch in a restaurant not far from Roy's office. While waiting for the server to bring their bill, Roy startled Curtis with an unexpected question, the primary reason he had asked his young friend to join him for a meal. "How would you like to go to Haifa?"[40] Curtis did not hesitate with his answer. He'd "like nothing better," but, he added, it was impossible for him to go. Roy then repeated the words Curtis had heard from him years

---

* Equivalence in 2022 dollars.

before in his Oregon basement: "Well, you never know about those things."[41]

Although Curtis had no formal training as an engineer or electrician, Roy had observed his work over the years and knew his young friend had an innate aptitude for detailed mechanical work. He had also come to know Curtis's character, and so he was confident Curtis was the right person to go to Haifa. Roy wrote to 'Abdu'l-Bahá and recommended the young man as the electrician he thought could do the job of installing the power plants. One generator was destined for the Shrine of Bahá'u'lláh, the sacred Qiblih of the Bahá'í world located outside of 'Akká, the second for the Shrine of the Báb in Haifa, and the third for 'Abdu'l-Bahá's Haifa home, the headquarters of the Faith.

Not long after the lunch with Roy, Curtis received a cable from 'Abdu'l-Bahá inviting him to come to the Holy Land. He sold his car and a few other belongings to raise funds for passage to Palestine. With this cash in hand, along with five hundred dollars given to him by Roy, Curtis paid for his travel expenses. His father, who was set against Curtis chasing halfway around the world for no financial compensation, went to the pier to see his son off and, in an unexpected gesture, slipped his son another $250 along with a Graflex camera, which would later be put to historic use.[42]

Once Curtis began his work in the Holy Land, 'Abdu'l-Bahá wrote to Roy of how pleased He was with Curtis's devotion, strong work ethic, and ability to get the electric generators up and running.[43] For the next eight months, Curtis labored on the slopes of Mount Carmel and around Haifa Bay, installing the Kohlers and stringing wires. At last, each evening there was steady light for the end of the day's routines and prayers. And, for the first time, a resplendent glow radiated from the side of that holy mountain. After sunset, the Báb's resting place was illumined for all to see—a symbolic compensation for His suffering.

With the Great War over, the victors gathered at Versailles in 1919 to redraw many lines on the map of the world, thereby creating new countries, new governments, and new international institutions such as the League of Nations. As 'Abdu'l-Bahá had predicted, the centuries-old ruling dynasties of the German, the Austro-Hungarian, the Ottoman, and the Russian Empires were swept away by the fighting. Even China's ancient monarchy was on its way out. The British and French empires were tottering as colonialism was dying, as independence movements emerged, emboldened by the instability of the world situation at the conclusion of the hostilities. When the Ottoman Empire was carved up at the Conference of Versailles, the British were given a mandate to administer Palestine and Iraq, while the French were handed neighboring Lebanon and Syria to govern. No longer under the rule of the despotic Sultan of Turkey, who had been both a secular leader and caliph of Sunni Islam, 'Abdu'l-Bahá was at last able to freely accept visitors and to travel. The new British overlords in the Holy Land visited Him and came to admire Him. They became very accommodating to 'Abdu'l-Bahá's needs and requests, especially after British and American believers interceded on His behalf.[44] Americans, such as Roy's friends Harry Randall and his family, and Corinne True and her daughter, Edna, seized the opportunity to make pilgrimages to Haifa.[45] At last, after four years of the horrors of mankind's first fully mechanized war, the world appeared to be a more peaceful, stable place.

With 'Abdu'l-Bahá's blessing, Roy was again traveling the country not only for business, but to assist the Bahá'í communities. As a middle-aged man, he had acquired habits that made him a distinctive house guest. In addition to his always-present bowtie, Roy had a few other eccentricities, such as carrying a cloth napkin in his luggage so his hosts would not be troubled with extra laundry after his departure. His hosts also discovered that he always ate a unique breakfast. While in Haifa in 1907, 'Abdu'l-Bahá instructed him in the preparation of a porridge made with a high-protein hard wheat. With the addition of goat's milk this breakfast regime gave Roy relief from the discomfort of his sensitive stomach. He made a point of shipping the ingredients required for his morning fare in advance of his travels.[46] His need for goat's milk undoubtedly explains his interest in goats, which he had begun to raise on his suburban property in West Englewood.

Roy's humility, amiability and keen sense of humor made him a welcome traveling teacher. He offered the believers loving encouragement and the opportunity to invite inquirers to hear him speak. His journeys provided opportunities to observe firsthand the state of the Bahá'í community from coast to coast, which not only served the Temple Unity Executive Board, but also 'Abdu'l-Bahá. On February 27, 1920, for example, Roy received the following cable that simply read, "HOW ARE FRIENDS? CONVEY MY GREETINGS ABBAS."[47]

'Abdu'l-Bahá was generally pleased with the progress His North American flock achieved in the years following His visit, writing to Roy in the summer of 1921 that "the present condition of the Cause in America cannot be compared to the former days. The Teachings of God and the heavenly characteristics are, day by day, gaining in strength." He added, however, that it was His "hope that the souls who are the cause of trouble may also repent and grow quiet."[48] This last comment most likely was referring to a small number of individuals causing great or minor difficulties. One especially challenging person was 'Abdu'l-Bahá's former translator and secretary, Dr. Ameen Fareed, who had had to be expelled from the Faith, along with those members of his family who continued to support him. Fareed had moved to Los Angeles, where he had gained sympathy among some of the American believers. He was perhaps the biggest challenge at the time, but there were others as well, especially well-intentioned Bahá'ís who had difficulty getting along with others or who insisted on following the Faith in their own way. A problem also began to emerge with a new Bahá'í journal, *Reality,* based in New York, when it came under new management and began running articles sympathetic to Covenant-breakers. Roy had a hand in alleviating all of these problems as a member of the Executive Board and of the New York Board of Counsel. Undoubtedly, no group of five thousand—the approximate number of North American Bahá'ís at the time—would be without problems arising from some of its members.[49]

169

On October 24, 1921, one of 'Abdu'l-Bahá's grandsons wrote to Roy about what was happening in Haifa, saying also that the friends there were very glad to learn that Roy was considering making another pilgrimage to the Holy Land. The letter included the good news that 'Abdu'l-Bahá was in "perfect health."[50]

Roy must have been puzzled when, two weeks later, on November 8, he received a personal message from 'Abdu'l-Bahá that put a forthright question to him: "How is situation and health of friends?"[51] Roy responded the next day by saying, "Chicago, Washington, Philadelphia agitating violation. Centering Fernald, Dyer, Watson. New York, Boston refused join, standing solidly constructive policy."[52] A few days later, Roy received a reply to his own cable that read:

> He who sits with leper catches leprosy. He who is with Christ shuns Pharisees and abhors Judas Iscariots. Certainly shun violators. Inform Goodall, True and Parsons telegraphically.
> (signed) Abbas[53]

That same day, Roy received another personal telegram from 'Abdu'l-Bahá that said simply, "I implore health from divine bounty. (signed) Abbas"[54]

These cables, presaging something important, must have seemed both curious and ominous to Roy. There was an underlying urgency to them.

He would not have long to wait.

7 / A NEW DAY

It was another Monday morning, the last one that November. The 1921 Thanksgiving holiday had just finished, and most Americans' attention was shifting to the rapidly approaching Christmas festivities. One easily imagines Roy's work week beginning in the same systematic routine he had strictly followed over the years. He would have been anxious to get back to work after the overindulgences that were part of his family's Thanksgiving feast. As usual, Roy would have stopped at his preferred newsstand, plunked down two cents for *The New York Times,* then made his way to his office. A light drizzle was falling that morning, and in the chilly, damp air of late November, snow seemed likely.[1] Although the heat for his office had been turned up a few hours before he arrived, arcs of silver frost still decorated the glass panes of his company's windows that looked out on Wall Street. Folding back the *Times,* he glanced at the front page—a terrible fire at the Rialto Theater in New Haven had taken four lives; the French were upset with the Americans for meddling in European affairs, again—all were tragic happenings, but not much was new. Turning to the financial section, Roy checked the schedules of arriving and departing steamships and saw that wholesale coffee prices were still rising. A weather sidebar indicated a storm was developing over the Atlantic.[2]

A short time later, a messenger for the Commercial Cable Company,* headquartered around the corner from his office, came through the door. Dripping little puddles on the floor, he probably handed the messages to one of Roy's staff then went back out into the wet weather to continue his deliveries. The dispatches were then placed into the inbox on Roy's desk. He picked up a small envelope with the cable company's familiar logo. The envelope was identical to the dozens he received each month with orders, invoices, or shipment notifications. Maybe it had information about a coffee consignment or a new order. Like most businesses in the city's financial district, Wilhelm & Co. had a distinct cable address that ensured messages were delivered to the proper recipient. Roy had chosen his last name with an added flourish of "ite" (wilhelmite) as his cable address, thereby inadvertently rendering it similar to the name of the Illinois village, Wilmette, where the Mother Temple of the West would soon rise from the sands along the shore of Lake Michigan. He opened the envelope and glanced down to scan the brief message. His body and spirit abruptly slumped as the cable dropped from his hand.

Hours before, half a world away on the eastern coast of the Mediterranean Sea, unending waves crashed against the shore while the city of Haifa slept. At the foot of Mount Carmel, windows of the shops and houses were dark; most, that is, except one house on the street of the Persians, where light from oil lamps could be seen flickering through the cracks of shuttered windows. Inside, a small group of friends, family, and pilgrims, overwhelmed by tears and sorrow, endured the early morning hours of November 28. Among the mourners were five of Roy's friends—John and Louise Bosch from California; Florian

---

*Cables (also called cablegrams) were international messages transmitted using the underseas cables laid beneath the rivers, estuaries, and oceans of the world. Telegrams usually referred to messages sent overland.

and Grace Krug from New York; and Curtis Kelsey. The five were in shock because a short time after 1 o'clock in the morning, 'Abdu'l-Bahá had unexpectedly ascended to God's other worlds.

As a medical doctor, Florian Krug had had a portent of how the night might end. He was among the first people summoned to 'Abdu'l-Bahá's bedside where he confirmed His passing and gently closed His eyes. Upon their arrival in Haifa just a few days earlier, Dr. Krug and his wife Grace had been escorted by 'Abdu'l-Bahá to His own chamber, whereupon, unaccountably, Grace "had a sudden feeling of apprehension and burst into tears."[3]

Curtis, accompanied by two other men, was instructed to drive to 'Akká to inform the Bahá'ís living there, especially members of 'Abdu'l-Bahá's family. In a milieu of weeping, fear, uncertainty, and grief, some were busy comforting those in need of comforting; some sat immobile, unable to comprehend the loss of their guiding star; while a few began the difficult task of notifying the authorities and the Bahá'ís throughout the world. What should they say? The sorrowful wailing emanating from the house was so intense that soon friends and nearby neighbors began arriving. 'Abdu'l-Bahá's beloved sister, Bahíyyih <u>Kh</u>ánum, the Greatest Holy Leaf, despite her own unfathomable grief at the loss of her Brother, the center of her world, was the captain directing everything. Now, the weight and significance of the moment, the future of the Faith, rested upon her delicate, indomitable, and heroic shoulders; her own mourning would have to wait.[4]

Picking up the cablegram, Roy reread the dozen words to confirm the unbearable news he had just received: HIS HOLINESS ABDUL BAHA ASCENDED TO ABHA KINGDOM INFORM FRIENDS GREATEST HOLY LEAF.[5] He paused, but not for long. He knew what he had to do.

Perhaps the most difficult task facing Roy that day was not informing the North American Bahá'ís that their leader was gone. No, it was the question of how to break this terrible, unanticipated news to his

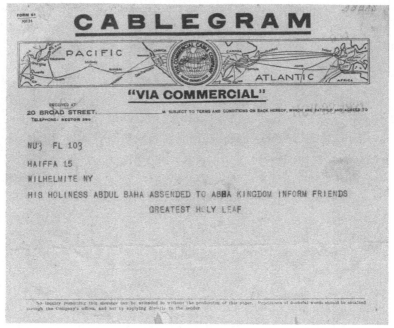

Cable from Bahíyyih Khánum announcing the passing of 'Abdu'l-Bahá.
Note Roy Wilhelm's cable address: Wilhelmite (USBNA)

mother. His heart was already broken, and her grief would no doubt rival if not surpass his own.

Roy remembered the letter assuring him of 'Abdu'l-Bahá's good health that he had received from the Holy Land just a few weeks before. What had 'Abdu'l-Bahá been trying to warn him about in His last messages when He used the analogy of the leper? Was there something in particular 'Abdu'l-Bahá had wanted Roy to understand about firmness in the Covenant? He needed to reflect more on those cautionary words and consider how this unfathomable loss would test all believers as to their submission to the Covenant. Surely, the Faith was now traveling through dangerous and turbulent waters. Then came that last personal telegram from 'Abdu'l-Bahá which simply said, "I implore health from divine bounty. (signed) Abbas."[6] Roy would need time for prayer and quiet reflection to comprehend that final cable's direct and transcendent meanings.

Once he had completed the task of notifying the North American Bahá'í community of their great loss, there was nothing for Roy to do but wait for further information and instructions from Haifa. For weeks, he went to his office, eagerly expecting something—a cable, a letter—anything that would reassure the Western flock they had not been left without a shepherd. Roy had great confidence in 'Abdu'l-Bahá's sister, the Greatest Holy Leaf, for she had expertly managed the immediate needs of the Faith in the Holy Land during her Brother's travels to Europe and America. She was, however, elderly, and therefore unlikely to be the long-term solution to the future leadership of the Cause. Perhaps the international governing body which Bahá'u'lláh had ordained, the Universal House of Justice, would be elected in the coming months. The anxiety born of this uncertainty weighed on the minds of the believers around the world.

Bahíyyih Khánum, titled the Greatest Holy Leaf, daughter of Bahá'u'lláh who served as regent several times during the ministries of her Brother, 'Abdu'l-Bahá, and her great nephew, Shoghi Effendi

On December 4, a cable did arrive at Roy's office, but it was from Tehran, not Haifa. The Persian believers sent a message of sympathy and encouragement to their brothers and sisters in North America and said simply, "LIGHT OF COVENANT TRANSFERRED FROM EYE TO HEART. DAY OF TEACHING, UNITY, SELF SACRIFICE."[7] This loving message must have touched Roy, but it could not allay his concerns about the future.

A cable, expressing condolences on behalf of the North American community, had been sent to 'Abdu'l-Bahá's family by the Executive Board of the Bahá'í Temple Unity.[8] The same day that the cable arrived from Tehran, Roy received another one conveying the gratitude of the Holy Family for the message of sympathy and asking the American believers to continue to serve the Cause. Yet no word was mentioned about what would come next.

There was a glimmer of hope when, three weeks after 'Abdu'l-Bahá's ascension, a cable, addressed to the Executive Board in response to its inquiry regarding a day to hold memorial services, arrived from the Greatest Holy Leaf.[9] Within her reply that a worldwide day of services would be held on January 7, she added that 'Abdu'l-Bahá had left instructions in His Will and Testament and that a translation would be forthcoming.[10]

Days later, on December 14, a cable arrived from the Greatest Holy Leaf addressed to Roy. It read, "Now is a period of great tests. The friends should be firm and united in defending the Cause. Nakeseens* starting activities through press other channels all over world. Select committee of wise cool heads to handle press propaganda in America."[11] Roy assumed that the cable was sent to him personally because it was addressed to him, so he immediately sprang into action, putting forward the names of three people capable of dealing with the news media to constitute the committee. To ensure

---

* *Nakeseens* was the word commonly employed at the time for Covenant-breakers, a designation that could only be made by 'Abdu'l-Bahá as Center of the Covenant.

that the matter was handled quickly, he brought it before the New York Board of Council, which approved his plan. Perceiving that "promptness seems essential," he asked that the Executive Board take necessary action as soon as possible.[12] However, Alfred Lunt, the Board's secretary, preferred to let the matter be decided only after the full membership of the Executive Board had had an opportunity to consult, and so was unwilling to implement Roy's plan.[13]

This hesitancy made any decision too late. 'Abdu'l-Bahá's archenemy, His half-brother, Muḥammad-'Alí, through his henchmen in the United States, approached prominent newspapers to spread misinformation about the new leadership of the Faith before the American believers could take steps to counter them, thereby gaining valuable publicity. The goal of the Board had to shift from prevention to damage control. This turn of events greatly vexed Roy, especially since it could have been avoided through instant obedience.[14]

On Monday, January 16, 1922, another cable arrived at Roy's office from Haifa. It contained the news he and every other believer had eagerly awaited. It read:

IN WILL, SHOUGHI [SIC] EFFENDI APPOINTED GUARDIAN OF CAUSE AND HEAD OF HOUSE OF JUSTICE. INFORM AMERICAN FRIENDS.

(SIGNED) GREATEST HOLY LEAF[15]

There was indeed a new shepherd, but many must have asked, who was Shoghi Effendi? Of the small number of American Bahá'ís who had met him, most had done so when he was a boy. The eldest grandchild of 'Abdu'l-Bahá, Shoghi Effendi had briefly served as his Grandfather's secretary and translator after graduating from the Syrian Presbyterian College in Beirut. At the time of 'Abdu'l-Bahá's passing, he was a graduate student at Balliol College at Oxford University in England, where he was refining his command of English. He had not returned to Haifa until the end of December, so the announcement about the contents of the Will and Testament of 'Abdu'l-Bahá could not be made until after he could examine and prepare to respond to the document. Prior to Shoghi Effendi's return home, only the Greatest Holy Leaf was familiar with the will's contents.[16]

Shoghi Effendi as a youth (USBNA)

Shoghi Effendi, born and raised in the Holy Land, was only twenty-four years old, and much more Western in his attributes and habits than the older members of his family who retained the cultural ways of Persia. He had never been to, nor would he ever visit, his ancestral homeland, Iran, the Cradle of the Faith. This new head of the Faith was mostly unfamiliar to Roy, who was more than two decades older. Yet Roy had unquestioning confidence in 'Abdu'l-Bahá and was ready to obey whatever He commanded in the Will and Testament.

On January 22, the North American believers received their first message from Shoghi Effendi. Sent to Roy's office, it said:

HOLY LEAVES [WOMEN OF THE HOLY HOUSEHOLD] COMFORTED BY AMERICANS UNSWERVING LOYALTY AND NOBLE RESOLVE DAY OF STEADFASTNESS ACCEPT MY LOVING COOPERATION

(SIGNED) SHOGHI.[17]

Shoghi Effendi wrote his first letter to the Bahá'ís of America, most likely the same day, January 21, he sent the cable. A few weeks later, on February 17, the letter arrived at Roy's office for dissemination in North America. This historic letter must have allayed any misgivings the Western believers harbored about one so young and inexperienced assuming the role of head of the Faith. He also held a new office, Guardian, which they did not yet understand or appreciate. His first message to the West was full of love and encouragement. It spoke of how 'Abdu'l-Bahá knew His time on this earthly plane was coming to an end and so made provisions for the next stage of the Cause of God. Shoghi Effendi called upon the grieving lovers of 'Abdu'l-Bahá to manifest and create unity:

Unity amongst the friends, selflessness in our labors in his path, detachment from all worldly things, the greatest prudence and caution in every step we take, earnest endeavor to carry out only what is his holy will and pleasure, the constant awareness of his presence and of the example of his life, the absolute shunning of whomsoever we feel to be an enemy of the Cause; these—and foremost among them is the need for UNITY—appear to me as our most vital duties should we dedicate our lives for his service.[18]

What must have struck the readers of that noteworthy letter was its depth, clarity, and beauty. It could have only been written by someone with profound spiritual insights, a true scion of the House of Bahá'u'lláh. Many hearts were lightened by its perusal. The full letter was later printed in the *Star of the West*.[19]

In the days after completing his initial messages to North America, Shoghi Effendi turned to another important message, the last letter 'Abdu'l-Bahá had written to the believers in the United States and Canada. A team of two Persians and one American present in Haifa were tasked with translating this letter into English. The original, though finished, lacked 'Abdu'l-Bahá's signature, so Shoghi Effendi affixed three of His seals upon it as certification of its authenticity and added a note in his own handwriting. Then the letter was dispatched to Roy's office for distribution.[20]

'Abdu'l-Bahá in 1920 (Bahá'í Media Bank)

This final, lengthy epistle of 'Abdu'l-Bahá to America can best be categorized as an admonition, a warning, to be diligent and watchful towards those seeking to undermine the Cause of God. The last paragraph foreshadows His imminent passing, speaking of the problems that were most likely to arise during the period of transition:

> In short the point is this: 'Abdu'l-Bahá is extremely kind, but when the disease is leprosy, what am I to do? Just as in bodily diseases we must prevent intermingling and infection and put into effect sanitary laws, because the infectious physical diseases uproot the foundation of humanity; likewise one must protect and safeguard the blessed souls from the breaths and fatal spiritual diseases, otherwise violation, like the plague, will become a contagion and all will perish. In the early days, after the ascension of the Blessed Beauty, the center of violation[21] was alone; little by little the infection spread, and this was due to companionship and association.[22]

While attacks on the Faith from within and without may have seemed an unusual topic for a message of farewell, as a caring father, 'Abdu'l-Bahá at the end of His life was preparing His Western flock to better understand His Will and Testament, and to fortify them against the inevitable tests to come. Over the course of the next decade, Roy, always a beacon of steadfastness as a member of the institutions charged with meeting these challenges when they affected the United States, would demonstrate that he had earned 'Abdu'l-Bahá's description of him as "like unto a solid mountain" and "unshakable in the Straight Path. . . ."[23]

Roy was not in his office the day 'Abdu'l-Bahá's last letter to America arrived, for he was already on his way to Haifa and had assigned the task of dispatching Bahá'í messages to his trustworthy assistant, Nellie Lloyd. When he had received a personal cable from Shoghi Effendi inviting him to the Holy Land, he had immediately made travel arrangements and had embarked on February 4 from New York for Southampton, England, aboard the Red Star Line's *S.S. Lapland.* His stated itinerary included England, France, Switzerland, Germany, Italy, Egypt, and Palestine. Hours before sailing, Roy sent a hurried letter to a Bahá'í friend in Washington, DC, saying of his trip to Haifa that "This thing came up so suddenly and there were so many things to be done that it kept me spinning like a top."[24]

Shoghi Effendi had also invited another member of the Executive Board, Mountfort Mills. For most of the trip, he and Roy would be companions. Mountfort was the son and grandson of coopers who specialized in the wooden staves used to make barrels. Born and raised in Boston, his family had deep roots in New England. Mountfort's parents were of modest means, so he lived in a boarding house when he was young. His father died while he was still a teenager, and he continued to live with his mother. His formal education ended after one year of college when he and his mother moved for a time to Minneapolis where he worked as a clerk. But Mountfort had ambitions. Probably by reading the law under the supervision of a licensed attorney, he passed the New York State bar and became a licensed lawyer. He quickly moved up in the legal world of New York City, where he specialized in international legal matters. He married a Frenchwoman living in the United States, Adele Mittant Mills. The couple remained childless, and Adele became adept at circulating within the upper circles of Manhattan society, which undoubtedly boosted her husband's own social standing. Mountfort had become a Bahá'í only a few years after Roy and was equally dedicated to the Faith. Levelheaded, with a lively sense of humor, he was often elected chairman of the Executive Board. The charming attorney with green eyes, a beard, and dark, graying hair—what was left of it—was only months older than Roy. Mountfort towered over most men, including Roy, and, like Roy, loved to sing. He had such a good singing voice that he was often asked to perform solos at Bahá'í gatherings. Roy could not have asked for a more agreeable traveling companion.[25]

Around noon on Tuesday, February 21, after almost three weeks of travel by land and sea, Roy and Mountfort arrived in Haifa on the train from Egypt.[26] The one-story stone train station was adjacent to

Mountfort Mills (left) and Fujita during the 1922 visit to the Holy Land. (USBNA)

the port where Roy and his mother had come ashore in 1907. In the years since, the original narrow-gauge tracks had been replaced with wider ones that made for a faster, smoother connection. Thus, the train had supplanted ships as the best way to travel north from Port Saeed. When the two Americans stepped onto the platform, they could see immediately that the Holy Land was under new management. For example, Turks were less visible because British soldiers and officials now oversaw the train station. New signage in their own language beckoned the English-speaking visitor. After the war ended in 1918, the British had lost no time building new infrastructure for the vital port. New piers were under construction as the port expanded to accommodate post-war prosperity and growth in global trade.

Waiting at the station for the two Americans were 'Abdu'l-Bahá's son-in-law, Mírzá Jalál, and Hippolyte Dreyfus-Barney, a lawyer who had become the first French Bahá'í.[27] When the group exited the station, the travelers must have paused briefly—at that spot at the foot of Mount Carmel just outside Haifa's ancient Eastern wall—to look up at the rocky hillside, where they would have seen, halfway up its slopes, the modest, one-story, stone Shrine of the Báb.

The four traversed the lower city, emerging through the western gate into an area that had been mainly laid out as gardens in 1907 but which had become filled with homes and shops in the interim. Haifa had a rapidly growing population of about twenty-five thousand people, many of whom were Jews escaping persecution in their homelands. Their arrival had created a more diverse citizenry. Some blocks away, Roy and Mountfort reached the Bahá'í residential properties on the Persian (now HaParsim) Street, the dominating feature of which was the imposing stone Master's House, whose northeastern lower wall adjoined a small commercial area. Situated across the unpaved lane was another walled property, in the center of which stood a two-storied stone building used as a hostel by Western pilgrims. That was where the Western visitors would be staying. It was simply and sparsely furnished, but comfortable.

Roy's friends, the Bosches and the Krugs, who had been present in Haifa the night of 'Abdu'l-Bahá's passing, had already left Palestine.

Curtis, of course, was still there and eager to see his mentor and friend. In addition to the Dreyfus-Barneys from Paris, Lady Sarah Blomfield and Ethel Rosenberg were already there from England. Roy's acquaintance, Emogene Hoagg, a native of California who often served as the hostess at the Western Pilgrim House, had hurriedly returned after time away from Haifa when she learned of 'Abdu'l-Bahá's passing. Ruth Randall from Boston, the wife of their friend and fellow Executive Committee member Harry Randall, arrived a few hours after Roy and Mountfort. The two were also pleased to become reacquainted with Fujita, a Japanese believer who, despite his advanced education at the University of Michigan, had served 'Abdu'l-Bahá as a gardener and host to the Western visitors. Also present in the Holy Land at the time was a young physician, Dr. Lotfu'lláh Hakím, trained in England, who years later would be among the original members of the Universal House of Justice. He was present to be of service to Shoghi Effendi.[28]

Roy must have been delighted to associate with such an assemblage of devoted believers, but he was not there specifically to meet with them. Shoghi Effendi was the primary reason he had made the long journey. The brief cable from Shoghi Effendi asking him to come at once—which, dropping everything, Roy had done—had given no hint of a reason. Roy soon learned that he was to take part in consultations about what to do next to move the Faith forward.

As soon as Roy met the youthful Guardian, he knew that Shoghi Effendi's appointment by his Grandfather was providential, for he was truly remarkable. Roy had been forewarned by members of 'Abdu'l-Bahá's household about the weight of the burdens Shoghi Effendi now carried. They told him that 'Abdu'l-Bahá's Will stated that Shoghi Effendi should be regarded as a young and tender shrub, who should be nurtured and protected by the believers.[29] At the time, Roy described the Guardian in these words:

> Shoghi Effendi is a most interesting character study. He is, I presume about twenty-three, small of stature, a singular sweetness of countenance and character, possessing extraordinary

185

brilliance of mind and perception, it seems to me for one of his years. His quickness too is remarkable. He makes it constantly evident that he wishes authority to rest in the body of the Bahá'ís at large. It seems to me that we should as far as possible shield him from the multitudinous perplexities which continually were presented and pressed upon 'Abdu'l-Bahá from all quarters of the globe—else his sympathetic mind will be so overburdened that his health may not be equal to the strain, and in any event his time and attention diverted from the most important matters—of bringing into operation the terms of the Will and Testament.[30]

Roy quickly surmised that Shoghi Effendi was wise beyond his years. During their travels on the way to the Holy Land, the artificial boundaries separating countries left an impression on Roy because he observed in place after place—most of which were still recovering from the recent war—that the inhabitants of each country thought only about their own homeland's problems rather than the problems of the entire planet. 'Abdu'l-Bahá had taught His followers not to look at the countries of the world in this manner, for there is only one country—the world—and the happiness of all is the business of everyone. Naturally, Shoghi Effendi had this same mindset, which Roy later remarked on, saying, "When one reaches Haifa and meets Shoghi Effendi and sees the workings of his mind and heart, his wonderful spirit and grasp of things, it is truly marvelous. Our world boundaries must fade!"[31]

The second day after his arrival, Roy participated in a meeting with Shoghi Effendi; the Dreyfus-Barneys; Mírzá Jalál; Dr. Hákím; Shoghi Effendi's younger cousin, Rúhí Afnán; Ruth Randall; and 'Abdu'l-Bahá's youngest daughter, Munavvar Khánum. Unfortunately, he did not record the topic under discussion that morning. Later that afternoon, he climbed steep dirt roads and rocky footpaths for his first visit to the Shrine of the Báb since the sacred remains of the Prophet-Herald had been laid to rest there. This short journey was especially poignant for him and released a multitude of emotions, because 'Abdu'l-Bahá had been buried in the front room of the Shrine less than three months before. There, beneath floors covered with exquisite Persian carpets upon which stood ornamental lamps, candelabras, and vases, were two of the three Central Figures of the Faith. He recalled 'Abdu'l-Bahá's words about the blessings of offering prayers at that holy spot. That evening, his first full day in Haifa was capped off by attending a memorable gathering of Persian men at the Master's House during which Shoghi Effendi, in his angelic voice, chanted a Tablet so beautifully that it touched the hearts of all of those present. The Guardian then accompanied the Westerners back to the Pilgrim House, and Mountfort was then given the bounty of reading aloud to them 'Abdu'l-Bahá's Will and Testament—the English translation that Shoghi Effendi had just completed.[32]

The first pilgrim house for Western Bahá'ís where Roy stayed in 1922.
(Bahá'í Media Bank)

The next morning, Roy was taken to Mírzá Jalál's home, located next to the Master's House, where he had the special privilege of meeting with the women from 'Abdu'l-Bahá's family. He was especially happy to see 'Abdu'l-Bahá's sister, Bahíyyíh Khánum, who had assumed responsibility for everything that had had to be accomplished during the interim between 'Abdu'l-Bahá's passing and the arrival, more than a month later, of Shoghi Effendi. She would continue to play a pivotal role in the years ahead, including serving as regent while her great-nephew withdrew to Europe to recuperate from the weight of the burdens he now carried and to prepare himself for the work ahead. Roy wrote that her face "is wonderful, in many ways much resembling that of 'Abdu'l-Bahá. It possesses wisdom, tenderness and power."[33] He was told that she also possessed a strong sense of humor, as had her Brother and mother.

The two hours with these amazing women, including 'Abdu'l-Bahá's widow, Munírih Khánum (called the "Holy Mother" by the Westerners) passed too quickly for Roy. His opportunities to be with these women of noble lineage were circumscribed because the culture of the East dictated that men who were not part of their family should never be allowed in their presence except under certain prescribed conditions. Roy and Mountfort were delighted later that day when the Greatest Holy Leaf sent them a gift: a "Bahá'í bouquet" with which to adorn their room at the Western Pilgrim House. It was a seven-foot-tall tree loaded with mandarins that were "large, juicy, and not only sweet and flavory but as fragrant as the rose."[34] The coast of the Holy Land has long had a reputation for superior citrus fruits, among the finest in the world. Roy confided that "I'm sure Mountfort would not want you to know how many of these wonderful fruits he surrounds in a day," and as to himself, "I do not usually eat more than three or four at a time—several times a day."[35] As they ventured out to explore the walled gardens of the Master's House, Roy and Mountfort discovered that its lemons, banana, and orange trees were at the height of harvesting time. But that was not all that excited the senses, for the borders along the pathways of that large home abounded in blooming flowers of all varieties:

. . . roses large and small—white roses, red roses, large golden roses, violets growing along the paths—a number of kinds of smaller flowers such as one finds in the old fashioned country gardens—all these fragrences [sic] blend together into a wonderful symphony of color and sweet smells. We find a great peace—what a contrast when one thinks of the world's cities. One day at our home 'Abdu'l-Bahá quoted from Bahá'u'lláh "The city is the abode of bodies—the country is the home of spirits."[36]

That afternoon, Roy had his first opportunity to speak with Shoghi Effendi when he took a walk with him accompanied by Mountfort and Rúhí Afnán. As the four of them enjoyed the early spring of the Holy Land, drinking in the clear air and the beauty of bright green tender leaves and grass, the Guardian discussed the Will and Testament of 'Abdu'l-Bahá, impressing upon them the importance of carefully studying it so that they would become thoroughly familiar with its details. Only two days after Roy's arrival, Shoghi Effendi had completed his full translation of the Will with the assistance of Emogene Hoagg and a Persian believer. A copy had been dispatched immediately to Roy's office, and the Guardian had requested that Roy cable his secretary, Nellie, with instructions about its distribution. She faithfully ensured that it was delivered to the Executive Board and New York Board of Council, and she conveyed that, for the time being, the Will was to be regarded as private and should only be shared with Bahá'ís. Shoghi Effendi informed his walking companions that, as soon as a few others arrived, consultation about the Will and its implications would begin in earnest.[37]

Shoghi Effendi elevated Roy's understanding of the importance of the Will and Testament, explaining to him that the true reality of the document was that it was not only intended for Bahá'ís, but for the whole of humanity, and that in the future it would become well known as it was put into effect. Certainly, the establishment of the Universal House of Justice ordained by Bahá'u'lláh was essential, but before its election could take place, much had to be done first to lay a proper foundation for that supreme institution. Shoghi Effendi continued his comments by asking many questions about the state of the community in America, while emphasizing to Roy and Mountfort the importance of the North Americans devoting their energies to spreading the Faith as well as to implementing the provisions of the Will. Everything else would have to be subordinated to this "most important work."[38]

Roy sent a postcard from Haifa to a friend in the United States, giving a brief impression of Shoghi Effendi. It reflected his own concerns that the new Guardian of the Faith was suffering already from overwork. Roy reported that, "Shoghi Effendi is a true grandson, but I hope he won't work himself to death . . . he cannot continue present pace without doing so, I'm afraid."[39] He had learned from Shoghi Effendi's cousin that the Guardian slept only about three hours a night and had even gone for a period of two days without eating.[40] The physical consequences of such an extreme schedule, even on one so young, were readily apparent to Roy. Even those who had been summoned to Haifa for consultation, like Roy, were busy and had found that there was "A mountain of work to be done."[41]

The work of carrying out the transition to the Guardianship continued apace, while at the same time pilgrims such as his friends Corinne and Katherine True from Chicago arrived in the Holy Land.[42] A group of nearly twenty pilgrims arrived from Iran after weeks of arduous travel. The sight of diverse believers from the Cradle of the Faith made a lasting impression on Roy:

> These pilgrims representing various religions and classes—some were light, others dark—some were merchants, other landowners of [sic] farmers—they wore various kinds of costumes—some had red fezes, some black, some tall others short—one or two big turbans, another the head covering and bands like the Sphinx. But their faces all shone. They expressed great love for us and asked us in turn to send their affections to America and to express the hope that as time goes on they may have the opportunity to meet American believers. Shoghi Effendi said that when arrangements are made for better contacts and closer acquaintances between America and Persia it would be productive of great good and make for spiritual progress in both countries.[43]

Because both pilgrims as well as consultants were present in the Holy
Land, on March 4, Shoghi Effendi arranged for all of them to spend
a day in ʻAkká, culminating with a visit to the Shrine of Baháʼuʼlláh
at Bahjí. The group caught a train in Haifa early that morning. The
Americans had been asked by the Guardian to be prepared to sing
ʻAbduʼl-Baháʼs favorite Christian hymn, *Nearer My God to Thee*, at
the Shrine, so they practiced during the hour journey along the outer
perimeter of the half-moon bay, singing that song and other Christian hymns as well as a few Baháʼí songs.[44]* Once they arrived at the
ʻAkká train station just outside the ancient walled city, most of them
proceeded to the northwest tower of the formidable citadel where
Baháʼuʼlláh and His companions were imprisoned for more than two
years. Then it was time to visit the holiest site of the Baháʼí World,
the Shrine of Baháʼuʼlláh at Bahjí.

After that spiritually uplifting day, the exhausted, exhilarated
Americans returned to the Western Pilgrim House in Haifa in the
mood for fun. A phonograph had been given to ʻAbduʼl-Bahá, and
Royʼs friend Ella Cooper had sent a stack of records—mainly dance
music. A record was placed on the player, and as Ruth Randall
reported, ". . . it started a very happy party. Roy discovered in his
belongings an instrument which he calls a "probasaphone." It fits
over the nose and mouth and is like a slide whistle. This afforded
great amusement, and then Emogene Hoagg danced and she can do
a most wonderful hula-hula, and we all nearly cried we laughed so
hard. It was a reaction and a much needed one."[45]

---

   * American believer Louise "Shahnaz" Waite composed a number of
Baháʼí songs, which were frequently used at national Baháʼí gatherings.
One of her compositions, *Benediction*, was extolled by ʻAbduʼl-Bahá and
routinely sung as part of every national Convention.

Once Consul Schwarz and his wife Alice reached Haifa from Germany, and the Englishman Wesley Tudor-Pole was finally well enough to endure the last leg of his travel after becoming ill in Egypt, the consultants began a series of confidential meetings with Shoghi Effendi. There were two consultants from each of the major western communities: England, North America, France, and Germany. Other Westerners, such as Corinne True and her youngest daughter Katherine, and Charles Mason Remey, summoned for his knowledge as an architect, were not invited to the sessions, although both Corinne and Mason were serving on the Executive Board with Roy and Mountfort. Three other consultants had yet to arrive, two from Iran and one from Burma, but the Guardian decided he could no longer wait to begin the sessions.[46]

The principal topic for consultation was whether it was timely to take steps to bring about the election of the Universal House of Justice—the international governing body of the Administrative Order decreed by Bahá'u'lláh.[47] The British authorities in Palestine were urging its election so that the governance of the Faith would be in the hands of an elected council, and not those of someone as young as Shoghi Effendi. At first, the consultants agreed that electing the House of Justice was the proper next step. But the more they consulted, they came to see that reality dictated otherwise. The House of Justice could only be elected by National Spiritual Assemblies, and despite North America and Iran each having an institution guiding their communities at the national level by default rather than by design,* there were no true National Spiritual Assemblies at that time. Nor had Local Spiritual Assemblies, as envisioned by the Will and Testament, been established. Local Houses of Justice mature enough to support National Assemblies were deemed to be a vital precondi-

---

* The Central Committee of Tehran, in essence, administered the Bahá'í community of Iran, as did the Executive Board of Temple Unity in North America even though neither had been founded to take on that level of responsibility.

tion to the election of national Houses of Justice, which could in turn elect the Universal House of Justice. The few existing committees at the local level, such as the New York Board of Council, had not been elected in conformity with Bahá'í principles and did not possess the full authority needed to take on the spiritual reins of their communities. Furthermore, the details of Bahá'í administrative procedures had never been expounded, for the Will offered only bare outlines. The consultants knew that the principle of consultation would underpin all Bahá'í institutions, but this general spiritual law could not answer many of the questions already being raised about how the institutions should function. It quickly became apparent that the election of the Universal House of Justice would have to be postponed until new conditions were created in multiple countries so that its establishment would be possible and timely. Furthermore, even after a number of National Assemblies and numerous Local Assemblies were in place, it would not be appropriate to elect the Supreme Institution if the largest Bahá'í community, Iran, then facing another wave of persecution, could not yet safely carry out a national election and establish a National Assembly.[48]

The idea of an administrative order that was worldwide and based upon the teachings of a religion was new to many believers, and it was not necessarily a concept welcomed by everyone, especially those familiar with the numerous instances of warfare caused in the past by misguided, ambitious people twisting religious dogma to gain positions of power. Among all His teachings, Bahá'u'lláh's call for a world government may have been the one component of the Faith that least interested the lion's share of believers. The majority of Bahá'ís most likely focused on the scriptures expounding on the oneness of mankind, spiritual transformation, and the mystical relationship between God and man. Yet, as Bahá'u'lláh made clear, His social and transformative teachings could never remake the world without a solid framework, a reordering of the organization of the life of humanity. God's Will could not be carried out without the necessary administrative machinery. It would be impossible to fully appreciate and assess Bahá'í administration until it was not only established, but had time to operate and mature many decades or centuries in the future. Only then would apprehensions and fears be truly allayed.

The Writings of Bahá'u'lláh called for the establishment of Bahá'í institutions, including an elected council for administering the world-wide Bahá'í community, the Universal House of Justice. Not only did the Will and Testament of 'Abdu'l-Bahá explicitly direct that this Supreme Institution should be established through an election by representatives of the worldwide Bahá'í community (National Spiritual Assemblies), He commanded the believers to obey its decisions and guidance without hesitation. This Universal House of Justice was described in the Will and Testament of 'Abdu'l-Bahá as "the source of all good and freed from all error . . ."[49] From the beginning of the promulgation of 'Abdu'l-Bahá's Will and Testament, there would be misgivings in some hearts as more became known about the Bahá'í administrative order, because unquestioning obedience was contrary to Western thinking about authority. Nor would it be easy for some people to accept that the House of Justice would be divinely guided and infallible in its judgment.

In His Will and Testament, 'Abdu'l-Bahá set forth a new institution, the Guardianship—a position to be held by Shoghi Effendi—that also had to be obeyed. Furthermore, the Will designated Shoghi Effendi as lifetime head of the House of Justice, as well as the only authorized interpreter of the Sacred Text. The Universal House of Justice could determine matters not found in the Holy Writings but would not have the authority to interpret the Writings. This relationship between the Guardianship and the Universal House of Justice was an unprecedented form of administration that was breathtaking, unique, and challenging. The relevant passages were emphatic and clear:

> The sacred and youthful branch, the guardian of the Cause of God as well as the Universal House of Justice, to be universally elected and established, are both under the care and protection of the Abhá Beauty, under the shelter and unerring guidance of His Holiness, the Exalted One (may my life be offered up for

them both). Whatsoever they decide is of God. Whoso obeyeth
him not, neither them, hath not obeyed God . . .[50]

One of those invited to participate in the consultations about the
future administration of the Faith, Wellesley Tudor-Pole, was profoundly disturbed by the shift in focus to Bahá'í administration, for
his primary interests were spiritualism, mysticism, and even the occult.
The closed-door meetings with Shoghi Effendi marked an inner turning point for him and led him to distance himself from the Faith soon
after he returned home to England, though he remained a friend of
the Cause and always held 'Abdu'l-Bahá up as his Master.[51] He would
not be alone in having misgivings about the implementation of the
Bahá'í Administrative Order. What the believers worldwide would
come to understand through study of the Will and Testament was
that, through acceptance of and obedience to the Bahá'í institutions,
they would be ensuring the unity and progress of the community and
preventing the development of schisms.[52]

One evening, when all the Western believers were present at the
Pilgrim House, Shoghi Effendi arrived with a bundle wrapped in silk.
Reverently, he placed it on a table and unwrapped layer after layer of
cloth surrounding something precious. At last, there before them,
was the original copy of the Will and Testament—all three parts.
The Guardian then called each of them one by one to come and
examine it, paying special attention to 'Abdu'l-Bahá's signature and
handwriting. They also studied the wax seals used to authenticate
documents in the East.[53] Everyone present had received numerous
letters and tablets from 'Abdu'l-Bahá and were familiar with both His
handwriting, signature, and seals. Their firsthand acceptance of the
documents' authenticity would prove to be important when rumors
spread in the United States that the Will was unsigned. Mountfort
and Roy quickly put that concern to rest by assuring those gathered at
the 1922 National Convention that they personally had witnessed the
signature and seals on the original copy of the Will and Testament.[54]

Shoghi Effendi provided the Western believers with the contents
of 'Abdu'l-Bahá's Will and Testament in two phases. The first doc-

ument he sent to the friends was composed of extracts. It contained what he considered to be the most significant provisions, especially those expounding aspects of the Administrative Order. Weeks after that collection of extracts was dispatched, when the friends had had time to become familiar with the abridged version's contents, he sent the English translation of the entire Will. Roy's initial impression was that "The Will and Testament gives us a mighty specification to measure up to—it just seems impossible to step up to."[55]

In addition to providing specifics about the House of Justice as well as national and local Bahá'í institutions, the Will provided specific information about Hands of the Cause of God. One of the four Hands appointed by Bahá'u'lláh, Mírzá 'Alí-Muḥammad (Ibn-i-Asdaq), was still alive but in 1922 was elderly. 'Abdu'l-Bahá had not appointed additional Hands but had announced that He had posthumously designated four stellar Persian believers to the ranks of Hands of the Cause of God.[56] The Will, however, envisioned the institution of the Hands taking an active role in carrying out the work of the Faith and stated that they were to be appointed exclusively by the Guardian. Their role was beyond the description of lofty:

The obligations of the Hands of the Cause of God are to diffuse the Divine Fragrances, to edify the souls of men, to promote learning, to improve the character of all men, and to be, at all times and under all conditions, sanctified and detached from earthly things. They must manifest the fear of God by their conduct, their manners, their deeds, and their words.[57]

Roy summarized the most important points he learned from Shoghi Effendi about the Will and Testament:

This may be and probably is a pattern and standard for the formation of the only World Government which will survive these times. Another point upon which Shoghi Effendi placed great emphasis was that the local Spiritual Assemblies are responsible for the spiritual affairs of the Cause in their respective centers and that likewise the Convention and the executive Committee are responsible for general spiritual matters. He said all this had become so well understood and established in Persia that there was no further question of trouble there; that while sometimes there were differing understandings about details—all were united in putting in first place the interest of the Cause itself.[58]

During the weeks Roy and his fellow consultants were in Haifa, other opportunities arose to spend private time with Shoghi Effendi, usually by taking walks with him. This made such an impression on Roy that he would later share those precious moments with the friends gathered at the 1922 National Convention:

Shoghi Effendi had a way of taking you out for a walk and talking to you as you were strolling up the rough mountain paths, or down through the fields at the foot of the mountains, or over through the olive orchards which were scattered around the foot of the mountains. He had a little personal way with him that was very interesting, too. At a point where he would be very earnest he would stop abruptly right in the road, right in the path and talk for a few moments. Then he would walk on, and then something else would strike him with particular force, and he would stop again, just as Abdul Baha did.[59]

At that Convention, days after he returned to the United States, Roy continued describing his encounters with Shoghi Effendi by first talking about the period when 'Abdu'l-Bahá was the head of the Faith. As important as that phase was, Roy left Haifa with the perception that the period the Faith had just entered was going to be of even greater significance. Before, the friends had always turned to 'Abdu'l-Bahá for guidance, but with His passing, each Bahá'í now had the responsibility to protect the Cause on behalf of 'Abdu'l-Bahá. As Roy put it, in the new day that had just dawned, "Abdul Baha was looking to us, each one of us, individually, to protect this Cause from unwisdom, over-earnestnesses [sic], to be responsible for the harmony of this Cause, and that nothing less than that was of such importance."[60] Roy felt that Shoghi Effendi was trying to impress upon those he had summoned to Haifa much the same message—namely, as Roy remembered 'Abdu'l-Bahá's guidance—that "the firmer a soul was, the less difficulty his opinions gave" and that "the thing of first importance was not how things were to be done or whether they were to be done or any of these things, but the harmony of the Cause."[61] By unhesitatingly turning to the youthful Guardian, the Bahá'ís and the Cause they loved would be protected.

Roy's stay in Haifa lasted well into March, one of the Holy Land's most delightful months of the year when the rains diminish, the temperatures become milder, and the preceding wet season causes the usual brown landscape to come alive with bright green grass dotted by flowers of all hues. Roy clearly enjoyed the beauty of springtime in Palestine. After others had retired for the night, Roy, Mountfort, and Mason would take advantage of the quiet to walk together near the Western Pilgrim House at the foot of Mount Carmel and discuss the monumental tasks before them. The moonlit nights were clear, and the lack of urban illumination made the sky brilliant with stars. Looking up the mountain, they could observe Curtis's handiwork. The soft glow from the electric lights he had installed outlined the Shrine of the Báb, making it not only a landmark, but a beacon for ships entering the port in the darkness. Years before, 'Abdu'l-Bahá had told them that a particular ancient olive tree on the outer edge of the German Colony had been blessed when Jesus sat beneath it two millennia before. Every time they took an evening stroll past that living witness to Christ, they recalled those remarks and paused to contemplate the significance of the spot. Finally, Roy could no longer contain his desire to have at least a leaf from that massive, gnarled old, old tree. He scampered over the enclosure surrounding it, and in short order returned to his friends with three sprigs, one for each of them, as a special souvenir.[62]

Mason Remey had been a frequent visitor to the Holy Land after making his first pilgrimage in 1901. He came from a distinguished family and had been brought up in Washington, DC within the elite milieu of the nation's capital. Though trained at the world's best school for architects, his business in that profession never seemed to thrive, possibly because he had inherited the financial means to travel the world as a Bahá'í teacher and, therefore, did not focus on his profession. This time, when he arrived in Haifa, he discovered that the primary reason he had been summoned was to provide Shoghi Effendi with advice about buildings. In the years just before His passing, 'Abdu'l-Bahá had accepted the offer of the Randall family to construct a much larger pilgrim house for the Western visitors on land where Bahá'u'lláh had pitched His tent in 1891 located across the street from the Master's House. Mason had already begun to draw up the plans for the building based upon 'Abdu'l-Bahá's descriptions of what He wanted, and Ruth Randall had come to Haifa to ensure that construction would soon begin, a desire also shared by the Guardian.[63]

When Shoghi Effendi arranged for Mason to meet with two of the Persian believers who also had expertise in the building trades, as well as two reputable building contractors from Haifa's German Templar Colony, Mason decided that others from America should take part so that more people would know and understand what needed to be done. He therefore asked Roy, who was an old friend of the donors, and Montfort to attend the meeting as well. Adding their business and legal perspectives, they contributed primarily to the consultation when it turned to the question as to who should hold the title to the property.[64] It was the first time, but it would not be the last, that Roy would become involved in the construction of buildings at the Bahá'í World Center.[65]

Charles Mason Remey, architect and member
of the Bahá'í Temple Unity Executive
Committee, who would later be named a
Hand of the Cause and break the Covenant.

One especially poignant event took place in Haifa in late February. At the same time as Roy was enroute to the Holy Land, Helen Goodall, the mother of his dear friend Ella Cooper, passed away on February 19, 1922. Helen was one of the first Bahá'ís in California and was informally considered that region's spiritual mother. She had served with Roy on the Executive Board during its first years and later would be honored with the title of "Disciple of 'Abdu'l-Bahá" by Shoghi Effendi. She had the same close relationship with Ella that Roy enjoyed with his own mother, as not only parent and child, but as devoted Bahá'í co-workers. Helen's final illness began when she learned of 'Abdu'l-Bahá's passing. Shoghi Effendi called together the hundred or so believers in the Holy Land and held a memorial service for that great handmaiden of the Cause.[66] As soon as Roy returned from that gathering, he wrote immediately to his "SisElla" to tell her about what a moving experience it had been and how Shoghi Effendi himself had chanted the prayer for her mother and then had spoken to the assembled friends of her good works. "Some one expressed the thought that Abdul Baha had called her to join Him and she had responded." He enclosed pressed flowers, which had been placed on the threshold of the Shrine of 'Abdu'l-Bahá, and then placed in his hands by Shoghi Effendi.[67]

There was much to reflect upon, to learn, and to experience during those swiftly passing days in Haifa, but one element was missing, the joy of sharing warm memories of 'Abdu'l-Bahá. With so much focus upon His passing and the serious issues facing the Faith at that moment, there had not been time to recall the many happy moments spent with the One they had all adored, Who was now gone from their midst. One evening, when no meeting with pilgrims was scheduled, Shoghi Effendi, accompanied by two of 'Abdu'l-Bahá's daughters, joined the Westerners for dinner. It became their one opportunity to reminisce about 'Abdu'l-Bahá together. No doubt, Shoghi Effendi and his aunts delighted in hearing new stories about 'Abdu'l-Bahá's time in the West. Then Shoghi Effendi and his relations asked the Westerners to sing, especially Mountfort and Ruth, who had good singing voices. Roy and Katherine True were also asked to sing. Then Fujita sang a Japanese song and finally one of the aunts chanted a Persian invocation. It was the first cheerful evening that members of the Holy Family had participated in since 'Abdu'l-Bahá's ascension, and thus, it was not only beautiful, but appreciated.[68]

After his extended 1922 trip, Roy would never again return to the Holy Land. When his time there was coming to an end, Shoghi Effendi arranged a very special day for the men from America. One morning, Shoghi Effendi, Roy, Mountfort, and Mason left Haifa before dawn in 'Abdu'l-Bahá's automobile. In the early hours, with the sun just peeking over the mountains of the Galilee to the northeast, they drove across the deserted open plain that separates Haifa and 'Akká. The Americans were surprised to see that others, including a camel caravan, were already making the same trek.[69]

A simple breakfast was waiting for them at Bahjí in the small building adjoining the Tomb of Bahá'u'lláh, which was used by visitors as a place to rest. Waiting for them as well was Curtis Kelsey. He had completed the wiring and lighting of the two Shrines and now had other electrical projects underway. Shoghi Effendi conferred with him as the little group enjoyed the repast spread before them that, no doubt, included freshly baked bread, local soft cheese, and steaming hot tea served along with lumps of sugar. They were allowed the privilege of visiting the corner room in that pilgrim house where 'Abdu'l-Bahá would stay when He visited Bahjí—left unaltered after His passing.[70]

Curtis Kelsey (far right) sitting on the steps of the pilgrim house
at Bahjí in October, 1921 with unknown Persian believers.
(USBNA)

With everyone refreshed and in a good mood, the group left the Pilgrim House and walked silently to the other side of the long, low building to the Tomb of Bahá'u'lláh, under guard by British sentinels. Unfortunately, because of the seizure of the keys by the Covenant-breaker members of 'Abdu'l-Bahá's family, the room where the sacred remains lay beneath the floor was locked, so they could only visit the central courtyard room. Though the attempt to wrest control of the Shrine by his enemies was a constant cause of anguish for Shoghi Effendi, on this morning he focused on lifting the spirits of the Americans. After they removed their shoes and reverently entered that sacred space, he chanted a prayer in Persian and allowed them all ample time for private prayer and reflection.[71]

After the group exited the holiest Bahá'í shrine, Shoghi Effendi turned to Curtis and asked him to put aside his work for the day and join the excursion. They all climbed back into the automobile and headed north along the coastal road. The sun was now high above the horizon, and their hearts must have been light after their time at Bahjí. Their next destination was the "Crimson Hill," so named by Bahá'u'lláh because of the wild red anemones that blanketed it in springtime. From that mound, they had a commanding view of the sea, the open countryside, and the mountains—Mount Carmel to the southwest, the hills separating Palestine from Lebanon to the north, and to the east, the mountains of the western Galilee within which was nestled the town of Nazareth, where Jesus had spent most of His life. The area was a place of beauty much loved by Bahá'u'lláh, and they all well understood His sentiments as they explored the low hill for almost an hour and meditated upon the many visits Bahá'u'lláh, accompanied by His followers, had made there.[72]

Back in the car, they retraced their tracks, but bypassed Bahjí and drove on toward 'Akká, where, on its outskirts, they entered the Garden of Riḍván—a lush, shaded garden that 'Abdu'l-Bahá had rented for His father to provide Him with respite from the Holy Land's oppressive summer heat. The garden, already familiar to Roy from his 1907 pilgrimage, was situated on a small, artificial island which, if viewed from above, formed the outline of a ship. A river had been diverted to form both the island and a millpond for the flour mill located on the other side of the stream. Bahá'u'lláh, shaded by towering mulberry trees, would often sit on a bench suspended above the millpond's gently flowing water. In front of Him, a tiered fountain cascaded constant streams of water and mist, making the garden a welcome refuge that eased the body and refreshed the soul. That day, the visitors, especially Mason, noted the property needed extensive restoration and upkeep, despite the well-tended and beautiful borders overflowing with flowering plants.[73]

While the Americans enjoyed the beautiful scenery and strolled along the pathways, the caretaker placed a table under the mulberry trees, decorated it with flowers, and spread their lunch, which they had brought in baskets from Bahjí, upon it. When they had finished their meal, the Americans were invited to visit the house on the southern end of the island. This moment was significant for Roy, as he remembered its connection with his life-changing vision. After offering prayers in Bahá'u'lláh's chamber, they returned to the table, where a simmering samovar and hot tea were awaiting them. They drank the tea in the charming manner of Persians, from tiny glass cups which showed off the tea's rich color.[74]

From there, the group drove to an adjoining Bahá'í property, the Ferdowsi Garden,* where they found to their delight that the caretakers had brought fruit from the orchards and had placed it for them on rugs spread around the side of the stone reservoir at the edge of that garden. The Americans enjoyed oranges and pomegranates as they visited with those devoted Persian friends and surveyed the surrounding countryside, with its view of the walls of 'Akká, the Mediterranean Sea, and Mount Carmel. The sun sat lower on the western horizon as they said their good-byes to those who had showered them with such genuine tokens of Bahá'í love. They then drove to the nearby land gate of 'Akká, where Curtis bid them farewell.[75]

---

* At the time of this writing, that location was under construction for the Shrine of 'Abdu'l-Bahá.

When they returned to Haifa, they did not go immediately to the Pilgrim House but instead drove up the road behind the Shrine of the Báb to the promontory at the top of Mount Carmel, where the mountain jutted into the sea to create the bay. A lighthouse stood guard at that point. They parked the car and stood for a time taking in the late afternoon view as the sun was heading toward the waters of the Mediterranean Sea. Then, led by Shoghi Effendi, they crossed the street to the Carmelite Monastery. Bahá'u'lláh and 'Abdu'l-Bahá had both visited the monastery, which had been built on a sacred site associated with the Prophet Elijah. Over the previous thirty years, this monastery had been visited many times by Bahá'ís, and a relationship had developed with the monks. The monastery was located near the area where the Guardian wished to build a House of Worship in the future, so he and Mason discussed this topic briefly. They visited the chapel and the cave under the high altar where, according to tradition, Elijah sought shelter. When a monk objected to Shoghi Effendi wearing his hat within the church, they all returned to the car and drove back down the mountain. They were tired but supremely happy, as it had been a day none of them would ever forget.[76]

Roy and Mountfort had a mission when they left Palestine. Their itinerary included another visit to Cairo and, afterward, to several Bahá'í communities in Europe. But they could not linger long at any one location because they were also asked by Shoghi Effendi to attend the upcoming National Convention in Chicago where they could convey the Guardian's message about the changes to the administration of the North American community and thereby help the delegates elect the first National Spiritual Assembly of the United States and Canada. Specifically, they were to help the friends understand that the new body—the National Spiritual Assembly—was unlike the more limited Temple Unity Executive Board. It would have the authority to administer the affairs of the Faith in North America as a legislative body, not simply as a committee to carry out the wishes of the delegates to the National Convention as before.[77]

When meeting with believers in Europe, Roy and Mountfort discovered that many of them had been disturbed about one aspect of the Will and Testament, and some American Bahá'ís would also raise this same concern during their own Convention. In its first section, 'Abdu'l-Bahá recounts at length the suffering He had endured at the hands of his half-siblings and cousins, especially the actions of Mírzá Muhammad-'Alí. It was an anathema to Westerners to use a last will and testament to set forth grievances and to expound upon a person's poor character. Fortunately, Roy and Mountfort were able to explain why it was essential for 'Abdu'l-Bahá to expose this tragic and appalling history of His family. Mountfort spoke to the Bahá'ís from the vantage point of a lawyer who had gained a rapid education in Middle Eastern laws of inheritance while in Haifa. In His Will, the Book of His Covenant, The Kitáb-i-'Ahd, Bahá'u'lláh had revealed that His second son, Muhammad-'Alí, had a station below that of 'Abdu'l-Bahá, so he would only be eligible to inherit the mantel of Head of the Faith after the passing of his older half-brother, 'Abdu'l-Bahá. This was in accordance with the usual practice of Islamic societies. However, in another of His tablets, Bahá'u'lláh warned Muhammad-'Alí not to "pass out from under the shadow of the Cause"; that is, to remain loyal to 'Abdu'l-Bahá during His ministry.[78] Rather than carry out his Father's wishes, Muhammad-'Alí tried repeatedly throughout 'Abdu'l-Bahá's years as Center of the Covenant to undermine his older Brother and to wrest control of the Faith from Him. He also repeatedly demonstrated through his public behavior that he was of poor character. 'Abdu'l-Bahá had no choice but to lay out to the world His brother's perfidy, including to emphasize the worst thing Muhammad-'Alí did—using his skills as a master calligrapher to alter Bahá'u'lláh's Sacred Texts. In league with his own siblings and cousins, Muhammad-'Alí had even tried to bring about 'Abdu'l-Bahá's death. It was vital that 'Abdu'l-Bahá ensure that the Faith not pass into His faithless half-brother's hands. This explanation fully satisfied most Bahá'ís, including Roy.[79]

Roy's return to the Holy Land and Europe had reinforced his belief in the oneness of humanity. As a businessman whose company was based on international commerce, he was closely following the directives of the 1922 Genoa Conference, which were being used to settle economic differences between nations. Shortly after returning to New York, he wrote a letter to the editor of the *New York Times* that gives an insight into not only his view of current events, but how he viewed mankind and religions as a result of his second visit to the Holy Land:

> During a recent trip to the Orient it was my fortune to come into closer and more friendly contact with some of the non-Christian peoples—particularly the Mohammedans, Jews and Zoroastrians—than is ordinarily possibly for the tourist class, and I was able to thereby gain some understanding of their point of view . . . and [was] impressed by their kindnesses and in many instances their breadth of outlook.
>
> The recent agreement of twenty-nine powers represented at the Genoa Conference strikes me with peculiar force . . . that after nineteen centuries of what we have been pleased to call "Christianity" we should have progressed to the point where we witness an agreement between twenty-nine Nations, that they will not engage in killing one another—during the next eight months.
>
> In God's Name, what would Jesus say? And when we send our teachers to instruct them in the principles of the "Brotherhood of Man," shall we blame these non-Christian brothers if they smile?

It all reminds one of the word of Abdul Baha: "The outward trapping of civilization without inward moral advancement is like unto confused dreams which cannot be interpreted."[80]

Not surprisingly, such a straightforward letter questioning Christian adherence to Jesus's teachings was not published.

Arriving at the Port of New York on the *SS Olympic* on Wednesday, April 19, Roy only had a short time to catch up on his business affairs and visit with his parents before repacking his suitcase and catching a train to Chicago for the annual Convention about to convene three days later. He was looking forward to the Convention, for it promised to be a gathering for the ages.

8 / HOUR OF TRANSITION

When Roy exited the Lasalle Street train station in downtown Chicago, he was already familiar with the route to the Auditorium Hotel. It was only a short walk east, toward Lake Michigan, to the same facility where previous Bahá'í Conventions had been held. Situated across from Grant Park, the magnificent hotel was not only a Chicago landmark, but was also located two blocks south of the Art Institute where, in 1893 at the Parliament of the World's Religions, the first recorded oral public mention in North America of the name *Bahá'u'lláh* had been made. The Art Nouveau architecture of the Auditorium Hotel* on Michigan Avenue combined the classic with the modern—a fitting bridge between the past and the future showcased in a building—befittingly demonstrating that spiritual bridge brought about by the coming of Bahá'u'lláh.

As the 1922 National Convention got underway, chatter from hundreds of indistinguishable voices echoed off the walls of the meeting room. The cacophony softened to a murmur when Mountfort Mills, the convention chairman, stepped up to the podium. Then the hall fell completely silent. Barely six months had elapsed since the passing of their Spiritual Shepherd, 'Abdu'l-Bahá, and uncertainty filled the hearts and minds of many of those gathered for this historic, world-changing meeting. The delegates and friends attending

---

* The Auditorium Hotel was designed by the renowned architectural firm Sullivan and Adler.

the conference knew Mountfort had just returned from Haifa, and all ears were tuned to him to catch his every word.

The Convention was called to order, but before the committee members responsible for checking the delegates' credentials could begin their duties, a modification to the customary opening agenda was announced. The usual opening items of business were put aside as Mountfort began the proceedings by reading Shoghi Effendi's March 5 letter addressed to the North American Bahá'í community.[1] This seminal letter, which outlined general policies about Bahá'í administration, was lengthy and contained newly translated quotations from the Bahá'í Sacred Writings. Much of its content was new to the listeners. After he finished reading, Mountfort took advantage of the moment to share the intimacy and gravity of his recent conversations with Shoghi Effendi in the Holy Land, as he related some of the guidance he had heard directly from the Guardian. He first spoke about how the Guardian had stressed the paramount necessity of every confirmed believer arising like never before to teach the Cause. Mountford went on to share how the Guardian had spoken of groundbreaking advances in the administration of the Faith—as set forth in his March 5 letter. Furthermore, he spoke of how Shoghi Effendi had emphasized the urgency of all believers remaining steadfast in the Covenant and that he wanted the friends to understand that these were perilous times, requiring the wholehearted recognition of the inviolability of 'Abdu'l-Bahá's Will and Testament. Moreover, Mountfort emphasized that each believer had to acknowledge, with both head and heart, that through the Will, 'Abdu'l-Bahá Himself had designated Shoghi Effendi as the head of the Universal House of Justice and the Guardian of the Cause.[2] Though alluded to in Bahá'u'lláh's own Writings, this new office of the Guardianship was now set forth in the Will.

Three other friends who had also recently returned from Haifa were then called, one by one, to the podium to share their own firsthand accounts and understanding of the March 5 letter. Corinne True, Mason Remey, and Roy Wilhelm confirmed Mountfort's report of Shoghi Effendi's statements as well as those of each other.[3]

They all underscored the significance of the contents of Shoghi Effendi's March 5 letter regarding the establishment of local and national institutions. The point each one of them emphatically made was that, going forward, the National Spiritual Assembly would be the sole Bahá'í institution with the authority and power to direct the affairs of the community in North America.[4] This represented a significant shift in the previous practice in which the authority to make decisions was invested in the Convention rather than in the Temple Unity Executive Board. Most of the participants in the room had already sensed that they were taking part in a historic event, and that this Convention would be nothing like previous Annual Conventions. Mountfort's words had stressed the hope "that we may become a channel for the spirit of God," and that they were indeed at a turning point; they had known the Faith as it was without Bahá'u'lláh's Administrative Order, and now, would look into the future toward new possibilities because of its establishment. The assembled delegates were about to make the first attempt at founding a National Spiritual Assembly for the United States and Canada—a divine institution ordained by Bahá'u'lláh.[5]

Unlike those Bahá'ís living in regions of the world lacking experience with democracy, the North American delegates came from peoples with histories of holding elections, of parliamentary procedures, nominations, campaigning, electioneering, and widespread participation in civic organizations. Many of those in attendance were steeped in the intricacies of *Robert's Rules of Order*—the administrative standards widely used by most American organizations—with its strict procedural guidelines of motions and seconds. The men and women assembled in Chicago were members and officers of women's clubs, business boards, and church, civic, and fraternal organizations. Throughout most of humanity's history, whenever voting for public office had been allowed at all, suffrage had been limited to those men who owned property, and who were of a certain class or race. The United States had been gradually lifting such restrictions and only two years before the 1922 convention had granted the right to vote to women through the adoption of a constitutional amendment. Those assembled at the Auditorium Hotel knew how to run a meeting, how to vote in a civic election, but they still had to learn how to conduct a Bahá'í election—something altogether different from the elections with which they were familiar.

For the first time, the delegates would be electing a spiritual entity, ordained by Bahá'u'lláh and wholly distinct, in essence, from the Executive Board for the Temple Unity. This elected body's mode of operation and relationship to the community it served would be unlike any governing institution that had ever existed before, and the delegates were cognizant that this election represented a new paradigm. The Executive Board had come into being solely to oversee the construction of the House of Worship; the new entity, on the other hand, would direct all affairs of the North American Bahá'í community. Up until then, the responsibilities and functions of the existing Executive Board were more like those for running a business: overseeing real estate development, signing contracts, letting bids, paying taxes, collecting funds, receipting contributions, and accounting for expenses. The vote taken at the convention would set in motion the creation of a National Spiritual Assembly that over time would evolve to become a secondary House of Justice ordained by Bahá'u'lláh in His Book of the Covenant. This institution would help usher in the Golden Age of Mankind.[6]

At the opening of the afternoon session on the second day, Louis Gregory, chairman of the Credentials Committee, reported that fifty-one delegates and thirty-three alternates, representing forty-nine Bahá'í communities from across the US and Canada, had been certified to officially represent their areas; thus, they were eligible to vote in the upcoming election.[7]

The election, however, was not the only business of the Convention. There was, as usual, a full agenda, because the Convention was the only annual opportunity for believers from across the continent

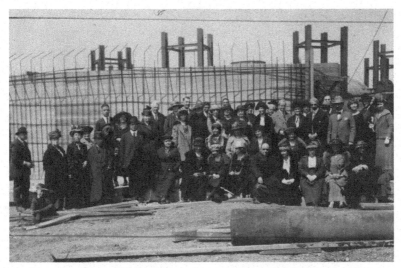

Participants from the historic 1922 National Convention visiting the
construction site of the House of Worship (USBNA)

to conduct business together. Various committees presented reports,
which were followed by consultation about the condition of the
building fund, teaching activities, and the latest efforts to publish
Bahá'í literature. By far, the largest project and expense for the North
Americans remained the Temple construction. Not unexpectedly,
reporting and consultation on its progress consumed the greatest
amount of the Convention's time.

Undoubtedly, the most poignant moments of the three days came
when time was allotted to several of the friends to tell of their experiences as witnesses to the events surrounding 'Abdu'l-Bahá's passing. Louise Bosch prefaced her remarks by reminding the audience
about how many of the soldiers returning from World War I were so
traumatized by the horrors of the battlefield that, when questioned
about their wartime experiences, they could not utter a word. She,
too, found the emotions of that night of sorrow at the Master's house
more difficult than her words could convey.[8]

Those gathered in Chicago not only wanted to learn more about
the death and funeral of 'Abdu'l-Bahá, but they were also keenly

interested to know about the Guardian, their new guiding star. Consequently, the returning pilgrims and consultants did their best to remember exactly what Shoghi Effendi said to them as they recounted their initial impressions of the youth who was now head of the Faith. "Stick to the plan" and "teach, teach, teach" were the battle cries of the beloved Guardian most commonly related by those who had been privileged to speak with him.[9] Katherine True, the daughter of Corinne True, when asked to speak of her own recent experience in the Holy Land, turned to Roy to corroborate her remarks. She recited Shoghi Effendi's words about staying firm in the Covenant and embracing the mandates set forth in the Tablets of the Divine Plan and trusting the Faith's institutions. Quoting the Guardian, Katherine's final words were, "the past is dead, and the future is important."[10]

Within the first three months of his ministry, Shoghi Effendi was already building on 'Abdu'l-Bahá's Tablets of the Divine Plan. He started the process by laying the groundwork and strategies needed for the eventual establishment of the Universal House of Justice. Never losing sight of 'Abdu'l-Bahá's admonition that 'The most important of all things is the guidance of the nations and peoples of the world. Teaching the Cause is of utmost importance for it is the head cornerstone of the foundation itself," the Guardian had determined that the time had come to establish the divinely ordained Administrative Order essential to carrying out the teaching work systematically.[11]

It was over the course of the Guardian's long evening walks in Haifa with the consultants and pilgrims and in the defining guidance found in his March 5 letter, that he outlined the teaching efforts and organizational steps needed to expand the Faith around the world. Among his directives was one that instructed that wherever there was a community with nine or more adult believers, they were obliged to form a Local Spiritual Assembly. The election of these Spiritual

Assemblies would bring about a conceptual change in the structure already extant in most of the larger Bahá'í communities, whose councils and committees prior to 1922 only attended to business and financial needs. In its place, each emerging divine institution would also be responsible for the spiritual health of the community it served. Dozens of small Bahá'í communities that had not felt the need to elect a governing committee would, for the first time, establish Local Assemblies that would strengthen their community life. This change would lead to a fundamental shift in how administrative bodies were viewed, for once local Spiritual Assemblies were established, the friends would be obliged to turn to them with questions or problems rather than to individuals in the community. Emphasizing the bedrock nature of the national and local Assemblies, the Guardian wrote, "These embryos of future Local Houses of Justice could then provide the foundation for the National House of Justice. Then, in the fullness of time, National Assemblies would serve as the pillars upon which the Universal House of Justice would be built."[12]

Inevitably, the new must be built upon the framework of the old. How were the American Bahá'ís going to reconcile Shoghi Effendi's guidance with the old requirements inherent in the Bahá'í Temple Unity organization and practices, especially since that entity had been incorporated so that how it functioned was as much a matter of Illinois law as of Bahá'í principles? Moreover, up until then, Bahá'í elections had often used a process of nominating candidates and, occasionally, used straw votes—a preliminary vote to bring to the attention of the electorate noteworthy and qualified candidates. The delegates discussed at length other questions about the organization of the National Assembly, especially whether or not it would be subject to the same legal constraints of Illinois corporate law that governed the Bahá'í Temple Unity Executive Board. What consideration should be given, when voting, to the great distances across the United States and Canada that members of the Assembly might have to travel to attend meetings? Should alternate or proxy members also be elected so a quorum would be more likely? Was a simple plurality of the votes cast to elect members sufficient, or was a majority vote necessary to elect each member? Roy's practical solution to the latter controversy was for the delegates to simply "make it unanimous . . . after the vote is taken" by acclamation, thereby satisfying the Bahá'í election requirements of a plurality and the State of Illinois requirements of a majority under the Temple Unity charter.[13]

The delegates and others assembled in the Auditorium Hotel, struggled to comprehend and accept these new approaches to managing the Faith, sensing they were on the cusp of a major transformation—though not one that was universally welcome. The March 5 letter expounded upon one unique aspect of the national and local institutions about to come into existence; namely, that in the Holy Writings it was promised that those bodies composed of fallible mortals would receive divine guidance through their deliberations. Furthermore, the voters were asked to prayerfully reflect and seek inspiration before marking their ballots, prompting one delegate to remark that there was a "certain element of superstition in believing that the spirit can tell us names and facts."[14]

After much wrangling, the delegates agreed to begin with a straw vote, rather than taking nominations. When it happened that eight of the top nine people receiving votes had more than a majority, a motion was put forward to accept the results as final. This motion was dismissed so that the delegates would have a clear understanding of when they were actually casting the ballot for the election. The actual vote for the members of the National Spiritual Assembly would thus be distinctive from a straw vote.

While the tellers counted the ballots in another room, the chairman asked Roy to speak about the Tablets he had brought from Haifa. Roy told how, when those assisting Shoghi Effendi were going through 'Abdu'l-Bahá's papers after His passing, a number of Tablets dictated by 'Abdu'l-Bahá for individuals in the West were found. Nearly all of them were unsigned, most undated, and only a few translated. Some Tablets went back as far as 1904, but most were ones that had not been sent during the war years because of unreliable mail service. After Roy announced the names of the recipients, the original Tablets were then given to individuals who knew the beneficiary or lived in the same community as the one to whom the Tablet was addressed. The distribution of the Tablets generated stories and consultation about the Will and Testament, which helped the friends to further grasp that Shoghi Effendi was now the head of the Faith and the one empowered to make a variety of decisions great and small.[15]

The convention then turned to the matter of how publishing the Sacred Writings, Tablets, and guidance from the World Center should be handled in the future. Translated and authenticated copies of Bahá'u'lláh's Writings and Tablets from 'Abdu'l-Bahá were treasures. Each one was often copied, studied, and shared with the friends before it was printed in *Star of the West*. It was decided that future general Tablets, as well as letters from Shoghi Effendi, should first go through the National Assembly before being distributed to the friends. Next, the Convention turned to other topics. Much of the consultation centered on the importance of teaching, especially children and youth, and plans for tackling the sensitive challenges of race relations. These projects, resolutions, teaching programs, and publishing agendas were readily endorsed by the Convention but almost never included a concomitant budget. Finally, Harry Randall, the exasperated treasurer of the Temple Unity Executive Board, stood up and reminded the gathering that as important and noble as each effort was, they all had a funding component. As the outgoing treasurer, he reminded them that the new national entity they were electing would need a treasurer—and treasure. As he so skillfully put it, ". . . there is a difference between, we want to sacrifice, love to sacrifice, and sacrificing."[16] Roy must have smiled while nodding his head to affirm his agreement with Harry.

Two years before, after the Temple design was chosen, the Executive Board had commissioned lithographic color reproductions of the Bourgeois design on paper the size of post cards. Basic principles of the Faith were printed on the back, making it suitable as a teaching card. A large quantity of these papers had never been distributed so, while the delegates waited for the voting results, Roy addressed the Convention and suggested the cards could serve as a fundraiser for the Temple if the friends vowed to contribute to the Temple Fund whenever they gave one of the small papers to an inquirer. Consequently, almost three decades before the Temple was dedicated, it became a "Silent Teacher."[17]

The tellers returned and announced the eagerly awaited election results. The outcome was almost the same as the straw vote, except that each of the top nine received a majority of the votes, thus satisfying both the incorporation and Bahá'í requirements.[18] Roy found that he and most of his colleagues from the Executive Board constituted the membership of the first National Spiritual Assembly. Of all those original members, he would be the one who would serve the longest. Roy and his fellow members were about to embark on laying the groundwork for a new way to order the affairs of humanity.

First known photograph of the National Spiritual Assembly of the United States and Canada that was taken at the Wilhelm home on July 1, 1923. Roy, absent from the photograph, most likely took the photo. From left to right: Alfred Lunt, Louis Gregory, Henry Randall, Agnes Parsons, Horace Holley, Corinne True, Charles Mason Remey, and a guest, Jenabe Fazel (Mírzá Asadu'lláh Fádil Mázandarání) (USBNA)

As the 1922 Convention came to its end, those who had been privileged to attend knew it had been truly a watershed event. Other than what had become a tradition of opening and closing each Convention by singing 'Abdu'l-Bahá's favorite Christian hymn, "Nearer My God to Thee," the Convention had been unlike any in the past, for the participants had taken the first steps into an unknown but bright future. Electing a National Assembly itself was a monumental achievement. Many more hours of consultation and untold effort would still be needed for the newborn Assembly to light the nation's administrative and spiritual beacons.[19] Despite clear guidance from the Guardian, it would be more than a decade before all Bahá'ís accepted the new paradigm that the Convention was no longer a decision-making body apart from its election of the National Assembly.[20] To add to that confusion, lawyers would determine that the Executive Board of Temple Unity would have to continue for some time due to its incorporation, even as the National Assembly would struggle to bring it fully under its control. Nonetheless, the reality was that the National Assembly's gestation period began, however imperfectly, during that Ridván of 1922.*

In Roy's mind, the structure and mechanics of the Bahá'í Administrative Order were much clearer than it seemed to be for others. One of

---

* It was not until 1925 that Shoghi Effendi pronounced the National Spiritual Assembly of the United States and Canada to be a National Assembly. He never explained his reasoning, though there are hints that as long as the Executive Committee of Temple Unity continued to openly function for legal reasons, the National Assembly could not carry out its full responsibilities. See Shoghi Effendi, *God Passes By*, p. 333. However, in all of his correspondence, the Guardian addressed the National Assembly as a National Assembly from the time of its first election in 1922.

his principal insights, which he often had to explain, was that certain matters within the Bahá'í community should be settled at the local level, while others should be decided at the national level, while still others needed to be referred to Haifa. Ever since receiving the letter from 'Abdu'l-Bahá about the need for the review of Bahá'í publications at the national level, he had been of the strong opinion that most matters regarding publishing should be under the supervision of a national governing body, first under the Executive Board of Bahá'í Temple Unity and now under the National Spiritual Assembly. The Guardian had re-emphasized this point in his March 5 letter. Despite this guidance, there continued to be controversy over the management of the *Star of the West*—at the time, the foremost worldwide Bahá'í newsletter. This dispute led Roy to stress to his colleagues that obedience was an essential quality of the Faith:

> Abdul Baha said that in Bahais there should be found "instant complete and exact obedience." This indisputable Command came for ALL matters of Publication to be under the control of the National Board. This did not mean that there should be any ifs buts and ands. It was not in any way ambiguous—it meant just what he said. It is not possible that <u>any soul</u> who does not promptly and wholly obey in such matters—however much we may admire them in general and personally—can find things working to their comfort and satisfaction.[21]

Roy did not think that obedience meant to carry out new commands in an unthinking, abrupt manner, but he could see that "with the ascension of Abdul Baha a new period is ushered in—with new requirements."[22] In Haifa, Shoghi Effendi had plainly outlined in his remarks to Roy what needed to be done to advance the Faith, and he echoed them in remarks to a fellow National Assembly member by saying, "It is the Cause itself which now must have our attention— with as much tact and kindness, of course, as possible to individuals. No one must be allowed to obstruct progress—as directed by the National Spiritual Assembly."[23]

Nonetheless, these principles, so evident to Roy, were neither understood nor easily accepted by many of his fellow believers. The National Spiritual Assembly, unlike the Executive Board, had the authority and power to make decisions for the growth, administration, and protection of the Faith, not just those related to the construction of the House of Worship. With this change came talk, rumors, misinformation as the friends began to realize the complexity and the comprehensive authority of this nascent institution. Roy shared his thoughts about this topic with his friend John Bosch in California and warned him not to be influenced by anything he heard from even well-meaning Bahá'ís by adding that, "half information and misinformation is responsible for a great deal of trouble now as heretofore, an[d] if we do not look out we will smother the Cause and keep it from influencing broad, progressive minds just the same as has been the case up to this point in orthodox Christianity."[24]

The pages were being rapidly torn off the 1922 calendar, and soon more than half a year had passed since that mid-night moment when 'Abdu'l-Bahá had taken His flight from this mortal plane. By late summer, the effects of 'Abdu'l-Bahá's ascension had evolved for most of the Americans who had loved Him from overwhelming grief to that of a dull ache. Ironically, the loss of 'Abdu'l-Bahá became a cause of renewal—of an emerging, wider vision guided by the delicate, yet exacting hands of Shoghi Effendi. Roy's mourning, interrupted by his journey to the Holy Land, was slowly replaced by the satisfaction of observing the growing evidence that the Faith's future had indeed been transferred to its exceedingly wise, capable, though youthful, Guardian.

Roy had returned to his routine of taking care of his prospering coffee business and serving the Cause both locally and nationally. His mother, Laurie—happy to have her family together in West Englewood—was busy as usual with teaching the Faith to those willing to listen and providing hospitality in their home to anyone who wanted to know more. Roy's father, Otis, at age 72 was still his son's partner in log cabin construction and, from time to time, helped with the coffee business. Most summer days, however, he could be found wielding his racket on the Wilhelms' tennis court. Except for a brief illness earlier that spring, Otis showed every sign of remaining vigorous and healthy at an age when most people of his generation were considered elderly and in decline.[25]

The happy family life of the Wilhelms was about to undergo an abrupt and sad change. Toward the end of August, Martha Root arrived from Green Acre for a visit with the family that had adopted her as one of its own. As they were enjoying the late summer greenery of New Jersey together, without warning, Otis suffered a massive stroke. A two-month ordeal for the Wilhelms had begun.

Day after day, Laurie and Roy nursed Otis with the assistance of their household help and medical staff. He never fully recovered consciousness. Some days he appeared a little better, and there seemed hope of recovery, but every improvement would only be followed by another downturn. Roy informed a friend in early October that his father's ". . . physical condition has improved a trifle so that it seems now he may recover if no other complications ensue, but still five weeks have passed and he does not recognize us yet. He of course is confined in bed under the constant supervision of nurses night and day."[26]

After being bedridden for two months, Otis died, surrounded by those who loved him, on October 30, 1922. To the end, he was a firm believer. Regrettably, Martha, with whom the Wilhelms had shared that delightful travel adventure in the REO eight years earlier, had left New Jersey before Otis' passing to attend to her own father who had taken a turn for the worse, and who would die only a few days after the man she called her second father.[27]

Laurie and Otis had been married for about forty-eight years. For her, it must have been agony to watch helplessly as the love of her life slowly ebbed from this material world to the next. Reflecting on the heart-wrenching difficulties of his father's passing, Roy thought about the time when he was with 'Abdu'l-Bahá and had asked if it was acceptable to give a dying person a "powder" to relieve their suffering by hastening death. 'Abdu'l-Bahá had replied that the Giver of life must be the one to take life.[28] That conversation must have replayed many times in Roy's head during the agony of tending to his father's unpleasant final illness. He wrote to the Bosches that he was grateful that his father had not seemed to be in pain and was now at last at peace, and he confided that "It is pretty hard to adjust to a loss like this which, from a human standpoint seems irreparable; yet mother and I do not grieve and feel we have many, many bounties; one of them is that had father recovered physically the doctors tell us he would not have been in possession of his mental faculties, and so we know that, all things considered, his taking in this way and without suffering is really pure mercy."[29]

Before laying Otis to rest in a local cemetery, Roy and his mother organized an uplifting memorial service at their home that included devotions accompanied by music played on an Italian harp. Mountfort Mills recited a prayer followed by words from Dr. Weir of the Unity Church in Montclair, New Jersey, the same church where 'Abdu'l-Bahá had spoken in 1912. As Roy said, they "tried to have a freedom from that deep sense of gloom which is so often present at funerals, and several remarked that it really seemed more like a beautiful spiritual wedding. . . ."[30] True to the inclusiveness of the Faith and of the family, Dr. Manuel Bolden, the Black pastor of a Harlem church and a member of the New York Local Spiritual Assembly,* officiated at the burial service.[31] It would be impossible to state how significant it was that a prosperous White family chose a Black clergy-

---

* At that time, it was possible to be a member of the Bahá'í community and a member of another religious group. This changed in 1935 when Bahá'ís were asked by Shoghi Effendi to relinquish their membership with other religions in recognition of the independent status of the Bahá'í Faith as a world religion.

man to conduct the funeral of their father and husband. At that time, this decision was perilous and risked opening Roy and his mother up to ridicule or being ostracized by many Whites and the institutions they controlled.

Roy was deeply committed to the equality of the races, which in the early 1920s in America meant standing up for and alongside any downtrodden and oppressed segment of the population, especially Black people.

The newly-established National Spiritual Assembly faced numerous challenges as it began to organize its work. Thus, like Roy, who had previously served on the Executive Board during its infancy, its members discovered the workload was not only heavier but more varied and complex than that of the Board. Shoghi Effendi, within his March 5 letter, emphasized the importance of using consultation in making decisions; but what quickly became apparent within the National Assembly was that consultation was a skill that had to be acquired through mindful effort, and it was inevitable that nine people would not always agree. To those members who were accustomed to making decisions on their own, consultation seemed to be only a hurdle that slowed progress.

The Guardian was also aware that wounds had never completely healed in the wake of the Chicago Reading Room controversy, and that a tendency to try to expose those who did not seem firm in the Covenant continued—like a slow-moving cancer—to infect the body of the community with the disease of mistrust. Notwithstanding the counsel of the Guardian in his March 5 letter to the American Bahá'ís to put the past behind them, even a few members of the National Assembly wanted to identify and expunge those who they believed were not firm, loyal believers. Roy called this behavior "Violation Hunting," and it was repugnant to him. During the years of the First World War, he had been upset by how unjustly the Chicago Reading Room incident had been handled and had let his views be known at the time, even though doing so had upset those behind the investigation of the wayward Chicagoans. He had not been alone in his judgment, which was shared by Mountfort Mills and Harry Randall, among many others. Serving with these three men became a test for the members of the National Assembly who had tried to expel the Chicagoans from the Faith during the war. Their attitudes and behavior, in turn, made service on the Assembly almost unbearable. Roy became so disheartened that he, as well as Mountfort and Harry, contemplated withdrawing from consideration for its membership in 1923. Word of this situation reached Haifa and prompted one of Shoghi Effendi's secretaries to write to Roy, probably with the blessing of the Guardian, encouraging him to persevere despite the challenges.[32] To clear up a misunderstanding of the situation, Roy wrote in response about how, over the course of the year, disunity had crept in:

> No, . . . , it was not because of any personal feeling or inconvenience that Mountfort and I had consulted with a few of the friends as to the advisability of withdrawing from the N.C.A. [sic], but rather was to try and find some way that the pivotal point of inharmony could be removed so that the harmony of the Cause could be preserved. Abdul Baha said it was better to be unified upon action not of the best, than to quarrel about something which might be better. (And this was made much of by our friends of other opinions). But, where so important a principle were at stake as Individualism v.s. consultation, and the prosecution of Violation Hunting with all the multiplying possibilities it involved—it seemed to us that the very heart of the Cause in America depended on saving it, particularly just now, from these things. I hope God will forgive us if our course was wrong.[33]

In the months prior to the next election of the National Assembly, both Roy and Mountfort were targeted by a handful of individuals who wanted them removed from the Assembly. Even though the teachings prohibiting electioneering prior to Bahá'í elections were not explicit as they would be later, the quiet rumors and backbiting used to try to prevent their reelection clearly contradicted the basic principles of the Faith, especially the stress upon maintaining unity. Those trying to remove Roy and Mountfort from the National Assembly were partially successful in that Mountfort, despite having served as Assembly chairman during its first year, was not reelected, though Roy was. Roy said that the failure of the delegates to reelect Mountfort was "a very great blow to me personally and I feel to the broader spirit in the Cause" because, in trying to understand how various people's minds worked, he "found <u>nowhere</u> his [Mountfort's] equal in analysis and breadth and <u>distance</u> of view." Mountfort had been an "admirable" chairman, with his "great moderation and refined qualities." Mountfort had confidentially predicted the election outcome, but Roy did not want to believe his assessment. Afterward, Roy concluded that, "There can be little question that a determined and well-planned effort brought it about . . ."[34] Many years would pass before the scourge of electioneering, brought into Bahá'í elections from the wider world, would be purged.

Left to right: Roy Wilhelm, unknown, Mountfort Mills, taken during the 1923 Convention at which Roy was reelected to the National Spiritual Assembly but Mountfort was not. (USBNA)

One bright spot of that election was that Horace Holley, a gifted published writer employed as a copywriter for a New York advertising agency, was elected to the National Assembly for the first time. Although Horace was twelve years younger, Roy had known him for many years from their service together on the New York Spiritual Assembly, and the two had become friends. Like Roy, he was quiet and had a devilish sense of humor, but unlike Roy, Horace was a New England Brahmin* who came from a well-to-do Connecticut family and who had received an elite education. The close working relationship they had established already would strengthen over the next quarter of a century through their joint service on the National Spiritual Assembly.[35]

'Alí Kuli-Khán and Horace Holley,
probably at the Wilhelm home.
(USBNA)

---

* "Brahmin" is often used to denote the upper levels of society. The expression encompasses more than simply wealth to include family heritage and educational attainment. The word derives from the classifications of Indian society, where the Brahmans were at the top of the caste system. The term is often used in the United States to describe the elite of the New England region.

Roy and his colleagues on the National Assembly were beginning to establish protocols and methods of operation for their meetings and tasks. What should they do about a letterhead and who could use it? What form should the minutes take? What should be done about accounting procedures, banking relationships, and financial records? What actions could be authorized by the officers and which ones needed the approval of the entire Assembly? Unsurprisingly, Roy wanted to incorporate efficient business practices into the Assembly's work. For example, tongue-in-cheek, with his inimitable wit, he gave Harry Randall instructions on how the Assembly members should traverse New York on their way to his home for a meeting. He suggested that Harry round up the others so they could travel across town together, so that members who were usually tardy would be on time: "It may still be well for you yourself to round up the gang and all start together, otherwise some of the sloweys may miss the connection and hold things up. Maybe you had better not mention my nice word for I think some of them consider me a bug on my constant insistence that we apply the methods <u>necessary</u> for <u>success</u> in <u>even</u> ordinary business affairs."[36]

A few years later, he chided his National Assembly colleagues by saying that it was his "earnest hope that as time goes on the N.S.A. will learn to handle still better, particularly more expeditiously, the business and the problems which may be presented."[37] The infant institution was learning to walk, but it was not yet ready to run.

As Shoghi Effendi settled into his work as Guardian and head of the Faith, he found Roy to be as much an assistant to him as he had been to his Grandfather. Roy kept him abreast of what was happening in North America through his letters to Haifa. In February 1924, about two years after his visit to the Holy Land, Roy received words of appreciation and encouragement from Shoghi Effendi:

The National Spiritual Assembly in session in 1929 at the Wilhelm home. Laurie Wilhelm is present. Shoghi Effendi would not clarify until the 1930s that only members could be present when an Assembly was conducting business. Often, the Assembly could only get a quorum and not the full membership due to the great distances some members had to travel to attend meetings. (USBNA)

My dearest Roy: -

It is such a joy to receive your letters. I shall never forget you in my prayers and pray to God to sustain you and guide you in your work. May your efficient labours, your disinterested efforts, your untiring activities be richly blessed by 'Abdu'l-Bahá who is tenderly watching over you from His station on high, who has received so much assistance from you in the past and whose hopes are so high for your future.

Your brother

Shoghi[38]

Less than two weeks later, Shoghi Effendi sent another letter to Roy concerning confidential problems within the American community. The letter gave Roy much credit for the unity of the New York community and said that "through your effort and that of a few others, New York is among the only cities that are free of all discord and anxiety, and it is only when this condition prevails that progress can really be made." His secretary noted in the main body of the letter that Shoghi Effendi "considers your presence there as an asset to the spread of the Cause in America. He certainly never thinks of ever repaying you for he is firm in assurance that in His Kingdom you shall have an ample share."[39] In his handwritten postscript at the bottom of the letter, Shoghi Effendi encouraged Roy to continue sending him reports because "I know full well the depth of your sincerity, your earnestness, your wisdom and your utter selflessness in His service."[40] The Guardian, like 'Abdu'l-Bahá before him, was happy to have Roy serve as his eyes and ears in North America.

The passing of 'Abdu'l-Bahá, Roy's lengthy journey to the Holy Land including the side trips to Egypt and Europe, his election to the National Assembly, and the death of his father—not to mention his other responsibilities—finally took their cumulative toll on his health and spirit. He needed a respite from the demands of business and the constant interruptions from telegrams and telephone calls. He also needed a break from the arduous trips to Chicago and other cities for meetings. Throughout his years as a member of the Executive Board and then the National Assembly, Roy conscientiously attended almost every meeting until the October, 1924 meeting of the National Assembly. Instead, he went camping in the autumn cold next to a stream full of trout so that he could get a "much needed rest."[41] Fortunately, the next National Convention would, for the first time, be held in a much more beautiful and relaxing spot, Green Acre.

The Convention of 1925 was truly a celebration. It was held on the tranquil slopes at Green Acre alongside the swiftly flowing Piscataqua River—a spot much beloved because it had been blessed by the visit of 'Abdu'l-Bahá. That year, after more than a decade of challenges, including litigation, the trustees of Green Acre were finally free to turn the property over to the management of the National Assembly.[42] But that was not the only reason to rejoice, for that year, Shoghi Effendi

Roy Wilhelm during a 1928 camping trip with friends. (USBNA)

affirmed that the National Spiritual Assembly of the United States and Canada was at last finally worthy of the name,* even though

---

* To this day, the National Spiritual Assembly of the United States considers 1925 as the year of its establishment rather than 1922, though viewed in practical terms, the earlier date was when it began to function.

231

a National Assembly had been elected every year since 1922. This recognition was in part possible because the Temple Unity Executive Board, still necessary under its Illinois incorporation, had come fully under the control and supervision of the National Assembly a few months earlier and was no longer functioning as a separate entity.[43] Furthermore, the voting procedures, which that year included absentee voting for the first time, more closely aligned with the guidance from the Guardian. Adding this one element to the electoral process greatly expanded the field for a broader, more representative selection of delegates. Roy, approaching age 50, was once again reelected.

In addition to his duties as a member of the National Assembly as well as the New York Spiritual Assembly, Roy had taken on another responsibility: ensuring that a grand annual picnic was held on his property the last Saturday of June without fail. 'Abdu'l-Bahá had even commented during that historic event that it marked the true establishment of the Faith in America,[44] and the idea that it would be celebrated and reenacted, centuries in the future, by thousands of such gatherings never left Roy's thoughts. Summer after summer, grateful New Yorkers and others from the region, lunch in hand, made the journey to New Jersey. By 1925, the annual outing was a prominent element of the Bahá'í calendar and eagerly anticipated by the Bahá'ís in the area. Yet hosting a crowd that seemed to increase yearly was also a monumental undertaking. Roy and his mother were aging, and the Bourgeois family were no longer neighbors. He first asked the New York Spiritual Assembly to take responsibility

---

From the statements of Shoghi Effendi, this seems to have been because of the continuation of the Bahá'í Temple Unity for those first years because of legal issues. See Shoghi Effendi, *God Passes By*, pp. 414, 527.

for the event, and it did. But as the gathering increasingly became a regional affair, the New York Assembly could no longer manage it. In 1930, Roy turned to the National Assembly—with its Secretariat based in New York—and asked that it sponsor the gathering, and the National Assembly unhesitatingly agreed to do so.[45]

1930 Souvenir Picnic (USBNA)

Martha Root was just as dedicated to the annual observance of the Souvenir Picnic as Roy. She had hardly stopped traveling from the time she had embarked on her South American adventures in 1919, yet, even when far away, she always celebrated the annual Souvenir Picnic on its anniversary and dedicated that day each year to extra service and prayer. While in Geneva, Switzerland on behalf of the Faith in 1925, she teasingly expressed her heartfelt appreciation for all that Roy had done for her and the Root family over the years, and she acknowledged even little tokens of friendship such as sending coffee to her sister-in-law. Nor had she forgotten that Roy and Laurie had surprised her with first-class passage for her first voyage to China. Practical Roy made sure Martha had a large travel trunk for her belongings and also gave her a little cloth security pouch to wear discretely around her neck to safeguard emergency funds. Much as a big sister, she discussed the picnic as she expressed her appreciation:

In anything big & little you have stood with me and one by one, each effort has been successful, it would have been very hard to go forward in China and here & everywhere without your help. Personally too, your message and meeting 'Abdu'l Baha and trying to live the Bahai life has brought me such happiness that I feel I am in Heaven all the time—except when I slip a cog and hate myself. Do you ever lose your temper, Roy, or feel "cranky" when you are sick, or have you become a saint? I'd like to see all your progress, couldn't you take a little vacation & come over to Geneva? You'd see . . . , and I hope you'd like to see me. Anyway I'd love to see you & your mother. . . . How I wish I could be at your feast today and see you all! But I see your hearts and feel your love and I thank 'Abdu'l Baha I could speak of His Teachings. . . . My heart is with you and I'm sure 'Abdu'l Baha and Mr. Wilhelm are very close to you. Your [sic] are standing "as His Command[."] I admire you & love you all and just pray to serve as faithfully as you do.[46]

There was one aspect to the Souvenir Picnic that worried Roy. If it was to be held every year in perpetuity, who would take care of the Teaneck property after he was gone, to make certain that the event could be held there long into the future? He was well into middle-age, still unmarried, and an only child. It seemed to him that the logical solution would be to turn ownership of his property over to the Faith. Initially, he intended to give it to the local Bahá'í community for use as a Bahá'í center, especially Evergreen Cabin. But over time, he changed his mind and made the decision to deed the land in stages to the National Assembly—an institution he felt had the greater resources needed to manage the property. He started the process in 1926 by conveying to the Assembly the lower two lots* where 'Abdu'l-Bahá had stood when He spoke to that first large crowd of picnickers. Roy offered to pay the taxes on the property for a few

---

* Roy did not own those bottom lots where 'Abdu'l-Bahá gave His talks in 1912. Over time, he acquired not only them but other lots intersecting his land until it was all contiguous.

years.[47] He began to think of his home and its land as a Bahá'í center for which he was merely the caretaker.

The original log cabin, completed in 1926, quickly became a hub for Bahá'í activities in the New York area. Besides the annual Souvenir Picnic, the grounds and building were the site of innumerable gatherings. Before long, despite its two large meeting rooms, which easily accommodated 150 people, Roy realized that a larger space was needed. Thus, he began to expand the cabin. Over time, he enlisted the help of several friends and Bahá'í neighbors, including William Bowen,[48] Albert Walkup,[49] Archie Tichenor,[50] and Donald Kinney.[51] Construction began on the north side of the original cabin with the addition of a substantial extension that included a sweeping second-floor interior balcony. The expansion project was finally completed in 1931.[52]

Martha considered the Wilhelm New Jersey property to be her other home and wanted to contribute in a small way to its development. She knew Roy was building an immense fireplace inside the new wing of the cabin, so in the course of her travels around the world, she hit upon a way she could participate in his latest project. Due to her efforts, what would have been an otherwise humdrum fireplace began to assume legendary status. Stories were told of how Martha collected rocks and stones from the places she visited which she then shipped to Roy. Following her example, Bahá'ís around the world sent stones to him from the homes and prisons of the Báb and Bahá'u'lláh in Persia and from 'Akká, Bahjí, Haifa, and Mount Carmel in the Holy Land. Martha's own contributions included stones from places such as the Great Wall of China, the Western Wall in Jerusalem, "emperor's gardens,"* and sites associated with the heroes and heroines of the Faith.[53]

A 1931 newspaper article extolled the craftsmanship and mysterious nature of the log cabin in the New Jersey suburbs.[54] It told of the conch shells that had been transformed into light fixtures,

---

* Most likely, the phrase *emperor's gardens* refers to palaces.

The National Spiritual Assembly often met at the Wilhelm home during the summer. The members present in 1932 posed beneath the torii on Roy's property. Far left: Allen Mc Daniel. Back row, left to right: Louis Gregory, Horace Holley, Carl Scheffler, Alfred Lunt. Front row, left to right: Laurie Wilhelm, Martha Root, Fred Schopflocher, Bertha Hertzlotz. Bertha Hertzlotz was the first administrative employee of the National Spiritual Assembly and mainly served under the treasurer. She and the other two women in the photo were not members of the Assembly. (USBNA)

and how Roy had used the polished ends of logs arranged in the outer floor to mimic Persian marquetry. It described how the broad second-floor balcony reached into "the limbs of the surrounding pine trees" and how the overall placement of exotic oriental vases and carpets accented the otherwise simple interior.[55] Near the north end of the cabin, a large boulder brought from nearby was set in the center of a concrete pool. Curtis Kelsey, who had been helping with the construction, drilled a hole through the rock to create an oriental fountain fed by water from a natural well a hundred feet below.*

---

* The pools were filled in by 1958 due to concerns small children might fall in and drown.

Above all, the newspaper writer, like many other visitors to the cabin, was enchanted by the great fireplace and its stones. Those historic rocks, contributed by well-wishers from so many countries, served as a talisman for visitors—a material token of their fatherlands—and "that Evergreen Cabin in its inner reality is a home of the spirit of all religions . . ." and where "the universality of this place impresses every guest."[56]

On his way to his office the last Tuesday morning in October, 1929, Roy would have noticed that it was not just the weather that seemed colder, but also the mood of the men and women scurrying along the sidewalks. From his office window, he and his staff looked out at a financial district that, since the previous Thursday, had been more volatile than coffee prices after news of a freeze in Brazil. Now, five days later, Roy and his staff watched as crowds of men—their coats unbuttoned, seemingly unconcerned with the abnormally frosty October weather—ran past his Wall Street office to gather in front of the Stock Exchange building a few blocks away. The falling price of stocks, often bought on speculative margins with borrowed funds, had settled back from the previous Thursday's uncontrolled freefall, so it had seemed at first glance that a serious disruption to the stock market had been sidestepped. To everyone's relief, the big banks had intervened quickly to support the wispy financial spiderweb— at least for the moment—so the market seemed stable again when it reopened on Monday. However, the next day, October 29, the market opened in chaos, stock prices plummeted, and the day would become known as "Black Tuesday." Despite widespread hope that this was a temporary setback, after this crash, the economy would not fully recover for a decade. Days would lead to weeks, and weeks to months until finally all hope of a return to prosperity was shattered.

On that fateful Tuesday, Herbert Hoover had only been in the White House for six months. When he had assumed the office the previous March, the stock market was the highest it had ever been, with no ceiling in sight. Few thought those days of seemingly endless profit taking would ever stop. However, a handful of clear-eyed business leaders, economists, and academics had foreseen an untenable future. To them, it seemed unlikely that the markets could continue to support the roulette wheel of margin calls, short selling, leverage, and other speculative investment activity then taking place on Wall Street. Their voices were just an unheeded irritant to the hundreds of thousands of men and women—tycoons and janitors, housewives and waiters—who had waved fists full of dollars at the hot stock of the day. For the first time, ordinary folks—anticipating that they too would be able to live in mansions, ride in chauffeur-driven limousines, and retire to Palm Beach—played the stock market. The notion of prosperity through buying and selling stock turned out to be a chimera, and these dreams ended the last Tuesday in October.[57]

For many people, the post-war years had been an escape from reality through unbridled self-indulgence. Declining moral standards and easy money in financial markets brought about a carelessness in the conduct of a young, liberated America. The 1920s had also marked the turning point when ordinary Americans truly became part of the Machine Age. Henry Ford made the automobile affordable for every middle-class family and no longer an extravagant plaything of the rich and powerful, so for the first time, most people could travel, and because of that freedom, they gained experiences that exposed them to new ideas and broadened their thinking. But that was not the only change that had occurred during that decade. The home of an average family now had an electric washing machine, oven, and refrigerator, and these inventions freed women from the drudgery of those domestic chores that sapped their time and energy. The development of commercial radio brought the world into more and more parlors thereby increasing the interconnectedness of people both in cities and in rural areas and allowing news to be received instantly. Films added sound, so evenings spent at movie houses became not only popular entertainment but further changed the average citizen's view of the world.[58] The stock market crash did not negate these positive and negative forces but took them in a new direction.

As the stock market tumbled, Roy would have seen desperation on the faces of men and women everywhere he turned. Mounted policemen pushed their way through a horde of the ten thousand frightened and angry men that congregated where Wall Street and Broad Street met. Like a human wave, men jumped to the sidewalk whenever a chauffeured limousine, its horn blasting, steered through the mélange of the distraught to usher a mogul away from what could easily turn into an angry mob. Roy needed to stay current with changes in the world, especially any news that might affect his business or life, so that day, after lunch, he probably bought an afternoon paper from a newsboy on the corner. Staked out on their turf, their caps pulled down around their eyes, the newsboys yelled out the calamitous headlines while waving their broadsheets in the faces of pedestrians on the street. A few blocks away at 18 Broad Street, throngs of men in fedoras—hopeful that the marble female "Integrity" in the center of the triangular pediment, with her clenched fist symbolizing honesty and sincerity, would be their salvation—stared up at the New York Stock Exchange building. At the railway station on his way home, Roy probably noticed the crowds gathered around a tickertape machine that continued to spew unending ribbons of buy and sell prices—now hours behind the trades executed on the exchange floor. That Black Tuesday was the beginning of a turbulent period at the stock exchange. For weeks, a mournful hum of the anticipated apocalypse could be heard and felt throughout the financial district.[59] The 1920s—the decade that roared—ended with a collective, painful groan.

What would the 1930s bring? Few understood that there had been a fundamental shift in the order of the world. There would be no return this time to the unbridled excesses of the previous ten years. October 29, 1929, came to represent the inception of the worldwide economic calamity known as the Great Depression. Its impact would hit the middle-class—who were often forced to live paycheck to paycheck—as well as working class families and the poor, who fell into destitution and homelessness.[60] Those last days of October marked the start of the stock market's financial descent that would not hit bottom until stock prices lost almost eighty percent of their value. The thirties would be a time of pulling back, introspection, and staying home.[61]

How did this devastating financial crisis affect Roy and his business? He had thrived without interruption since the Great War as coffee prices rose to unprecedented levels. There is no evidence that Roy had speculated in the stock market or lost money that terrible day, but all around him was the visible devastation of ruined lives. Even if his wealth was diminished, he had his Faith, and a growing understanding of his own true reality that had little to do with the material world. Yet, as he exited his office that historic day, he entered a different world—one for which he would need to adjust.

9 / TESTS AND LOSSES

Roy was in a good mood the summer of 1930, despite the country's economic troubles. A few months after attending the Annual Convention in Chicago, he wrote a playful letter to his friends John and Louise Bosch in California in which he mused about approaching old age now that he was turning fifty-five, saying, "As to getting old—huh! Why 'Abdu'l-Bahá told us <u>some</u> fruits do not even attain to ripeness until after they leave the tree. I'm not exactly a spring capon myself, but I'm having the busiest happiest and <u>I hope</u> most fruitful time of my life."[1]

Why should he not be contented and happy at that time? The previous decade had been a period of unmitigated prosperity during which he became wealthy, as coffee prices soared. He and his mother were generally in good health and living contentedly in their spacious suburban home. Neither wanted for any material comfort. Their teaching efforts had been rewarded with the establishment of a growing local Bahá'í community that in 1926 had elected a Local Spiritual Assembly for the first time. Roy's Evergreen Cabin,* though always a project that could be improved, had become the center for those Bahá'í activities in New Jersey, as well as the New York City region, when a larger venue was required. The National Spiritual Assembly had successfully passed through its formative years and solidified poli-

---

* Roy named the New Jersey log cabin "Evergreen Cabin." The street which his home faces is now named Evergreen Place.

cies and practices for administering its affairs. Moreover, the National Assembly—and Roy—had developed a close working relationship with Shoghi Effendi, who had now been serving almost nine years as head of the Faith. His direction of the affairs of the Cause worldwide was nothing less than masterful. For Roy, the Faith continued to be the catalyst for him to improve as a spiritual being, to draw closer to his Creator, and to channel his desires to serve his fellow man. Roy remained attuned to world affairs and was paying close attention to the ominous developments in other regions of the world, especially Europe. The worsening economy aside, so far, life in the United States had promised to be unaffected by those trouble spots. Yes, in his sixth decade, Roy was happy with his world.

Even the 1930 National Convention seemed a harbinger of better things to come for the Bahá'í Faith in North America—for there were signs of greater unity and that nascent institutions were beginning to improve Bahá'í community life. His enthusiasm apparent, Roy described the gathering as "the largest, most harmonious and most progressive Convention." Held in the completed lower level of the House of Worship, that year's meeting "stretched the capacity of Foundation Hall."[2] When the newly elected National Assembly held its initial meeting during the Convention, Roy was, for the first time, voted into a new role—treasurer—a post he would hold intermittently until advanced age and a terminal illness required his resignation more than fifteen years later. From the time of his service on the Temple Unity Executive Board more than twenty years earlier, he had been involved in the Faith's finances and had often served on the Executive Board's finance committee when Harry Randall served as its treasurer. Harry had continued that service during the first two years after the National Spiritual Assembly was established.[3] Then in 1924, the first woman to hold that office, Florence Morton, was elected treasurer—an office most often accorded only to men at the time. A friend of Roy's, Florence was a capable businesswoman and the owner of a large factory in the Boston area.[4] For a few months in 1926, when she could no longer manage the treasury for personal reasons, Roy had served as treasurer until his friend, Carl Scheffler from Chicago, was elected to that office. During the early years of the National Assembly, Roy had usually been elected vice-chairman and had often had to preside over meetings because of the frequent absences of the chairmen. This was particularly true when Mountfort held this office and was travelling on behalf of Shoghi Effendi.[5] Through experience, Roy became intimately familiar with all the work of the National Assembly, especially matters related to finance, property, and the business aspects of publishing.

Library of Evergreen Cabin, 1930, which that year became the headquarters for the work of the National Assembly. (USBNA)

When the National Assembly was electing its officers during the Annual Convention in 1930, Carl asked to be relieved as treasurer for personal reasons. At the same time, Horace Holley, who was coping with a sensitive family crisis, announced he could no longer serve as secretary.[6] This situation led to a lengthy consultation regarding how the business affairs of the National Assembly should be managed. Roy was subsequently elected treasurer, and the Assembly decided to create a secretariat to carry out the role of secretary.[7] Alfred "Fred" Lunt resumed his earlier position of secretary but shared the work with Horace and Nellie French, a wealthy matron from Pasadena,

California, who had a head for administration. This new arrangement presented the Assembly with the dilemma of where to locate its administrative operations. For the previous three years, the secretary and treasurer had carried out their duties from their homes—urban residences with limited space. Roy offered the Assembly the use of his log cabin. It would be the natural place for him to do his work as treasurer and it had ample room for additional desks and for storing records. The secretariat could share it as much as necessary. He also suggested that the publishing operations be based out of the cabin. His offer was gratefully accepted, and the Assembly agreed to continue to pay Bertha Herzlotz of the New York Bahá'í community to carry out clerical tasks on a part-time basis. Furthermore, it decided to hire Roushan Wilkinson on a part-time basis[8] because she lived in the Boston area near Fred Lunt. Thus, for a number of years, Evergreen Cabin became the official headquarters of the National Spiritual Assembly, though much of the work continued to be carried out in the residence of the secretary.[9]

The National Assembly in front of Roy's fountain and Evergreen Cabin in the early 1930s, along with its employee, Bertha Hertzlotz. (Front left to right) Allen McDaniel, Bertha Hertzlotz, Amelia Collins, Siegfried Schopflocher, Nellie French; (back left to right) Leroy Ioas, Alfred Lunt, Horace Holley, Roy Wilhelm. (USBNA)

Expanded Evergreen Cabin and Roy's garage with its attached apartment
as they appeared in 2015. (Courtesy of Bryan Weber)

After the 1930 Convention, Roy decided to get away for a holiday
at summer's end—a camping trip—which would provide him an
opportunity to contemplate the changes happening in the United
States as well as his added Bahá'í responsibilities. The further he drove
into New England's wooded hills, the more he must have been mull-
ing over many nagging questions: was it possible the excesses of the
Roaring Twenties and the days of the great New York stock market's
reckless gambling had ended? How were the financial challenges of
the past year going to affect his business and the Faith? Few yet recognized that the ebullient days of careless investing and easy money were
indeed finished. What had happened to those predictable economic
cycles of ups and downs in the market that quickly adjusted to make
everything right again? In the past, if someone such as Roy engaged
in business was patient, inevitably within a few months, the business
climate would rebound and even exceed the levels it had reached prior
to the downturn. After all, that is what had happened during the
recession that came on the heels of the Great War. Was that not
how capitalism worked if left unencumbered?[10] The aftershocks of
the stock market collapse on Black Tuesday had rippled through the

245

economy, even into segments that had not been rife with speculative practices, including commodity sales, such as coffee.

But the history of the past was not a good predictor of the future, for the country was entering an extended period of crisis that would not end until a worldwide war was won. Nonetheless, the equities market did seem to momentarily ease back from the precipice in the early months of 1930, as stocks regained much of their lost value. In September, when Roy confidently pitched his tent in quiet solitude beneath a canopy of trees with only a campfire and a cup of coffee for company, he could relax, certain that all was well back at his Manhattan office.* The White Mountains offered the backwoods escape he needed to distance himself from his responsibilities and cares.

When Roy told his friends about his forthcoming vacation in Maine, he said he was "going to Gilead." There was a town of that name in the vicinity of where he camped, but more likely he drew upon the inspiration of the Biblical trope. The Book of Jeremiah in the Old Testament told of the healing balm of Gilead, enjoining that one must "Go up to Gilead" to receive its curative remedy. He could probably sing the popular Christian hymn, "There's a Balm in Gilead," from memory. He loved and coveted the agrarian life; for him, the best kind of holiday was a camping trip into the wilderness, splitting wood for a fire or pitching a tent by a stream. Immersion in nature was Roy's balm and the White Mountains his Gilead.[11]

Roy enjoyed his camping trip so much that even before returning home where he could consider his decision more carefully, he purchased acreage at the eastern end of the White Mountain Range

---

* During the Great Depression, coffee prices fell, so despite the effects of the Depression, sales of the beverage, which had become such an integral part of American life, remained strong. Information regarding the effect of the stock market crash of 1929 on Roy's finances was unavailable to the writers. Given his cautious nature, he may not have been heavily invested in equities. Inherent in the financial calamity of 1929 was the collapse of the real estate bubble. Land values tumbled, and bargained-price property in Maine became readily available during the summer of 1930.

on Maine's Speckled Mountains. Far from paved roads and the amenities of modern life, his new property sat midway up a peak called Stoneham Mountain. Undeterred by advancing age, Roy wanted to create a camp of sorts, to try his hand once again at building another log cabin and to experience the life of a dairy farmer. In the years ahead, Evergreen Camp,* as he called his Maine property, would become his primary home and his final resting place.

Following his acquisition of real estate in Maine, Roy became more involved in the teaching work in New England, a region where the few widely scattered Bahá'í communities were composed primarily of elderly believers. It had long proven to be a difficult area in which to teach because the lingering vestiges of Protestant Puritanism, combined with the reserved, conservative culture of the descendants of the first European settlers to that northern region, made it difficult to attract the local citizenry to anything new. The Guardian was especially grateful for Roy's personal teaching work in that area where, as Roy reported, ". . . frozen New England is gradually melting."[12] Roy must have expressed impatience with the slow pace of the teaching work in the United States, for the response he received from Shoghi Effendi commented that

> We should not be too impatient. The Cause of God has, throughout all the ages, developed gradually and slowly, unlike all other man-made institutions and movements which rise and develop only to sink after some while into the darkness of oblivion. Speedy development is not always a sign of vitality. It is even sometimes but the prelude to inevitable decline.[13]

---

* The cabin in New Jersey was "Evergreen Cabin" and the property in Maine was "Evergreen Camp." The use of the name "Evergreen" makes it somewhat confusing to distinguish the two.

Unlike Roy, few Bahá'ís were fortunate enough to be directly involved in bringing about the implementation of all three major Charters of the Faith.* The Universal House of Justice quoted Shoghi Effendi's explanation of the Charters and their importance.

> Shoghi Effendi explained that the revelation by Bahá'u'lláh of the Kitáb-i-Aqdas "preserves for posterity the basic laws and ordinances on which the fabric of His future World Order must rest." And he referred to "the triple impulse generated through the revelation of the Tablet of Carmel by Bahá'u'lláh and the Will and Testament as well as the Tablets of the Divine Plan bequeathed by the Center of His Covenant—the three Charters which have set in motion three distinct processes, the first operating in the Holy Land for the development of the institutions of the Faith at its World Center and the other two, throughout the rest of the Bahá'í world, for its propagation and the establishment of its Administrative Order." These three processes, although distinct, are closely interrelated. Developments at the World Center of the Faith, the heart and nerve-center of the Administrative Order, must necessarily exert a pronounced influence on the organic body of the worldwide Bahá'í community, and be affected by its vitality. The Administrative Order may best be viewed as the chief instrument for the prosecution of the Divine Plan, while that Plan has become recognized as the most potent agency for the development of the administrative structure of the Faith. It follows that, for the sound and balanced growth of the Faith and the speedy attainment of world order, due attention must be paid to all three processes.[14]

'Abdu'l-Bahá's Tablets of the Divine Plan, discussed previously, which set forth the battle plan for the spiritual conquest of the planet,

---

* Shoghi Effendi designated Bahá'u'lláh's Tablet of Carmel and 'Abdu'l-Bahá's Tablets of the Divine Plan and Will and Testament as the three Charters of the Faith.

had been of particular interest to Roy since 1916, when Tablets specifically addressed to regions of North America reached the United States. During periods when he could not personally travel or consider moving his residence to further the spread of the Cause, Roy assisted those who could, especially Martha Root, who more than anyone was carrying out the mission entrusted to the North Americans in this great Charter. He continued to work on the production of introductory Bahá'í literature and gave talks on the Faith whenever possible. He also arranged for other speakers to present the Faith at Evergreen Cabin. The annual picnic always received good local newspaper coverage, further spreading word of the Faith. Of particular note were Roy's radio talks at a time when that medium was just becoming widespread.[15] Even though records have not survived of all that Roy did to promote the teaching work around the world, his efforts were praised with gratitude by Shoghi Effendi in a postscript to a 1936 letter: "The services you are rendering and the generous and unfailing assistance you are extending in various countries to isolated believers, travelling teachers, and sympathizers and friends of the Cause are highly meritorious, and constitute a very important aspect of your manifold activities and high endeavors. I am truly proud of and grateful for such eminent accomplishments."[16]

Roy became intimately involved in promulgating and carrying out another Charter—the Will and Testament of 'Abdu'l-Bahá, which laid out the Administrative Order—immediately following his return from his second visit to the Holy Land in 1922. Foremost, he took part in raising up the nascent institutions elected that year, especially the National Assembly for the United States and Canada, which later would be used as an administrative model by other countries as they too elected National Assemblies. He was also among the original members of the first Local Spiritual Assembly of New York, which was established at about the same time. That Local Assembly, notably during its first years, set the policies for many of the practices that in the future would be adopted by other Local Assemblies around the world. Roy not only contributed to the establishment of policies and procedures for local and national institutions, but he also served on the National Assembly at the time it was drafting the Declaration of Trust, which would become the template constitution used by all National Assemblies worldwide. Shoghi Effendi referred to North America as the cradle of the Administrative Order, and Roy was there assisting as a midwife at its birth.[17]

Perhaps the most important of the three Charters was the Tablet of Carmel, because it was revealed by Bahá'u'lláh Himself as the foundational document for the establishment of the World Center of the Faith in the Holy Land. All believers could directly participate in the execution of this Charter through making contributions to the International Fund, but Roy's contributions to its implementation during the formative years of the development of the World Center went far beyond making financial donations. As another of his essential contributions, during the ministry of Shoghi Effendi, Roy became closely associated with the development of the buildings and grounds as well as the acquisition of the land at the World Center.

Following the Great War, a growing tide of Jewish immigrants, fleeing from increasing antisemitism in Europe, flooded Palestine. These refugees quickly changed the demographic makeup of the Haifa area. To accommodate them, Jewish neighborhoods were hastily constructed on the slopes above the Muslim and Christian quarters of the old city. Multistory apartment buildings sprang up ever closer to the land needed for the environs of the Shrine of the Báb and future World Center buildings. Shoghi Effendi found himself in a relentless race with developers to acquire the real estate necessary to fulfill Bahá'u'lláh's vision for the future great international center for the spiritual development of humanity. Without the ready availability of funds, this divinely decreed project would be impeded for generations.

Not surprisingly, the Guardian knew he could always turn to Roy for help with any aspect of the requirements of the World Center. A decade earlier, Roy had underwritten a significant portion of the expenses related to the electrification of the Shrines and the Master's House. In 1922, he had participated in the consultation concerning the erection of the Western Pilgrim House. This vital structure would later serve as the temporary seat for the Universal House of Justice and other institutions. In 1925, Roy provided money to purchase land adjacent to the Shrine of the Báb, as well as funds needed to restore the sacred Mansion of Bahjí, where Bahá'u'lláh lived at the end of His life and passed away.

Roy's contributions to the World Center did not stop with providing funds for these projects. Sometimes Shoghi Effendi considered it prudent to hold certain properties in the name of an individual to safeguard them from the vagaries of unstable governments. Roy was always willing for his name to be used on legal documents in Haifa, even if that meant becoming a party in a lawsuit. After 1930, the National Spiritual Assembly of the United States and Canada was incorporated, and this legal entity, once it was registered as a religious society with the commissioner's office in Haifa, was also used to hold title to land in British-held Palestine.[18] The Guardian frequently confided to Roy details of particular plots and land transactions. After becoming the National Assembly's treasurer, Roy assumed an institutional role in assisting the Guardian with the transfer of funds and the timely assistance with legal matters in the newly established nation of Israel. Often, when he transferred money from the National Fund to the International Fund as treasurer, Roy would add an additional amount from his own pocket. Shoghi Effendi could always count on him to do what was needed in an expeditious manner without need of recognition or thanks—though the Guardian unfailingly told him of his immense appreciation.[19]

As with the generators needed to light the World Center in 1921, Roy was always thinking of practical items he could donate to the Guardian. In 1934, he offered to send irrigation equipment for watering the gardens around the Shrines, and this offer was gratefully accepted.[20] Once the sprinklers were operational, a member of the staff in Haifa reported that, "They are, indeed, most beautiful and practical, and tremendously add to the beauty of the gardens, especially at night when they produce a most impressive effect."[21] Next, Roy sent Shoghi Effendi an electric refrigerator, a gift that, no doubt, pleased all the members of the Guardian's household, especially his cook.[22]

Roy's wide-reaching services to the Cause were further extolled by the Guardian in his own hand in a postscript to a 1933 letter: "Few, if any among the believers of East and West, have been privileged to serve as effectively the varied and ever-increasing branches of Bahá'í activity, whether local, national or international, as your own precious self. No one, certainly has supported them as generously and continuously as have your own contributions in the past."[23]

During the early 1930s, as financial woes increasingly affected the activities of the Faith worldwide, Roy received a letter from Shoghi Effendi informing him that he would have to suspend making contributions toward the construction of the North American House of Worship from the International Fund. Increasingly, the government of Iran was placing severe political and fiscal restrictions on the Persian Bahá'í community. The Guardian had relied upon funds contributed by the Iranian community to promote "the vital interests of the community at its world centre."[24] Only a few months earlier, as the Great Depression continued to tighten its grip over the American economy, Roy had reported to Shoghi Effendi that contributions coming into the National Fund had slowed, making it difficult to meet payment demands for the Temple construction or to reduce their bank loan balances. He attributed this problem to believers being out of work and of others needing to recoup their own finances before contributing again. Alas, there was an additional cause: factions had split the community at the national level, due in large measure to the misguided activities of a member of the National Assembly. That disunity had affected contributions. Yet, Roy continued to be an optimist, reporting to Shoghi Effendi that he felt that the 1934 Convention had marked a turning point during which, after frank consultation, the foundations had been laid for better understanding that would ultimately bring the disunity to an end.[25] He would do whatever he could to get the Cause through that period of trouble.

From about 1927, Shoghi Effendi began to provide the Western believers with two gifts that were precious beyond measure. First, using his extensive mastery of English, Arabic, and Persian, he translated many of the most significant Sacred Texts into English, from which they would later be rendered into other languages.[26] At long last, Westerners had a plethora of authoritative and carefully translated Bahá'í Writings. Better yet, because Shoghi Effendi had been designated in 'Abdu'l-Bahá's Will and Testament as the only authoritative interpreter of the Sacred Texts, in effect, the Guardian's English translations served also as his interpretations. Shoghi Effendi's translations rose to the level of exquisite works of literature rather than being simply the rendering into English of religious texts. The second gift, beginning in 1929 and ending in 1936, was a series of annual letters—better termed expositions—which as a collection were given the title *The World Order of Bahá'u'lláh*. These majestic commentaries set out the vision of the Faith and placed it into the context of history and the currents of thought afoot at the time. Embedded within these timeless, magnificent compositions were a multitude of newly translated quotations from Bahá'u'lláh, the Báb, and 'Abdu'l-Bahá. The most important section of this weighty compilation was a subset of essays later titled "The Dispensation of Bahá'u'lláh," which explained the verities of the Faith, especially the stations of the three Central Figures—an unresolved issue that had caused much confusion among Western believers. Included in "The Dispensation of Bahá'u'lláh" was one essay that explained the spiritual significance of the Administrative Order and what it would mean in the future when the Bahá'í World Commonwealth was established.

"The Dispensation of Bahá'u'lláh" alone presented a breathtakingly inspiring vision of the future of the Faith, but the collection together was eye-opening and exciting.

As the friends studied these new texts, the community became firmer overall in its devotion and steadfastness, and thereby, through concerted effort both individually and collectively, began to exemplify the teachings more closely. The Bahá'ís had not only developed a deeper love for the Faith but also now had a mission. At the time these Writings were taking hold of hearts, the rise of the superstructure of the House of Worship had brought to a close the demoralizing period when it seemed as if the Temple would never be built. Now, though still unclad by ornamentation, the soaring dome dominated the north shore skyline of Chicago. With such positive advances in the fortunes of the Faith, even as the gloom of economic chaos cast its shadow over the United States, believers who had not been seen for some years began to reconnect with the Bahá'í community, drawn by its renewed vibrancy. Roy reported this phenomenon to the Guardian, who, in a letter written on his behalf, commented:

> You mentioned in one of your letters that some of the old believers who for many years had kept away are now coming back and attending the meetings. How wonderful it would be if all such persons together with all those who met the Master and whose life was changed through His influence would come along and help us in spreading these divine teachings! Perhaps the friends should take the initiative and make their meetings so inspiring and their activities so interesting and far reaching in importance that they would of their own accord come forward and lend us their help. Anyhow they would be a large army.[27]

Despite the exuberance created by old friends reconnecting to the Faith, 1932 turned out to be one of the most painful years of the Depression as the economy went into freefall. Due to ill-advised government policies under the administration of President Herbert Hoover, especially the imposition of draconian tariffs which crippled international trade, the Depression not only deepened but inadvertently spread to other countries. The situation became dire for multitudes. Unemployment soared, and the value of many assets, including real estate, plummeted. More and more people lost their homes, businesses, or farms. Long lines of well-dressed, former businessmen waiting for meager handouts from "soup kitchens" in Manhattan became commonplace. Homeless squatters had set up camps, christened "Hoovervilles," in New York's Central Park, while others could be found sleeping in the subways. Unable to find work, many men spent their days sitting on public benches, their heads lowered as they stared vacantly at the ground, too embarrassed to make eye contact with passersby.[28] Bahá'ís were not immune from the hardships surrounding them. One friend told Roy about the situation of many American Bahá'ís: "Quite a few are living on poor orders, and others not quite that bad, are not able to buy anything except necessary food and enough clothes to cover for them. Yes, there are some who go to the movies, have their own cars, etc, although they <u>feel</u> poor, but a good many of the friends <u>are</u> poor."[29]

Both Local Assemblies and the National Assembly increasingly received appeals for material assistance.[30] In hindsight, Roy must have been especially grateful that the Guardian had insisted on strict austerity and the channeling of funds into the Temple account during the waning years of prosperity before the economic collapse. Because of the National Assembly's strict and cautious husbanding of funds, money was available to ensure that the superstructure of the House of Worship could be completed—a monetary goal that had been accomplished only through great effort. Absent a miracle, raising this same amount of money in 1932 would have been impossible. The economic landscape had undergone a dramatic change; the old rules no longer applied. What a time it was for Roy to serve as national treasurer!

Roy's predecessors had already set high standards as capable national treasurers. Each of them had well understood the sanctity and the need for careful stewardship of what would be referred to by Shoghi Effendi as the "life blood of the Cause."[31] They had established proper protocols for receipting and disbursing funds, as well as accounting procedures for administering the contributed funds for the construction of the House of Worship and later the general National Fund. They were aided in their work by a trustworthy, competent Bahá'í accountant living in the Chicago area. Corinne True had also continued to assist with raising funds to complete the Temple by sending forth her own steady stream of letters to the friends across North America and lovingly acknowledging donations.

The integrity of the treasury was essential. Americans knew of too many cases where those entrusted with other people's money at charitable institutions, churches, and nonprofit organizations had mismanaged or stolen funds from their donors because precautions—such as carrying out regular audits and ensuring transparent bookkeeping—had not been taken. Those entrusted with the work of the office of treasurer needed to embody the attributes of honesty, strength of character, integrity, trustworthiness, and knowledge of the proper procedures for safeguarding of money and other tangible assets such as real estate. All who had been able to observe how Roy conducted his personal affairs and his business would have agreed that he possessed these essential traits. He had acquired a high level of understanding of finance, accounting, and banking. Because his coffee import company was not confined within the borders of the United States, he also knew how money could be safely moved around the globe. Sending funds to Brazil or Costa Rica for a consignment of green coffee, for example, was a routine part of his day. 'Abdu'l-Bahá, and now Shoghi Effendi, depended on Roy's ability to get money to the Holy Land to meet the expenses of a growing World Center and to continue the ever-expanding teaching activities across the planet. They knew Roy could manage these vital transactions successfully and in a timely manner.

During Roy's lifetime, pennies—even just one cent—mattered. When he was a small boy, Roy could go to a corner store and buy a piece of candy for a penny. Profit margins on items sold were more often measured in cents rather than dollars, so unsurprisingly, he kept meticulous financial records. When he was a young man, Roy had learned a valuable lesson when, after saving a substantial sum of money, he had been swindled out of it, losing what had taken him a great effort to accumulate. He never forgot that lesson. He became accomplished at creating savings and cautious about expending them. The vigilance he applied to his business's bookkeeping naturally extended to his custodianship of the funds of the Faith. In a note to a former treasurer, he lamented the lack of oversight over some of those pennies:

> I don't know where the trouble lies but you will remember a while back we had some bills overlooked and lost the discount besides being scolded on two of them because they were weeks over-ripe. This is really too bad. The discount on two of these recent bills amounted to at least $1.50, some perfectly good money which should be in our till. Some poor washerwomen worked pretty hard to scare up that many pennies for the fund.
> . . . I am not going to be happy over losing discounts even only a dime,* also we want the good will of those who have served us and they should be paid promptly.[32]

Thus, Roy's unspoken message was that the meticulous accounting for every sacrificially contributed cent conveyed to contributors a spirit of integrity and care. The funds of the Faith belonged to God.

---

* A ten-cent coin in United States, one tenth of a dollar.

After purchasing his Speckled Mountain real estate, Roy immediately set to work developing it. The world was falling apart, but Roy continued to build. In the early 1930s, the rugged state of Maine, with its hundreds of miles of jagged Atlantic coastline and inland granite mountains, remained largely rural. Forestry and farming drove its economy, and it boasted an enticing natural beauty—rocky shores along the Atlantic, and lakes set like brilliant blue jewels in the green meadows spread between the craggy rolling hills shaded by thick pine woodlands. These wonders of nature beckoned hardy vacationers, including famous film stars and the wealthy.[33] They spent the summers boating and swimming in the ocean and lakes, the springs and autumns hiking along wooded trails, and the winters skiing down the mountainsides. The residents of the mountain region, which had been settled by Scandinavian immigrants, loved winter and were long accustomed to using skis and snowshoes, not for sport, but to get from place to place when it snowed. Indeed, not far from Roy's Evergreen Camp was the factory of the country's leading snowshoe maker.[34] Caught up in the spirit of his new neighbors, Roy began to spend more and more of the colder periods of the year at his second home.

Roy cleared large swathes of his Stoneham Mountain property and used the felled trees to construct another log cabin, although this time it was fashioned in the style of a Swiss mountain chalet. The chalet was much larger than his New Jersey cabin and had wonderful views from its front porches. When it was first completed, Roy was probably able to see the lake at the bottom of the hill, but as trees grew, that view disappeared.

Lower down the mountain, Roy built a smaller cabin designated the "sugarhouse." From late winter through early spring, hundreds of maple trees growing on his property were tapped, and the buckets of sap were delivered to the sugarhouse, where it was boiled down until it became maple syrup. Evergreen Camp boasted fine local fare: pancakes drenched in maple syrup, wild blueberry ice cream made from goat's milk, and fresh butter from his dairy cows. To Roy, it was heaven.

Front view of Evergreen Camp's chalet in 1934. Roy is in the middle with the dark sweater. (USBNA)

Side view of the chalet showing its porches in 1934 (USBNA)

And then there was Roy's goat herd. Roy adored goats! It is presumed he first began raising a few of them on his suburban property in West Englewood because goat's milk was a key ingredient of the porridge 'Abdu'l-Bahá had recommended that he eat each morning. Now he had enough acreage in Maine to own a herd. Where the land flattened out closer to the lake, he constructed a shed for the hundreds of Oberhasli goats he eventually owned. This particular breed had been recommended by his dear Swiss friend, John Bosch, because these goats were renowned for producing plentiful and rich milk. They were the same variety of Alpine goats that he was already raising on a smaller scale in New Jersey. With hillside meadows on his Maine country estate, Roy also had room for a herd of rusty-orange and white Scottish Ayrshire cattle. To complete his menagerie, prize-winning German Shepherds patrolled the property and kept Roy company on his walks through the countryside.

Roy holding the tether of a goat in 1936 at Evergreen Camp
(USBNA)

Roy not only loved animals, but all his life was also enamored by automobiles, so over the years, he indulged his fancy by owning several iconic models. Although some were luxury cars, he was always prudent when spending money and so usually bought them secondhand. One such acquisition was his powerful twelve cylinder "twin six" Packard Roadster. Perched on the radiator, with her outstretched arms pointing the way, rode Nike, the Greek winged goddess of speed and victory. Roy delighted in driving into town to retrieve friends coming to Stoneham Mountain for a visit. On sunny days with no rain in the forecast, he would lower the car's top. Two guests could squeeze into the tiny rumble seat, and another would sit up front next to him. With his guests' suitcases securely strapped onto the fold-down luggage rack above the rear bumper, Roy would race through villages and past farms with the wind blowing through the hair of his passengers. Wearing his signature khaki suit, a bowtie snug around his neck, and with the impressive long hood of his sporty roadster stretched out in front of him, Roy could have easily been mistaken for one of the vacationing Hollywood *bon vivants* enjoying the refreshing, crystal-clear lake at the foot of Stoneham Mountain. Branching off the main road, the way to the chalet was located up a bumpy dirt farm lane. It was dusty unless rain turned it into a river of mud. If the road was too slick to climb the last mile and a half, Roy would abandon the car beside a small cement bridge, and a horse and wagon would be summoned to carry his guests up the last leg to the chalet.[35] Visiting Roy had become an adventure—one that the National Spiritual Assembly as a group would undertake only once.

By spring of 1932, construction on the chalet was underway though, as usual, additions and expansion would continue for the next fifteen years. Roy wanted his many overnight guests to be comfortable, so each of the five bedrooms situated off the birch-railed balcony had a sink and an oil lamp; however, everyone had to share the cabin's only bathroom, which was located down a hallway. Meals in the dining room were served at a huge table beneath a large wagon wheel converted into a chandelier. On warm summer days, visitors sat with Roy in his numerous rocking chairs or along the built-in mandars* on the long front porch that offered an endless panorama of the mountains. The log cabin was heated by a massive stone fireplace that could take away the chill of an autumn or spring evening, even though it offered little comfort in the dead of winter.[36] Many hours of chopping and sawing were needed to put aside the thirty to fifty cords of wood used each year to keep Roy's visitors and staff from freezing. The Kohler generators he sent to the Holy Land a decade before had performed well, so he had one installed at the chalet to operate a few appliances and to supplement the oil lamps with electric lights for several hours in the evening.

Despite its lack of modern amenities, his mountain home was always a place for hospitality where Roy's guests could wander his grounds or sit on his porch even if they did not stay the night. Thousands of guests, both invited and uninvited, eventually passed through his property as hikers or tourists who had heard about his unusual retreat. In later years, during cold wintry days, one of his staff, Helen Blakely, would gather white bark from the many birch trees growing on the property, cut them into small attractive shapes, and gilt the edges. Then she would affix a passage from the Bahá'í Writings on each one. These small tokens of hospitality given to the thousands of visitor to Evergreen Camp became known as "Barkies."[37] Small wonder then that Roy became a legendary local curiosity.[38] No matter, he made everyone feel welcome. His farm became the physical heart that served as a spiritual platform for his indefatigable teaching activities. With copies of his teaching pamphlets, the Bens, always present in his pocket, he never missed an opportunity to share Bahá'u'lláh's message with a visitor or someone at a village shop.[39]

Florence Morton, an old and cherished friend, enjoyed spending time at Evergreen Camp because it gave her an opportunity to get

---

* Most likely, Roy first encountered mandars on his 1907 pilgrimage to the Holy Land. They were long boxes situated against a wall, usually covered by rugs or pillows to make them more comfortable for sitting. As boxes, they were also used for storage.

away from her large New England factory and to enjoy fresh air and greenery. Although she trained in college to be a landscape architect, life's demands intervened, requiring her to set aside that passion to run the family business she inherited after her father died. Florence quickly learned to manage production, staff, and finances to keep the family's business operating. She was someone who could have enjoyed a leisurely life of privilege but chose instead to carry on her father's legacy. The Depression had been particularly hard on her, especially during government-imposed bank holidays when she and other depositors were denied access to their money. As a result, she struggled to fund her factory and pay her hundreds of employees.[40] At Evergreen Camp, she could dig in the dirt, create flower gardens, and otherwise revel in the natural beauty of the property and rid herself—at least for a few days—of the stress that came with hard times. She wrote to a friend about one of her visits when she worked diligently to landscape Roy's grounds:

> Went to "Evergreen" with Hebe Struven & for ten days, excepting three days of down pour, shrouded in clouds, I worked as a day-laborer in that central garden, terracing it to prevent wash, planting 102 perennials, making it permanent as far as possible—the work I intended doing last spring, but couldn't get there. We saw the foliage far & near gradually take on its autumn beauty. Each day more beautiful than the last, and last Wednesday I drove home in such a maze of beauty, mountains, lakes and swollen streams that many times my praise came out audibly. It was a marvelous panorama![41]

Florence delighted in her work at Evergreen Camp but was disturbed at the obviously deteriorating state of Roy's health, the cause of which was unclear to her. Nonetheless, she observed that his welcoming countenance and folksy humor had already made him a favorite among his neighbors. She marveled at his steady influx of visitors. No matter that Roy had built a home in the middle of nowhere;

Florence Morton, first woman to serve as treasurer of the National Spiritual Assembly, landscape architect, businesswoman, and friend of Roy Wilhelm. (USBNA)

people came to him anyway and provided him with a large audience to introduce to Bahá'u'lláh:

> People stream there, rainy days as well as sunny days, and so many have learned about The Cause, came back and ask for more literature, bring gifts of cakes, apples, vegetables, and take away a handful of, and we hear them say, "Oh, My God, Mr. Wilhelm, how are you! & "How glad we are to see you look-ing better." From the farmers as we drive by & Roy waves his hands, they come out to speak & show great friendliness. In the stores, in the bank, always goes a "little Ben" & if they have [indecipherable word] one, he brings out the ides [sic] & they

are all interest, add "extras for luck" etc. His method is a telling one. Soon he'll have a good big group there for a fine public meeting.[42]

In 1936, after his chalet was mostly complete, he invited the villagers from nearby Lovell to tour his property. By that time, Evergreen had become a showplace according to a description in the local newspaper:

As one approaches this mountain home he realizes it's commanding position. Visitors, and there are hundreds of them, are met by the perfect host Mr. Wilhelm. They are first brought to the wide porch with its excellent view. The logs on the wide overhanging balconies are huge in size. The garden in the front of the house and a fountain inlaid with rose quartz set off the immediate surroundings. On the most sultry days there is always a cooling breeze at the lodge because of its high location . . . and at every turn one finds something unique amusing or interesting.[43]

His guests from Lovell must have been especially amazed that one living so simply could show them movies at his remote home. However, it demonstrates Roy's longstanding passion for photography and motion pictures. Indeed, he had been one of those primarily responsible for the creation and maintenance of the films of 'Abdu'l-Bahá's 1912 visit.

His event for the town, held on September 13, was reported in the Lovell newspaper. What seemed to fascinate the reporter the most were the goats: "Mr. Wilhelm is very much interested in the raising of milk goats. Goat's milk is said to be even healthier and more nutritious than cow's milk and the goat eats only one-seventh as much as a cow. The goat will provide all the milk one family can use and at the same time make an ideal family pet. After inspecting the dairy, goat's milk was served to the guests. It tastes exactly like cow's milk—only slightly sweeter."[44]

The large barn at Evergreen Camp (USBNA)

Though the work on the chalet and farm were well underway, Evergreen Camp was not yet Roy's new permanent home. He still needed to spend time at his property in Teaneck and to attend to his brokerage business in New York. As long as he was well enough to travel between the two places he loved, he would continue to make regular journeys between New Jersey and Maine. But Roy was also detaching himself from the many administrative activities he had formerly undertaken in Teaneck, and was slowly transferring his property there to the National Assembly. He could not yet relinquish his responsibilities to continue nurturing his New Jersey Bahá'í children, even when they created challenges.

Between 1922 and 1927, Shoghi Effendi wrote a series of significant letters to the North American community and its National Spiritual Assembly, explaining many aspects of Bahá'í administration as well

266

as setting forth governing principles and policies for its functioning. The Guardian provided guidelines on topics such as how elections should be conducted; who was eligible to vote and to serve; and how records should be kept. He addressed the subject of the importance and structure of the Nineteen Day Feast and gave guidance on how the business of the local community should be conducted during that important meeting. These and many other subjects related to the management of the community were explored in his letters. Horace Holley collected them and, with the approval of the Guardian and the National Assembly, had them published together in the *Bahá'í Newsletter*, then later as a book, *Bahá'í Administration*, a publication that continues to be the foundation for all later guidance on Bahá'í administration. The National Assembly, especially during those early years, assumed the responsibility of educating those it served about the basic principles of Bahá'í administration and of overseeing the establishment and development of Local Spiritual Assemblies.

Prior to Shoghi Effendi's ministry, Roy had served on the New York Board of Council for more than a decade. When, in 1922, that community elected a Local Spiritual Assembly rather than a Board for the first time, he was elected a member. At the outset of the establishment of local Bahá'í institutions, the issue of geographic jurisdiction remained an open question. It was common for those living in neighboring civil jurisdictions to serve on the Local Assembly of the community where they preferred to attend meetings. In 1926, Roy put the question to the National Spiritual Assembly: Was it proper for those living outside a city or town to vote for and serve on that city or town's Local Spiritual Assembly? Part of his motivation for raising this issue was that, over the years, through the efforts of his family, a large number of believers resided in Teaneck Township (which included the neighborhood of West Englewood). Roy felt the time had come for Teaneck to have its own Assembly. The National Assembly agreed, and with the approval of Shoghi Effendi, it determined that Roy, because he did not reside in New York, should no longer be eligible to serve on that Assembly. Because of his question, a new policy regarding the jurisdiction of a locality and its membership was established. From this point onward, believers would be considered voting members only in the civil community in which they resided. Unsurprisingly, Roy was elected to the first Teaneck Assembly in 1926.

In a letter to Shoghi Effendi in 1932, Roy reported with pride that the West Englewood community was actively involved in teaching the Faith and that it had a good Bahá'í spirit. The Guardian's response gave him much of the credit for the health of that community:

> He is very glad to hear of the activities of the West Englewood friends in spreading the Cause and manifesting its spirit. He sincerely hopes that through God's grace and loving kindness their hopes will be fully realized and that they will attract the attention and admiration of all that town. Much of the success they achieve undoubtedly stands to your credit and kind attention. The Master often said that if in a community one person is found who leads a truly Bahá'í life soon the whole of that community will be won over to the Cause. I believe that this remark seems to be true of West Englewood and your life of service.[45]

At the end of a letter to Roy, written only two days later, Shoghi Effendi included a brief note in his own hand and further commented on the activities of West Englewood by saying that he especially welcomed "their exemplary activity in associating themselves with the social and humanitarian efforts exerted by the local authorities in that centre, and in demonstrating, in a tangible manner, the universality of the Cause of Bahá'u'lláh and the vitality of His Faith." The Guardian went on to express the hope that other communities would learn from their example.[46]

At the time Roy decided to build Evergreen Cabin during the 1920s, he was still serving on the New York Spiritual Assembly. He observed that a need existed for a facility that could accommodate large crowds, and he knew that renting such spaces in and around New York City was exceptionally expensive. Furthermore, the annual picnic mandated by 'Abdu'l-Bahá required a large shelter to ensure that it could be held regardless of the weather. So Evergreen Cabin was constructed partially to fill the needs of the metropolitan New York Bahá'í community, as Roy saw them.[47] There was not yet a Local Assembly in Teaneck to which he could bring the proposal of constructing a building for large meetings, and there was therefore no way to determine through consultation if his idea was not only good, but timely. When his local community outgrew the parlors of average homes, his largess allowed the Teaneck friends to move most of their activities to his newly constructed cabin, except during the coldest months, when it was prohibitively expensive to heat the large, drafty building. He continued to own Evergreen Cabin, located only a few steps from his house, despite his stated intention in the early 1930s to convey his New Jersey property to the National Spiritual Assembly.[48] Roy's property was a blessing to the growing suburban community, yet, also presented new issues that helped the community mature.

The first Local Spiritual Assembly for Teaneck Township was established in 1926 just as the friends in the West were learning to understand two important administrative principles: first, decisions for the communities were to be made by duly elected Assemblies; and second, those decisions must be obeyed, even when a particular decision seemed to be in error. These developing institutions were laying the groundwork for the future, ploughing furrows in unturned soil. Even though some members of newly established Local Assemblies had had years of experience serving social, community, political, and ecclesiastic organizations, they had to learn how to manage and follow Bahá'í administration, which was something entirely new. The conduct of Bahá'í institutions was based upon the principles of consultation. No coercion, lobbying, or insistence upon a point of view was to be used to arrive at decisions. Consultation was a search for truth, and a decision based on a search for truth was different from a decision reached through compromise. Moreover, those elected to serve had to see themselves as trustees and servants of their community, and the process of adopting this mindset inevitably led to challenges. The Teaneck Spiritual Assembly experienced the same internal growing pains that other Assemblies were working through, and Roy learned from this as he tried to guide his Local Assembly toward greater unity.[49]

As the work of the Local and National Assemblies rapidly increased in the early 1930s, and Roy was getting well into middle age, his service at both levels of Bahá'í administration became increasingly taxing, even to the point of affecting his health. The National Assembly brought this matter to the attention of Shoghi Effendi, who made clear that national service should take precedence over local service. This new policy would be applied in other similar situations. Reluctantly, Roy resigned from the Teaneck Assembly. In a letter to his local community, he said that "This is to me a matter of profound regrets," for "It is always grievous to be compelled to decide between different avenues of Bahá'í service."[50]

'Abdu'l-Bahá had trained Roy to manage difficult situations and people, and He had relied upon him more than once to do so on His behalf. Shoghi Effendi understood this and, from time to time, also asked Roy to meet with individuals who were of special concern. The Guardian was particularly anxious about those who were reluctant to sever connections with Covenant-breakers. For example, some believers had continued to associate with Dr. Fareed, who had been expelled from the Faith by 'Abdu'l-Bahá, as well as with Ahmad Sohrab, Roy's former acquaintance, who had rebelled against the authority of the Bahá'í institutions and, in the process, had attracted a number of active believers from the New York Bahá'í community to his public gatherings. Roy was called upon to meet with specific people to resolve problems created by these two adversaries of the Faith and to draw them back into the fold. These were delicate assignments "warranting careful handling." But as the Guardian's secretary said to him, "you are experienced enough in the Cause to take care of such matters," because "An old war horse can accomplish any feat."[51] Yet, Shoghi Effendi added in his own hand that Roy needed to take care of his health, for he was "an invaluable and in many respects a unique, international asset to the Cause, and these days through which we are passing are days of intense stress, of unprecedented turmoil and agitation."[52]

Despite his years of experience and tutelage under 'Abdu'l-Bahá, Roy still had much to learn. When he asked Shoghi Effendi to clarify the requirements for admission into the Bahá'í community, he was given new insights into the concept of obedience—one of the strongest traits that exemplified his own character. The response he received must have surprised him because it stated that new believers need not rigidly accept everything in the Bahá'í Writings but instead that "This should be done gradually as the friends become more familiar with the literature of the Cause," for the reason that "Mere mechanical obedience is not only without any enduring benefit but is actually harmful."[53] He was learning that the Faith was organic and flexible in every respect except its core principles.

Roy's mother, Laurie, ever faithful to the Cause she loved dearly, was fading with age and, like her husband, suffered a stroke, most likely in 1935. That December, Roy explained in a letter to Shoghi Effendi how, despite her physical limitations, "her mind is always upon plans for extending the Faith."[54] The Guardian replied that though he grieved at Laurie's "helplessness," her spirit had always been a "great encouragement" to him.[55] On January 21, 1937, Laurie had another stroke and became unconscious. Earlier that day, Martha Root, who was recovering from a life-threatening case of influenza far away in upper New York State, had a vision of Laurie—her other mother—as she herself lay in bed. She felt that Laurie had made a spiritual journey to her adopted daughter to say goodbye.[56]

Roy and his mother, Laurie (USBNA)

Laurie passed away peacefully at the age of eighty-six on the morning of January 26. Roy was "thankful" that his mother did not suffer and "to have had her so many years." At the time of his mother's passing, Roy was also ill with influenza and so was unable to be at her side.[57] The following day, this steadfast Bahá'í handmaiden was laid to rest next to her husband Otis at the nearby Hackensack, New Jersey Cemetery after a Bahá'í funeral service.[58]

Shoghi Effendi was effusive in his praise of Laurie. He sent a cable of condolence to Roy followed by a letter which said in part, "Your loss is indeed irreparable, so also is the loss which the American Bahá'í community has come to suffer. They all cannot but deeply mourn your dearly beloved Mother's departure from their midst. She was to them a living example of virtue, of utter devotion to the Cause. And now that the hand of destiny has so cruelly removed her from their sight, it is hoped they will nevertheless continue for long to cherish her dear memory, and draw from it the strength, faith and confidence she so beautifully exemplified all through her earthly life."[59] The Guardian penned a postscript which must have consoled Roy for it assured him that his mother was with 'Abdu'l-Bahá:

The cable I addressed to you conveys most inadequately my sentiment of profound sympathy and tender affection for you in the severe loss you have sustained. I know how close your dear mother was to you, and I am well aware of her share in the services you have rendered the Cause. I am conscious of your loneliness and feel genuinely concerned for the state of your health. No need to assure you that when I lay my head on the Sacred Threshold, I will most fervently pray for your dear Mother who, I am sure, is now enjoying near access to our Beloved who loved you and her so dearly.

Affectionately,

Shoghi[60]

10 / TWILIGHT ON STONEHAM MOUNTAIN

Following Laurie's passing, Roy, though only in his early sixties, began to disengage from many of his routine endeavors. He spent less and less time in New Jersey, preferring instead his retreat in the mountains of Maine to the West Englewood home so redolent with sweet memories of 'Abdu'l-Bahá's visits as well as other loved ones who were now gone. But he did not let the loneliness to which Shoghi Effendi referred in his letter of condolence when Laurie passed away consume him; instead, he continued to make new friends and created a substitute family of sorts at his Maine home.

Evergreen Camp continued to be a magnet for thousands of people for a variety of reasons. Rather than post "no trespassing signs" and place fences around his land, Roy welcomed and encouraged visitors, especially the many hikers who stopped to see his unusual showpiece home, taking advantage of the spectacular views from the front porch of the chalet. In 1937, Roy wrote to Martha Root that nearly 2,800 "callers" had come to Evergreen Camp and had given him and the other Bahá'ís there many opportunities to tell countless numbers of people about the Faith. He boasted to Martha that they were "giving out more literature than ever before."[1] The number of visitors continued rising until by 1940, Roy was able to inform John Bosch that the Camp had had over 3,300 "callers." He jokingly told his Swiss friend that much of the curiosity sprang from interest in the unique herd of Swiss goats John had recommended to him. Best of all, people from all over the United States and even other countries had heard rumors that Roy was interested in "some strange thing," which drew those who wanted to learn about the Bahá'í Faith to his hillside retreat.[2] He was delighted by the interest his mountain home generated in the Cause and wrote to John that "The other day the Ladies Club, about 50 of our nearby farm and town women sent word and asked if they could meet here and learn about this Faith we believe in. Whoopla! And so it goes. Well, between the whole business I hardly can find time to keep my chin smooth—and now and then have to go back to N.Y.—for a rest."[3]

Despite the remoteness of his Maine home, Roy continued to keep abreast of what was happening throughout much of the rest of the world by scouring the pages of the *New York Times* every day. He carried on extensive official and unofficial Bahá'í correspondence from the chalet while serving as national treasurer. He wrote letter after letter in longhand while standing several hours each day at his draftsman's desk.* He also often dictated letters to a stenographer (a Bahá'í) who would then type the drafts for his approval before getting them promptly off to the postman making his afternoon stop at the Wilhelm farm. If a request from the Guardian arrived, Roy would take immediate action, sometimes sending someone from his household to the nearest large town more than twenty miles away to dispatch a message to the national office in Wilmette. The cables sent by the Guardian arrived first at Roy's New York City office and were then retransmitted by telegraph to North Lovell. The little store in town was the telephone service hub for the area. Before the telegraph operator could send or receive Roy's messages, everyone else had to get off the many telephone lines.[4] And so it went.

---

* A draftsman's desk is built so that the top can be tilted, raised, or lowered depending on whether the user wishes to work sitting or standing.

Roy remained particularly interested in the issue of racial justice even though his Stoneham Mountain neighbors were almost exclusively White. Nonetheless, from that isolated retreat, he found ways to continue his advocacy for the elimination of racial prejudice and the betterment of life for the Black citizens of the country. Over many decades of engagement with this issue, he developed a friendship with the famous Black scientist, educator, and civil rights leader George Washington Carver and introduced him to the Faith.[5] The two remained longtime friends, exchanging correspondence over a period of several years. At one point, Dr. Carver, a renowned botanist, proposed that Roy spend time at Tuskegee Institute, where Carver could observe Roy and hopefully find plant-based remedies for his many ailments.[6]

Because of its intense concern about relations between Black people and White people, the National Spiritual Assembly held special meetings in Nashville and Knoxville, Tennessee, where the members, including Roy, could assess firsthand the existing appalling racial conditions that were impeding the Faith's ability to hold mixed race gatherings. Across the country there were Bahá'í teachers who advocated the oneness of mankind and the importance of the eradication of racial prejudice—bedrock Bahá'í teachings—but the National Assembly knew more had to be done. Social mores and laws existing at the time, especially in the Southern states, made it virtually impossible to hold integrated Bahá'í gatherings because they not only violated local laws and ordinances in many areas, but could likely place the participants in physical danger. For those reasons, White believers in the South were often afraid to participate in integrated gatherings.[7] Frequently, the police, who shared the attitudes of most White citizens, could not be counted on to protect the friends in such a hostile environment. Roy offered his perceptions of the situation as he observed it in Tennessee in a letter to Shoghi Effendi and said that, in his opinion, the problem could only be solved through educating the White race:

> Our trip South was interesting and very instructive. My personal observation is that the fruitful approach will be almost if not quite exclusively with the Whites in the beginning. Once the Whites accept, the problem fades, but in the beginning I am afraid a mixed Spiritual Assembly for instance would prove an almost impassable barrier for a majority of the Whites. In Tennessee the Blacks are said to be approximately one-fourth of the population. They tell me that they are well treated but are deprived of earning in the trades, professions, etc. A colored person is not permitted in hotel corridors, elevators, public gatherings, etc. Further South it is said the colored outnumber the whites ten to one, with some unrest. If a colored man becomes educated, he must come North to find suitable employment. The question seems to be the education of the white race.[8]

In 1938, Shoghi Effendi wrote a lengthy letter to the American community, which was later published as a book, *The Advent of Divine Justice*. In his concise yet amazingly accurate exposition of the state of American society coming from one who had never set foot in North America, he included frank remarks about the scourge of racism, which he termed the "most vital and challenging issue" facing the United States.[9] Directly addressing sentiments such as those expressed by Roy, the Guardian emphasized that both the Black and White races had roles to play in eliminating the deep-seated racism which was destroying the moral and spiritual fiber of the nation.[10] Good intentions would never be enough; courageous action was required. Roy and his colleagues took this guidance to heart and redoubled their efforts to raise up integrated Bahá'í communities, free of prejudice, throughout the country—especially in the Southern states.[11]

At the forefront of the work of bringing the Faith to the Black population was Roy's esteemed colleague, Louis Gregory, for whom

Roy had developed not only great admiration but sincere brotherly affection. They both served many years together on the National Assembly, and Louis was always a welcome guest in Roy's New Jersey and Maine homes. In 1943, Roy was given an opportunity to speak up on Louis' behalf when his dear friend was treated unjustly solely because of his race. In the Southern states, "Jim Crow" laws existed at the time that prohibited the mixing of races in public places, including requiring that Black and White people be separated on public transportation. A situation arose following a National Assembly meeting when Louis bought a more expensive train ticket than usual for his trip from Chicago to Nashville because he was not feeling well. His ticket entitled him to a seat in one of the more comfortable Pullman cars, where he could rest. Though he was undisturbed during the first leg of his journey, problems arose for him when the train reached Cincinnati, where a conductor informed him that he would have to move to the car reserved for Black passengers even though he had paid for a better seat. Louis refused to move. When the train crossed the Ohio river and entered the southern state of Kentucky, he was removed from the train, arrested for violating a "Jim Crow" law, and forced to spend a night in jail. Taking advantage of the unexpected opportunity to meet new people, even though under adverse circumstances, Louis taught the Faith to his jailer that evening. The next day, the judge dismissed the case, and Louis was permitted to proceed to his destination on the condition that he had to sit in the car reserved for Black passengers.[12]

Roy responded to this outrageous treatment of his friend. Rather than write a scolding letter to those responsible for Louis's arrest, he wrote to the judge in Kentucky to praise him for his wise and appropriate action in dismissing the charges against Louis. In his letter, Roy sought to elevate the judge's thinking about Black people by telling him of Louis's attainments and sterling character, for if the judge looked beyond Louis's color, he would see before him an outstanding citizen of note. His letter, however, also reminded the judge that the laws invoked to harass Louis violated national laws regarding impeding interstate travel.[13] Tactfully, he approached the

Louis Gregory, a close friend to Roy Wilhelm who stayed as a guest at both the Wilhelm home in Teaneck and at Evergreen Camp in Maine. (USBNA)

matter by praising the positive rather than condemning those who charged Louis unjustly. Years earlier, 'Abdu'l-Bahá had tutored Roy about how to manage troubling situations—to stress the good over the bad—and Roy always tried to apply this principle.

It always made Roy happy when, from time to time, Martha Root returned to the United States from her global travels. She tried to keep those visits to friends and family brief so that she could resume her teaching work, but she generally liked to include a visit to Roy's New Jersey home. Over the years, this single woman, traveling alone—something frowned upon at the time—took the Faith to an extraordinary number of countries in every corner of the globe. If needed, Roy was ready to send aid to Martha. She, however, was only willing to accept his financial assistance when there was no other choice but to do so, and she most often insisted upon reimbursing him whenever she was able.[14] Once Roy tried to send her emergency funds and ended up having to wire money to three different countries before she finally received it.[15] She appreciated his role as her trusted friend and financial safety net and sent him details of her expenditures, even recounting how she was restricting her food purchases, so that he could see that she was managing by herself. His love and admiration for Martha grew all the more. In his mirthful yet practical fashion, Roy reminded her that his financial resources were for the service of the Cause and said, "'Wilhelmite' is thus far a spring in which Bahá'u'lláh deposits as fast—even faster than the water is withdrawn. . . . Keep me informed at all times as to your financial outlook say for sixty to ninety days ahead of you."[16]

While traveling in Sweden in December 1935, Martha suffered an accident from which she was slow to recover.[17] Roy offered his home as a place for her to rest and recuperate and offered to pay her expenses to get there. Shoghi Effendi had learned of her situation and had judged from photographs of her that she had become "extremely weak and frail." Through his secretary, he wrote Martha to endorse Roy's offer and urged her to accept the invitation.[18]

When Martha returned to the United States the following July, in 1936, Roy, along with a delegation of National Assembly members, was at the New York City dock to welcome her. The Guardian had asked the National Assembly to ensure she received an appropriate reception worthy of the indefatigable, historic, and sacrificial work she had performed on multiple continents.[19] After a visit to her family in Pennsylvania, she joined Roy at his new log home at Stoneham Mountain for a two-month-long rest—a rest ordered by Shoghi Effendi himself. The National Assembly established a subcommittee composed of Mountfort Mills,* Horace Holley, and Roy to ensure that no Bahá'í activities be scheduled for her without her doctor's consent.[20] The breast cancer that had afflicted her for more than two decades was taking its toll, as was her age. Adding to her health problems were the burdens she imposed on herself by traveling third-class, enduring unheated hotel rooms, and eating a sparse diet. She was worn out.

Martha Root addresses the 1936 Souvenir Picnic, the last time she would attend it. (USBNA)

---

* Mountfort Mills had come to know Martha well when both were sent as a team by Shoghi Effendi to represent the Faith at international conferences at The Hague.

This was Martha's first and only visit to Evergreen Camp. She must have found it beautiful, delightful, and peaceful while relaxing on its front porch gazing out beneath the trees and across stunning mountain vistas to catch glimpses of the lake below. Roy and his staff were loving and solicitous of her every need. Life at the chalet without modern amenities must have reminded her of her childhood. For almost two months, she had little to do except rest. Most of the time, she stayed in bed.[21]

Though neither Roy nor Martha seemed to have written much about that extended time together, no doubt they spent hours discussing the work of the Faith and Martha's travels. One can well imagine those two saintly believers—Roy and Martha—warming themselves by the fire in the chalet's huge stone fireplace, sitting and talking together in the evening, and sharing their mutual love of the Faith, sprinkled with a copious dose of Roy's humor.

One of the few friends allowed to visit Martha was the daughter of Harry and Ruth Randall, Margaret, called Bahíyyih, a name bestowed upon her by 'Abdu'l-Bahá. She found her dear Bahá'í sister Martha sitting up in an upstairs bedroom—a tiny figure enveloped by a mammoth bed. Having known her for many years, Bahíyyih was alarmed as soon as she got a good look at Martha and asked her why she had refused to see a doctor. The reason should have been obvious—Martha was afraid a doctor would order her to stop traveling for the Faith, and she was not willing to do that as long as she could muster the strength to go on. Martha sensed her time was short and did not wish to waste a moment. She was only willing to try to restore her health if she knew she had any hope of traveling again.[22]

By October, thanks to the clear mountain air, sleep, and the tender care she received under Roy's supervision, Martha was given a doctor's permission to resume some of her activities, including a limited public speaking schedule in the United States.[23] As a member of the committee that had to approve her resumption of Bahá'í work, Roy must have had to delicately balance his concern about her health with her powerful desire to promote the Faith. He wanted her safe and well cared for. She, of course, wanted to tell the whole world about Bahá'u'lláh.

Speckled Mountain Sept 1936   Mrs Howard Struven
Roy Wilhelm
Martha Root

Roy, Martha Root, and others getting fresh air and exercise in the fields of Evergreen Camp, September 1936. She had been ordered to rest to restore her health. (USBNA)

After her lengthy stay with Roy, Martha remained in the United States for several months before embarking again for foreign shores, sailing from California. Treating her as a concerned brother, Roy chided her about her habit of traveling without exercising caution and wisdom: "There is one remark in your letter that deserve [sic] a challenge. You say, Well anyway Bahá'u'lláh "will go" with me. No, Martha Bahá'u'lláh goes with us just to the extent that we use cautiousness & wisdom. We can't blame things on Bahá'u'lláh if we strain that law in any degree. I know too well that a good many of my troubles this past two years were avoidable I am going to be wiser now!"[24]

Roy passed his care for Martha into the hands of Shoghi Effendi when, upon sailing to the Far East in June 1937, she resumed her travels. Roy knew the political situation in that region was deteriorating as Japan's war machine was ramping up, so he expected war to break out at any moment. He advised Martha that "If in the future serious developments should take place, I am certain Shoghi Effendi will advise and make provision for you."[25] He could not, however, resist adding some of his own suggestions as to how to cope with seasickness—mal de mer, as he called it. Martha, who had sailed far more than Roy, hardly needed that brotherly advice.[26]

There is no record of where Roy and Martha last said good-bye to each other as she headed into the sunset on what she intended to be another global tour. They both no doubt sensed that their future connection would be a purely spiritual one, and that they would never see each other again in this world.

When 1938 arrived, the United States was still in the grip of the Great Depression, while Europe and the Far East on the other sides of the Atlantic and Pacific Oceans were tinderboxes, with the matches already lit by land-hungry authoritarian regimes. In time, those international crises would affect the Bahá'í community, though not immediately. Despite ominous war clouds and continued financial austerity, the American Bahá'í community was doing well overall, and the mood among the believers was generally optimistic as many answered the call of the Seven Year Plan to arise to spread the Faith to new territories and countries. Over the previous decade, the National Assembly had emerged stronger and wiser despite struggling through a series of severe tests a few years earlier. Notable among those tests had been the public defection of Ahmad Sohrab, which had taxed Roy's spiritual strength when he was called upon to carry out attempts to rescue those caught in Sohrab's web. But those tests were, for the most part, resolved, and the National Assembly was moving forward as an institution with confidence.[27] Furthermore, Local Assemblies, particularly those serving the larger Bahá'í communities, were gaining the necessary experience and maturity to better direct the affairs of their communities. Roy, as always, focused on these positive developments, rather than the remaining deficiencies.

With the North American Bahá'í community's successful completion of the first year of their Seven Year Plan, Roy's report to Shoghi

Effendi about the 1938 Convention was upbeat and full of hope. This first true national teaching plan* had three ambitious goals: continue to build the House of Worship by erecting the superstructure of the dome; open all of the countries in Central and South America to the Faith; and establish at least one center of Bahá'í activities in every state of the United States and every province of Canada.[28] Reports from newly settled pioneers and traveling teachers lifted everyone's spirits, which seemed to magically make the teaching work in older communities more successful. The erection of the House of Worship was continuing apace; indeed, it had become one of the few monumental buildings under construction in the nation during the Depression. Pleased, Shoghi Effendi wrote an encouraging letter to Roy extolling the many achievements of the North American community. He also took the opportunity to praise Roy's sound judgment and remarked that "The views you have expressed, although personal, are so sound, and so high above the plane of egoistic feelings and selfish considerations" that he had "derived considerable delight and illumination in sharing them."[29] As to the North American community, the Guardian remarked to Roy as to how it had proven its worth:

> This year's Convention, indeed, as you have judiciously remarked, bore one more striking witness to the fact that the Administrative Order in America has achieved such a unity of understanding and action among the believers that no storm, however mighty, can any longer shake, much less undermine, their one basic loyalty to the Cause. The Faith, unhampered by the perpetual and inevitable forces of disintegration that assail it, both from within and without, is forging ahead, its

---

* The first plan adopted by the North American Bahá'í community was called the Plan of Unified Action. It was devised by the National Spiritual Assembly with the enthusiastic blessing of Shoghi Effendi. Its defect was its vagueness. Despite that deficiency, it was a good beginning, for it required the National Assembly to learn to manage the teaching work and the construction of the Temple more systematically.

growth maintained nay steadily increased, its unity unimpaired, and the Divine destiny, with which it has been invested by the Almighty Providence as the one ark of salvation in a rapidly declining world, becoming increasingly evident to the eyes of an unbelieving humanity.[30]

Even though these growing Bahá'í achievements raised Roy's spirits, they came at a time when his health was deteriorating at a more rapid pace than in the past. While there are no records of his exact ailments, various reports make clear that he had experienced chronic digestive problems from the time he was in his thirties and that he had contracted influenza three times in three months during 1937, which indicated that he had a repressed immune system.[31] For most of his life, Roy had also suffered continual pain from a back injury. When he was a teenager, he had jumped from a barn loft into a wagon full of straw, unaware of a hidden pitchfork that impaled his back. The result was back pain that plagued him the rest of his life. To reduce his chronic pain, he used a custom-made draftsman's desk that allowed him to sit on a tall stool or stand while he wrote.[32] Over the years, he tried a variety of treatments for his aches and pains, including unconventional ones, but only received limited relief.[33] Finally, with his health failing, during the late summer of 1938, he wrote to Shoghi Effendi seeking permission to resign from the National Assembly. Though fully aware of Roy's poor health, the Guardian begged him to reconsider. He knew Roy would never ask to resign unless his health problems made his service unbearable, especially arduous travel to attend meetings. In the letter written on his behalf, Shoghi Effendi said that he considered such a resignation from membership in a Bahá'í Assembly as contrary to the principles of the Administration, and he strongly felt that Roy's presence on the National Assembly at that crucial time was a considerable asset to that body. To reinforce this message, Shoghi Effendi said in a postscript: "To dissociate yourself, even temporarily and officially from the deliberations and strivings of the National Assembly, would, I assure you, cause me infinite regret and sadness. Your presence is such a stabilizing factor, your participation such a source of strength and progress. I do not feel, however, if your health does not permit it, that it would be necessary for you to take a strenuous part in its manifold activities." The Guardian, as he usually did, assured Roy that he would offer prayers for his health and continued service.[34]

What could Roy do but, like a good soldier, carry on. Immensely pleased, Shoghi Effendi wrote that, "I am aware of the burden you carry and of the responsibilities you shoulder, but I am fully convinced that you fulfil a role and contribute a share to the common task that the Faith can ill afford to dispense with these days."[35] The Guardian signed the postscript, "Affectionately, Shoghi."

Adding to his other cares, Roy had Martha's personal safety on his mind. It is easy to imagine how worried Roy must have been reading one dire headline after another about the calamities and dangers in cities where his dear Martha was sojourning. She experienced the bombing of Shanghai in China, fled to the Philippines just as a major earthquake struck, and then headed to British-controlled India at the same time as England was trying to avert being drawn into war with Germany. Roy must have felt the pangs that come from being helpless, for even though she was keeping the National Assembly informed of her whereabouts as best she could, his ability to assist her often became impossible. Finally, in 1939, she determined it was time to return home to America.[36]

On her voyage back across the Pacific, Martha sent messages ahead to the Bahá'ís living at ports where she would be making stops. When her ship docked in Honolulu, two Bahá'ís came on board to welcome her: Katherine Baldwin and Henriette From. They found her so ill that they insisted that she accompany them ashore to obtain proper medical treatment. Katherine opened her home to Martha and gave her a loving environment in which to rest and recover her health.

From that point on, through cables and letters from Katherine, Roy was kept closely informed of Martha's condition and living arrangements. When she was able, Martha sent letters addressed jointly to a handful of her closest friends, including Roy. He, of course, offered to do whatever he could, especially to send money if needed. Martha, as usual, sent a detailed record of her mounting medical expenses, while insisting on paying for them from her own resources. She was determined to get better. If war forced her to remain away from the Far East, she envisioned traveling throughout Central America. Alas, it was not to be. The breast cancer she had held at bay for decades finally overcame her.[37]

At the end of July, in a confidential letter to Roy, Katherine informed him that the doctors treating Martha saw no hope of her recovery and could only make her as comfortable as possible. She assured Roy that caring for Martha was a blessing for her and the other Bahá'ís in Honolulu:

> Naturally I have felt a great responsibility because she does belong to the Baha'i world, in addition to my own personal love for her. But I want to reassure you again that every thing we can possibly think of will be done for this glorious Soul, whose name will pass down in history from age to age as the outstanding teacher of this present age. Often I find myself wondering why we in Hawaii have been so outstandingly blessed as to be given the tremendous privilege to care for our beloved Martha during her last illness. The thought is almost more than I can stand at times![38]

Roy responded to that letter by informing Katherine that he had notified Shoghi Effendi about Martha's condition and circumstances. Roy added words that probably comforted not only Katherine, but Martha as well, when his letter was shared with her.

> . . . I have compared Martha's herculean efforts to the beetle which in the writings was said to have even striven to attain

the <u>musk-sac</u>. 'Abdu'l-Bahá went with me to a hospital to see a woman who was in the advanced stages of this trouble and who had been somewhat attracted. He greatly comforted her by saying that this world seemed a long and important experience to us, but in reality it was less than an instant as God reckoned time and was hardly more important than the wing of an insect. A smile came over her tired face . . . the following day she passed from this "vale of tears."[39]

On August 28, Katherine wrote to Roy to learn the wishes of the National Assembly regarding funeral arrangements for Martha. A week later, Martha sent a letter to Roy and a few others with details about the distribution of her estate and directing that her will and testament be entrusted to Roy. She added that, "I am so near the shore of eternity . . ."[40] During her last days, in moments of delirium, she called out Roy's name numerous times.[41]

Roy wrote one last letter to his dear friend, but she never had an opportunity to read it for she peacefully passed away on September 28, the day after it was written.[42] Based on all reports, Roy informed Katherine that he was satisfied that Martha's finances had been taken care of and that, as she desired, Honolulu would be an appropriate resting place. He also forwarded funds from Shoghi Effendi designated to be used for a fitting monument for her grave.[43] His note evinced deep gratitude for all that the Hawaiian friends had done for his spiritual sister.[44]

Shoghi Effendi sent a message to the North American Bahá'í community on October 3 announcing Martha's passing, extolling her extraordinary heroic service—the "finest fruit" the Formative Age had yet produced—and naming her the foremost of the Hands of the Cause of God as she joined the galaxy of Bahá'í immortals.[45] He was well-aware of how close Roy had been to Martha. In a later letter, he expressed his own words of condolence to him for the loss of one who was like a member of Roy's family. In a letter written on the Guardian's behalf, he said that "To you, & to all the dear American friends who are now so profoundly deploring beloved Martha's passing, the

Guardian feels moved to convey the assurances of his deepest & most loving sympathy in your great bereavement."[46] He added in his own hand that he rejoiced "at the glory & joy that must be hers & which she fully deserves, in the Abha Paradise."[47] Roy must have taken great comfort in that assurance, though he had undoubtedly reached the same conclusion about her worth many years before. Years later, Roy penned his own tribute to his longtime coworker and devoted friend saying, "Martha was a unique [sic]. She seemed to have been born for her special work. I doubt if there is another who has brought attention to the Faith to so many tens of thousands over so many corners of the earth. I sometimes think my chief reason for being born was to get Martha started."[48]

Having already lost his parents, Roy must have felt much more alone in the world after Martha's death. Following his mother's death, when his beloved Martha had headed off into the dangers of the Far East, Roy went through a brief spurt of researching his own family's genealogy.[49] He found he had no remaining blood relations other than distant cousins. He once remarked during the last years of his life that he envied those who had children.[50] Other people would need to replace those whose memories he held tightly within his heart.

Other major changes—particularly to the work of the officers of the National Assembly—occurred in Roy's life at around the same time as Martha's passing in the autumn of 1939. As far back as 1930, Evergreen Cabin had served as a hub for Bahá'í administration, especially for Roy's work as treasurer. It was also the headquarters for the production and distribution of Bahá'í publications. Over the years, with both men living and working in the New York metropolitan area, Roy and Horace Holley, as treasurer and secretary of the Assembly, had developed a strong relationship and had worked together at their desks in the national office Roy had created on the second floor of the cabin. Over time, however, the National Assembly concluded that its secretariat should be transferred nearer to the House of Worship in Wilmette. That way, being more geographically central for its disparate membership, the offices would be anchored at a headquarters and no longer move to wherever the officers resided. Obediently, as secretary, Horace agreed to relocate to Illinois and made the move in October 1939. A few months later, once the secretariat was firmly established in Wilmette, the National Assembly decided to also move the treasury and publishing work there as well. Roy's cabin was no longer needed as a national office once Bertha Herklotz (who served primarily as Roy's assistant handling the clerical work of the treasury) and Clara R. Wood (who ran the publications office) moved to the Chicago area.[51]

Under Horace's on-site supervision on behalf of Roy, Bertha organized the Office of the Treasurer in its new space with the help of Sophie Loeding, a newly hired aide to the secretary.[52] Whenever Roy was in Wilmette for National Assembly meetings, in keeping with his responsibilities as treasurer, he took time to review and manage work being done on his behalf at the new national center. A few years after relocating, his longtime friend Bertha was injured in an accident, requiring her to return to New York where she could be cared for by her family. Loretta Voeltz, a young woman from a dedicated Kenosha, Wisconsin, Bahá'í family, was hired to replace her. Loretta remembered that Roy wrote her a letter of welcome, which congratulated her for working for the Faith.[53]

Meeting the ongoing expenses of an office, especially the salaries of the staff, placed an added burden on the Faith's already overly stretched finances. A construction contract could be deferred, but not payroll and office expenses. Loretta said Roy was often visibly discouraged when there were insufficient contributions to cover bills because he had nowhere to turn for help. In despair, he would put his head down on a piece of furniture and then, after that moment of grief passed, pay many of the bills out of his own pocket.[54]

Roy, with his keen mind, attention to detail, understanding of business methods, and practical mindset, was especially suited for the work of Bahá'í administration. Over the years, these traits served the national governing body well, especially as the National Assembly developed its treasury and National Fund. Correspondence between 'Abdu'l-Bahá, Shoghi Effendi, and Roy, plus a legion of notations in National Convention and National Assembly minutes, highlighted his unwavering role as a financial safety net and wise advisor when it came to finance and business matters. Just as he was generous with his gifts to Shoghi Effendi and to Martha, Roy was always ready to help the National Assembly with his checkbook. For example, on one occasion, he supplied two dozen folding chairs for the 1925 National Convention at Green Acre; another time he contributed the money needed to publish an issue of *Bahá'í Magazine* when a shortfall in funds occurred.[55] Sometimes he provided loans to the National Assembly, for which he usually did not ask to be repaid. He used his connections and experience in the financial world to cement good relations between the Bahá'í institutions and banks. Because of the international nature of his business, he knew how to move funds not only to Palestine but to the Bahá'í pioneers working to bring the Faith to countries throughout the Western Hemisphere.

Roy understood the important principle of universal participation in giving to the funds of the Faith and that, for the Faith to truly grow, it could not rely solely on the largess of a handful of wealthy believers. The secretary of the Chicago Assembly, Keith Ransom-Kehler, reported "that out of about 130 members, at least 90 were contributors and all were poor."[56] To which Roy responded as a New Yorker that, "this beats our record in regard to numbers which is the essential thing in order to bring about unity in giving."[57] Another time, Roy spoke on the importance of supporting the treasury and stated, "there are certain cities where a few people are known to have means and possibly some have felt that it did not make much difference whether they gave much or not."[58] He added that, unfortunately, "believers ignored the reality and assumed things would be taken care of anyhow . . . a tendency to let a few take the responsibility of giving and doing the work."[59] Roy felt that it was important for the friends to understand that "most of the people who have means are doing all they can . . . and it is quite possible that some of them are doing more than some on our list who are doing nothing. We must take our obligations seriously and if there is not enough to meet the rent we must get down to meet our incomes."[60] He added that "We would stop at nothing to stop a big war if we knew it were coming. I would be in favor of letting things come to a level where they belong until we can come to the point where we arise to our responsibility and privilege."[61]

From the time of the Temple Unity Executive Committee to the end of his service on the National Assembly, Roy played a significant role in managing the real estate of the Faith. In 1927, when the National Assembly gained possession of Green Acre, it had to establish a legal method of holding property since it was not yet incorporated. The National Assembly set up an Indenture of Trust, and Roy was made one of the three trustees legally responsible for that Maine property. This responsibility would grow in the following years as more and more real estate was given to or purchased by the National Assembly.[62]

Roy's administrative contributions were not limited to finances and property. He brought up important issues that he felt the Assembly needed to better understand. One such topic was the requirement of maintaining the Assembly's confidentiality—which was vital to retaining the trust of those it served. Roy told his colleagues that if anything discussed in their meetings was repeated away from the council table, it made public something that should remain private and could prove to be injurious. He emphatically stated that, "We must consider private any reference to the opinions expressed and personalities mentioned in an Assembly meeting, must remain confidential."[63] This was a new concept to those accustomed to American organizations, which generally prized transparency.

Martha's passing occurred less than a month after Germany invaded Poland in September 1939, marking the full onset of World War II in Europe, Africa, and the Near East; though in truth, however, the war had already been raging in other parts of the world, especially in Asia.[64] When Great Britain declared war on Germany, Canada, as a member of the British Commonwealth of Nations, was drawn into the conflict. Palestine, under British administration, also soon became a theater of war. Though still officially neutral, the United States adopted a war footing. (The United States would not enter the conflict directly until attacked by Japan in Honolulu in December, 1941.) This turn of events had immediate repercussions for the North American Bahá'ís, especially the Canadian believers whose travel arrangements were subjected to wartime restraints. Bahá'ís the world over worried about the personal safety of the Guardian and his household as well as the holy places in Israel. They had not forgotten World War I when 'Abdu'l-Bahá was cut off from the world and in constant mortal danger.

Roy had anticipated that war was inevitable for years before it began, because he knew that 'Abdu'l-Bahá and Shoghi Effendi had alluded to the coming of another great war after World War I.[65] In 1935, he wrote to Shoghi Effendi to suggest that funds be sent to the World Center in case Palestine was cut off. During the darkest days of World War I, sending much-needed funds to 'Abdu'l-Bahá became impossible. Roy recounted the time when he had tried to send gold to 'Abdu'l-Bahá during that period, and that those who agreed to transmit it between Beirut and Haifa had demanded half of it as payment for their services. In his role as the North American Bahá'í postman for the Faith, Roy was also interested in devising means to transmit delicate communications during a crisis. He proposed a system to alert the Guardian with a code word if he heard that war had broken out: "Should war be declared, New York might know of it in advance of the East—if everything were not immediately blocked I would try and penetrate with the word FULFILLED, perhaps errand fulfilled."[66]

In his personal response, Shoghi Effendi replied that he was "deeply touched by these ever-recurring evidences of your watchful care, your unfailing solicitude and eagerness to promote and safeguard the interests of our beloved Faith at its world centre."[67] Nonetheless, he did not wish to deflect the resources of the friends from fulfilling the more urgent needs of the hour, especially the teaching work. He agreed that the world situation was indeed serious but did not anticipate the closing of communications in the immediate future.[68] In the body of the letter, his secretary expressed the Guardian's thoughts about a coming war: "Regarding the next war; . . . He feels . . . that there is at present no danger of any immediate outbreak, although the international situation is causing much fear, and is growing more and more agitated. There are certainly many dark clouds on the horizon, but it is very improbable that the general cataclysm we are all expecting some day to take place will happen in the <u>immediate</u> future."[69]

After England and Canada entered the war in 1939, life at the chalet and the nearby small mountain communities continued with little change. Roy tended to his goats, cattle, and the dwindling number of guests as before. At night, he gathered close to the radio with friends to listen to the somber voices of broadcasters reporting about the worsening situations as war spread from country to country. An unrestrained Germany had already invaded Poland to the east, had marched west through Belgium, and from there had invaded France. For many Americans, the conflict was Europe's problem alone and should stay its problem.

American entry into the war was, nonetheless, inevitable. Everything changed for Roy and the country early on Sunday morning, December 7, 1941, with the Japanese attack on the US Navy at Pearl Harbor, followed a few days later by Germany declaring war against the United States. The nation was now forced into the war, and its mood shifted accordingly. Words of patriotism, duty, and honor filled the newspapers and airways. Factories emptied of young men, as multitudes enlisted or were drafted into military duty. Machines producing essential war materials were almost immediately turned over to a sea of women who took on the jobs vacated by men. Men of all ages from the small towns of Maine's mountains went to work in the shipyards by the coast. The snowshoe factory located near his chalet ramped up production to outfit troops soon to be fighting in the frigid zones of the conflict.[70] The war created a labor shortage, which required Roy to make difficult decisions—the most painful of which was to drastically cull his goat herd because he lacked the staff to tend it and the military had no need of goat's milk. He kept just enough goats to start breeding them again when the war was over.[71] Like all civilians too old to be drafted, the war still required sacrifices of men like Roy.

In early 1942, after the United States entered the war, just at the same time as Roy was first contemplating making his Maine chalet his primary residence, he wrote to Shoghi Effendi and offered the use of his New Jersey home as a place of refuge for him if the situation in the Holy Land became dangerous.[72] Grateful, the Guardian responded by cable, saying "Extremely touched further evidence valued solicitude. Your home my home, if occasion arises."[73]

The war had a big effect upon Roy's coffee brokerage. New orders for coffee for the military filled the inbox in Roy's Wall Street office, though coffee became a rationed commodity for civilians. Even though war was hell, some businesses, such as Roy's, prospered because of it.

War can stimulate feelings of common purpose and loyalty to one's side, but it can also provoke paranoid mistrust of the unfamiliar. This unjustified paranoia can also be spurred on by deep-seated racism and anti-immigrant sentiment. Longtime friends and colleagues may suddenly seem suspicious if they or their ancestors sprang from the same group as the enemy. Viewed through the lens of well-intended hypervigilance during a period when fears of invasion were well founded, German and Japanese Americans came to be perceived as potential spies or saboteurs. German submarines were operating along the Atlantic and Gulf of Mexico coasts of the United States and sinking ships. There were reports of German submarines coming up rivers in New England to deliver saboteurs. In the interest of national security during the war, thousands—Japanese Americans, German Americans and Italian Americans—were unjustly interred in camps around the country.[74]

In this milieu of fear stoked by misguided xenophobia and paranoia, people with German-sounding surnames came under closer scrutiny, especially if the individuals seemed odd. What about that wealthy man from New York who lived a sheltered life on a mountain in the back country of Maine, who entertained a constant stream of strange visitors, and who raised an odd variety of goats? His unusual life and German-sounding last name raised suspicions. Who would be more likely to be up to no good than a mild-mannered, friendly fellow named Wilhelm, who regularly sent telegrams worldwide and wired money to Palestine and other faraway places from the Lovell general store?[75] To a few of Roy's neighbors in Maine, these factors seemed to be more than a coincidence. Someone concluded that he was a German spy who was transmitting shipping secrets to submarines in Portland Harbor by flashing lights from his chalet high on a hillside in Western Maine. Roy was anonymously reported to the Federal Bureau of Investigation. As one who remembered those rumors stated, they were unfounded and absurd:

> . . . a rumor started that Roy Wilhelm was a German spy, it was reported that lights were frequently observed flashing at night, some type of signaling. The false story continued that Wilhelm, a German name, was spying on shipping in the Atlantic and sending that info to a German contact. That is ridiculous because his home was 100 miles from the Atlantic Ocean. The FBI came to investigate anyway. Roy had just installed in the barn several large overhead fans. The FBI took measurements of the barn and concluded there was a secret room. They partially dismantled the building looking for the hidden room.

There was no hidden room or secret spy activities, just jealous neighbors.[76]

What were the flashing lights? Nothing more than a game Roy played with local boys camping on Rattlesnake Island in nearby Kezar Lake. The boys would flick their flashlights on and off, and sometimes Roy would playfully flash back to them from his porch. The incident, no doubt, caused Roy and the ones who loved him a great deal of anguish. Even after the FBI decided that there was nothing to the rumors, envious neighbors remained suspicious. Years after the war, when reviewing that period, the Lovell Historical Society's journal went on to point out that "a Bahá'í leader seeking privacy and spirituality in the Maine woods was much less intriguing than a putative German spy."[77]

That was not the only trouble that erupted during the war. The international cables and letters flowing through Roy's office from the Holy Land also attracted the attention of government wartime censors. To mitigate their concerns, the National Spiritual Assembly provided him with an official letter to explain that, in his capacity as a member of the National Assembly, he was directing correspondence for transmission to individuals, and that the National Assembly took full responsibility for all this correspondence.[78]

Roy commented on the state of the world a month after the United States entered the war saying in exasperation: "Such a sick old world but hardly ready yet to listen to the Remedy."[79]

In 1942, during America's first year at war, Roy decided it was time to hand over the day-to-day responsibility of managing his business to a trustworthy business associate, though he never completely divorced himself from it.[80] This accomplished, he made Evergreen Camp his primary residence and allowed the National Assembly to find tenants for his New Jersey home. He continued to attend National Assembly meetings as best he could and to keep abreast of what was happening in the wider world. For years, he had supplied Shoghi Effendi with newspaper clippings, a practice which was appreciated and encouraged. That would not stop. But his declining health required him to have less stress, less strenuous activity and, above all, less travel. He had extra firewood cut for the sugarhouse—called Evergreen Cottage—to make it suitable for winter and hunkered in.[81]

Roy on the porch of the chalet. (USBNA)

No matter where Roy resided, Shoghi Effendi made clear that he continued to be among those whom he trusted, especially when it came to shoring up those who had difficulty with firmness in the Covenant. Writing on his behalf, Shoghi Effendi's secretary explained how the Guardian saw Roy's position in the North American community:

> He is always happy to hear from you, as he values both your affection and your opinions very highly, indeed he wishes you would feel free to write him in more detail of any matters you feel are important, as your views concerning the general progress of the Cause and state of the friends. You are a very old believer, one might say an immovable pillar of the Faith in America, and the Guardian likes to have these old and trusted ones keep in close touch with him. The winds of test and trial have blown upon our Faith more than once, and he strongly feels the old believers like yourself should do everything in their power to protect the younger Bahá'ís, to strengthen their faith, deepen them in the Covenant, and enable them to take full refuge in the Will and Testament of the beloved Master, that impregnable fortress He built for our safety when He Himself should have gone from our sight.[82]

Despite the war, the Bahá'ís in North America continued to carry out the Seven Year Plan, which was scheduled to conclude at the time of the celebration of the 100th anniversary of the Declaration of the Báb in 1944. Achieving the Plan's goals became especially difficult once the war broke out; however, it continued to be possible to dispatch pioneers and traveling teachers to most goal areas because most of the fighting never spread to the Western Hemisphere. Raising funds for the House of Worship was especially challenging when the Plan began in 1937 at the height of the Depression; however, by 1940, the economy had not only improved but had begun to roar back as industries and agriculture ramped up production. With funds available and travel difficult but not impossible, international pioneers dispatched home exciting reports about the receptivity they were finding in place after place. New Local Spiritual Assemblies were established not only in Central and South America but in the United

States and Canada due to the sacrificial efforts of the pioneers. It was a heady time to be an American Bahá'í. Roy was in the thick of it as not only the National Assembly treasurer but as an avid correspondent ready to be of assistance to pioneers and travel teachers working in the field. In 1941, Shoghi Effendi wrote to him as treasurer that "conscious of the state of the National Fund and realizing the urgency of the task facing its administrators," he did not wish for Americans to continue making contributions to the International Fund for the remainder of the Plan, so that those limited funds could be used for "the work which is now vitally facing and challenging the friends in the teaching field."[83]

It must have seemed like a miracle when, in April 1944, Bahá'ís from all over the Americas gathered for the first time beneath the dome of the House of Worship to celebrate the centenary of the establishment of the Faith. The gathering was held during the darkest days of World War II when most of the other Bahá'í communities across the world could only dream of publicly celebrating such a momentous anniversary. Fully aware of the unfulfilled longing of their sister communities, the North Americans made their celebration the best festival possible. The interior of the House of Worship was far from complete, yet they were able to place folding chairs on the floor of the cavernous sanctuary, even though it remained a construction site.[84] The greatest thrill was not only seeing the resplendent beauty of the completed exterior dome but seeing the Temple illumined in all its ethereal glory at night. Floodlights had been installed at the last minute for the centenary.[85] Roy, who had helped with planning and carrying out of the occasion—even chairing one of its sessions—must have been overjoyed![86] Since being elected to the Executive Board of Temple Unity in 1909 (or 1910), he had worked relentlessly to bring the House of Worship into reality. Finally, the amazing, unique edifice stood as a beacon of hope in a hopeless world.

The members of the National Assembly during this pivotal period of the Seven Year Plan were indeed a stellar group. In addition to the old timers—Horace, Roy, Siegfried (Fred) Schopflocher, and Louis Gregory—there were other exemplary leaders of the Cause: Dorothy Baker, Allen McDaniel, Amelia Collins, Leroy Ioas, and George Latimer. All but George and Allen would later be named Hands of the Cause by Shoghi Effendi. George was a distinguished international travel teacher from the time of 'Abdu'l-Bahá; and Allen, a civil engineer, was invaluable as the member with the professional expertise required to oversee the construction of the Temple. Roy must have relished the time he spent with such esteemed colleagues. He had become the National Assembly's longest serving member and, as such, was much beloved; but his time serving at the national level was drawing to a close.

In September 1945, Roy was diagnosed with colon cancer. He again wrote to the Guardian and asked permission to resign from the National Assembly. This time, Shoghi Effendi reluctantly gave his consent.[87] Roy's resignation required a by-election, which was held in 1946, the first by-election in the history of the National Assembly.

The National Assembly membership during the period of World War II, 1941–1944. They were a distinguished group, seven of whom would be named Hands of the Cause of God. Front left to right: Siegfried Shopflocher, Dorothy Baker, Amelia Collins, George Latimer. Back left to right: Leroy Ioas, Horace Holley, Louis Gregory, Roy Wilhelm, Allen McDaniel. (USBNA)

Elsie Austin, an accomplished young Black attorney, became its newest member, and Roy was delighted with the choice of his replacement. Within the next year, Louis Gregory would also be unable to continue to serve because of cancer, and Allen McDaniel, suffering from ill health, would not be reelected. A generation of mighty pillars was beginning to be replaced by exceptional believers from the next generation who would carry on the ever-expanding work.

Nonetheless, despite his resignation from the National Assembly and failing health, Roy's service to the Cause was far from concluded. The Faith remained the first responsibility of his life, and he always carried out his personal business with the goal of serving the Faith. For example, even though he had wanted to make improvements to his Maine homestead, he knew that funds were more urgently needed to complete the superstructure of the Shrine of the Báb, so he put aside his personal interests and desires to save money for that project. In big ways and small, he found opportunities to be of service to the Guardian. Even at remote Stoneham Mountain, Roy read the *New York Times* every day in order to look for news and articles he thought important to send as clippings to the Holy Land.[88] He continued to receive letters from Shoghi Effendi, though less frequently.

Longtime friends—members of the Struven family—became Roy's second family during the last years of his life. He could not have connected with a better clan, for it included the legendary Bahá'í teacher, Lua Moore Getsinger, one of the earliest believers in North America. She and her husband, Edward Getsinger, were the first Western believers to meet 'Abdu'l-Bahá. Subsequently, the title "Herald of the Covenant" was bestowed on her by 'Abdu'l-Bahá, and Shoghi Effendi referred to her as the "Mother Teacher of the American Bahá'í Community."[89] Roy came to know Lua during his early years attending Bahá'í gatherings in New York. In 1897, Lua taught the Faith to Edward Struven, a university student from Baltimore, Maryland, who in turn introduced it to his younger brother, Howard Struven. Years later, Edward worked full time in Wilmette as supervisor of the construction and maintenance of the House of Worship. Lua's mother and siblings, the Moore family, also became active believers. Howard married Lua's younger sister, Ruby Jean Moore, whom everyone called Hebe. As newlyweds, Howard and Hebe lived in Baltimore, where they worked diligently to raise up a Bahá'í community. When 'Abdu'l-Bahá visited that city for a few hours in 1912, the Struvens hosted a luncheon for Him at their modest rowhouse.[90]

At age 27, Howard, an expert in building construction, in the company of Mason Remey circled the globe in 1909 to spread the Faith. He was an ardent Bahá'í teacher and became a capable administrator through service on Bahá'í institutions and committees. He was often elected a delegate to the National Convention and was considered a pillar first of the Maryland Bahá'í community and later the Worcester, Massachusetts community, which he and his wife established. During the 1940s, Howard became Roy's handyman, looking after electrical and plumbing work at the Maine farm.[91] He also managed Roy's gardens and greenhouse and often supervised other staff.

Roy Wilhelm with members of the Struven family, which became his second family after his relatives were gone. They posed at Evergreen Camp. Back left to right: Roy Wilhelm, Howard Struven, Hebe Struven. Front left to right: Cora Pomeroy, Bea Eardley, Ellen Struven, Esta Struven, Douglas Struven Junior, baby Roberta Struven, Douglas Struven. (USBNA)

Hebe first crossed paths with the Wilhelms when they were all on pilgrimage in 1907. Like her older sister, she loved to teach the Faith and was instructed by 'Abdu'l-Bahá as to how to give talks—He told her not to prepare but to turn to Him in prayer, and He would give her the words to say. Selfless and always willing to be helpful, no matter how lowly the task, Hebe became Roy's hostess at the chalet and managed his farm operation overall. She made the staffing decisions. Immersed in the teachings of the Faith, she understood the importance and power of love, and showered it upon everyone who came to Evergreen Camp.[92] Together with their children, grandchildren, nieces, and nephews, the Struvens (and Moore descendants) took loving care of Roy up until his last breath.

One member of that family recounted fond memories of Roy's personality from those last years on Stoneham Mountain and said that Roy as an elderly man was consistently dignified, liked to laugh, and always loved a good story. Roy was by nature a quiet person, but when he did speak, whatever he said was worth listening to.[93] However, even though he was unfailingly courteous and considerate, he could be very direct if need be. He never used popular slang and preferred instead to use "proper English," even when saying something funny (unlike in his letters to close friends). Roy never tolerated coarse language, and the Struvens heard that he even left a National Assembly meeting once during a heated moment when unseemly language was spoken by his colleagues.[94] All in all, he was remembered as an amiable person who was always pleasant to be around. One of Roy's comments stuck fast in the memory of that nephew of Lua Getsinger, because he repeatedly said: "The Bahá'ís are the most important people in the world because they can teach the Bahá'í Cause."[95]

A story from his last years demonstrated how Roy's adherence to the concept of the oneness of humanity affected his everyday actions. One of those who visited Evergreen Camp as a tourist was a person of means who arrived by chauffeur-driven automobile. The man instructed his driver to remain with the car while he enjoyed the property and visited with Roy. This seemed to Roy to be demeaning treatment of the driver. At one point after he began visiting with the tourist, Roy excused himself, fetched the driver, and then seated that man next to him in a place of honor while continuing his visit with the affluent tourist. Class and status prejudice was just as wrong to Roy as racial prejudice.[96]

In 1948, after Roy spent a few weeks in New York tending to business, Hebe's nephew, Walter Blakely, drove him back home to Maine. During the last hours of the journey, Roy began to suffer from intense pain, so Walter took him to a hospital in Lewiston. There, he endured three operations over the course of several weeks to correct an intestinal blockage. For the next three years, Roy's health worsened, even as he struggled to continue serving the Faith any way possible.[97]

Generosity was an integral part of Roy's character from the time he first accepted the divine teachings of Bahá'u'lláh. Whether it was providing the generators used to illumine the Holy Places, sending needed funds for countless other projects in and around Haifa or to advance the Cause across the continents, 'Abdu'l-Bahá and then Shoghi Effendi knew they could always turn to Roy for both funds and needed equipment. This would be no less true during the years immediately following the Second World War.

When the conflict ended in 1945, Europe was a wasteland; its infrastructure, factories, and cities were in ruins. So was much of Asia. The North Americans did not suffer the same fate and were able to quickly pivot from wartime to peacetime production. Factories in America transformed from building tanks, planes, and guns to producing automobiles, refrigerators, and washing machines. Pent-up demands from war-weary men and women in the United States and abroad created a nation about to experience unprecedented prosperity during the coming two decades—perhaps the fastest accumulation of personal wealth in the history of humankind. But much of the rest of the world was not so fortunate.

Palestine after the War was in turmoil even as the artillery in the rest of the world fell silent. In the twenty years since the end of World War I, previously cordial relations between Arabs and Jews had come to a boil as both vied for control over the same territory. At midnight, on May 14, 1948, the suzerainty of the British mandate over Palestine came to an end. That same afternoon, David Ben-Gurion, on behalf of Palestine's Jewish population, declared the creation of the State of Israel. The following day, a war for survival began as the nascent country was attacked on three sides by Arab armies.

In such a state of constant warfare and uncertainty, supplies, including precious building materials needed at the time to erect the superstructure of the Shrine of the Báb, would not always be available. Concerned about the quality and the economy of the construction, Shoghi Effendi could often be seen walking among the workers, consulting with them, and taking measurements. Even when a shipment of building materials did arrive safely, it did not necessarily mean the workers had everything they needed to continue the sacred project.[98] Rúḥíyyih Khánum described some of the challenges they experienced with the arrival of consignments of marble and stone that had been carved in Italy. She wrote, "The chaos at the port included: dropping boxes of stone into the water, ships leaving before they are fully unloaded, delivery trucks departing before their cargo is secured, and boxes of stones arriving damaged etc."[99] She recounted that those problems all were satisfactorily solved after much trouble, adding,

> Well Roy dear, I trust this has raised your spirits too and cheered you up? Why do you suppose God has this remarkable technique of creating problems so He can solve them by some mysterious spiritual slight of hand? It must be because we are so stupid and immature we need such things to convince us He does do it all![100]

At that time, transportation throughout Israel was unreliable and dangerous. Aware of this situation, in 1947, Roy sent a contribution to the National Fund to be used to purchase an automobile for Shoghi Effendi to facilitate his trips between Haifa and 'Akká, as well as around the region. A Buick Roadmaster was selected and shipped to Israel. Billed as an "executive car,"[101] Roy felt the Buick had an aura of unpretentious dignity, without the ostentatiousness inferred from luxury vehicles such as General Motor's Cadillac or the Ford Motorcar Company's Lincoln Continental models. With its shining chrome, baleen grille and wide whitewall tires, it seemed a suitable automobile for the station of the Guardian. Its powerful straight-eight engine would make the steep climb up Mount Carmel seem effortless. Shoghi Effendi wrote: "The car arrived safely and I drove yesterday to the Shrine remembering you all the time and wishing you were seated by my side. It is a daily reminder of your dear self, your fine and rare spirit, your long record of splendid achievement . . ."[102] Roy's largess didn't end with the Buick. He stood at the ready to supply spare parts for the car at any time, which became necessary later.[103] He also offered to send a smaller, more fuel-efficient car if needed. That second offer was declined, though appreciated.[104]

Especially after the war, Roy dispatched dozens of canisters of 16mm film so that the Guardian could have movies made of the Holy Places. He arranged shipments of hundreds of gallons of blue, green, brown, and white paint—unavailable in Israel at the time—needed to preserve and beautify the sacred properties around Haifa Bay. He also sent little things; for example, he sent a supply of pen nibs so the ink would flow uninterrupted onto the Guardian's many charts, directives, and letters.[105] Sometimes Roy offered to send items simply to make life easier for Shoghi Effendi, such as an electric razor. He would usually receive a response thanking him for the kind offer but suggesting he might send other items in short supply instead. And he kept the Guardian's household supplied with maple syrup produced on his Maine farm to the great enjoyment of Shoghi Effendi and his Canadian wife.[106] His anticipation of the material needs of those at the World Center well illustrated the thoughtful, compassionate, and loving bond they shared with him for over forty-five years.

In one final demonstration of his great love for Shoghi Effendi, Roy wrote a will leaving the bulk of his estate to the Guardian. When received after his death, the funds were used to purchase a significant property of six and a half acres, which extended the belt of land surrounding the Shrine of the Báb, property which forever will be a silent testimony to a generous, devoted heart.[107] The Guardian publicly acknowledged Roy's final contribution to the World Center saying:

> International endowments surrounding the tomb of the Prophet-Herald of the Faith on the bosom of God's Holy Mountain are considerably extended through the acquisition, after thirty years' effort, of a wooded area of over twenty-three thousand square meters, including a building overlooking the sacred spot, made possible through the estate bequeathed to the Faith by the herald of Bahá'u'lláh's Covenant, Roy Wilhelm, raising the total area within the precincts permanently dedicated to the Báb's Sepulcher to almost a quarter million square meters.[108]

During his last years, Roy seldom ventured outside the chalet. Even though, in 1948, his property was at last connected to the electrical grid, he continued his practice of going to bed early and rising early to save on the expense of lighting his home. He had a cook, farm hands, and the Struvens to take responsibility for his personal needs, buildings, and livestock, which in addition to the ever-present goats, included pigs, chickens, dairy cows, and a prize bull. He also had his faithful German Shepherd, Koh-Talis,* as a companion.

---

* *Koh-Talis* is Hindu for *Mountain of Good Omen.*

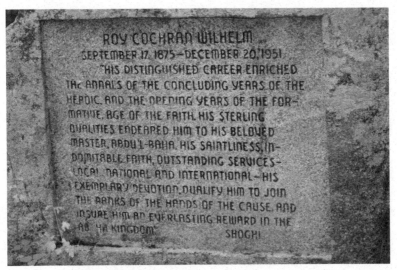

Grave marker at Roy Wilhelm's resting place on Stoneham Mountain
(Joel Nizin photographer)

After the Thanksgiving holiday of 1951, when winter had arrived in the Maine woods, Roy was taken again to a local hospital, this time in the town of Norway. He knew his time was coming to an end. Earlier that year, he had given burial instructions to one of the Struvens and had specifically directed that he wanted a grave that would not fill with water, as this had happened during the funeral of a friend, and it had deeply upset Roy.[109] The time had now arrived when the Struvens had to locate a spot at Evergreen Camp for a resting place that would comply with Roy's wishes.

Like his beloved Martha, Roy had suffered the effects of cancer for years. On December 20, 1951, at the age of seventy-six, after weeks of hospitalization with the Struvens by his bedside, Roy peacefully joined his loved ones and the Bahá'í immortals waiting for him in the other worlds of God. No doubt, knowing his end was rapidly approaching, Roy must have taken comfort in the by then so familiar words of Bahá'u'lláh:

O Son of Spirit!
With the joyful tidings of light I hail thee: rejoice! To the court
of holiness I summon thee; abide therein that thou mayest live
in peace for evermore.[110]

Curtis Kelsey visiting the grave of his friend, Roy Wilhelm (USBNA)

EPILOGUE: LEGACY

Four days after Roy Wilhelm's passing, Shoghi Effendi sent a cable to the Bahá'í world that, for the first time since Bahá'u'lláh's ascension, named living Hands of the Cause of God. Among those honored with that title were Roy's friends: Amelia Collins, Horace Holley, William Sutherland Maxwell, Charles Mason Remey, Dorothy Baker, and Leroy Ioas. All except Sutherland Maxwell had served with Roy on the National Assembly of the United States and Canada.[1] The same day that cable was sent, Shoghi Effendi announced in another cable that Roy had become the last individual to be named a Hand of the Cause posthumously.

Shoghi Effendi's deeply abiding love and admiration for Roy was reflected throughout the cable message he sent as a tribute to his faithful servant.

HEART FILLED (WITH)* SORROW (FOR) LOSS (OF) GREATLY PRIZED, MUCH LOVED, HIGHLY ADMIRED HERALD (OF) BAHÁ'U'LLÁH'S COVENANT, ROY WILHELM. DISTINGUISHED CAREER ENRICHED ANNALS (OF) CONCLUDING YEARS (OF) HEROIC (AND) OPENING YEARS (OF) FORMATIVE AGE (OF) FAITH. STERLING QUALITIES ENDEARED HIM (TO) HIS BELOVED MASTER, 'ABDU'L-BAHÁ. HIS SAINTLINESS,

---

* This cable was written in the space and cost-saving format that omitted words that would naturally occur but that were only implied. Horace Holley, as secretary of the National Spiritual Assembly, was allowed to insert the omitted words to make the text of cables easier to read.

INDOMITABLE FAITH, OUTSTANDING SERVICES LOCAL, NATIONAL, INTERNATIONAL, (HIS) EXEMPLARY DEVOTION, QUALIFY HIM (TO) JOIN RANKS (OF) HANDS (OF) CAUSE, INSURE HIM EVERLASTING REWARD (IN) ABHÁ KINGDOM. ADVISE HOLD MEMORIAL GATHERING (IN) TEMPLE BEFITTING HIS UNFORGETTABLE SERVICES (AND) LOFTY RANK.
—SHOGHI[2]

His impassioned message was dated December 24, 1951, the same day as his announcement of the living Hands.

In the "In Memoriam" article for *The Bahá'í World*, Roy's friend and colleague, Horace Holley, stated that Roy "was first and foremost a man of integrity who applied the high Bahá'í standards of conduct to himself before he applied them to others."[3] The article, extolling Roy's life of service, also noted his unprecedented membership on the nationally elected bodies of the United States (and Canada), from the establishment of the Temple Unity Executive Board in 1909 until his resignation for health reasons from the National Assembly in 1946. Referring to Roy's role of many years as the National Assembly's treasurer, Horace remarked that "the integrity of his character and the simple, direct humanness of his exposition of financial matters brought about a rapid development of the Bahá'í fund as an organic institution of the community."[4] In the early years of the development of the administrative order, Roy was one of the few Assembly members with hands-on business experience; plus he had an inherent inclination to organize its activities in a businesslike manner. His quiet contributions to the management of the day-to-day practical work of the National Assembly were significant and were partially responsible for setting it on a firm foundation. Utilizing the National Assembly of the United States and Canada as an example, Shoghi Effendi directed other National Assemblies to learn from the North Americans, and he designated the United States as the "Cradle of the Administrative Order." During Roy's last decades of service on the National Assembly, he also provided institutional memory to the consultation around the council chamber table, which was a vital contribution to the progress and maturation of its work.

Those who knew Roy, with his especially saintly character cloaked in wit, were not surprised that he was named a Hand of the Cause. Others from among his good friends already had been named Hands of the Cause after their passing, including Martha Root, Louis Gregory, and Keith Ransom-Kehler.[5] Roy, however, with his characteristic modesty, no doubt would have thought himself unworthy to be included in that august list of friends he held in high regard. Those three of his friends had distinguished themselves through their courageous journeys to promote the Faith and its interests. Roy's role had been different from those intrepid travelers, but equally crucial. Though he had not undertaken arduous travels that would have placed him in physical distress or danger, he possessed other sacrificial qualities—notably his immovable firmness in the Covenant and his instant obedience to 'Abdu'l-Bahá and Shoghi Effendi, no matter the costs to himself—that set him apart. With his sound judgment, he had served both 'Abdu'l-Bahá and the Guardian well, not only as their eyes and ears in North America but as one on whom they could count to carry out delicate assignments to protect the Cause of God while maintaining confidentiality.

From 1951 up to the passing of the last Hand of the Cause in 2007, the Hands appointed by Shoghi Effendi provided extraordinary, selfless service to the Faith—first, under the direction and guidance of Shoghi Effendi himself until his death in 1957, then after 1963 under the auspices of the newly established Universal House of Justice. During the precarious six-year interregnum between the Guardian's passing and the election of the House of Justice, the Hands of the Cause, serving as either Custodians in the Holy Land or at their posts around the world, forever earned the inexpressible gratitude of the global Bahá'í community for continuing to promote the progress of the Faith and serving as a central point of temporary guidance that prevented the community from splitting into factions.[6]

The work of the Hands did not include making decisions or setting policies. In the Writings of Bahá'u'lláh and 'Abdu'l-Bahá, the authority to carry out these responsibilities had been left to the elected institutions. Instead, the Hands focused on their twin responsibilities of promoting the teaching work and the protection of the Faith. It is evident, through this brief glimpse into the life of Roy Wilhelm, that he carried out both of these responsibilities again and again over the course of many decades.

Included in the praise Shoghi Effendi showered on Roy was the title *Herald of the Covenant.* The Guardian used that title rather than that of Hand, when referring to Roy in the message he issued to announce to the Bahá'í world that funds Roy had bequeathed to the Faith had been used to purchase important parcels of land adjoining the Shrine of the Báb. Both 'Abdu'l-Bahá and Shoghi Effendi had previously bestowed the title *Herald of the Covenant* on a small number of outstanding believers. Neither of them defined the qualities of a Herald of the Covenant, but it can be inferred that the title reflected the individual's exceptional promotion of and adherence to the Covenant of Bahá'u'lláh, and these qualities certainly defined all aspects of Roy's life of service. One only has to look at Roy's 1922 visit to the Holy Land to grasp his awareness of the imperative duty of all believers to proactively ensure that the Will and Testament of 'Abdu'l-Bahá be not only widely disseminated but studied and followed, and Roy was repeatedly requested to unobtrusively guide and counsel those having difficulty remaining firm in the Covenant. This mountainlike steadfastness and complete submission to the Covenant became an inseparable part of Roy's being.

Any summary of Roy's life would be incomplete without considering his material affluence. The Bahá'í Writings speak of how difficult it is for a wealthy individual to attain a position of great spirituality because the powerful force of materialism can easily draw that soul away from the straight path. Roy exemplifies the passage that "the best of men are they that earn a livelihood by their calling and spend upon themselves and upon their kindred for the love of God, the Lord of all worlds."[7] An examination of his life shows that he never allowed his prosperity to impede his spiritual development. This, according to 'Abdu'l-Bahá, made him especially favored in the Kingdom of the Spirit, for

> It is easier for a camel to go through the eye of a needle, than for a rich man to enter into the Kingdom of God. If, however, the wealth of this world, and worldly glory and repute, do not block his entry therein, that rich man will be favoured at the Holy Threshold and accepted by the Lord of the Kingdom.[8]

Each year, on the last Saturday of June, the legacy of a tangible contribution that Roy made to the Faith lives on when hundreds of believers travel by automobile, ferry, train, bus, or on foot to the West Englewood suburbs of New Jersey for the annual Souvenir Picnic. While most come from the environs of New York City and Philadelphia, some venture from distant locations around the country and even from other countries. The Souvenir Picnic is one of two annual events in the United States ordained by 'Abdu'l-Bahá Himself* and the only one specifically designated to serve as a living memorial to His visit to North America.

Rain or shine, the day is always filled with a combination of joyous laughter and prayerful recollection of 'Abdu'l-Bahá's long ago visit. The friends enjoy a picnic lunch on the lawn, explore the grounds and Evergreen Cabin, and stop to take pictures in front of the old REO Touring Car still parked in Roy's garage. And with their thoughts fixed on that hot humid day in 1912, when 'Abdu'l-Bahá was the host, they can say a prayer in the room inside the Wilhelm home where He stayed as the family's honored guest. The crowd, sitting quietly on blankets beneath the ancient pines, listens reverently to the annual reading of one of 'Abdu'l-Bahá's talks from that first picnic. One can easily imagine Roy's spirit permeating each of

---

* The other annual event ordained by 'Abdu'l-Bahá is a visit to the resting place of the first American Bahá'í, Thornton Chase. Interestingly, he is laid to rest in Inglewood, California.

these gatherings, moving among the guests, invariably dressed in a suit and signature bowtie, ensuring that each and all feel the warmth and welcome of his loving hospitality.

APPENDIX A:
THE ANNUAL SOUVENIR PICNIC

"O thou my dear son! Thy letter, dated July 13, 1913, was received. Its contents indicated the firmness and steadfastness of the believers in God and told of the holding of a divine meeting in your radiant charming country place. Praise be unto God, that that day was spent in the utmost joy and happiness. That annual memorial meeting will be the souvenir of 'Abdu'l-Bahá, especially when it is passed with infinite delight and gladness." August 2, 1913, letter from 'Abdu'l-Bahá to Roy Wilhelm[1]

'Abdu'l-Bahá's request that a picnic be held annually as a "souvenir" of His visit to North America has been faithfully carried out for more than a century except for three years when it was not possible to do so.* Throughout that period, it has drawn sizeable diverse crowds, usually in the hundreds, and featured many renowned speakers and performers. Of the fifty Hands of the Cause, at least sixteen attended no less than once, and of these, many were featured as speakers. This annual gathering, held on the last Saturday of June, has become a much-loved part of the rhythm of the Bahá'í calendar for the friends in the Greater New York Metropolitan Area, even as it serves as an

---

* In 2020, when the worldwide Covid-19 pandemic required the suspension of gatherings, the picnic was commemorated with a program conducted by way of the Internet, rather than in person.

annual reminder for the entire North American Bahá'í community of the privilege and blessing bestowed upon it through the 1912 visit of 'Abdu'l-Bahá.

Beginning in 1913, a pattern developed of holding a program in the area known as "the Grove," which was adjacent to the spot where 'Abdu'l-Bahá stood as He spoke to the crowd in 1912. One of His talks from that historic afternoon is read at each picnic to those seated on the grounds on the sloping lawns or in the shade of Evergreen Cabin. This highlight of the day is usually supplemented by musical performances and a talk by a Bahá'í of note.

Throughout the years, the picnic has garnered significant publicity in the immediate area, especially through articles in New Jersey publications.

A number of the picnics in the early years were especially noteworthy, among which were the following:

- In 1919, those who attended were permitted to view—in most cases for the first time—the plaster model of the future Bahá'í House of Worship that would be raised up in Wilmette, Illinois. It was on display at the home of the architect, Louis Bourgeois, a short walk from the Wilhelm property.[2]
- The entire National Spiritual Assembly of the United States and Canada, elected for the first time only months earlier, attended as a group and addressed the crowd at the 1922 picnic.
- The 1928 picnic's program deviated from its format to become a symposium on the teachings of the Faith intended for those who were inquirers and guests. The illustrious speakers that day included Amelia Collins, Louis Gregory, Horace Holley, Siegfried Schopflocher, and Roy Wilhelm, all of whom would later be named Hands of the Cause of God. That occasion also included performances of a Negro spiritual by Dorothy Richardson from Boston and an address on racial unity by a Black clergyman, Rev. Dr. George E. Haynes, who was secretary of the Commission on Church and Race Relations of the Federal Council of Churches of Christ in America.[3]

In 1933, a special ceremony took place to ensure that the historic and spiritual significance of 'Abdu'l-Bahá's visit to the site would never be forgotten. A copper box, made by Curtis Kelsey and containing a copy of 'Abdu'l-Bahá's 1912 talk at the original picnic, was reverently placed underneath a granite stone where He had spoken that unforgettable June day. The box also contained a written statement authenticating the location, which was signed by many of those who were present in 1912, including Isabella Brittingham (named a Disciple of 'Abdu'l-Bahá), Bertha Clark, Mary Hanford Ford, Maude Gaudreaux, Gertrude Harris, Hooper Harris, Ann Hoar, Edith Magee Inglis, Allah Kalantar, Bertha Herklotz, Edward "Saffa" Kinney, Carrie "Vaffa" Kinney, Grace Krug, Esther (Etta) Magee, Rita Mazel, Charlotte Segler, Irwin Smith Amalie Tyler, and Roy Wilhelm.[4] In 1992, with the permission of the National Spiritual Assembly, the box was opened.

Following the erection of the marker, Shoghi Effendi provided guidance about any future tangible memorials to 'Abdu'l-Bahá's visit to America and stated that the only one that should be raised up should be one at the Wilhelm property in West Englewood.

Concerning the proposed erection of a memorial in West Englewood to commemorate the place where the Master stood when addressing the friends of the Metropolitan New York district in 1912, the Guardian wishes me to express his full approval of such a plan, but wishes also to make it quite clear that this should in no way be considered as establishing a precedent for other cases in the future. For although the Master, while on His journey to America, did visit many places and centers, He attached a special significance to His visit to West Englewood, and this is therefore why the friends should feel justified in choosing this place rather than any other one to commemorate His visit by erecting on that spot a permanent memorial. . . .[5]

A year after he advised that there should only be one memorial, the Guardian further explained that it should be a monument, not a building.

. . . when a Memorial is constructed to commemorate in the pine grove at West Englewood 'Abdu'l-Bahá's visit to America, the Memorial should take the form a of a monument and not of a building. This reminds us of the Guardian's previous instruction, that on account of the Unity Feast which the Master held on that spot, the sole Memorial commemorating His American visit is to be constructed there. The Guardian's views in this matter would seem to answer a question raised locally from time to time in various cities, namely, where the Local Spiritual Assembly should not take steps to acquire permanently some house which had been blessed by the Master's Holy Presence."[6]

The annual gathering is often concluded with evening prayers in front of the Wilhelm home, similar to what occurred when darkness fell that glorious Saturday in 1912.

The Wilhelm property is owned and managed by the National Spiritual Assembly of the United States, which also oversees the annual picnic with assistance from Local Spiritual Assemblies and appointed task forces.

Hands of the Cause of God
who spoke at or otherwise attended the Souvenir Picnic

Amatu'l-Bahá Ruḥíyyíh Khánum	1935
Amelia Collins	1926, 1928
Charles Mason Remey	1922
Corrine True	1922
Dorothy Baker	1937, 1939
Horace Holley	1924, 1926, 1928, 1930, 1932, 1936, 1937, 1938
Keith Ransom-Kehler	1926
Leroy Ioas	1937, 1950

Louis Gregory	1922, 1928, 1930
Martha Root	1919, 1928, 1931
Roy Wilhelm	most between 1912 and 1945
Siegfried Schopflocher	1924, 1926, 1928, 1932
Ugo Giachery	1942
William Sears	1959, 1960, 1978, 1987
William Sutherland Maxwell	1928
Zikru'lláh Khádem	1965, 1984

APPENDIX B

COLLIER'S MAGAZINE
JANUARY 10, 1914, VOLUME 52, NUMBER 17

STORY BY ROY WILHELM & MARTHA ROOT
GASOLINE GYPSIES FOUR (TRANSCRIPT)

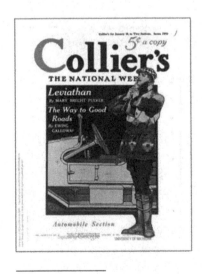

To Those who wish to journey a little apart from beaten motoring paths and to those who would travel at nominal expense, close to nature, this simple account of a gypsying* trip may prove a mental run into a terra incognita. It brings one into a land filled with the delicacy and charm of roadside feasts, of camp life, of wild mountains and glorious sunsets, and incidentally, it recounts the caprices of a motor car.

---

* The word *gypsy*, meaning a nomadic or free-spirited person, has also been used with a capital "G" as a name for the Roma people. In the twenty-first century, the appellation *Gypsy*, when applied to the Roma, is considered a racial slur. The Wilhelms and Martha Root used the term in the more general sense of happy wanderers.

It was like this: a young man decided to take his parents and a friend on a gypsying trip through New England. Having been surfeited with the usual tours he declared he wouldn't give a cent a mile for the big hotels. He wished a real camp of his own, one which could be squeezed into his motor car somewhat as snugly as a shoehorn might turn the trick. He held memories of quaint farmhouses, where the owners were often "original pieces" whose Yankee dialect and many kindnesses made "blends" as fragrant as his own coffee bean.

The Outfit

With the earliest days of spring, during hours of inactivity, his mind would begin the trekking in his office. He often found himself driving tandem, coffee trade and motor car, over roadways lined with woods and tangled underfoot with fringes of fragrant wild grape and bright corn flowers. He was so chockful of sporting zest to get the outfit mentally stored into the family car that he forgot his figures in pounds, and began to reckon in ounces and inches. Recalling opportunely the phrase, "If business interferes with pleasure, cut out the business," he still managed to save some time for the acquirement of "compressed cash" for future gasoline. He appointed himself Chief of the "engineering department." His mother was to be the Poet-Cook, his father Commissary, and his friend could act as "Peelot." The car was designated "The Lady."

The entire baggage weighed 325 pounds. Each "officer" was limited to twenty-five pounds. Every true caravaner knows the importance of packing snugly, so even at the risk of being prosaic I detail the load. If it seems too liberal, it is because Chief quoted the old saw: "'Tis better to cry over a thing than for it." Three heavy waterproof bags were securely strapped to the running boards. The bottoms were placed forward to prevent rain from entering and a square of thin oilcloth "aft" to keep out the dust. The first bag contained the wall tent, fly, thirty feet of rope, and two army blankets. The second held the two pneumatic mattresses and bedding of which an ample supply is advised. These were balanced on the other side by the tent poles, the big umbrella, and the third waterproof bag, containing the cooking utensils, large waterproof cloth, and sundries. It was likewise strapped to the running board.

The Tent on the Running Board

A shoebox of tightly compressed waste was tied to the frame under the hood in front, and on the opposite side were three quart cans of lubricating oil. (It is better to use the oil which one knows to be good than to chance the "sorghum" sometimes sold by wayside garages.) there was also kerosene for the lamps and for the compressed air blue-flame oil stove. Tent pins were carried in a small grain bag under the rear seat. A luggage rack in the back would have been useful, but this space was for the spare tires. The tent poles were "scarfed" (jointed in the center) to fit the running board, a scheme that was also applied to increase the height of the big umbrella, which, in its waterproof cover, was fastened along the top frames.

Every Inch of Space Utilized

This umbrella was to serve the purpose of a small extra tent to shelter the supplies from the dew and to relieve the congestion which would occur by having everything under the fly. A large portion of the fly is always necessarily occupied by the table. The umbrella could also be utilized if grim necessity required the changing of a tire during a storm. An army blanket and a heavy comfort were carried under the rear cushion and two smaller blankets under the forward cushions. Tucked in with the bedding were white net curtains which could be hooked to the inner tent walls at both front and rear, making the place as comfortable and dainty as a Juliet's chamber.

The wood frame under the front seat was cut out an additional inch on both sides, to allow the carrying of extra lubricating oil and small cans of a certain grease in the few inches thus gained between the sides and gas tank. An important item not to be overlooked in the cargo was a dozen boxes of Swedish safety matches. Small pouches 9x12 inches, made of ticking purchased at a ten-cent store, were attached to the four doors of the car as well as to the dash, the wire hooks at the sides going through little screw eyes inserted for the purpose. These were for small articles, the "hand bags" of the four nomads.

The Pantry Under the Seat

The most novel feature was the combination pantry and table, built by Chief exactly to fit the space in the back seat. It was half-inch basswood, eighteen inches high, with hinged leaves folding at the back and front. The latter could be raise when luncheon was served in the car. The lower front section was removable so that it could be passed to those in front for use as a lap-tray. The lower corner was partitioned to hold the compressed air oil lamp. This space was lined with tin, and four layers of blotting paper were also carried under the stove. To allow the escape of any aroma of kerosene, several holes were bored in the outer wall. Three-eight-inch material was used for the remaining partitions. The whole was securely fastened together with screws, as nails would not have stood the continued strain. Handles were placed on the ends and these were securely tied to the guardrail.

Other little accessories were two one-quart vacuum bottles and one pint bottle. Empty cloth sugar sacks were also put in for carrying potatoes, onions, and other vegetables. A dozen ten-pound paper sacks were to be used for all scraps of paper and food, so that no trace of luncheons need be left to mar even woodsy spots. Specially useful were two one-gallon flannel-covered canteens, each having a shoulder band for carrying. When the flannel is wet, evaporation cools the water, reducing the temperature several degrees.

What Is So Rare—

Little square pillows were carried in a small khaki pouch suspended between the roof frames, and in front of it was a second pocket for carrying sweaters and raincoats. Small suit cases were strapped at the top of the back seat and larger ones were wedged in the middle of the back seat. When everybody was packed in, each was as "comfy" as a pea in a pod, and had fully as much room!

After rolling out of the busy hubbub of the metropolis, the first day's course was steered through the beautiful Croton Lake district of New York State and on up into Connecticut. Lowell would have found out what is so rare as a day in June if he had been along that splendid August morning.

Each turn in the road brought some unexpected glimpse of distant wooded hills, and the flashing waters in the sunlit lakes lay like meadows of diamonds far below. Cowbells tinkled from the pastures and occasionally squirrels chattered a protest.

Chief hinted that possibly after three weeks his crew might become "toughened to the joys of the country." But instead of their artistic sinews being overtrained, they attained, Chief later declared, a development almost Samsonian with each day's marvelous changes in landscape.

The Spirit of Adventure

A flurry was caused the first afternoon by Poet-Cook losing her heavy black petticoat, which blew from the upper pouch. It was rescued by Peelot and safely restored. Chief ejaculating: "That's nothing, we shall probably lose several years off our shoulders before we get back home if this spirit of adventure is as 'catching' every day."

There was a "lay-off" for luncheon at one o'clock. This was the premier of a long series of delicious banquets served in Nature's spacious dining rooms where appetite and mind and soul can truly feast. Conventional motorists speed from place to place and dine in fashionable hotels, where perhaps six strong men stand to refill one's glass. Only gypsies know the joy of foraging and the tonic of wood smoke. This band ate leisurely in the privacy of the great outdoors. After each meal they explored the rocks and hills, culling wild flowers new to them, and studying strange birds. "Space annihilators" probably swept up the main road, their cars passing "The Lady" without so much as poking their noses toward hers in friendly greetings, but they missed scenery and that sacred feeling Nature accords to those who vibrate in tune with her.

After a genial day's run, the first night was spent at a little inn in Cornwall, Conn. The head of the house and Poet-Cook found themselves domestic affinities and the Cornwall woman agreed to dry some corn and express it to the city home. The whole family, quite naturally, seemed to go hunting for winter spoils. In four weeks they arranged for so many delicious foods to be sent home that their December table must constantly remind them of the summer's pursuit. A Vermont farmer's wife canned blueberries. (Chief was very particular that the crew said "blubury" just as did the natives, but the Vermonters were never to be fooled!) a Massachusetts woman made blackberry jam and a New Hampshire friend parcel-posted a box of the wonderful apples, "Yellow Transparencies." Camping comrades freighted little cedars, hemlocks and tamarack trees to plant, as well as big slices of birch bark for picture frames. Pine pillows were slipped in just for good measure, one bearing the touching words: "I pine for you and sometimes balsam!" In Vermont Poet-Cook engaged a capable housekeeper.

Leaving Cornwall that second sparkling morning, the petroleumites fared forth in mood hilarious. Commissary stood and called out greetings to boys in the barren bewildered sheep pastures, just to keep from "bustin with joy." The little phrase, "Best day of all," appeared that morning and was worn daily to something worse than silk stockings in blackberry brambles, but it held until the day of disembarking, when each one purposely refrained.

Delectable ozone was in everybody's spirits except "The Lady's." Chief thought it was the carburetor, and he mixed the "gal" every variation of gasoline breakfast from "lean" to "fat". For two hours, with lightning nerves and steel muscles, he worked to discover the cause of such intermittent balking. The running board was too full to open the "fore" door on his side – and, unfortunately, he was not twins! He tried to relieve his tension by stopping work a moment and taking a picture of some fragrant clover-blossomed meadows. "Does this bit of country bring us nearer heaven or does it only seem to? The bees hum so rhythmically and the clovers are so heavily laden with bright color and perfume. I will pinch Peelot to see if I am only dreaming.

Another grind at the sulking motor brought Chief back to his common senses. He was resigned, though, this time, and said to the "deck hands": "Ten miles from here there is a lovely spot 1,600 feet above sea level. It is the home of a well-known New York surgeon. From its novel bungalow, fashioned after a sixteenth century eight-sided wool market in London, we can look sixty miles and see New York, Connecticut, and Massachusetts. We will make the detour and have a short day, and I will take this pesky car to a garage early this evening.

Romany Rye

The trip was almost ended when "The Lady," wholly indifferent to her faux pas, had the impertinence to stall forty feet from the porte-cochere of the stately country house. As Chief was preparing to present his card, the surgeon himself came out to greet the visitors. His wife was away, but he called his son, who took the guests in the doctor's big touring car over the estate, and then up to the wigwam.

This bewitching little wigwam set on a high Connecticut hilltop in a grove of birches, was a regular "Sun-in-the-Face" kind of place where totem-pole charm had truly brought real China to the dining room, wood wild flowers to the table, and a white man's range in the kitchen. We were insistently invited to camp overnight, and the surgeon's son, who probably never before had shelled a pea, plunged actively into the supper getting. After everybody had enjoyed a bountiful supper—because each had worked to get it—the surgeon and his wife, who had now returned, came up to spend the evening—and brought a maid to assist with the dishes.

Chief slipped out to play airs on his ocarina, an effect which was exquisite in that sylvan wonderland. The surgeon a little later invited all to join him around an immense watch fire guarded by sentinel torches. Meantime, the chauffeur, a real "motor surgeon," had been down in the driveway making several exploratory incisions and various adjustments on our stalled motor and had finally rolled her back to the garage, as he hoped, cured.

A Fairy Grandmother in the Right Place

The third day's run was up through the picturesque Berkshire hills. The roads resembled a continuous billiard table. Leaving Lenox, the journey was continued up through Massachusetts towards the White

Mountains. In Lincoln, Mass., the gate of a comely grandmother's residence swung inward to the gypsies as cheerily as if they were her own kin. It was house a century old. The table was laden with the delicious bounties of the whole countryside, and after a big supper the dear soul took the motorists out to see her kitchen. With the brasses of the sixties ranged a 1913 electric toaster, bread mixer, flatiron, and beyond, in the woodhouse, was a new electric washing machine.

She opened a great pantry cupboard and handed out peppermints, which only she could have made so toothsome.

"These toasted almonds I have made for you, too." She added, "but I am keeping them to pack with your lunch tomorrow." In the front parlor later she told of her life in Lincoln, and how the cordial Congregationalists completely wore out her white kid gloves the very first Sunday she went among them as a bride. Her stories were rare pictures of the very heart of ideal New England.

Next morning the motherly New Englander arranged that the automobilists should have the spice of journeying behind that almost extinct animal, the horse.

This one was laughingly called Threffs, which the son of the house explained was "fair, fat, and forty." In the comfortable carryall they were jogged along to historic Lexington, where the hostess showed them the "old, ancient relics of antiquity"! A trip through the thirteen original colonies is so filled with historic interest that travelers should carry along "spare" brains to help them catch all the echoes of fact and fancy which reverberate from hill and valley.

The first Saturday out the gypsies had the joy of pitching camp on Lake Winnisquam south of Lake Winnepesaukee, in New Hampshire. With the zest of playhouse days the canvas was coaxed from the bag and the little khaki house stretched up into reality.

The fly formed a front porch overlooking this still, cameolike stretch of water with its fairy islands and marvelous changes in coloring. The gypsies troubled themselves little about its Indian history and traditions. They were not rediscovering America that afternoon, not even remembering schoolbook knowledge, for their eyes were too ravished at every turn by the graceful scenic pictures.

Poet-Cook make apple sauce from red Astrakhans. She cooked peas, corn and potatoes and boiled bacon over compressed air blue-flame oil lamp. To Commissary's marvelous supplies friends and farmers had added gifts of angel food, blueberry muffins, homemade bread, and blackberry jam.

The pantry table from the car, surrounded by artists folding tripod seats, made the "dining room" exceedingly attractive. A farmer boy rowed up to the bank and, as a welcome, tossed from his boat a few white lilies, delicately kissed with pink. As a feast progressed, motor launches and canoes kept passing by, their occupants singing salutes, one calling out to the campers an invitation for a ride.

The farmer on whose land the tent stood, a "husky" of 245 pounds, brought down an old one-piece buffalo robe, the kind almost vanished now, and said: "This may come in handy before morning."

Just before retiring, the gypsies took a swim in the tranquil water. The sun had added its warmth to the cooler mountain waters, and complementing the comfortable bathing was the bracing air. A full moon looked joyously down on the playful swimmers. Strenuous days led to nights of deep sleep. If occasionally one woke, it was only to feel thankful he could look out upon a starlit lake, dotted with little isles of paradise, and then know he could roll over and take another sleep. There were no alarm clocks to jar or jolt the vacationists from their natural rest. It was truly a timeless month for no one ran on schedule: no calendar was carried and no member of the crew ever bought a newspaper, except for wrapping purposes.

There is much to do in camp. Commissary scurried for food: Chief motored over to Laconia for more table luxuries: the Poet-Cook evolved dishes fit for an emperor but not a whit too good for her little family. Peelot steered the pots and pans, often assisted by the men for they were real suffragettes.

Stevenson says: "To journey happily is better than to arrive," and so it seemed.

After packing the tent nicely on Monday, they moved along to larger joys. Each time Chief would suggest an early start, but with a whole house to be bagged and "The Lady's" "toilet" to be made, it was usually ten o'clock before the party had exchanged good-bys (sic) with their farmer friends and anchor was actually weighed.

The Gypsies Seize a Cottage

In North Woodstock, N.H., "some class" was show by taking "a cottage" for the night.

"Idlewild," the two-room log cabin, was situated in a grove of spruces on high ground, commanding a majestic view of Franconia Notch and the White Mountains.

From Woodstock, the way was through Twin Mountain, Profile Mountain, Bretton Woods and down to Crawford Notch. The return was made through Bethlehem, and then westward to Montpelier, Vt.

In Montpelier, Chief had friends. The home of these people affords a fine view of the Green Mountains, and the family has sleeping porches build like double-decked staterooms on a large veranda, facing the imposing ranges. Japanese latticed curtains can be drawn to keep out the morning sun. the arrangement was so novel that Chief drew a map of it for he will build one similar in his country home when he puts up an al fresco dining room, also fashioned a little like the Vermonters' breakfast room. Ideas seemed to project themselves into focus at every turn of the journey, and the gypsies' eyes were not so preoccupied but they could see truths which looked at them from man-made products. As well as from birds and sunsets.

One night Chief said: "Poet, are you asleep?" and she replied: "No, son, but my soul is motoring in those far-off mystic star spheres."

"Oh, come, mother, apply the emergency – with gee-whiz juice at twenty-two cents!"

Taking the road again and leaving the billowy fields with peaks on either side farther and farther behind, the gypsies went on toward Lake Champlain. Any automobilists who have rolled its length know the scenic pleasure of this jaunt. As Peelot had never been in Canada, the party went up through Rouse Point to old Fort Blunder, and then over to lunch on the Canadian side. By this time even Commissary, who had required considerable coaxing to leave the comforts of New York, love the motor for itself alone. As all climbed into their "pod" and each "pea" sank comfortably into the spring seat which just "fitted" each gypsy, in luxurious ease, smiled at the others in the sheer, sensuous joy of restful motion. "The Lady," too, settled down to a steady hum which quietly sang of perfectly adjusted machinery. The afternoon was young and every incident harmonious.

The Enchanted Campers

The crossing of the ferry at Chazy was a quaint little "curtain raiser," preparatory to the joyous comedy of camping by Lake Champlain. Longfellow's kind of barefooted boy pulled up a white wood curtain which signaled to a raft in the mid-lake, and when it laboriously moved over to shore it took "The Lady" and her cargo right into its lap. The two little engines had a full load, but they kept chugging aloud: "We think we can do it!" and, sure fire, and the khaki-clothed group sang wild Russian airs around it, even trying to dance some Marsovian steps. Then they wrapped themselves in blankets and stretched out before the blaze. It was poetic to watch the dancing pine flames flirt with the harvest moon and entice her beams over the waters to their very embers.

Next day the crew went out in a boat with a real honest-to-goodness fisherman. As he paddled along ahead of the wind, Chief asked: "About how fast are we going?" The Champlain seer viewed the heavens and the lake, then, shifting his weed, slowly ejaculated: "Wall, I should say we be goin' pretty good hickory, pretty good hickory, Chief!"

As camp was only a mile from a large creamery, cream 60 per cent fat, delicious buttermilk, and milk (always ordered one-third cream throughout the trip) added to the supplies. Poet-Cook felt that the occasion of Lake Champlain demanded Lucullan banquets, so she concocted dishes which would place a "Spitz-Charlton" in second row of famous restaurants.

Ticonderoga

Chief and Commissary worked like master mechanics to build a dining table, bench, chairs, cupboards, dressing tables, and washstands. They cut a forty-foot slender pine to furl a ten-cent flag! An incandescent bulb which was found upon the beach, probably jettisoned from some passing yacht, was carefully suspended by Chief above the dining table, its humor causing a smile.

So complete was "Camp Champlain," with its "Broadway," "Fifth Avenue," and "Wall Street" features that the gypsies never would have been content to leave it at the end of one week, if a hurricane had not come along on Thursday and breezily bidden them "pack and be off."

As they were not due at a professor's camp near Orwell, Vt., also on Lake Champlain, until Saturday they took to the road again and stopped for the night at a farmhouse near Ticonderoga. Here they met some fellow travelers who were going to explore Ticonderoga fort thoroughly. The militant spirits looked their disdain at peace-loving Poet-Cook, who said she would enjoy having one free day to sew a little, gather some poppy seeds, and wander about with nothing special planned.

The Professor at the Supper Table

Sunday in the professor's camp was novel. The place is called the "Singing Cedars." He and his children, with their children, have bungalows fringing a grove of a thousand cedars. The cabins stand on rocky points, facing the Adirondacks and overlooking a mile and a half of Champlain beauty. In the evenings all gather in his big living room before the massive fireplace, which weighs fifty tons. It is of glacial boulders, with a big, three-hundred-pound meteorite over the mantel.

Music, corn popping, dancing, clay modeling, original verse, and finally, swimming all find a place in the night's diversions.

How They Lived on the Cream of the Land

From Lake Champlain the journey was continued to Bennington, Vt., and down the Hudson through the Catskills. The gypsies reached New York after thirty days. Their total expenditure was $1.21 per day each, including hotel and all forage and 20 cents each for expense of car. They lived on the cream of the land. Fruit, often at 40 to 60 cents a dozen, melons, ice cream, green corn, at 35 cents per dozen, and candy, will give some ideal of what they had; yet these in abundance and occasional bills at the inns were covered by the investment of $1.21 per person per day.

Anyone would have considered Chief a consummate "tight wad" about "The Lady's" gasoline, so closely did he watch her consumption of gas and oil every day, but her entire cost was only 20 cents per day for each of the party. Some persons may prefer to camp every night, but as it requires two hours of very active work to get a tent pitched and everything in order, and again two hours to repack one, it seemed advisable to the New Yorkers not to camp, except for stops of two or more days. The inexpensiveness of this outing is such that families even in moderate circumstances can go. All that is necessary is to plan carefully to avoid waste,

The Effects of Ozone
These flitting witchfolk had only a four weeks' journey, yet it meant 1,300 miles of beautiful pictures.

A little rain, a few bad roads—yes but such incidents were accepted as part of the "chance" which lent interest to a wholesome adventure. Physically the New Yorkers are brown as pine cones; mentally, they are rugged and wide awake to color and movement. Poet-Cook says they are more susceptible to fine spiritual impressions since roving, light as thistledown, in the splendid outdoors.

The Metropolitan gypsies too, have become real comrades, drawn together by kindred desires and appreciations.

Each happy "best day yet" of the journey stands out to them as passionately fine because of cherished experiences, wonderful scenery, madcap pranks in camp, delightful motor runs, and plenty of God-given ozone.

NOTES

Prologue

1. Cable dated December 24, 1951, from Shoghi Effendi, in "Roy C. Wilhelm" by Horace Holley, *The Bahá'í World, Vol. XII, 1950–1954*, p. 662.

1 / A Fragrant Bean

1. A coauthor of this book, Gary Hogenson, lived several years in Costa Rica, including a time spent on a coffee farm. He became familiar with the geography, language, customs and culture of the country and its coffee plantations. Angelina Allen, one of the readers of the manuscript, lived in the port city of Limón. This firsthand knowledge has been used throughout the section of this book regarding Roy Wilhelm's time in Costa Rica. The authors also wish to acknowledge and thank Rodrigo Tomás, of San José, Costa Rica who, together with his family, searched in vain for tax and property registry records for confirmation of Roy's two years as a coffee grower in the country. Photographs and the testimony of those who knew Roy remain the sole evidence available of his sojourn in Central America.

2. Watt Stewart, *Keith and Costa Rica: The Biography of Minor Cooper Keith, American Entrepreneur.*

3. Florencia Quesada, "Urbanism, Architecture, and Cultural Transformations in San Jose, Costa Rica, 1850–1930," in Arturo Almandoz, ed., *Planning Latin America's Capital Cities, 1850–1950*, p. 241.

4. The information about Roy's family background comes from *History of Muskingum County, Ohio, Illustrations and Biographical Sketches of Prominent Men and Pioneers*; the website http://ancestry.com, and the Hugh M. Cochran Bible, including genealogical charts found in the Roy C. Wilhelm papers, USBNA, M-46, Boxes 2 & 3.

5. *History of Muskingum County, Ohio, Illustrations and Biographical Sketches of Prominent Men and Pioneers*, p. 67.

6. 1880 US Census.

7. Ibid.

8. 1900 US Census.

9. The family spelled Laura's nickname both as *Laurie* and *Lourie*. Her tombstone has *Lourie* inscribed on it.

10. "Mrs. L. Wilhelm Dead in Teaneck," *The Record* (Hackensack, New Jersey), January 27, 1937.

11. Interview with Walter Blakely, who came to know Roy well during his later years while serving as Roy's butler. Personal archives of book's coauthor, Joel Nizin.

12. Ibid.

13. There are hints in the records that Roy traveled to Brazil—then one of the world's primary coffee exporters—but this is not confirmed.

14. News story appearing in the *North Adams Transcript Newspaper* (North Adams, Massachusetts), July 28, 1898.

15. William H. Uker, *All About Coffee.* Much of the background information about growing, harvesting, processing, grading, and roasting coffee came from this excellent history.

16. Certificate of Incorporation for R. C. Wilhelm & Co., filed and recorded on July 9, 1903, held at the "Division of Old Records" located at 31 Chambers Street, NYC, Department of Records/Municipal Archives, County Clerk Records, Historic Records, Business Records, Corporation Certificates. The business started about a year before the incorporation.

17. For a discussion of this wave of immigration and its impact on New York, see Edward Robb Ellis, *The Epic of New York City: A Narrative History,* pp. 416–17.

18. For a discussion of the coming of the automobile to New York, see ibid., p. 462.

19. For a discussion of New York City during the opening years of the twentieth century, see Paul Johnson, *A History of the American People,* pp. 575–79.

20. Certificate of Incorporation for R. C. Wilhelm & Co., filed and recorded on July 9, 1903, held at the "Division of Old Records" located at 31 Chambers Street, NYC, Department of Records/Municipal Archives, County Clerk Records, Historic Records, Business Records, Corporation Certificates. The incorporation certificate includes Roy's new partners.

21. Business records for R. C. Wilhelm & Co., held at the "Division of Old Records" located at 31 Chambers Street, NYC, Department of Records/Municipal Archives, County Clerk Records, Historic Records, Business Records, Corporation Certificates.

22. http://www.coffeetime.wikidot.com/standard-coffee-sack-weights-green-coffee/. Depending on the country of origin, green coffee was shipped in jute bags weighing between 50 and 70 kg.

23. "History of Coffee," Timeline, http://www.historyofcoffee.net/coffee-history/timeline-of-coffee/.

24. Gloversville (NY) Business School, "A Bookkeeping & Stenographer School, 1906–1907 Annual Catalog."

25. "A Green Coffee Shrinkage Table," compiled by Roy Cochran Wilhelm, *Tea & Coffee Trade Journal*, vol. 31, no. 4 (October 1916): 321–26.

26. Roy Cochran Wilhelm, "On Cup Characteristics," *Tea & Coffee Trade Journal*, vol. 31, no. 2 (August 1916): 142; Roy Cochran Wilhelm, "The Color of the Roast," *Tea & Coffee Trade Journal*, vol. 31, no. 5 (November 1916): 428–29; Roy Cochran Wilhelm, "Drip, The Best Method," *Tea & Coffee Trade Journal*, vol. 31, no. 4 (October 1916): 338–39.

27. Donald N. Schoenholt, "Clarence Bickford: The man who discovered Central America," *Tea & Coffee Trade Journal*, November 1, 1993, and The Free Library. 1993 Lockwood Trade Journal Co., Inc. Accessed January 22, 2022. http://www.thefreelibrary.com/The+man+who+discovered+Central+America.-a014608186.

28. Donald N. Schoenholt, "Clarence Bickford: The man who discovered Central America," *Tea & Coffee Trade Journal*, November 1, 1993, and The Free Library. 1993 Lockwood Trade Journal Co., Inc. January 22, 2022. http://www.thefreelibrary.comThe+man+who+discovered+Central+America.-a014608186.

29. "9 Most Consumed Beverages Around the World," http://www.haleysdailyblog.com/9-most-consumed-beverages-around-the-world/.

2 / Turning Point

1. Roy C. Wilhelm, "Mrs. Laurie C. Wilhelm," *The Bahá'í World, Vol. VII, 1936–1938*, p. 539.

2. "Rich Merchant Returns $50 Received for Singing When a Youth," *Washington Post*, February 10, 1910. Newspaper article about Roy Wilhelm returning his wages with interest to that church years later.

3. Handwritten genealogical chart of Roy Wilhelm's ancestors, with notes by Roy C. Wilhelm in his own handwriting. USBNA, Roy C. Wilhelm papers, M-46, Box 3.

4. Roy C. Wilhelm, "Mrs. Laurie C. Wilhelm," *The Bahá'í World, Vol. VII, 1936–1938*, p. 539.

5. Ibid.

6. Ibid.

7. The first public mention in the West was during a speech read before the Parliament of World Religions, which was held as part of the Colombian Exposition in Chicago in September, 1893. However, even though this speech generated interest in the Faith, no one became a Bahá'í in America until after Kheiralla began his classes in 1894. For a more thorough discus-

sion of the establishment of the Faith in the United States, see Robert Stockman, *The Bahá'í Faith in America: Origins 1892–1900, vol. 1*, pp. 26–38, and
Kathryn Jewett Hogenson, *Lighting the Western Sky: The Hearst Pilgrimage
and the Establishment of the Bahá'í Faith in the West*, pp. 21–22.

8. Robert Stockman, *The Bahá'í Faith in America: Origins 1892–1900,
vol. 1*, pp. 26–38, and Kathryn Jewett Hogenson, *Lighting the Western Sky:
The Hearst Pilgrimage and the Establishment of the Bahá'í Faith in the West*,
pp. 21–22.

9. Roy C. Wilhelm, "Mrs. Laurie C. Wilhelm," *The Bahá'í World, Vol.
VII, 1936–1938*, p. 539.

10. May 19, 1909 letter from Roy Wilhelm to Ahmad Esphahani
[Mírzá Aḥmad-i-Iṣfahání known as Ahmad Sohrab], USBNA, Ahmad Solis
Collection, M-955, Box 8.

11. Arthur Pillsbury Dodge was a publisher of literary journals, lawyer,
inventor, entrepreneur, businessman who made and lost fortunes. For more
about his life and establishment of the Faith in New York City, see Robert
H. Stockman, *The Bahá'í Faith in America: Origins 1892–1900, Vol. I*, pp.
116–17.

12. For a comprehensive discussion of Ibrahim Kheiralla's rebellion
against 'Abdu'l-Bahá, see Kathryn Jewett Hogenson, *Lighting the Western
Sky: The Hearst Pilgrimage and the Establishment of the Bahá'í Faith in the
West*, pp. 191–207.

13. For a more thorough discussion of the establishment of the Faith
in the United States, see Robert Stockman, *The Bahá'í Faith in America:
Origins 1892–1900, Vol. I*, and *The Bahá'í Faith in America: Early Expansion,
1900–1912, Vol. 2*. Please also see Kathryn Jewett Hogenson, *Lighting the
Western Sky: The Hearst Pilgrimage and the Establishment of the Bahá'í Faith
in the West*, pp. 21–22.

14. Even though Roy Wilhelm was uncertain about the year he first
attended a Bahá'í gathering and would give it as either 1901 or 1902, his
memory that May Maxwell was present dates it to at least the summer of
1902, as she was in France throughout 1901.

15. Roy's account is unclear about the year of this meeting, but if his
recollection that May Maxwell was present was correct, then it occurred in
1902. May had been asked by 'Abdu'l-Bahá to remain in Paris during the
year 1901, which she did. This period of May's remarkable life is recounted
in Violette Nakhjavání, *The Maxwells of Montreal: Early Years 1870–1922*.

16. Roy C. Wilhelm, "Mrs. Laurie C. Wilhelm," *The Bahá'í World, Vol.
VII, 1936–1938*, p. 540.

17. Robert H. Stockman, *The Bahá'í Faith in America: Early Expansion, 1900–1912, vol. 2*, pp. 101–2. See also Nathan Rutstein, *He Loved and
Served: The Story of Curtis Kelsey*, p. 25 for Roy Wilhem's comments about
his mother's friends' interest in the metaphysical.

18. Letter dated May 19, 1909 from Roy Wilhelm to Ahmad Esphahani, USBNA, Ahmad Solis Collection, M-955, Box 8.

19. Roy C. Wilhelm, "Mrs. Laurie C. Wilhelm," *The Bahá'í World, Vol. VII, 1936–1938*, p. 539.

20. Tablet from 'Abdu'l-Bahá to Roy C. Wilhelm, translated by Moneer, son of Z. M., probably 1904, USBNA, Roy C. Wilhelm papers, M-46, Box 1.

21. Tablet from 'Abdu'l-Bahá to Roy C. Wilhelm, translated by Moneer, son of Z. M., received October 18, 1904, USBNA, Roy C. Wilhelm papers, M-46, Box 1.

22. Tablet from 'Abdu'l-Bahá to Roy C. Wilhelm, translated by Mirza A. U. Fareed, received December 21, 1904, USBNA, Roy C. Wilhelm papers, M-46, Box 1.

23. In March 1907, Roy Wilhelm listed 415 W. 115th Street in New York as his residence on his US passport application, http://www.ancestry.com.

24. For a discussion of the development of the Morningside Heights neighborhood during the time Roy Wilhelm lived there, see Mike Wallace, *Greater Gotham: A History of New York City from 1898 to 1919*, pp. 368–70.

25. Nathan Rutstein, *He Loved and Served: The Story of Curtis Kelsey*, pp. 24–25.

26. Ibid., p. 25.

27. Ibid.

28. In His Book of Laws, the Kitáb-i-Aqdas, Bahá'u'lláh enjoined on all believers the obligation to make a pilgrimage if they can afford to do so. However, He conditioned this law on one's being free of debt, in good health, and on first gaining permission to come. At the time, the Americans would not have been aware that this was a requirement of the Faith.

29. Tablet from 'Abdu'l-Bahá to J. O. Wilhelm, translated June 2, 1905, by Ameen U. Fareed, USBNA, Roy C. Wilhelm papers, M-46, Box 1.

30. Corinne True, "Notes taken at Acca," p. 18.

31. Ibid., p. 28.

32. Both Wilhelms applied for US passports while in Westminster, England. They had not needed them to visit the British Isles but would require them to enter the Ottoman Empire. Please see http://www.ancestory.com.

33. Most likely, they boarded the ship in Italy, but this is not known with certainty.

34. Earl Redman, *Visiting 'Abdu'l-Bahá, Vol. 1: The West Discovers the Master, 1897–1911*, p. 170. The four were Thornton Chase; Carl Scheffler, who would serve with Roy in Bahá'í administration and become a close friend; and Arthur and Mary Agnew. See also Roy Wilhelm, "Knock, and It Shall Be Opened Unto You, 1907," republished in *In His Presence: Visits*

to 'Abdu'l-Bahá: Memoirs of Roy Wilhelm, Stanwood Cobb, Genevieve L. Coy, p. 6.

35. Roy Wilhelm, "Knock, and It Shall Be Opened Unto You," 1907, republished in *In His Presence: Visits to 'Abdu'l-Bahá: Memoirs of Roy Wilhelm, Stanwood Cobb, Genevieve L. Coy,* p. 6. This was also published in other forms, including in *The Bahá'í World, Vol. IX, 1940–1944,* pp. 802–7.

36. Ibid.

37. Ibid., pp. 6–7.

38. Ibid., p. 7.

39. Ibid., pp. 7–8.

40. Ibid., p. 8.

41. The description of April in the Haifa / 'Akká area and what flowers are in bloom during this month comes from the co-authors' many years living in this area.

42. Roy Wilhelm, "Knock, and It Shall Be Opened Unto You," 1907, republished in *In His Presence: Visits to 'Abdu'l-Bahá: Memoirs of Roy Wilhelm, Stanwood Cobb, Genevieve L. Coy,* pp. 10–11.

43. Ibid.

44. Most likely, these words were said in English. 'Abdu'l-Bahá spoke many basic English phrases, especially greetings. One of the other tenants at the House of 'Abdu'lláh Pá<u>sh</u>á was a British doctor, who operated a medical clinic there. 'Abdu'l-Bahá and the members of His household would have had opportunities to learn some English words from association with the doctor's household and visitors.

45. Nathan Rutstein, *He Loved and Served: The Story of Curtis Kelsey,* p. 26.

46. Roy Wilhelm, "Knock, and It Shall Be Opened Unto You," 1907, republished in *In His Presence: Visits to 'Abdu'l-Bahá: Memoirs of Roy Wilhelm, Stanwood Cobb, Genevieve L. Coy,* pp. 1–22.

47. Ibid., p. 17.

48. 'Abdu'l-Bahá was allowed to move about within the walls of 'Akká, but He was cruelly deprived of leaving the city, even to visit His Father's nearby resting place.

49. Roy Wilhelm, "Knock, and It Shall Be Opened Unto You," 1907, republished in *In His Presence: Visits to 'Abdu'l-Bahá: Memoirs of Roy Wilhelm, Stanwood Cobb, Genevieve L. Coy,* pp. 1–22.

50. Earl Redman, *Visiting 'Abdu'l-Bahá, Vol. 1: The West Discovers the Master, 1897–1911,* p. 170.

51. Roy Wilhelm, "Knock, and It Shall Be Opened Unto You," 1907, republished in *In His Presence: Visits to 'Abdu'l-Bahá: Memoirs of Roy Wilhelm, Stanwood Cobb, Genevieve L. Coy,* p. 14.

52. Betty D'Arujo, personal recollections. Oral interview by Joel Nizin. Betty was the daughter of Carl Scheffler, member of the National Spiritual

Assembly of the United States, close friend, and frequent host to Roy Wilhelm during his travels. See also Robert H. Stockman, *The Bahá'í Faith in America: Early Expansion, 1900–1912, Vol. 2*, pp. 317–18. Years later, during the ministry of Shoghi Effendi, the spelling of Bahá'u'lláh would be standardized, with the "o" in the center changed to a "u."

53. Roy Wilhelm, "Two Glimpses of 'Abdu'l-Bahá," *The Bahá'í World, Vol. IX, 1940–1944*, p. 803.

54. Interview of Betty de Araujo by Joel Nizin.

55. Roy Wilhelm, "Knock, and It Shall Be Opened Unto You," 1907, republished in *In His Presence: Visits to 'Abdu'l-Bahá: Memoirs of Roy Wilhelm, Stanwood Cobb, Genevieve L. Coy*, pp. 17–18.

56. Ibid., pp. 17–18.

57. Ibid., pp. 3–4.

58. Mathew 26: 26–28; Luke 22: 19–20.

59. Roy Wilhelm, "Knock, and It Shall Be Opened Unto You," 1907, republished in *In His Presence: Visits to 'Abdu'l-Bahá: Memoirs of Roy Wilhelm, Stanwood Cobb, Genevieve L. Coy*, p. 19.

60. Ibid.

61. Nathan Rutstein, *He Loved and Served: The Story of Curtis Kelsey*, pp. 25–26.

62. Passenger list of the *S.S. New York*, http://www.ancestry.com.

63. Roy Wilhelm, "Knock, and It Shall Be Opened Unto You," 1907, republished in *In His Presence: Visits to 'Abdu'l-Bahá: Memoirs of Roy Wilhelm, Stanwood Cobb, Genevieve L. Coy*, p. 21.

64. Letter dated May 19, 1909 from Roy Wilhelm to Ahmad Esphahani (Ahmad Sohrab), USBNA, Ahmad Solis Collection, M-955, Box 8.

65. Ibid.

66. Ibid.

67. Tablet from 'Abdu'l-Bahá to Roy Wilhelm, translated on August 14, 1909 by Mirza Ahmad Sohrab. Roy C. Wilhelm papers, USBNA M-46, Box 1.

68. Ibid.

3 / Flowering in New Jersey

1. Letter dated October 18, 1907, from Mírzá Moneer Zane to Roy Wilhelm, USBNA.

2. Tablet from 'Abdu'l-Bahá to Roy Wilhelm, revealed in 'Akká on September 3, 1907, and translated by Mírzá Aḥmad-i-Iṣfahání (Sohrab) on October 9, 1907, Roy C. Wilhelm papers, USBNA, M-46, Box 1.

3. Ibid.

4. M. R. Garis, *Martha Root: Lioness at the Threshold*, pp. 39–40.

5. Ibid., pp. 40–41.

6. Ibid., p. 41.

7. Researchers have thus far been unable to establish the exact familial relationship between Elihu Root and Martha Root, though the two did know each other. Martha used whatever their connection was whenever it assisted her work, especially when dealing with foreign diplomats or officials of other countries. M. R. Garis, *Martha Root: Lioness at the Threshold*, pp. 5, 93, 124, 165.

8. Martha was born on August 10, 1872, in Richwood, Ohio, the youngest of the three children of Timothy T. Root and Nancy Hart Root. Her family were active members of the Baptist Church. While still an infant, Martha's family returned to live in their former community, Cambridgeboro (now Cambridge Springs), Pennsylvania. As a teenager, some of her years studying at Oberlin College would later be considered secondary school (high school). At both Oberlin and University of Chicago, she focused on writing. M. R. Garis, *Martha Root: Lioness at the Threshold*, pp. 7–16.

9. Ibid., p. 41.

10. Martha Root investigated the Bahá'í Faith for about a year and was aided on that journey by a visit to Chicago, where she was greatly touched when she attended a Bahá'í gathering. For an in-depth account of her life, including her first meeting with Roy, her study of the Faith and her acceptance of it and confirmation within it, see M. R. Garis, *Martha Root: Lioness at the Threshold*, especially pp. 39–48.

11. Tablet from 'Abdu'l-Bahá to Roy Wilhelm, translated July 15, 1908, by Mírzá Aḥmad-i-Iṣfahání (Sohrab) in Washington, DC, USBNA, Roy C. Wilhelm papers, M-46, Box 1.

12. Letter from 'Abdu'l-Bahá to Roy Wilhelm, translated on August 11, 1911, by Ahmad Sohrab, USBNA, Roy C. Wilhelm papers, M-46, Box 1.

13. "Mary Hanford Ford," Wikipedia, https://en.wikipedia.org/wiki/Mary_Hanford_Ford.

14. Mildred Taylor, "The William Walter Phelps Mansion 'The Grange,'" History of Teaneck Township, https://archive.teanecklibrary.org/phelps/grange.html.

15. "Teaneck, New Jersey 40 years of Progress 1895–1935," reference section, Teaneck Historic Collection.

16. Mildred Taylor, "The William Walter Phelps Mansion 'The Grange,'" History of Teaneck Township, https://archive.teanecklibrary.org/phelps/grange.html.

17. R. Jackson Armstrong-Ingram, "Bourgeois, Jean-Baptiste Louis (1856–1930)," 1997, https://bahai-lbrarycom/armstrong-ingram_jean-baptiste_louis_bourgeois.

18. Ibid.

19. Bruce W. Whitmore, *The Dawning Place: The Building of a Temple, the Forging of the North American Bahá'í Community*, pp. 76–77.

20. "Paul De Longpré," https://en.wikipedia.org/wiki/Paul_de_Longpr%C3%A9.

21. Bruce W. Whitmore, *The Dawning Place: The Building of a Temple, the Forging of the North American Bahá'í Community*, p. 78.

22. The Institution of the Mashriqu'l-Adhkár. A Statement and Compilation prepared by the Research Department of the Universal House of Justice, September 2017.

23. Bruce W. Whitmore, *The Dawning Place: The Building of a Temple, the Forging of the North American Bahá'í Community*, pp. 24–35.

24. 'Abdu'l-Bahá, quoted in Shoghi Effendi, *God Passes By*, p. 437.

25. R. Jackson Armstrong-Ingram, *Music, Devotions, and Mashriqu'l-Adhkár: Studies in Bábí and Bahá'í History, Volume Four*, pp. 166–67.

26. Tablet from 'Abdu'l-Bahá to Roy C. Wilhelm, translated by Mirza Ahmad Sohrab on August 14, 1909, USBNA, Roy Wilhelm papers, M-46, Box 1.

27. April 4, 1910, letter from Roy Wilhelm to John Bosch, USBNA; see also Angelina Diliberto Allen, *John David Bosch: In the Vanguard of Heroes, Martyrs, and Saints*, p. 300.

28. Years later, National Spiritual Assemblies were given authority to decide upon issues of membership status, subject to the approval of the Universal House of Justice. Local Spiritual Assemblies are not authorized to make such determinations, only to make recommendations and present information.

29. For a more thorough discussion of the establishment and development of the New York Board of Council, see Kathryn Jewett Hogenson, *Infinite Horizons: The Life and Times of Horace Holley*, pp. 101–105.

30. *Bahá'í News* vol. 1, no. 1 (March 21, 1910): 17. The annual election of the Board of Council recently took place. Those elected to serve for the ensuing year were Messrs. Mills, Kinney, Brittingham, Wilhelm, (Wm.) Dodge, Baker, Marshall, Woodcock and Mírzá Raffie.

31. Nathan Rutstein, *He Loved and Served: The Story of Curtis Kelsey*, pp. 8–9.

4 / Joyous Days: 'Abdu'l-Bahá in America

1. 'Abdu'l-Bahá, *Promulgation of Universal Peace: Talks Delivered by 'Abdul-Bahá during His Visit to the United States and Canada in 1912*, p. 289.

2. The overthrow of the Sultanate government in 1908 led to the release of all political and religious prisoners in the Ottoman Empire. A telegram was sent to inquire if 'Abdu'l-Bahá was included in this release, and an affirmative response was quickly received. However, until His own release was officially confirmed by telegram, 'Abdu'l-Bahá continued to consider Himself a prisoner. This took time. Shoghi Effendi, *God Passes By*, pp. 271–72.

3. Earl Redman, *Visiting 'Abdu'l-Bahá, Volume 1: The West Discovers the Master, 1897–1911*, pp. 254–55.

4. See for example, the general Tablet 'Abdu'l-Bahá sent to "the members of the Assemblies [Communities] of Bahais in America" which was translated on December 8, 1910, discussing the conditions which had to be met for Him to journey to North America. *Bahá'í News*, vol. 1, no. 16 (Dec. 31, 1910): 1–2. See also a Tablet to Dr. Amin Fareed, *Bahá'í News*, vol. 1, no. 17 (Jan. 19, 1911): 2–3.

5. Undated letter from the Executive Board Bahá'í Temple Unity, *Bahá'í News*, vol. 1, no. 12 (Oct. 16, 1910): 6.

6. Ibid.

7. Ibid.

8. Tablet from 'Abdu'l-Bahá to "The Friends of God and the Maidservants of the Merciful in America," translated Dec. 16, 1911, in *Star of the West*, vol. 2, no. 16 (Dec. 31, 1911): 1.

9. Tablet from 'Abdu'l-Bahá to Roy Wilhelm, translated by Mirza Ahmad Sohrab on August 11, 1911. USBNA, Roy C. Wilhelm papers, M-46, Box 1.

10. Tablet from 'Abdu'l-Bahá to Roy C. Wilhelm, translated by Mirza Ahmad Sohrab on February 21, 1912. USBNA, Roy C. Wilhelm papers, M-46, Box 1.

11. Tablet from 'Abdu'l-Bahá to Roy C. Wilhelm, translated by Hippolyte Dreyfus and received by Roy Wilhelm on March 5, 1912. USBNA, Roy C. Wilhelm papers, M-46, Box 1.

12. "To the Bahá'í Assemblies of America," *Star of the West*, vol. 2, no. 16 (Dec. 31, 1911): p. 10.

13. "To the Bahá'í Assemblies of North America, and all Friends in the Cause of God," letter from the Executive Board Bahá'í Temple Unity, *Star of the West*, vol. 2, no. 18 (Feb. 7, 1912): 1–2.

14. Wendell Phillips Dodge, "'Abdu'l-Bahá's Arrival in America," *Star of the West*, vol. 3, no. 3 (Apr. 28, 1912): 2.

15. For accounts of the Church of the Ascension address on April 14, 1913, see "'Abdu'l-Bahá's First Public Address in America," *Star of the West*, vol. 3, no. 3 (Apr. 28, 1912): 5–6; *Maḥmúd's Diary: The Diary of Mírzá Maḥmúd-i-Zarqání Chronicling 'Abdu'l-Bahá's Journey to America*, p. 43; Juliet Thompson, *The Diary of Juliet Thompson*, pp. 242–48.

16. For a discussion of the establishment of the Faith in North America, see Kathryn Jewett Hogenson, *Lighting the Western Sky: The Hearst Pilgrimage and the Establishment of the Bahá'í Faith in the West*, throughout.

17. 'Abdu'l-Bahá, *The Promulgation of Universal Peace: Talks Delivered by 'Abdu'l-Bahá during His Visit to the United States and Canada in 1912*, p. 89.

18. Ibid.

19. Nathan Rustein, *Corinne True: Faithful Handmaid of 'Abdu'l-Bahá*, pp. 101–103.

20. "The stone the builders rejected has become the cornerstone." New International Version Bible, Psalms 118: 22.

21. Bruce W. Whitmore, *The Dawning Place*, pp. 42–48.

22. Tablet from 'Abdu'l-Bahá to Roy Wilhelm, translated by Hippolyte Dreyfus and received by Roy Wilhelm on March 5, 1912. USBNA, Roy C. Wilhelm papers, M-46, Box 1.

23. Ibid.

24. Ibid.

25. Mírzá Maḥmúd-i-Zarqání, *Mahmúd's Diary*, pp. 43–149.

26. Ibid. p. 140.

27. Recollections of Roy Wilhelm, USBNA, Walter H. Blakely Papers, M-285, Box 2, pp. 9–10.

28. Ibid.

29. According to the written recollections of Edward "Saffa" Kinney and his wife, Vaffa Kinney, 'Abdu'l-Bahá requested that the menu be fried chicken, lamb, rice, eggplant and many other vegetables.

30. 'Abdu'l-Bahá, *The Promulgation of Universal Peace: Talks Delivered by 'Abdu'l-Bahá during His Visit to the United States and Canada in 1912*, p. 289.

31. *The Bahá'í World, Vol. VII, 1936–1938*, p. 540.

32. Recollections of Vaffa Kinney regarding the Unity Feast held on June 29, 1912.

33. Audio recording of a 1942 interview of Roy Wilhelm, Curtis Kelsey, and Edward Struven, made at Speckled Mountain, Maine. The tape was obtained from Douglas Struven, Squaw Valley, California, 1993.

34. Ibid.

35. Recollections of Vaffa Kinney regarding the Unity Feast held on June 29, 1912.

36. Audio recording of a 1942 interview of Roy Wilhelm, Curtis Kelsey and Edward Struven made at Speckled Mountain, Maine. The tape was obtained from Douglas Struven, Squaw Valley, California, 1993.

37. See Special to the *New York Times* / Montclair, NJ, June 29, 1912.

38. Mírzá Maḥmúd-i-Zarqání, *Mahmúd's Diary*, pp. 149–50.

39. Juliet Thompson, *The Diary of Juliet Thompson*, p. 322.

40. "A Memorable Feast: 'Abdu'l-Bahá the Host" by Ester Foster, *Star of the West*, vol. 3, no. 8, pp. 16–18.

41. Audio recording of a 1942 interview of Roy Wilhelm, Curtis Kelsey and Edward Struven made at Speckled Mountain, Maine. The tape was obtained from Douglas Struven, Squaw Valley, California, 1993.

42. Allan L Ward, *239 Days: 'Abdu'l-Bahá's Journey in America*, p. 102.

43. Juliet Thompson, *The Diary of Juliet Thompson*, pp. 322–23.

44. Ibid., p. 323.

45. While the Bahá'í Faith plays down the miracles of the Báb, Bahá'u'lláh, and 'Abdu'l-Bahá, those who were with 'Abdu'l-Bahá witnessed many scenarios which seemed miraculous, including His healing the sick and His knowledge of the past and future. He knew what people were thinking without being told. For accounts of these "miracles," see any of the growing number of books, pamphlets and articles which include accounts of His life. One of the authors, Kathryn Jewett Hogenson, heard stories of miraculous healing, miraculous knowledge and other seemingly preternatural events from two people who experienced them firsthand while they were with 'Abdu'l-Bahá: Edna True and Stanwood Cobb. See also, for examples of seeming miraculous happenings scattered throughout the following accounts of encounters with 'Abdu'l-Bahá: Juliet Thompson, *The Diary of Juliet Thompson*; Howard Colby Ives, *Portals to Freedom*; and Bahíyyih Randall-Winckler, *William Henry Randall.*

46. Audio tape Ed Struven and Curtis Kelsey and Roy Wilhelm, Maine 1942. Transcription by Joel S. Nizin, October 1992.

47. The detail of the table arrangement is taken from the recollections of Vaffa Kinney about the Unity Feast.

48. Ibid. 'Abdu'l-Bahá gave the 4-ounce bottle of attar of rose to Mrs. Grace Ober, who donated it to the Teaneck, New Jersey Bahá'í Archives. Curtis Kelsey, "Notes on development of property of the late Roy C. Wilhelm, Hand of the Bahá'í Faith at West Englewood, New Jersey." See also "Recollection of the June 29, 1912, Unity Feast" by Edward B. Kinney, pp. 3–4, 6.

49. 'Abdu'l-Bahá, *The Promulgation of Universal Peace: Talks Delivered by 'Abdu'l-Bahá during His Visit to the United States and Canada in 1912*, p. 300.

50. Juliet Thompson, *The Diary of Juliet Thompson*, p. 322.

51. 'Abdu'l-Bahá, *The Promulgation of Universal Peace: Talks Delivered by 'Abdu'l-Bahá during His Visit to the United States and Canada in 1912*, pp. 298–99.

52. Dr. Amin Farid's translation of 'Abdu'l-Bahá's third talk at the 1912 picnic:

> . . . Praise be to God! Our gathering is the gathering of love and this assemblage of ours is for the sake of unity; this association of ours is in order to bring about and proclaim the oneness of the world of man; these efforts of ours are extended towards quickening eternally the world of humanity; these words that we speak are in order to cause the coming forth of the virtues of the human world. We have no personal desire; we have no essential purpose which is of a selfish nature. We have no material feelings; all our feelings tonight are spiritual; all our

purposes this evening are of the Kingdom. Our whole wish consists in the coming forth of the Divine virtues from men. All our wish is to bring about the Guidance of God.

Were one to look fairly, we would say that today upon this planet no such gathering, such an assemblage exists. This gathering is distinguished above all the other gatherings held in the world, because this is a spiritual gathering, a shining gathering, a divine gathering, a heavenly gathering. All of you are turning towards God, and you have no purpose or wish except His Love. All of us are exerting towards benefiting the world of humanity, so that the world of humanity may become illumined, so that the eternal life may become manifest, so that the power of Divinity may come forth, so that the Fragrance of God may become diffused—that the world may become another world, the universal resuscitation may come to pass, the most great resurrection may become manifest, that the dead may be raised, the blind may see, the deaf may hear, the withered may become verdant and refreshing, the sick may receive healing, the ignorant may become knowing, those in darkness may receive light, those earthly may become heavenly. This is our purpose. This is our utmost desire. Our wish is that by the Grace and Providence of God, this most mighty gift may become manifest.

I pray in behalf of you all, and I pray to God to send this most great gift to every individual among you. It is my hope that ye shall become the cause of transforming this material world into another world, so that the teaching of all the prophets may become realized and fulfilled; so that this earthly world may be transformed into the Paradise of Abhá.

The third speech was recorded by Maḥmúd and translated by Dr. Amin Farid. It appears in the National Archives of the Baháʼís of the United States in both the Roy Wilhelm collection and the Martha Root collection.

53. ʻAbdu'l-Bahá, *The Promulgation of Universal Peace: Talks Delivered by ʻAbdu'l-Bahá during His Visit to the United States and Canada in 1912*, p. 299.

54. Audio recording of a 1942 interview of Roy Wilhelm, Curtis Kelsey, and Edward Struven made at Speckled Mountain, Maine. The tape was obtained from Douglas Struven, Squaw Valley, California, 1993.

55. Ibid.

56. Mírzá Maḥmúd-i-Zarqání, *Maḥmúd's Diary*, p. 151.

57. Juliet Thompson, *The Diary of Juliet Thompson*, p. 324.

58. Ibid.

59. Audio recording of a 1942 interview of Roy Wilhelm, Curtis Kelsey, and Edward Struven made at Speckled Mountain, Maine. The tape was obtained from Douglas Struven, Squaw Valley, California, 1993.

60. Ibid.

61. Áqá Siyyid Assadu'lláh.

62. Audio recording of a 1942 interview of Roy Wilhelm, Curtis Kelsey, and Edward Struven made at Speckled Mountain, Maine. The tape was obtained from Douglas Struven, Squaw Valley, California, 1993.

63. Ibid.

64. Mírzá Maḥmúd-i-Zarqání, *Maḥmúd's Diary*, p. 153.

65. Allan L Ward, *239 Days: 'Abdu'l-Bahá's Journey in America*, p. 103.

66. Amin Egea, *The Apostle of Peace*, Vol. I, pp. 376–77.

67. Mírzá Maḥmúd-i-Zarqání, *Maḥmúd's Diary*, p. 153.

68. Amin Egea, *The Apostle of Peace*, Vol. I, pp. 376–77.

69. Mírzá Maḥmúd-i-Zarqání, *Maḥmúd's Diary*, p. 168.

70. Ibid., p. 169.

71. Charlotte Segler, "Little Personal Touches," January 1935, Early Believer Collection of papers, New York, New York Bahá'í Archives.

72. Ibid.

73. Ibid.

74. Ibid.

75. Ibid.

76. Ibid.

77. For more details of this relationship between Sarah Farmer and Phoebe Hearst and their joint interest in Green Acre, see Kathryn Jewett Hogenson, *Lighting the Western Sky: The Hearst Pilgrimage and the Establishment of the Bahá'í Faith in the West*, pp. 42, 261–62.

78. Walter Blakely recollection, USBNA, Walter H. Blakely papers, Box 2.

79. For more about Fred Mortensen, see Earl Redman, *'Abdu'l-Bahá in their Midst*, pp. 168–75.

80. Robert Stockman, *'Abdu'l-Bahá in America*, pp. 298–99.

81. Tablet from 'Abdu'l-Bahá to Roy C. Wilhelm translated on September 7, 1912, in Montreal, Canada by Ahmad Sohrab. At the close of this letter, 'Abdu'l-Bahá sends greetings to Roy's parents and to his neighbor, Louis Bourgeois. USBNA, Roy C. Wilhelm papers, M-46, Box 1.

82. Juliet Thompson, *The Diary of Juliet Thompson*, pp. 376–77.

5 / Twin Duties

1. For general discussions of Hands of the Cause of God, see "The Institution of the Hands of the Cause of God, *The Bahá'í World Vol. XIX, 1963–1968*, pp. 459–65; Barron Harper, *Lights of Fortitude*, pp. ix–xi; Kathryn Jewett Hogenson, *Infinite Horizons: The Life and Times of Horace Holley*, pp. 322–24.

2. Handwritten recollection of Walter Blakely, USBNA, Walter H. Blakely papers, M-285, Box 2.

3. Letter dated November 16, 1922, from Roy Wilhelm to Alfred Lunt, USBNA, Alfred Lunt papers, M-10, Box 11.

4. Handwritten note of extract from tablet from 'Abdu'l-Bahá to Roy Wilhelm which Roy received on March 5, 1912, which was translated and dispatch by Hippolyte Dreyfus. The note is attached to the typed copies of tablets Roy received from 'Abdu'l-Bahá in March 1913. USBNA, Roy C. Wilhelm papers, M-46, Box 1.

5. The authors have chosen to not provide any information that would identify the individual in question. The Tablet is discussed as an example of how 'Abdu'l-Bahá managed a difficult person. USBNA, Roy C. Wilhelm papers.

6. Tablet dated May 22, 1913, from 'Abdu'l-Bahá to Roy Wilhelm, written in Paris, France and translated by Ahmad Sohrab. USBNA, Roy C. Wilhelm papers, M-46, Box 1.

7. Letter dated December 18, 1917, from Roy Wilhelm to Agnes Parson. USBNA, Agnes Parsons papers, M-32, Box 16.

8. Ibid.

9. Ibid.

10. Copy of cablegram from 'Abdu'l-Bahá to Roy Wilhelm and sent to other communities by Roy on December 30, 1912. USBNA, Roy C. Wilhelm papers, M-46, Box 1.

11. Letter dated December 30, 1912, from Roy Wilhelm to *Star of the West* editor Albert Windust. USBNA, Albert Windust papers.

12. Letter dated March 26, 1913 from Ahmad Sohrab to Roy Wilhelm. USBNA, Roy C. Wilhelm papers, M-46, Box 2.

13. Tablet dated August 2, 1913, from 'Abdu'l-Bahá to Roy Wilhelm. *Star of the West*, vol. 4, no. 14 (November 23, 1913): 240–41.

14. Tablet from 'Abdu'l-Bahá to Roy Wilhelm, translated on January 23, 1913 by Ahmad Sohrab. Tablet from 'Abdu'l-Bahá to Roy Wilhelm, translated on September 6, 1920, translated by Azizullah S. Bahadur. USBNA, Roy C. Wilhelm papers, M-46, Box 1.

15. Tablet dated April 22, 1913, from 'Abdu'l-Bahá to Roy Wilhelm, revealed in Vienna, Austria. Translated by Ahmad Sohrab on May 4, 1913, in Paris, France.

16. Tablet from 'Abdu'l-Bahá to Roy Wilhelm, translated on August 2, 1913, in Ramleh, Egypt, printed in *Star of the West*, vol. 4, no. 14 (November 23, 1913): 240–41.

17. Tablet from 'Abdu'l-Bahá sent through Roy C. Wilhelm to the friends of God and the maid-servants of the Merciful, United States, translated by Ahmad Sohrab on April 19, 1914. USBNA, Roy C. Wilhelm papers, M-46, Box 1.

18. See for example, Tablet from 'Abdu'l-Bahá to Roy Wilhelm, translated by Ahmad Sohrab on August 12, 1914. USBNA, Roy C. Wilhelm

papers, M-46, Box 1. Tablet from 'Abdu'l-Bahá to Roy Wilhelm, September 7, 1912; Tablet from 'Abdu'l-Bahá to Roy Wilhelm March 25, 1913; Tablet from 'Abdu'l-Bahá to Roy Wilhelm, May 4, 1913; Tablet from 'Abdu'l-Bahá to Roy Wilhelm, May 22, 1913; Tablet from 'Abdu'l-Bahá to Roy Wilhelm, August 2, 1913; Tablet from 'Abdu'l-Bahá to Roy Wilhelm, February 14, 1914. USBNA, Roy C. Wilhelm papers, M-46, Box 1.

19. Tablet from 'Abdu'l-Bahá to Roy Wilhelm, translated by Ahmad Sohrab on August 12, 1914. USBNA, Roy C. Wilhelm papers, M-46, Box 1.

20. Tablet from 'Abdu'l-Bahá to Roy Wilhelm, translated on August 12, 1914. USBNA, Roy C. Wilhelm papers, M-46, Box 1.

21. The authors do not know who the Covenant-breaker was or any details of the encounter.

22. Tablet from 'Abdu'l-Bahá to Roy Wilhelm, October 1914. USBNA, Roy C. Wilhelm papers, M-46, Box 1.

23. "The Main Sessions of the Convention: A Digest from the Minutes," *Star of the West*, vol. 7, no. 7 (July 13, 1916): 60.

24. *Star of the West*, vol. 8, no. 10, p. 133.

25. Technically, Big Ben is the name of the largest bell of the clock at the top of a tower of the Houses of Parliament building in London, though in popular usage it has come to mean the tower, clock, and its bells. Little Ben is a smaller replica of the landmark tower near Victoria Station in central London. It is unclear if by "Big Ben" and "Little Ben," Roy was referring to the towers or the bells. Certainly, the bell analogy ringing forth the good news of new Divine Guidance was apt.

26. Martha Root, "Pot-Pourri of Convention Fragrances," *Star of the West*, vol. 8, no. 9 (August 20, 1917): 108.

27. General letter to the Bahá'í community from Roy Wilhelm. Written in 1917, the letter is otherwise undated. Lunt papers, USBNA.

28. Ibid.

29. At the bottom of the letter, Roy quotes 'Abdu'l-Bahá as saying, "Find thou always time to say some earnest word between the idle talk." Ibid.

30. Ibid.

31. Tablet from 'Abdu'l-Bahá to Roy Wilhelm, translated by Shoghi Rabbani on December 12, 1918. *Star of the West*, vol. 10, no. 1 (March 21, 1919): 10.

32. Tablet from 'Abdu'l-Bahá to Roy Wilhelm, translated by Shoghi Rabbani on April 26, 1919. USBNA, Roy C. Wilhelm papers, M-46, Box 1.

33. Tablet from 'Abdu'l-Bahá to Roy Wilhelm, translated by Shoghi Rabbani on December 12, 1918. USBNA, Roy C. Wilhelm papers, M-46, Box 1.

34. Robert Stockman, *The Bahá'í Faith in America, Vol. 2*, p. 321.

35. 1916 records of the Executive Committee of Bahá'í Temple Unity. These are held as part of the records of the National Spiritual Assembly of the United States.

36. Letter dated August 13, 1915, from Roy Wilhelm to P. B. Coyne, USBNA, Albert Windust papers, M-21, Box 12.

37. This instruction would be changed years later by Shoghi Effendi, who standardized the transliteration of Persian and Arabic into English. He directed that pronouns or other words referring to 'Abdu'l-Bahá be capitalized, the practice followed in this work.

38. Letter dated August 13, 1915, from Roy Wilhelm to P. B. Coyne, USBNA, Albert Windust papers, M-21, Box 12.

39. Tablet dated April 11, 1916 from 'Abdu'l-Bahá to Roy Wilhelm, translated by Ahmad Sohrab. USBNA, Roy C. Wilhelm papers, M-46, Box 1.

40. June 29, 1913, *New York Times*, weather report on page 2.

41. Tablet from 'Abdu'l-Bahá to Roy Wilhelm, translated on August 2, 1913 by Ahmad Sohrab in Ramleh, Egypt. *Star of the West*, vol. 4, no. 14 (November 23, 1913): 240–41.

42. Like Roy, Martha Root would be posthumously named a Hand of the Cause of God by Shoghi Effendi.

43. November 12, 1912, letter from Roy Wilhelm to Martha Root. USBNA, Roy C. Wilhelm papers, M-46, Box 2.

44. Ibid.

45. Letter dated February 1, 1914, from Roy Wilhelm to Ella C. Cooper. USBNA, Ella G. Cooper papers, M-7, Box 10. Daddy-longlegs are a variety of harmless spider with very long legs that are easy to pick up. "Spud-de-pommes" are potatoes.

46. Ibid. To "stand pat" is to stubbornly refuse to move or waiver from one's opinion or decision.

47. See, for example, "Follower of Bahá'í died on West Side; Cult Rites Observed," *Atlantic City Daily Press*, February 10, 1914, which concluded with a paragraph with the subheading "Predict a War." The article went on to say of the Bahá'ís that "They look forward to a great European war in the near future—a war that will change the map of the world—and it is their belief that this will be the last war under our present civilization."

48. For background on this period and President Woodrow Wilson's response to the onset of World War I as well as that of various groups within the United States, see Larry Schweikart and Dave Dougherty, *A Patriot's History of the Modern World: From America's Exceptional Ascent to the Atomic Bomb: 1898–1945*, pp. 110–19; and Thomas J. Knock, *To End All Wars: Woodrow Wilson and the Quest for a New World Order*, pp. 32–38, 55–67.

49. Tablet dated June 1, 1914, from 'Abdu'l-Bahá to Roy Wilhelm, translated by Ahmad Sohrab. USBNA, Roy C. Wilhelm papers, M-46, Box 1.

50. Ibid.

51. Ibid.

52. Tablet from 'Abdu'l-Bahá to Roy Wilhelm, translated by Ahmad Sohrab on April 30, 1914. USBNA, Roy C. Wilhelm papers, M-46, Box 1.

53. M. R. Garis, *Martha Root: Lioness at the Threshold*, pp. 58–63.

54. Ibid., pp. 63–71.

55. Ibid., pp. 72–73.

6 / Moving Forward

1. See Kathryn Jewett Hogenson, *Infinite Horizons: The Live and Times of Horace Holley*, p. 92 and Ahmad Sohrab, *The Story of the Divine Plan*, pp. 5–43, which contains a detailed account of the revelation of the Tablets of the Divine Plan as remembered by the one then serving as the secretary and translator of 'Abdu'l-Bahá, Ahmad Sohrab. (Sohrab later rebelled against the Bahá'í Administrative Order and became estranged from the Faith. He was designated a Covenant-breaker.)

2. This first group of Tablets, collectively referred to as "The Tablets of the Divine Plan" were printed in the September 8, 1916 *Star of the West*, vol. 7, no. 10, pp. 87–91. The names of those these were mailed to are included along with other specifics about the dispatch and translation of the Tablets from Haifa.

3. "The Teaching Campaign—A Suggestion," *Star of the West*, vol. 7, no. 12 (October 16, 1916): 112–13.

4. The information in this paragraph is derived from the institutional records of the United States National Spiritual Assembly, including those of the Temple Unity Executive Committee held within the US Bahá'í Archives.

5. Tablet dated August 26, 1919, from 'Abdu'l-Bahá to Roy Wilhelm, translated by Shoghi Rabbani, USBNA, Roy C. Wilhelm papers, M-46, Box 1.

6. Politicians born during the heyday of the log cabin, such as President Abraham Lincoln, promoted their births in such frontier homes to emphasize their humble beginnings as a badge of honor.

7. Letter dated January 19, 1919, from Roy Wilhelm to 'Abdu'l-Bahá, USBNA, Roy C. Wilhelm papers, M-46, Box 1.

8. See deeds found in the Bergen County land records.

9. "Teaneck, New Jersey 40 years of Progress 1895–1935," reference section Teaneck Historic Collection p. 17.

10. Tablet from 'Abdu'l-Bahá to Roy Wilhelm, translated on December 12, 1918 by Shoghi Rabbani, *Star of the West*, vol. 10, no. 1, p. 9.

11. Ibid.

12. Tablet from 'Abdu'l-Bahá to Martha Root, translated on January

10, 1919, by Shoghi Rabbani, *Star of the West*, vol. 10, no. 2, p. 30.

13. Adib Taherzadeh, *The Covenant of Bahá'u'lláh*, pp. 343–44.

14. For more about Sohrab and his breaking of the Covenant, see Kathryn Jewett Hogenson, *Infinite Horizons: The Live and Times of Horace Holley*, pp. 146–59.

15. Ibid.

16. During World War I, the "Reading Room" conflict drained the vibrancy of the North American Bahá'í community by generating ill feelings among a number of active members of the Faith at the national level. For more about this division, see Kathryn Jewett Hogenson, *Infinite Horizons: The Life and Times of Horace Holley*, pp. 137–38.

17. Ibid, pp. 92–93.

18. The last places mentioned by name in the Tablets of the Divine Plan to be opened to the Faith in 1989 and 1990 were Mongolia and the Sakhalin Islands, respectively. This systematic process of taking the Bahá'í Faith to the farthest corners of the world began in earnest with the 1919 promulgation of the Tablets of the Divine Plan.

19. M. R. Garis, *Martha Root: Lioness at the Threshold*, pp. 89–110.

20. Records of the Temple Unity held by the National Spiritual Assembly of the United States.

21. For a thorough discussion of the Bourgeois, Remey, and Maxwell designs, see R. Jackson Armstrong-Ingram, *Music, Devotions, and Mashriqu;l-Adhkár*, pp. 175–92.

22. Ibid, pp. 220–21

23. February 13, 1950, letter from Roy Wilhelm to Horace Holley, USBNA, Horace Holley papers, M-2, Box 5. Roy also showed 'Abdu'l-Bahá a photograph of the ornamentation of windows at the palatial home Louis designed in Hollywood, California for his father-in-law.

24. Tablet from 'Abdu'l-Bahá to Roy Wilhelm, translated by Shoghi Rabbani on December 12, 1918. It was reproduced in *Star of the West*, vol. 10, no. 1 (March 21, 1919): 9.

25. Ibid.

26. Tablet from 'Abdu'l-Bahá to Roy Wilhelm, translated by Shoghi Rabbani on April 26, 1919. It was reproduced in *Star of the West*, vol. 10, no. 5 (June 5, 1919): 95.

27. "Twelfth Annual Masrekol-Azkar Convention and Bahai Congress," by Louis G. Gregory, *Star of the West*, vol. 11, no. 4 (May 17, 1920): 59–60.

28. For more detailed information about the design of the House of Worship and the process of choosing it, see Bruce W. Whitmore, *The Dawning Place: The Building of a Temple, the Forging of the North American Bahá'í Community*, pp. 76–95; R. Jackson Armstrong-Ingram, *Music, Devotions, and Mashriqu'l-Adhkár: Studies in Bábí and Bahá'í History, vol. 4*, pp. 175–192.

29. Letter dated June 23, 1919 from Roy Wilhelm to Gertrude Bukiema, Albert Windust papers, USBNA, M-21, Box 14.

30. Tablet dated May 25, 1919 from 'Abdu'l-Bahá to Roy Wilhelm, USBNA, Roy C. Wilhelm papers, M-46, Box 1. The document makes no mention of the translator, nor is the Tablet signed.

31. Letter dated January 14, 1920, from Roy Wilhelm to Ella Cooper, USBNA, Ella Goodall Cooper papers, M-7, Box 10.

32. Nathan Rutstein, *He Loved and Served: The Story of Curtis Kelsey,* p. 28.

33. Letter dated August 4, 1921, from Roy Wilhelm to Alfred Lunt, USBNA, Alfred Lunt papers, M-10, Box 10.

34. Tablet written by 'Abdu'l-Bahá to Roy Wilhelm, translated by Azizullah S. Bahadur on November 4, 1920, USBNA, Roy C. Wilhelm papers, M-46, Box 1.

35. The 1936 Congressional Act funded the initiative to bring electric power to the homes and barns of rural Americans.

36. Curtis Kelsey, "Notes on development of property of the late Roy C. Wilhelm, Hand of the Bahá'í Faith at West Englewood, New Jersey" (Bradenton, Florida, 1967) audio recording held by Joel Nizin. See also another transcript of an oral history of Curtis Kelsey at http://paintdrawer.co.uk/david/folders/Research/Bahai/Abdul-Baha/kelsey_transcript_abdulbaha_guardian.htm.

37. Ibid. See also Tablet from 'Abdu'l-Bahá to Roy C. Wilhelm, translated on June 25, 1920 by Azizullah S. Bahadur, USBNA, Roy Wilhelm papers, M-46, Box 1.

38. Tablet from 'Abdu'l-Bahá to Roy C. Wilhelm, translated on June 25, 1920 by Azizullah S. Bahadur, USBNA, Roy Wilhelm papers, M-46, Box 1.

39. Curtis Kelsey, "Notes on development of property of the late Roy C. Wilhelm, Hand of the Bahá'í Faith at West Englewood, New Jersey" (Bradenton, Florida, 1967) audio recording held by Joel Nizin. See also recollections of Walter Blakely, USBNA; and Tablet from 'Abdu'l-Bahá to Roy C. Wilhelm dated June 14, 1921 and translated by Azizullah S. Bahadur, USBNA, Roy Wilhelm papers, M-46, Box 1.

40. Ibid.

41. Ibid.

42. See Nathan Rutstein's account of his father-in-law in the 1982 biography *Curtis Kelsey: He Loved and Served.*

43. Tablet from 'Abdu'l-Bahá to Roy Wilhelm dated October 13, 1921, USBNA, Roy Wilhelm papers, M-46, Box 1.

44. For more on this period see, H. M. Balyuzi, *'Abdu'l-Bahá: The Centre of the Covenant of Bahá'u'lláh,* pp. 425–35; and Earl Redman, *Visiting 'Abdu'l-Bahá: Vol. 2, The Final Years, 1913–1921,* pp. 78–88.

45. See Earl Redman, *Visiting 'Abdu'l-Bahá: Vol. 2, The Final Years, 1913–1921*, pp. 102.

46. This information about the porridge and napkin comes from an interview with Betty d'Araujo by Joel Nizin. She was the daughter of Roy's close friend and fellow member of the National Spiritual Assembly, Carl Scheffler. As a child, she knew Roy as "Uncle Roy."

47. Cable from 'Abdu'l-Bahá to Roy Wilhelm received on February 27, 1920. "Cablegram from Abdul-Baha," *Star of the West*, vol. 10, no. 19 (March 2, 1920): 344.

48. Tablet dated August 12, 1921, from 'Abdu'l-Bahá to Roy Wilhelm, translated by Aziz 'Ullah S. Bahdur, USBNA, Roy Wilhelm papers, M-46, Box 1.

49. For a more thorough discussion of these problems, see Hogenson, *Infinite Horizons: The Life and Times of Horace Holley*, pp. 136 48.

50. Letter dated October 24, 1921, from Rouhi Afnan to Roy Wilhelm, USBNA, Roy Wilhelm papers, M-46, Box 1.

51. Cable dated November 8, 1921 from 'Abdu'l-Bahá to Roy Wilhelm, *Star of the West*, vol. 12, no. 14 (November 23, 1921): 232.

52. Cable dated November 9, 1921 from Roy Wilhelm to 'Abdu'l-Bahá, *Star of the West*, vol. 12, no. 14 (November 23, 1921): 232.

53. Cable dated November 12, 1921 from 'Abdu'l-Bahá to Roy Wilhelm, *Star of the West*, vol. 12, no. 14 (November 23, 1921): 232.

54. Second cable dated November 12, 1921 from 'Abdu'l-Bahá to Roy Wilhelm, *Star of the West*, vol. 12, no. 14 (November 23, 1921): 232.

7 / A New Day

1. The weather for that day comes from *The New York Times*, vol. LXXI, November 28, 1921, frontpage and page 17.

2. Ibid., frontpage.

3. Earl Redman, *Visiting 'Abdu'l-Baha: Volume 2, The Final Years, 1913–1921*, p. 200.

4. In addition to the book by Earl Redman cited above, for a full account of the passing of 'Abdu'l-Bahá and its aftermath, see Angelina Diliberto Allen, *When the Moon Set Over Haifa*, throughout.

5. Photograph of the cable of November 28, 1921 sent to Roy Wilhelm's cable address (WILHELMITE) from Greatest Holy Leaf, *Star of the West*, vol. 12, no. 15, p. 245.

6. November 12, 1921, second cable from 'Abdu'l-Bahá to Roy Wilhelm, *Star of the West*, vol. 12, no. 14 (November 23, 1921): 232.

7. Cable from Tehran signed by Rouhani (from the House of Spirituality) to Bahai Assemblies, care of Roy Wilhelm's cable address, received December 4, 1921, reproduced in *Star of the West*, vol. 12, no. 16 (December 31, 1921): 253.

8. December 3, 1921, cable from the Executive Board to the Family of 'Abdu'l-Bahá Abbas, *Star of the West*, vol. 12, no. 19 (March 2, 1922): 303. See also December 4, 1921, letter from Roy Wilhelm to Alfred Lunt in which he mentions the cable Lunt sent as Secretary of the Executive Board, and Roy's summary of the reply, which was printed in *Star of the West*, vol. 12, no. 14 (December 12, 1921): 243.

9. December 22, 1921, cable from Bahíyyih Khánum to the Executive Board of Temple Unity, *Star of the West*, vol. 12, no. 19 (March 2, 1922): 303.

10. Ibid.

11. Rúhíyyih Rabbani, *The Priceless Pearl*, p. 49.

12. Letter dated December 19, 1921 from Roy Wilhelm to Alfred Lunt, USBNA, Alfred Lunt papers, M-10, Box 10.

13. Letter dated December 21, 1921 from Alfred Lunt to Roy Wilhelm, USBNA, Alfred Lunt papers, M-10, Box 10.

14. Letter dated January 9, 1922 from Roy Wilhelm to Alfred Lunt, USBNA, Alfred Lunt papers.

15. Copy of cablegram received January 16, 1922, from Bahíyyih Khánum care of Roy Wilhelm, *Star of the West*, vol. 12, no. 17 (January 19, 1922): 259.

16. The best source of information about Shoghi Effendi is Rúhíyyih Rabbani's *The Priceless Pearl*, pp. 1–56.

17. Copy of cablegram received January 22, 1922, from Shoghi Effendi care of Roy Wilhelm, *Star of the West*, vol. 12, no. 18 (February 7, 1922): 273.

18. The First Letter from Shoghi Effendi to the Bahá'ís of America, mailed January 21, 1922, received by Roy Wilhelm's office on February 17, 1922, *Star of the West*, vol. 13, no. 1 (March 21, 1922): 17–18.

19. The First Letter from Shoghi Effendi to the Bahá'ís of America, mailed January 21, 1922, received by Roy Wilhelm's office on February 17, 1922, *Star of the West*, vol. 13, no. 1 (March 21, 1922): 17–18. The letter is also in Shoghi Effendi, *Bahá'í Administration*, pp. 15–17.

20. Most likely, Roy did not see 'Abdu'l-Bahá's final Tablet to America when it first arrived because he was en route to Haifa. Once there, the Tablet was probably shared with him. During his absence, his Bahá'í employee, Nellie Lloyd, faithfully made certain that all incoming Bahá'í mail was dispatched appropriately. Such a Tablet would have been sent to Alfred Lunt, secretary of the Temple Unity Executive Board, and also to Horace Holley, secretary of the New York Board of Council. It would have also been sent to the editors of *Star of the West*.

21. This is probably a reference to Muhammed 'Alí, 'Abdu'l-Bahá's eldest half-brother.

22. The last Tablet revealed by 'Abdu'l-Bahá for the Bahá'ís in America, *Star of the West*, vol. 13, no. 1 (March 21, 1922): 25.

23. Tablet dated June 1, 1914 from 'Abdu'l-Bahá to Roy Wilhelm, translated by Mirza Ahmad Sohrab, USBNA, Roy Wilhelm papers.

24. Letter dated February 2, 1922 from Roy Wilhelm to Agnes Parsons, USBNA, Agnes Parsons papers, M-32, Box 20.

25. Information about Mountfort Mill's life comes primarily from public records found on the website http://www.ancestry.com. He was born on December 27, 1874, to Henry F. Mills and Annie Taylor Mills. His wife, Adele Mittant Mills, who was from France, did not seem to be an active member of the New York Bahá'í community, so little is known about her other than a few brief mentions of her in the society pages of *The New York Times*. Her information derives as well from http://www.ancestry.com.

26. February 23, 1922, Roy Wilhelm Pilgrimage Notes, USBNA, Roy Wilhelm papers, Box 7, Folder 44.

27. Ibid.

28. Ibid. See also Earl Redman, *Shoghi Effendi Through the Pilgrim's Eye, Vol. 1, Building the Administrative Order, 1922–1952*, pp. 30–32.

29. Ibid.

30. Ibid.

31. Louis Gregory, "The Bahá'í Congress for Teaching and the Fourteenth Annual Convention," *Star of the West*, vol. 13, no. 4 (May 17, 1922): 69.

32. Ibid. See also Earl Redman, *Shoghi Effendi Through the Pilgrim's Eye, Vol. 1, Building the Administrative Order, 1922–1952*, p. 32.

33. February 23, 1922, Roy Wilhelm Pilgrimage Notes, USBNA, Roy Wilhelm papers, Box 7, Folder 44.

34. Ibid.

35. Ibid.

36. Ibid.

37. Ibid.

38. Ibid.

39. February 22, 1922, postcard from Roy Wilhelm to Agnes Parsons, USBNA, Agnes Parsons papers, M-32, Box 20.

40. Louis Gregory, "The Bahá'í Congress for Teaching and the Fourteenth Annual Convention," *Star of the West*, vol. 13, no. 4 (May 17, 1922): 89.

41. Ibid.

42. Nathan Rutstein, *Corinne True: Faithful Handmaid of 'Abdu'l-Bahá*, pp. 154–55.

43. February 23, 1922, Roy Wilhelm Pilgrimage Notes, USBNA, Roy Wilhelm papers, Box 7, Folder 44.

44. Bahíyyih Randall-Winckler, *William Henry Randall: Disciple of 'Abdu'l-Bahá*, pp. 210–11.

45. Ibid.

46. Earl Redman, *Shoghi Effendi Through the Pilgrim's Eye, Vol. 1, Building the Administrative Order, 1922–1952*, pp. 44–46.

47. Letter dated 26 February 1922 from Roy Wilhelm to Ella Goodall Cooper, USBNA, Ella Goodall Cooper papers, M-7, Box 10.

48. Transcript of 1922 National Convention, pp. 27–29, record of the National Spiritual Assembly of the United States.

49. 'Abdu'l-Bahá, *Will and Testament of 'Abdu'l-Bahá*, p. 14.

50. Ibid., first section.

51. Robert Weinberg, *Ethel Jenner Rosenberg: The Life and Times of England's Outstanding Bahá'í Pioneer Worker*, pp. 213–14.

52. Please see Shoghi Effendi, *The World Order of Bahá'u'lláh*, pp. 143–57.

53. Charles Mason Remey, *A Pilgrimage to the Holy Land: CMR, 1922*, p. 10, unpublished document, USBNA, Mary Rabb papers, M-466, Box 7.

54. Transcript of 1922 National Convention, pp. 241–42, record of the National Spiritual Assembly of the United States.

55. Letter dated February 26, 1922, from Roy Wilhelm to Ella Goodall Cooper, USBNA, Ella Goodall Cooper papers, M-7, Box 10.

56. Barron Harper, *Lights of Fortitude*, pp. 3–49.

57. 'Abdu'l-Bahá, *Will and Testament of 'Abdu'l-Bahá*, first section.

58. February 23, 1922, Roy Wilhelm Pilgrimage Notes, USBNA, Roy Wilhelm papers, Box 7, Folder 44.

59. Transcript of 1922 National Convention, p. 35, USBNA, National Spiritual Assembly papers.

60. Ibid., p. 36.

61. Ibid.

62. Charles Mason Remey, *A Pilgrimage to the Holy Land: CMR, 1922*, pp. 15–16, unpublished manuscript, USBNA, Mary Rabb papers, M-466, Box 7.

63. Ibid., pp. 28–33. See also Earl Redman, *Shoghi Effendi Through the Pilgrim's Eye, Vol. 1, Building the Administrative Order, 1922–1952*, pp. 42–43.

64. Ibid., pp. 28–30.

65. Ibid.

66. Robert Weinberg, *Ethel Jenner Rosenberg: The Life and Times of England's Outstanding Bahá'í Pioneer Worker*, pp. 206–7.

67. Letter dated February 26, 1922, from Roy Wilhelm to Ella Goodall Cooper, USBNA, Ella Goodall Cooper papers, M-7, Box 10.

68. Bahíyyih Randall-Winckler, *William Henry Randall: Disciple of 'Abdu'l-Bahá*, p. 212.

69. Charles Mason Remey, *A Pilgrimage to the Holy Land: CMR, 1922,* pp. 20–21, unpublished manuscript, USBNA, Mary Rabb papers, M-466, Box 7.

70. Ibid., p. 21.

71. Ibid.

72. Charles Mason Remey, *A Pilgrimage to the Holy Land: CMR, 1922,* pp. 23–24, unpublished document. USBNA, Mary Rabb papers, M-466, Box 7.

73. The restoration of the Garden of Riḍván was one of the matters that Shoghi Effendi and Remey consulted upon during that 1922 visit. Ibid., pp. 24–25.

74. Ibid., pp. 24–25.

75. Charles Mason Remey, *A Pilgrimage to the Holy Land: CMR, 1922,* pp. 25–26, unpublished manuscript. USBNA, Mary Rabb papers, M-466, Box 7.

76. Ibid., pp. 26–27.

77. Rúḥíyyih Rabbani, *The Priceless Pearl,* p. 56; Robert Weinberg, *Ethel Jenner Rosenberg: The Life and Times of England's Outstanding Bahá'í Pioneer Worker,* p. 209.

78. 'Abdu'l-Bahá, *Light of the World,* no. 40, paragraph 8.

79. Transcript of 1922 National Convention, pp. 237–40.

80. Letter dated May 22, 1922 from Roy C. Wilhelm to the *New York Times,* USBNA, Ella Goodall Cooper papers, M7–10.

8 / Hour of Transition

1. Transcript, proceedings of the 1922 National Convention, pp. 9–21, USBNA, National Spiritual Assembly papers.

2. Ibid., pp. 23–25.

3. Ibid., pp. 30–35.

4. Ibid.

5. Ibid., p. 23.

6. Shoghi Effendi, *The World Order of Bahá'u'lláh,* pp. 204-6.

7. Transcript, proceedings of the 1922 National Convention, pp. 73–86. At the time of the election, sixty-four delegates would be seated.

8. Ibid., pp. 116–19.

9. Ibid.

10. Ibid., pp. 143–44.

11. 'Abdu'l-Bahá's *Will & Testament.*

12. Transcript, proceedings of the 1922 national convention, pp. 150–52. USBNA, National Spiritual Assembly papers.

13. Ibid., p. 212.

14. Ibid., p. 214, comment by Harlan Ober.

15. Ibid., pp. 234–36.

16. Ibid., p. 350.

17. Ibid., pp. 357–58.

18. Ibid., p. 271. Corrine True, Alfred Lunt, Henry Randall, Helen Goodall Cooper, Louis Gregory, Mountfort Mills, Roy Wilhelm, Charles Mason Remey, and Zia Bagdadi were elected.

19. Ibid., p. 332.

20. Kathryn Jewett Hogenson, *Infinite Horizons: The Life and Times of Horace Holley*, pp. 233–40. This issue of the role of the Convention came to a head in 1933–1934.

21. Letter dated August 11, 1922 from Roy Wilhelm to Alfred Lunt, USBNA, Alfred Lunt papers, M-101, Box 11.

22. Ibid.

23. Ibid.

24. Letter dated October 2, 1922 from Roy Wilhelm to John Bosch, USBNA, John Bosch papers, M-289, Box 8.

25. Obituary, *The Spice Mill*, vol. XLV, no. 12 (December 1922): 2278.

26. Letter dated October 2, 1922 from Roy Wilhelm to John and Louise Bosch, quoted in Angelina Diliberto Allen, *John David Bosch: In the Vanguard of Heroes, Martyrs, and Saints*, p. 307. USBNA, John Bosch papers, M-289, Box 8. The authors used the original document.

27. M. R. Garis, *Martha Root: Lioness at the Threshold*, p. 149.

28. Bahíyyih Randall-Winckler, *William Henry Randall: Disciple of 'Abdu'l-Bahá*, p. 214. Roy related this conversation while in Haifa in 1922 during a dinner when Shoghi Effendi was present.

29. Letter dated November 6, 1922 from Roy Wilhelm to John and Louise Bosch, quoted in Angelina Diliberto Allen, *John David Bosch: In the Vanguard of Heroes, Martyrs and Saints*, p. 309. USBNA, John Bosch papers, M-289, Box 8. The authors used the original document.

30. Ibid.

31. Angelina Diliberto Allen, *John David Bosch: In the Vanguard of Heroes, Martyrs and Saints*, pp. 307–9.

32. Letter dated April 13, 1923 from Aziz Bahadur to Roy Wilhelm, USBNA, Roy Wilhelm papers, M-46, Box 1.

33. Letter dated May 7, 1923 from Roy Wilhelm to Aziz Bahadur, USBNA, Roy Wilhelm papers, M-46, Box 1.

34. Ibid.

35. For an in-depth study of the life of Horace Holley, see Kathryn Jewett Hogenson, *Infinite Horizons: The Life and Times of Horace Holley*, throughout.

36. Letter dated June 7, 1923 from Roy Wilhelm to Henry Randall, USBNA, Alfred Lunt papers, M-101, Box 11.

37. Letter dated December 24, 1925 from Roy Wilhelm to Friends of the N.S.A., USBNA, Roy Wilhelm papers, M-46, Box 1.

38. Handwritten postscript dated February 5, 1924 from Shoghi Effendi to Roy Wilhelm, USBNA, Roy Wilhelm papers, M-46, Box 1.

39. Letter dated February 18, 1924 written on behalf of Shoghi Effendi to Roy Wilhelm, USBNA, Roy Wilhelm papers, M-46, Box 1.

40. Ibid., handwritten postscript written by Shoghi Effendi to Roy Wilhelm, USBNA, Roy Wilhelm papers, M-46, Box 1.

41. Letter dated October 28, 1924 from Roy Wilhelm to Carl Scheffler, USBNA, Scheffler papers, M-28, Box 4.

42. Anne Gordon Perry, *Green Acre on the Piscataqua* (third edition), p. 166; "Old and New Paths at Green Acre" by Mariam Haney, *Bahá'í Year Book*, Volume One (April, 1925–April, 1926): 87–94.

43. This weaning the Executive Board from the Temple fund management and other aspects of that work was gradual, but significant progress was made in this regard when a joint meeting of the National Assembly and Executive Board was held in the autumn of 1924. Records of the National Spiritual Assembly of the Bahá'ís of the United States.

44. See "Roy C. Wilhelm," by Horace Holley, *The Bahá'í World*, Vol. XII, p. 662.

45. 1930 records of the National Spiritual Assembly of the Bahá'ís of the United States and Canada.

46. Letter dated June 27, 1925 from Martha Root to Lourie Wilhelm and Roy Wilhelm, USBNA, Mabel Garis papers, M-1170, Box 3.

47. 1930 records of the National Spiritual Assembly of the Bahá'ís of the United States and Canada.

48. William Bowens (1878–1947) of Riverton, NJ accepted the Faith in 1910 in Washington, DC. He met 'Abdu'l-Bahá in 1912.

49. Albert Walkup (1879–1977), attorney, moved to Teaneck in 1919, became a Bahá'í in 1926 and gave the opening prayer at the Souvenir Picnic just a month after that declaration. He served on the Teaneck Local Assembly for ten years and as a delegate to National Conventions.

50. Archie Tichenor (1896–1981), was taught the Faith by Roy Wilhelm and Curtis Kelsey and subsequently enrolled in the Faith in the Wilhelm home. An intrepid speaker and teacher of the Faith, he moved in the 1930s to Teaneck into the house where 'Abdu'l-Bahá had stayed overnight.

51. Donald Kinney (1911–1988), served on the Western Hemisphere Committee and the Spiritual Assemblies of Teaneck and Bergenfield, New Jersey. He helped form the first Bahá'í Audio-Visual Aids Committee.

52. Curtis Kelsey, "Notes on development of property of the late Roy C. Wilhelm, Hand of the Bahá'í Faith at West Englewood, New Jersey," Bradenton, FL 1967.

53. Ibid.

54. "Bergen Evening Record," April 28, 1931.

55. Ibid.

56. *Star of the West* (Bahá'í News Service 1922), vol. 22, no. 5 (August): 146.

57. Frederick Lewis Allen, *Only Yesterday, an Informal History of the 1920s*, pp. 279–309.

58. Ibid.

59. Ibid.

60. "History of Poverty & Homelessness in NYC," http://nychome-lesshistory.org/era/great_depression/. For a comprehensive look at the Great Depression, see Amity Shlaes, The Forgotten Man: A New History of the Great Depression.

61. Frederick Lewis Allen, *Since Yesterday: The 1930s in America,* throughout.

9 / Tests and Losses

1. Letter dated April 30, 1930 from Roy Wilhelm to John and Louise Bosch, USBNA.

2. Ibid.

3. Records of the National Spiritual Assembly of the United States and Canada.

4. Kathryn Jewett Hogenson, *Infinite Horizons: The Life and Times of Horace Holley*, p. 259.

5. 1926 records of the National Spiritual Assembly of the United States and Canada.

6. Kathryn Jewett Hogenson, *Infinite Horizons: The Life and Times of Horace Holley*, pp. 208–10.

7. Records of the National Spiritual Assembly of the United States.

8. Ibid.

9. This period, and the arrangements are discussed in part in Kathryn Jewett Hogenson, *Infinite Horizons: The Life and Times of Horace Holley*, p. 210, 279–80.

10. For a full treatment of the financial issues of the 1930s with the advantage of hindsight, see Amity Shlaes, *The Forgotten Man: A New History of the Great Depression.*

11. "Gilead," https://en.wikipedia.org/wiki/Gilead.

12. Letter dated September 19, 1933 written on behalf of Shoghi Effendi to Roy Wilhelm. USBNA, Roy C. Wilhelm papers, M-46, Box 1.

13. Ibid.

14. Letter dated January 4, 1994, from the Universal House of Justice to all National Spiritual Assemblies, quoting the letter dated April, 1955 of Shoghi Effendi; Shoghi Effendi, *Messages to the Bahá'í World*, pp. 84–85.

15. *Bahá'í News,* April, 1936, p. 4.

16. Postscript dated May 25, 1936 by Shoghi Effendi, attached to a letter written on behalf of Shoghi Effendi to Roy Wilhelm, USBNA, Roy C. Wilhelm papers, M-46, Box 1.

17. Shoghi Effendi, *God Passes By,* p. 522.

18. *The Bahá'í World,* Vol. 4 (April 1930–1932): 165.

19. Records of the National Spiritual Assembly of the United States.

20. Letter dated November 26, 1934 written on behalf of Shoghi Effendi to Roy Wilhelm. USBNA, Roy C. Wilhelm papers, M-46, Box 1.

21. Letter dated May 26, 1935 written on behalf of Shoghi Effendi to Roy Wilhelm. USBNA, Roy C. Wilhelm papers, M-46, Box 1.

22. Ibid.

23. Letter dated January 18, 1933, written on behalf of Shoghi Effendi to Roy Wilhelm. USBNA, Roy C. Wilhelm papers, M-46, Box 1.

24. September 30, 1934, postscript from Shoghi Effendi to Roy Wilhelm on a letter written on behalf of Shoghi Effendi to Roy Wilhelm, records of the National Spiritual Assembly of the United States and Canada.

25. Copy of handwritten card dated June 12, 1934 from Roy Wilhelm to Shoghi Effendi. USBNA, Roy C. Wilhelm papers, M-46, Box 1.

26. These included *Gleanings from the Writings of Bahá'u'lláh, Epistle to the Son of the Wolf, Prayers and Meditations,* as well as numerous Tablets and prayers. For a discussion of Shoghi Effendi's translation work, see Rúḥíyyih Rabbani, *The Priceless Pearl,* pp. 202–3.

27. Letter dated September 3, 1932 written on behalf of Shoghi Effendi to Roy Wilhelm. USBNA, Roy C. Wilhelm papers, M-46, Box 1.

28. For a firsthand account of this period, see Frederick Lewis Allen, *Since Yesterday: The 1930s in America, September 3, 1929–September 3, 1939,* as well as Amity Shlaes, *The Forgotten Man: A New History of the Great Depression.*

29. Letter dated May 26, 1932 from Elizabeth Bowen to Roy Wilhelm, USBNA, Roy C. Wilhelm papers, M-46, Box 1.

30. Records of the National Spiritual Assembly of the United States and records of the Spiritual Assembly of New York, New York.

31. Letter dated December 31, 1935 from Shoghi Effendi to an individual, *Lights of Guidance,* no. 838.

32. Letter dated May 10, 1937 from Roy Wilhelm to Carl Scheffler, USBNA, Carl Scheffler papers, M-28, Box 4.

33. Virginia Wright, *Endless Summer,* Down East Magazine, July 2016.

34. "About Us," https://tubbssnowshoes.com/en-us/support/about-us. Founded in Norway, Maine, Tubbs Snowshoes is a pioneer of the American snowshoeing industry.

35. Boston Globe, January 20, 1952, Walter Blakely Collection, Box #2, National Spiritual Assembly of the Bahá'ís of the United States, Archives.

36. "Wilhelm's Chalet by Deborah," http://westernmainedaytrips.blog-spot.com/2014/01/wilhelms-chalet-by-deborah.html.

37. Recollections of Walter Blakely, USBNA, Walter Blakely papers, Box 2.

38. Combined interviews: Douglas Struven, Phone Interview, 1993, by James Mangan and Diane Iverson and in person interview with John (Jack) Hawley, 2004, by Frances Pollitt.

39. Letter dated October 15, 1934 from Florence Morton to Horace Holley. USBNA, Horace Holley papers, box 3.

40. Kathryn Jewett Hogenson, *Infinite Horizons: The Life and Times of Horace Holley*, pp. 258–59, 268.

41. Ibid.

42. Ibid.

43. From a story in the community newsletter, *The Kezar Kat*, Vol. 1, No. 2, August 1938. USBNA, Ella Cooper papers, Box m7–10.

44. *The Lovell News*, Vol. 2, No. 24 (September 25, 1936).

45. Letter dated November 12, 1932 written on behalf of Shoghi Effendi to Roy Wilhelm. USBNA, Roy C. Wilhelm papers, M-46, Box 1.

46. Letter dated November 14, 1932 written on behalf of Shoghi Effendi to Roy Wilhelm. USBNA, Roy C. Wilhelm papers, M-46, Box 1.

47. Records of the National Spiritual Assembly of the United States.

48. Ibid.

49. Records of the Spiritual Assembly of Teaneck Township, New Jersey.

50. Letter dated December 12, 1933 from Roy Wilhelm to the Friends of the West Englewood Community, USBNA.

51. Letter dated March 5, 1933 written on behalf of Shoghi Effendi to Roy Wilhelm. USBNA, Roy C. Wilhelm papers, M-46, Box 1.

52. Ibid. Handwritten postscript by Shoghi Effendi to Roy Wilhelm. USBNA, Roy C. Wilhelm papers, M-46, Box 1.

53. Letter dated December 24, 1933 written on behalf of Shoghi Effendi to Roy Wilhelm. USBNA, Roy C. Wilhelm papers, M-46, Box 1.

54. Letter December 21, 1935 from Roy Wilhelm to Shoghi Effendi. USBNA, Roy C. Wilhelm papers, M-46, Box 1.

55. Postscript dated January 7, 1936 by Shoghi Effendi on a letter written on his behalf to Roy Wilhelm. USBNA, Roy C. Wilhelm papers, M-46, Box 1.

56. M. R. Garis, *Martha Root: Lioness at the Threshold*, p. 423.

57. "Mrs. L. Wilhelm Dead in Teaneck: Succumbs to 2-Year Illness—Hold Services Today," *The Record* (January 27, 1937): 2.

58. "Mrs. Louise Wilhelm Long a Bahá'í Leader, Dies at the Age of 86: Entertained Abdul Baha at Her Home on His Visit in 1912," *Englewood Press* (January 28, 1937).

59. Letter dated January 20, 1937 written on behalf of Shoghi Effendi to Roy Wilhelm. USBNA, Roy C. Wilhelm papers, M-46, Box 1.

60. Handwritten postscript dated January 20, 1937 by Shoghi Effendi to Roy Wilhelm, in letter written on behalf of Shoghi Effendi to Roy Wilhelm. USBNA, Roy C. Wilhelm papers, M-46, Box 1.

10 / Twilight on Stoneham Mountain

1. Letter dated September 27, 1937 from Roy Wilhelm to Martha Root, USBNA, Mabel Garis papers, M-1170, Box 4.

2. Letter dated November 4, 1940 from Roy Wilhelm to John Bosch, USBNA, John Bosch papers, M-289, Box 8; see also Angelina Diliberto Allen, *John David Bosch: In the Vanguard of Heroes, Martyrs, and Saints*, pp. 317–18.

3. Ibid.

4. Walter Blakely memoirs, USBNA, Walter Blakely papers, M-285, Box 2.

5. McKay, *Fires in Many Hearts*, p. 183. No information has been found as to how Roy first met Carver.

6. Letter dated January 14, 1937 written by G. W. Carver to Roy C. Wilhelm, USBNA, Roy C. Wilhelm papers, M-46, Box 1. The letter laments not seeing Roy during his visit to the South and implies that a donation to the work of the Tuskegee Institute would be appreciated. See also McKay, *Fires in Many Hearts*, p. 183.

7. Records of the National Spiritual Assembly of the United States. For a discussion of racism and the teaching work in the South during the 1930s, see Kathryn Jewett Hogenson, *Infinite Horizons: The Life and Times of Horace Holley*, pp. 296–98.

8. Letter dated January 22, 1937 from Roy Wilhelm to Shoghi Effendi, USBNA, Roy C. Wilhelm papers, M-46, Box 1.

9. Shoghi Effendi, *The Advent of Divine Justice*, p. 33.

10. Ibid., p. 34.

11. Records of the National Spiritual Assembly of the United States. For a discussion of racism and the teaching work in the South during the 1930s, see Kathryn Jewett Hogenson, *Infinite Horizons: The Life and Times of Horace Holley*, pp. 296–98.

12. Walter Blakely memoirs, USBNA, Walter Blakely papers, USBNA, M-285, Box 2.

13. Letter dated January 18, 1943 from Roy Wilhelm to a judge in Fulton County, Kentucky, Walter Blakely papers, USBNA.

14. M. R. Garis, *Martha Root: Lioness at the Threshold*, pp. 226, 315, 382–83.

15. Ibid., pp. 324–26.

16. Ibid., pp. 382–83.

17. Martha Root fell at a hotel and received inadequate medical treatment. M. R. Garis, *Martha Root: Lioness at the Threshold*, p. 406.

18. Letter dated August 3, 1935 written on behalf of Shoghi Effendi to Roy Wilhelm, Roy C. Wilhelm papers, USBNA, M-46, Box 1.

19. August 1 & 2, 1936, p. 3 minutes of the National Spiritual Assembly of the Bahá'ís of the United States and Canada, USBNA, National Spiritual Assembly papers. (Access was granted to the authors by the National Spiritual Assembly of the United States.)

20. September 19, 20, 21, 1936, p. 7, minutes of the National Spiritual Assembly of the Bahá'ís of the United States and Canada, USBNA, National Spiritual Assembly papers.

21. Douglas and Esta Struven 1993 telephone interview, conducted by James Manga and Diane Iverson. Transcript in possession of Joel Nizin.

22. M. R. Garis, *Martha Root: Lioness at the Threshold*, pp. 418–19.

23. Ibid.

24. Letter dated May 3, 1937 from Roy Wilhelm to Martha Root, USBNA, Mabel Garis papers. Quote is taken from the original letter. The Garis book does not have the underlining.

25. Letter dated September 27, 1937 from Roy Wilhelm to Martha Root. USBNA, Mabel Garis papers, M-1170, Box 4.

26. Ibid.

27. Kathryn Jewett Hogenson, *Infinite Horizons: The Life and Times of Horace Holley*, pp. 146–59.

28. Ibid., pp. 293–94.

29. Letter dated July 3, 1938 written on behalf of Shoghi Effendi to Roy Wilhelm. USBNA, Roy C. Wilhelm papers, M-46, Box 1.

30. Ibid.

31. Letter dated May 3, 1937 from Roy Wilhelm to Martha Root, USBNA, Mabel Garis papers.

32. O. Z. Whitehead, *Some Early Bahá'ís of the West*, p. 87. In a 1993 telephone interview with James Manga and Diane Iverson, Howard "Douglas" Struven said that "You know what a draftsman desk is like? It has a tilt to it. He had one of those. You know he had a bad back and he had a tall stool made and he would kind of stand and sit and write on that draftsman table. He wrote longhand." Transcript in the possession of Joel Nizin.

33. Letter dated October 15, 1934 from Florence Morton to Horace Holley. USBNA, Horace Holley papers, M-2, Box 3.

34. Letter dated September 28, 1938 written on behalf of Shoghi Effendi to Roy Wilhelm with a postscript by Shoghi Effendi. USBNA, Roy C. Wilhelm papers, M-46, Box 1.

35. Letter dated December 2, 1938, written on behalf of Shoghi Effendi to Roy Wilhelm with a postscript by Shoghi Effendi. USBNA, Roy C. Wilhelm, M-46, Box 1.

36. This period is covered in detail in *Martha Root: Lioness at the Threshold*, by M.R. Garis, pp. 441–52.

37. Ibid., pp. 472–86.

38. Letter dated July 30, 1939 from Katherine Baldwin to Roy Wilhelm, USBNA, Mabel Garis papers, M-1170, Box 4.

39. Letter dated August 7, 1939 from Roy Wilhelm to Katherine Baldwin, USBNA, Mabel Garis papers, M-1170, Box 4.

40. Letter dated September 9, 1939 from Martha Root to unnamed multiple recipients, USBNA, Mabel Garis papers, M-1170, Box 2.

41. Letter dated October 2, 1939 letter from Katherine Baldwin to Roy Wilhelm, USBNA, Mabel Garis papers, M-1170, Box 4.

42. Letter dated September 27, 1939 from Roy Wilhelm to Martha Root, USBNA, Mabel Garis papers, M-1170, Box 4.

43. Just before Martha's passing, Shoghi Effendi, through Roy, dispatched money to Hawaii to assist with her expenses. Once he learned of her passing, he asked that it be used for her memorial. Roy had also sent money to Hawaii. Letter dated November 22, 1939 from Roy Wilhelm to Katherine Baldwin, USBNA, Mabel Garis papers, M-1170, Box 4.

44. Letter dated September 28, 1939 from Roy Wilhelm to Katherine Baldwin, USBNA, Mabel Garis papers, M-1170, Box 4.

45. Cable dated October 3, 1939 from Shoghi Effendi to the Bahá'ís of the World, M. R. Garis, *Martha Root: Lioness at the Threshold*, p. 493.

46. Letter dated October 20, 1939 written on behalf of Shoghi Effendi to Roy Wilhelm, USBNA, Roy C. Wilhelm papers, M-46, Box 1.

47. Ibid.

48. M. R. Garis, *Martha Root: Lioness at the Threshold*, p. 494.

49. The Roy C. Wilhelm papers at the USBNA include many letters with government record offices and distant relatives about his genealogy. It includes information from a Cochran family Bible held by another family member and a few hand-drawn genealogical charts with Roy's notes on them in his handwriting.

50. January 27, 2012 telephone interview by Kathryn Jewett Hogenson with Loretta Voeltz.

51. This transition of moving the national headquarters from the New York area to the Chicago area is explored in Kathryn Jewett Hogenson, *Infinite Horizons: The Life and Times of Horace Holley*, pp. 279–86. Another source for the authors were the records of the National Spiritual Assembly of the United States.

52. Ibid.

53. January 27, 2012, telephone interview by Kathryn Jewett Hogenson with Loretta Voeltz.

54. Ibid.

55. Minutes, National Spiritual Assembly, March 28-29, 1925, USBNA, National Spiritual Assembly papers.

56. Report, open conference, Spiritual Assembly of New York, New York, April 2, 1925, New York City Bahá'í Archives (held at the USBNA).

57. Ibid.

58. Report, open conference, Spiritual Assembly of New York, New York, August 6, 1925, New York Bahá'í Archives (held at the USBNA).

59. Report from Open Conference Meeting in New York, New York, April 2, 1925, New York Bahá'í Archives (held at the USBNA).

60. Report, open conference, Spiritual Assembly of New York, New York, August 6, 1925, New York Bahá'í Archives (held at the USBNA).

61. Ibid.

62. Records of the National Spiritual Assembly of the United States.

63. Minutes, Spiritual Assembly of New York, New York, January 14, 1926, New York Bahá'í Archives (held at the USBNA).

64. General background information for the run up to World War II and the war years comes from multiple sources, including Frederick Lewis Allen, *Since Yesterday: The 1930s in America, September 3, 1929–September 3, 1939*; Doris Kearns Goodwin, *No Ordinary Time: Franklin and Eleanor Roosevelt: The Home Front in World War II*; Victor Davis Hanson, *The Second World Wars: How the First Global Conflict was Fought and Won*; Paul Johnson, *A History of the American People*; Larry Schweikart, *A Patriot's History of the Modern World: From America's Exceptional Ascent to the Atomic Bomb: 1898–1945*.

65. See 'Abdu'l-Bahá's Tablets to the Hague, https://www.bahai.org/library/authoritative-texts/abdul-baha/tablets-hague-abdul-baha/.

66. Letter dated December 21, 1935 from Roy Wilhelm to Shoghi Effendi, USBNA, RCW papers, M-46, Box 1.

67. Handwritten postscript dated January 7, 1936 by Shoghi Effendi to Roy Wilhelm, USBNA, Roy C. Wilhelm papers, M-46, Box 1.

68. Ibid.

69. Letter dated January 7, 1936 written on behalf of Shoghi Effendi to Roy Wilhelm, USBNA, Roy C. Wilhelm papers, M-46, Box 1.

70. "Norway was Once America's Snowshoe Capital," https://www.mrlakefront.net/newsdetails.taf?date=01/19/2015&link=norway-was-once-americas-snowshoe-capital.

71. John [Jack] Hawley, Lovell, Maine, Recording made in spring, 2004. Interviewer: Frances Pollitt, Transcription: Spring, 2005, Frances Pollitt.

72. Cable dated January 30, 1942, from Roy Wilhelm to Shoghi Effendi, USBNA, Roy C. Wilhelm papers, M-46, Box 1.

73. Cable dated February 4, 1942 from Shoghi Effendi to Roy Wilhelm, USBNA, Roy C. Wilhelm papers, M-46, Box 1.

74. While the internment of Japanese Americans is well known, the internment during the war of German and Italian Americans is less well known, probably because the numbers were less and the racial element was not a factor. However, 11,000 ethnic Germans were detained. https://en.wikipedia.org/wiki/Internment_of_German_Americans.

75. Kathryn Skelton, *Lewiston Sun Journal*, April 11, 2009, and FBI subject: 298088 Freedom of Information Act.

76. Ibid.

77. Ibid.

78. 1943 records of the National Spiritual Assembly of the United States and Canada.

79. Postcard dated January 14, 1942 from Roy Wilhelm to Mr. and Mrs. John D. Bosch, John & Louise Bosch papers, USBNA, M-289, Box 8.

80. Roy retained 85% ownership in his company after 1942 and had always ensured that each of his staff owned at least one share of the company stock. The person running the company in his absence was the largest minority shareholder. Douglas Struven, 1993 telephone interview, conducted by James Manga and Diane Iverson. Douglas was the son of Howard and Hebe Struven.

81. The chalet had high ceilings and balconies around the main rooms, and this design made it difficult to heat during the winter. The smaller building, originally constructed to boil sap for maple syrup, was transformed into a winter cottage.

82. Letter dated October 26, 1941 written on behalf of Shoghi Effendi to Roy Wilhelm, USBNA, Roy C. Wilhelm papers, M-46, Box 1.

83. Ibid.

84. *The Bahá'í World*, Vol. X, 1944–1946, pp. 158–70.

85. "Bahá'í Temple Floodlighted for Centenary Gatherings," *The Bahá'í World*, Vol. X, 1944–1946, p. 172.

86. *The Bahá'í World*, Vol. X, 1944–1946, p. 163.

87. Letter dated March 11, 1946, from Shoghi Effendi and Amatu'l-Bahá Rúḥíyyih Khánum to Roy Wilhelm.

88. Douglas Struven, 1993 telephone interview, conducted by James Manga and Diane Iverson.

89. Shoghi Effendi, *This Decisive Hour*, no. 101; Velda Piff Metelmann, *Lua Getsinger: Herald of the Covenant*, p. 158.

90. For a history of the Struven family, see Deb Clark, "The Bahá'ís of Baltimore, 1898–1990," *Community Histories: Studies in Bábí and Bahá'í Relitions*, Vol. 6, pp. 115–128. See also https://worcesterbahais.org/content/struven-family, "Struven Family" on the website about the history of the Worcester, Massachusetts Bahá'í community.

91. Spring 2004 interview with John Hawley conducted by Frances Pollit.

92. Hebe's understanding of the power of love is well-illustrated in a story found in *Fires in Many Hearts*, by Doris McKay, p. 42.

93. Rúḥíyyih Khánum wrote Roy a loving letter, which gives insight into how many viewed him during his own twilight years. She said that, though Roy's "words are few," yet he was "one of those people who don't have to say anything" to his friends because they could feel his love and sympathy. Letter to Roy dated February 9, 1949, from Amatu'l-Bahá Rúḥíyyih Khánum. USBNA, Roy C. Wilhelm papers, M-46, Box 1

94. Douglas Struven, 1993 telephone interview, conducted by James Manga and Diane Iverson.

95. Walter Blakely memoirs, p. 8, USBNA, Walter Blakely papers, M-285, Box 2.

96. Ibid.

97. Walter Blakely memoirs, USBNA, Walter Blakely papers, M-285, Box 2.

98. This period of the post-World War II years and the building of the superstructure of the Shrine of the Báb is recounted in great detail in *Coronation on Carmel: The Story of the Shrine of the Báb, Vol. II, 1922–1963* by Michael V. Day.

99. Letter dated February 9, 1949 from Rúḥíyyih Khánum to Roy Wilhelm, USBNA, Roy Wilhelm papers.

100. Ibid.

101. A British term for a larger car, targeted at successful professionals and middle-to-senior managers. Referred to as a "full-sized car" in the United States. https://en.wikipedia.org/wiki/Executive_car.

102. Letter dated February 18, 1948 written on behalf of Shoghi Effendi to Roy Wilhelm, USBNA, Roy C. Wilhelm papers, M-46, Box 1.

103. It was impossible to get a radiator for the car in Israel, so Roy sent one. Otherwise, whenever Buick parts were unavailable, the Guardian's driver improvised as best he could.

104. Letter dated February 18, 1948 written on behalf of Shoghi Effendi to Roy Wilhelm, USBNA, Roy C. Wilhelm papers, M-46, Box 1.

105. Letter dated January 16, 1951 written on behalf of Shoghi Effendi to Roy Wilhelm. And April 13, 1945, August 6, 1946 and December 17, 1950 letters from Amatu'l-Bahá Rúḥíyyih Khánum to Roy Wilhelm. All are found at USBNA, Roy C. Wilhelm papers, M-46, Box 1.

106. Letter to Roy dated December 25, 1949, written on behalf of Shoghi Effendi by Amatu'l-Báhá Rúḥíyyih Khánum.

107. Anita Ioas Chapman, *Leroy Ioas: Hand of the Cause of God*, p. 209.

108. Cablegram dated March 21, 1953 from Shoghi Effendi to the Bahá'í World, Shoghi Effendi, *Messages to the Bahá'í World*, no. 26.

109. Douglas Struven, 1993 telephone interview, conducted by James Manga and Diane Iverson.

110. Bahá'u'lláh, The Hidden Words of Bahá'u'lláh, Arabic no. 33.

Epilogue

1. Cablegram dated December 24, 1951 from Shoghi Effendi, in Shoghi Effendi, *Messages to the Bahá'í World 1950–1957*, pp. 18–20.

2. "Roy C. Wilhelm," by Horace Holley, *The Bahá'í World: A Biennial International Record*, Vol. XII (1950–1954): 662.

3. Ibid.

4. Ibid., p. 664.

5. Keith Ransom-Kehler was sent to Iran by Shoghi Effendi to plead with the government to end its persecution of the Bahá'í community. This was a delicate and dangerous assignment. While there, she became ill and died.

6. See tribute to the Hands of the Cause of God in a letter dated November 26, 2007 from the Universal House of Justice to the Bahá'ís of the World.

7. Bahá'u'lláh, The Hidden Words of Bahá'u'lláh, Persian no. 82.

8. 'Abdu'l-Bahá, *Selections from the Writings of 'Abdu'l-Bahá*, no. 163.9.

Appendix A: The Annual Souvenir Picnic

1. This Tablet was published in *The Star of the West*, vol. 4, no. 14 (November 23, 1913).

2. Martha Root, "Eighth Annual Feast of Commemoration," *The Star of the West*, vol. 10, no. 7 (July 13, 1919): 134–135.

3. *The Star of the West*, vol. 19, no. 5 (August 1928): 147–49.

4. *Bahá'í Magazine*, vol. 24, no. 5 (August 1933): 150.

5. Letter dated August 7,1934, written on behalf of Shoghi Effendi to the National Spiritual Assembly of the United States and Canada.

6. *Bahá'í News*, April 1935, Issue #92.

Appendix B: Collier's Magazine

Collier's Magazine is a registered trademark of

JTE Multimedia, LLC
435 Devon Park Drive, Bldg 500
Wayne, PA 19087

BIBLIOGRAPHY

Works of Bahá'u'lláh

The Kitáb-i-Aqdas: The Most Holy Book. Wilmette, IL: Bahá'í Publishing Trust, 1993.

Works of 'Abdu'l-Bahá

Light of the World: Selected Tablets of 'Abdu'l-Bahá. Haifa, Israel: Bahá'í World Centre, 2021.

Promulgation of Universal Peace: Talks Delivered by 'Abdu'l-Bahá During His Visit to the United States and Canada in 1912. Wilmette, IL: Bahá'í Publishing, 2012.

Tablets of the Divine Plan. Wilmette, IL: Bahá'í Publishing Trust, 1993.

Will and Testament of 'Abdu'l-Bahá. Wilmette, IL: Bahá'í Publishing Trust, 1944.

Works of Shoghi Effendi

The Advent of Divine Justice. New ed. Wilmette, IL: Bahá'í Publishing Trust, 2006.

Bahá'í Administration: Selected Messages, 1922–1932. 7th ed. Wilmette, IL: Bahá'í Publishing Trust, 1974.

God Passes By. Wilmette, IL: Bahá'í Publishing Trust, 1965. Revised edition 1974. Ninth printing 2018.

Message to the Bahá'í World, 1950–1957. Wilmette, IL: Bahá'í Publishing Trust, 1971.

This Decisive Hour: Messages to America 1932–1946 (originally published as *Messages to America*). Wilmette, IL: Bahá'í Publishing Committee, 1947.

The World Order of Bahá'u'lláh. Wilmette, IL: Bahá'í Publishing Trust, 1991.

Other Works

Allen, Angelina Diliberto. *John David Bosch: In the Vanguard of Heroes, Martyrs, and Saints.* Wilmette, IL: Bahá'í Publishing, 2019.

Allen, Frederick Lewis. *Only Yesterday: An Informal History of the 1920s.* New York: Harper Perennial Modern Classics, 1931.

———. *Since Yesterday: The 1930s in America.* New York: Harper & Row, 1939.

Almandoz, Arturo, ed. *Planning Latin America's Capital Cities, 1850–1950.* New York: Routledge, 2002.

Armstrong-Ingram, R. Jackson. *Music, Devotions, and Mashriqu'l-Adhkár: Studies in Bábí and Bahá'í History, Volume Four.* Los Angeles: Kalimát Press, 1987.

The Bahá'í World. Vols. VII (1936–1938), IX (1940–1944), X (1944–1946), XII (1950–1954), and XIX (1963–1968). Haifa, Israel: Bahá'í World Centre.

Bahá'í Year Book: Volume One, April, 1925–April, 1926. Wilmette, IL: Bahá'í Publishing Trust, 1926 (reprinted 1980).

Balyuzi, H. M. *'Abdu'l-Bahá: The Centre of the Covenant of Bahá'u'lláh.* Oxford: George Ronald, 1971.

Chapman, Anita Ioas. *Leroy Ioas: Hand of the Cause of God.* Oxford: George Ronald, 1998.

Davis, Victor Hanson. *The Second World Wars: How the First Global Con-*

flict was Fought and Won. New York: Basic Books, 2017.

Day, Michael V. *Coronation on Carmel: The Story of the Shrine of the Báb, Vol. II: 1922–1963*. Oxford: George Ronald, 2018.

Ellis, Edward Robb. *The Epic of New York City*. New York: Old Town Books, 1966.

Garis, M. R. *Martha Root: Lioness at the Threshold*. Wilmette, IL: Bahá'í Publishing Trust, 1983.

Gloversville (NY) Business School, A Bookkeeping & Stenographer School. *1906–1907 Annual Catalog*.

Goodwin, Doris Kearns. *No Ordinary Time: Franklin and Eleanor Roosevelt: The Home Front in World War II*. New York: Simon & Schuster, 1994.

Harper, Barron Deems. *Lights of Fortitude: Glimpses into the Lives of the Hands of the Cause of God*. Oxford: George Ronald, 1997.

History of Muskingum County, Ohio, Illustrations and Biographical Sketches of Prominent Men and Pioneers. J. F. Everhart & Co., 1882.

Hogenson, Kathryn Jewett. *Infinite Horizons: The Life and Times of Horace Holley*. Oxford: George Ronald, 2022.

———. *Lighting the Western Sky: The Hearst Pilgrimage and the Establishment of the Bahá'í Faith in the West*. Oxford: George Ronald, 2010.

Hollinger, Richard, ed. *Community Histories: Studies in the Bábí and Bahá'í Religions*. Volume Six. Los Angeles: Kalimát Press, 1992.

Ives, Howard Colby. *Portals to Freedom*. Oxford: George Ronald, 1983.

Johnson, Paul. *A History of the American People*. New York: Harper Collins, 1997.

———. *Modern Times: From the Twenties to the Nineties, rev ed*. New York: Harper Collins, 1991.

Knock, Thomas J. *To End All Wars: Woodrow Wilson and the Quest for a*

New World Order. Princeton, NJ: Princeton University Press, 1992.

Maḥmúd-i-Zarqání. *Maḥmúd's Diary: The Diary of Mírzá Maḥmúd-i-Zarqání Chronicling 'Abdu'l-Bahá's Journey to America.* Translation by Mohi Sobhani. Oxford: George Ronald, 1998.

McKay, Doris. *Fires in Many Hearts.* Oxford: George Ronald, 2021.

Metelman, Velda Piff. *Lua Getsinger: Herald of the Covenant.* Oxford: George Ronald, 1997.

Nakhjavani, Violette. *The Maxwells of Montreal: Early Years 1870–1922.* Oxford: George Ronald, 2011.

Perry, Anne Gordon. *Green Acre on the Piscataqua.* Third edition. Wilmette, IL: Bahá'í Publishing Trust, 2012.

Rabbani, Rúḥíyyih. *The Priceless Pearl.* Rutland, UK: Bahá'í Publishing, 2000.

Randall-Winckler, Bahíyyih. *William Henry Randall: Disciple of 'Abdu'l-Bahá.* Oxford: Oneworld Publications, 1996.

Redman, Earl. *'Abdu'l-Bahá in Their Midst.* Oxford: George Ronald, 2011.

———. *The Knights of Bahá'u'lláh.* Oxford: George Ronald, 2017.

———. *Shoghi Effendi Through the Pilgrim's Eye, Vol. 1: Building the Administrative Order, 1922–1952.* Oxford: George Ronald, 2015.

———. *Visiting 'Abdu'l-Bahá. Vol. 1: The West Discovers the Master, 1897–1911.* Oxford: George Ronald, 2019.

———. *Visiting 'Abdu'l-Bahá. Vol. 2: The Final Years, 1913–1921.* Oxford: George Ronald, 2020.

Rutstein, Nathan. *Corinne True: Faithful Handmaid of 'Abdu'l-Bahá.* Oxford: George Ronald, 1987.

———. *He Loved and Served: The Story of Curtis Kelsey.* Oxford: George Ronald, 1982.

Schapira, Joel, David, & Karl. *The Book of Coffee & Tea.* New York: St. Martin's Press, 1982.

Schweikart, Larry. *A Patriot's History of the Modern World: From America's Exceptional Ascent to the Atomic Bomb: 1898–1945.* New York: Sentinel (Penguin Group), 2012.

Shlaes, Amity. *The Forgotten Man: A New History of the Great Depression.* New York: Harper Perennial (Harper Collins Publishers), 2007.

Sohrab, Ahmad. *The Story of the Divine Plan: Taking place during and immediately following World War I.* New York: The New History Foundation, 1947.

Stewart, Watt. *Keith and Costa Rica: The Biography of Minor Cooper Keith, American Entrepreneur.* Albuquerque: University of New Mexico Press, 1964.

Stockman, Robert H. *'Abdu'l-Bahá in America.* Wilmette, IL: Bahá'í Publishing, 2012.

———. *The Bahá'í Faith in America: Origins 1892–1900, vol. 1.* Wilmette, IL: Bahá'í Publishing Trust, 1985.

———. *The Bahá'í Faith in America: Early Expansion, 1900–1912, vol. 2.* Oxford: George Ronald, 1995.

Taherzadeh, Adib. *The Covenant of Bahá'u'lláh.* Oxford: George Ronald, 1992.

Thompson, Juliet. *The Diary of Juliet Thompson.* Los Angeles: Kalimat Press, 1983.

Uker, William H. *All About Coffee.* Second edition. New York: The Tea & Coffee Trade Journal Company, 1935.

Wallace, Mike. *Greater Gotham: A History of New York City from 1898 to 1919.* Oxford: Oxford University Press, 2017.

Ward, Allan L. *239 Days: 'Abdu'l-Bahá's Journey in America.* Wilmette, IL: Bahá'í Publishing Trust, 1979.

Weinberg, Robert. *Lady Blomfield: Her Life and Times.* Oxford: George Ronald, 2012.

———. *Ethel Jenner Rosenberg: The Life and Times of England's Outstanding Bahá'í Pioneer Worker.* Oxford: George Ronald, 1995.

Whitehead, O. Z. *Some Early Bahá'ís of the West.* Oxford: George Ronald, 1976.

Whitmore, Bruce W. *The Dawning Place: The Building of a Temple, the Forging of the North American Bahá'í Community.* Wilmette, IL: Bahá'í Publishing Trust, 1984.

Wilhelm, Roy, Stanwood Cobb, and Genevieve L. Coy. *In His Presence: Visits to 'Abdu'l-Bahá.* Los Angeles: Kalimat Press, 1989.

INDEX

ABOUT THE AUTHORS

Joel Nizin is a northern New Jersey, double-boarded colorectal surgeon who has been in practice for nearly forty years. He is blessed with one wife, two daughters, and five grandchildren, with one currently on the way. Research on Bahá'í history, family genealogy, photography, travel, and hiking are among his diverse interests. He has served on numerous Bahá'í institutions, including the Regional Bahá'í Council for the Northeastern States, and as a delegate to the Bahá'í National Convention. He has created several multiyear programs for youth, including "Badasht," "Badasht Prep," and "Turning 15." This is his first book.

Kathryn Jewett Hogenson, a native of Virginia and resident of Florida, is a lawyer by profession and a historian by choice, as well as a wife, mother, and grandmother. She and her husband Gary Hogenson served many years at the international headquarters of the Bahá'í Faith, and she has also served as a staff member of the US Bahá'í National Center. A frequent lecturer, she authored *Lighting the Western Sky: The Hearst Pilgrimage and the Establishment of the Bahá'í Faith in the West* and *Infinite Horizons: The Life and Times of Horace Holley,* as well as other published works.

Gary Hogenson, originally from Michigan, currently lives in Florida and has a degree in international management. He enjoyed a global career in engineering and finance, which included a decade in Latin America and eighteen years in the Finance Department at the Bahá'í World Center. He has served on numerous Spiritual Assemblies in the US and Costa Rica, as well as teaching committees in Virginia and Florida. In retirement, he discovered the joy of writing and has published a number of items in professional journals. He is married to Kathryn Hogenson, and they have two daughters and three grandsons.